P9-CDH-782

Praise for *Spy:*
The Inside Story of How the FBI's
Robert Hanssen Betrayed America

"As America's premier writer on espionage and the intelligence bureaucracy, David Wise has over the years introduced us to some very weird and dangerous civil servants. But for weirdness, the others couldn't touch Robert Philip Hanssen. . . . As always, Wise offers his readers the excitement of spying on the spies."

—*The Washington Post*

"David Wise reports a tale of monstrous treachery. . . . Of several books published about the Hanssen case, *Spy* is the most authoritative. . . . Gripping reading."

—*The New York Times*
Book Review

"Thoroughly researched and replete with new information. With so much junk being written these days about the intelligence world, Wise's books have one overarching virtue: What he says in them is actually true. . . . The blockbuster of Hanssen's betrayal . . . was how the FBI came into possession of Hanssen's KGB case file [that] led directly to Hanssen's arrest. Well, Wise breaks the story."

—washingtonpost.com

"The best account of this extraordinary coup—and of much else—is to be found in David Wise's *Spy*. Wise . . . has been writing about American intelligence for nearly forty years and it appears that he has never forgotten the name or lost the phone number of a source."

—*The New York Review of Books*

"Wise . . . has expertly studied and written about spies for a life-time. . . . *Spy* provides substantial evidence of a troubled intelligence community."

—*Los Angeles Times*

"David Wise has unparalleled sources in the quarrelsome bureaucracies of the 'intelligence community.' No one knows as much background on the . . . wilderness of mirrors and can put Hanssen's work into perspective the way Wise does. The book, for the first time, describes the hunt and the hunted."

—*The Palm Beach Post/*
Cox News Service

"A fascinating look into the mind of the secret agent and into the strengths and weaknesses of the United States' intelligence community . . . [Wise] provides a critical analysis of the flaws of the U.S. intelligence community."

—*Rocky Mountain News*

"The KGB marketed [Hanssen] for $7 million . . . putting the former FBI agent in prison for the rest of his life. Such is the remarkable revelation in . . . *Spy,* by David Wise, indisputably the dean of American espionage writers. [*Spy* is] the inside story of how our intelligence agencies finally tracked [Hanssen] down and brought him to justice."

—*The Washington Times*

"Solidly paced, richly detailed . . . a first-rate true-crime story that gets inside the shadowy . . . world of spooks, moles, and ops."

—*Kirkus Reviews*

PHOTO: © JON WISE

DAVID WISE is America's leading writer on intelligence and espionage. He is coauthor of *The Invisible Government,* a number one bestseller widely credited with bringing about a reappraisal of the role of the CIA in a democratic society. He is the author of *Cassidy's Run: The Secret Spy War over Nerve Gas, Nightmover: How Aldrich Ames Sold the CIA to the KGB for $4.6 Million, Molehunt, The Spy Who Got Away, The American Police State,* and *The Politics of Lying,* and coauthor with Thomas B. Ross of *The Espionage Establishment* and *The U-2 Affair.* He is also the author of three espionage novels, *The Samarkand Dimension, The Children's Game,* and *Spectrum.* A native New Yorker and graduate of Columbia College, he is the former chief of the Washington bureau of the *New York Herald Tribune* and has contributed articles on government and politics to many national magazines. He is married and has two sons.

Also by David Wise

Nonfiction

The U-2 Affair (with Thomas B. Ross)

The Invisible Government (with Thomas B. Ross)

The Espionage Establishment (with Thomas B. Ross)

The Politics of Lying

The American Police State

The Spy Who Got Away

Molehunt

Nightmover

Cassidy's Run

Fiction

Spectrum

The Children's Game

The Samarkand Dimension

SPY

SPY

The Inside Story of How the FBI's Robert Hanssen Betrayed America

David Wise

Random House Trade Paperbacks
New York

2003 Random House Trade Paperback Edition

Copyright © 2002, 2003 by David Wise

This work was originally published in hardcover by Random House,
an imprint of The Random House Publishing Group,
a division of Random House, Inc.,
New York, in 2002.

Library of Congress Cataloging-in-Publication Data

Wise, David.
Spy: the inside story of how the FBI's Robert Hanssen betrayed
America / David Wise
p.   cm.
Includes index.
ISBN 0-375-75894-1
1. Hanssen, Robert.   2. Spies—Russia (Federation)—Biography.
3. Intelligence agents—United States—Biography.
4. United States. Federal Bureau of Investigation—Biography.
I. Title

UB271.R92 H3723 2002   327.1247073'092—dc21   2002031867
[B]

Printed in the United States of America

Random House website address: www.atrandom.com

6897

Book design by Mercedes Everett

To Thomas B. Ross

Contents

1- The Mole Hunter - 3

2- The Man Who Was Sunday - 5

3- "Oh, My Son, My Son" - 9

4- "On Second Thought, Give the Money to Mother Teresa" - 19

5- Headquarters - 28

6- The Year of the Spy - 37

7- "Soon, I Will Send a Box of Documents" - 47

8- "For Sale, Dodge Diplomat, Needs Engine Work" - 58

9- Anybody Here Seen a Mole? - 66

10- The Spy - 74

11- Hanssen's Gods - 85

12- Diamonds Are a Spy's Best Friend - 94

13- Let's Play MONOPOLY - 100

14- "A Contagious Disease Is Suspected" - 111

15- "Oh My God, Look What He Leaves Lying Around!" - 120

16- "Life Is Becoming Too Fast" - 132

17- Play It Again, Sam - 143

18- "He Was Dragging Me by the Arm, Screaming at Me" - 153

19- Hibernation - 159

20- "There Has to Be Another" - 168

21- Mole Wars - 178

22- Recontact - 183

23- BUCKLURE - 196

24- The Wrong Man - 205

25- GRAYDAY - 219

26- Sleeping Tiger - 233

27- The Arrest - 240

28- Sex, Lies, and Videotape - 251

29- The Plea Bargain - 261

30- The Mind of Robert Hanssen - 270

31- "You Would Have to Be a Total Stupid Fucking Idiot
to Spy for the KGB" - 282

Author's Note - 295

Afterword - 301

Index - 305

SPY

1

The Mole Hunter

Disaster.

Inside the Soviet counterintelligence section at FBI headquarters in Washington, there could be no other word for what had happened: the two KGB agents who were the bureau's highly secret sources inside the Soviet embassy in Washington had somehow been discovered. Valery Martynov and Sergei Motorin had been lured back to Moscow and executed. Each was killed with a bullet in the head, the preferred method used by the KGB to dispatch traitors.

There would be no more visits to the candy store by the FBI counterintelligence agents; M&M, as the two KGB men were informally if irreverently known inside FBI headquarters, were gone, two more secret casualties of the Cold War. The year was 1986. The FBI quickly created a six-person team to try to determine what had gone wrong.

Meanwhile, the CIA, across the Potomac in Langley, Virginia, was having its own troubles. It was losing dozens of agents inside the Soviet Union, some executed, others thrown into prison. The agency formed a mole hunt group.

Two years later, in 1988, the FBI still had no answer to how Martynov, whom the bureau had given the code name PIMENTA, and Motorin, code name MEGAS, had been lost. Something more had to be done, and the FBI now began thinking the unthinkable. As painful, even heretical, as it might be to consider, perhaps there was a traitor—a Russian spy—inside the FBI itself.

To find out the truth was the job of the bureau's intelligence division, which was in charge of arresting spies, penetrating foreign espionage services, and, when possible, recruiting their agents to work for the FBI. The division was divided into sections, one of which, CI-3 (the CI stood for counterintelligence), housed the Soviet analytical unit, the research arm of the bureau's spycatchers. Perhaps, the division's chiefs reasoned, something might be learned if the analysts, looking back to the beginning of the Cold War, carefully studied every report gleaned from a recruitment or a defector that hinted at possible penetrations of the FBI by Soviet intelligence. Perhaps a pattern could be seen that might point to a current penetration, if one existed.

Within the Soviet unit, two experienced analysts, Bob King and Jim Milburn, were assigned to read the debriefings of Soviet defectors and reports of Soviet intelligence sources who had, over the years, been recruited as spies by the FBI. The two shared a cubicle in Room 4835 with their supervisor.

The supervisor, a tall, forty-four-year-old, somewhat dour man, was not a popular figure among his fellow special agents, although he was respected for his wizardry with computers. He had been born in Chicago, served for a while as a police officer in that city, and joined the FBI twelve years before, in 1976. Now he was responsible for preparing and overseeing the mole study.

For the supervisor, directing the analysis to help pinpoint a possible mole inside the FBI was a task of exquisite irony. For he knew who had turned over the names of Valery Martynov and Sergei Motorin to the KGB. He knew there was in fact an active mole inside the FBI, passing the bureau's most highly classified secrets to Moscow. He knew the spy was a trusted counterintelligence agent at headquarters. He knew, in fact, that the spy was a supervisory special agent inside the Soviet analytical unit. He knew all this but could tell no one. And for good reason.

Robert Hanssen was looking for himself.

2

The Man Who Was Sunday

Jack was visiting that Sunday in February 2001, as he did every chance he got when business took him to Washington from his home in Trier, Germany. He was, as usual, staying with Bob and Bonnie Hanssen in their modest brown-shingle home in Vienna, Virginia.

Jack Delroy Hoschouer—"Uncle Jack" to the Hanssens' six children—was Bob Hanssen's closest friend; they had met in high school in Chicago. Hanssen was an only child, but Jack considered himself closer than a brother. He had been best man at Bob and Bonnie's wedding and was godfather to one of their children. He was so close that he telephoned Hanssen every day, without fail, from wherever he was.

They had bonded almost immediately at Taft High School in Chicago's Norwood Park, the bookish, bespectacled Hoschouer and his taller, somber friend. Both were quiet and not drawn to sports, but they shared an interest in Formula One racing and girls. As adults, both were avid surfers of Internet porn sites; they were connoisseurs of the wide range of naked women, appealing to various sexual appetites, depicted in cyberspace. Hanssen would e-mail Hoschouer in Germany: had Jack seen this or that website? Check it out, Hanssen would suggest, the women and the sexual acrobatics on display were awesome.

Bob Hanssen, as Hoschouer well knew, was fascinated by sex and pornography, and not only on the Internet. When Jack was in Washington, they often secretly slipped away to visit strip clubs.

They also spent hours discussing philosophy, religion, and literature. Their career paths had diverged. Hoschouer was a military man; he had commanded an air infantry company in Vietnam and went into the arms business after he retired from the Army. Hanssen, meanwhile, was in Washington and New York, building his career in FBI counterintelligence.

The two friends talked about more than sex and salvation. Intelligence was another subject of mutual interest. At the bureau, it was Hanssen's daily preoccupation. And Jack had served five years as an Army attaché at the United States embassy in Bonn, a job in which he had a lot to do with intelligence. In Germany, Hoschouer had often met with his Soviet opposite number in an accepted, familiar game of trading intelligence tidbits.

Now, in northern Virginia on this February 18, Hoschouer was enjoying the last day of his visit. The quiet winter Sunday had begun like any other. The Hanssens, as usual, went to church. To those who knew the family, the Roman Catholic Church appeared central to their lives. Born a Lutheran, Hanssen had converted to Catholicism at the behest of his wife soon after their marriage. Their three boys and three girls attended Catholic schools. Hanssen not only went to mass frequently—often daily—he was a dedicated member of Opus Dei, a secretive, highly conservative, and somewhat mysterious Catholic group that emphasizes spirituality and prayer in the daily lives of its lay members. Hanssen frequently tried to persuade Catholic friends to come with him to Opus Dei meetings.

Hoschouer was about to join the Hanssens as they were leaving for church when his wife, Aya, called from Germany. He decided to talk to her rather than accompany the Hanssens.

After lunch, Hoschouer and Hanssen lazily threw the Frisbee for Bob's dog, Sunday, a black mixed breed, part mastiff, part Labrador. Around 3 P.M., back inside, Hanssen handed his friend a copy of *The Man Who Was Thursday*, G. K. Chesterton's novel about seven men who are apparent anarchists—the early twentieth-century version of today's terrorists. Hanssen urged Jack to read it.

Each of the characters in the novel is named for a day of the week. Sunday, their leader, is a massive, outsize figure with supernatural powers who represents nature or the universe. But in the dreamlike fantasy, nothing is as it first appears. All six of Sunday's followers turn out to be undercover Scotland Yard detectives, recruited in a dark room by a mysterious, unseen man who, of course, was really Sunday. But why was a senior police official leading such a convoluted, complex double life?

Hoschouer, later reflecting on that day, thought he understood why the book held a special attraction for Hanssen. Not one of the characters was what he first seemed to be; all were secretly somebody else. There were other intriguing bits. Of Gabriel Syme, the first police detective introduced to the reader, Chesterton wrote: "It never occurred to him to be spiritually won over to the enemy."*

In midafternoon, it was time for Hoschouer to head for the airport. He was flying to Phoenix to visit his elderly parents in Mesa, Arizona. The two friends climbed into the Hanssens' three-year-old silver Ford Taurus for the trip to Dulles.

They reached the airport, but Hanssen did not follow their customary routine. "Usually he'd park and he'd come in and we'd have a cup of coffee," Hoschouer recalled. "Actually, he didn't drink coffee, he'd have a Coke. This time he just dropped me off. I didn't think anything about that because I knew his daughter Jane and his son-in-law were coming for dinner, so it seemed perfectly normal." Richard Trimber, Jane's husband, was a young associate in a downtown Washington law firm. The Trimbers had four children; Bob Hanssen, at fifty-six, was a grandfather.

With a wave, Hanssen was gone. Hoschouer checked in and about 6 P.M. boarded his flight to Phoenix.

*   *   *

From the airport, Hanssen did not return directly to his home at 9414 Talisman Drive. He drove instead to Foxstone Park, a few blocks from his house.

There, he placed a piece of white adhesive tape in a vertical position on one of the poles that supported the park sign. Like some malign doppelgänger of Clark Kent, Special Agent Robert Hanssen of the FBI had figuratively changed costume and stepped into his other, secret life as "Ramon," ace agent of the Sluzhba Vneshnei Razvedki, or SVR, the successor to the KGB. The tape was a signal to the Russian spy agency that secret documents would be waiting at a dead drop, a hiding place inside the park, ready for them to pick up.

---

*G. K. Chesterton, *The Man Who Was Thursday,* annotated by Martin Gardner (San Francisco: Ignatius Press, 1999), p. 105. Originally published in 1907. In retrospect, Hoschouer wondered whether Hanssen had even named his dog for Chesterton's character Sunday.

This was no sudden transformation of loyalties to Moscow by Robert Hanssen. He did not have an epiphany in Foxstone Park. He had secretly been a Russian spy, on and off, for almost twenty-two years. He was Moscow's mole, operating from within the very heart of American counterintelligence. He had turned over more than six thousand pages of classified documents, including many of the nation's most sensitive secrets, to the Russians. In return, he had been paid more than $600,000 in cash and diamonds, and told that another $800,000 had been deposited to his account in a Moscow bank, for a total of $1.4 million.

As Hanssen's reward this day, the Russians had stashed $50,000 in used hundred-dollar bills in dead drop LEWIS, a hiding place in Arlington beneath a wooden stage in an outdoor amphitheater in the Long Branch Nature Center.

From his car, Hanssen removed a large plastic garbage bag, tightly secured at the top with clear tape. To anyone watching, it might appear, at worst, that someone was furtively dumping unwanted trash in the park. The garbage bag, however, contained not trash but a computer disk and seven FBI documents, each classified SECRET. These would be of great interest to the SVR's leaders in Yasenevo, the agency's headquarters on the Moscow ring road. They revealed the FBI's current and proposed counterintelligence operations against certain Russian officials and installations in the United States.

It was just after 4:30 P.M. Hanssen made his way along the path through the trees to a wooden footbridge that crossed over Wolf Trap Creek, the narrow stream that meanders through the park. To the Russians and Hanssen, this was dead drop ELLIS. Carefully, he placed the bag out of sight, just under the bridge.

It took him another four minutes to emerge from the woods and walk to his car.

At that instant, he knew.

The men moving toward him were armed with submachine guns.

Hanssen had realized the risks. He had reminded the Russians in a letter just three months earlier that the espionage laws in the United States had been changed. If caught, he warned, he might not just be sent to prison.

He might face the penalty of death.

3

"Oh, My Son, My Son"

Norwood Park is a working-class, predominantly white area on the northwest fringe of Chicago. "It was the only neighborhood in Chicago that looked like the suburbs, with one-family houses set on lawns," recalled James D. Ohlson, who grew up nearby and later became a friend of Hanssen when both served in the FBI.

The neighborhood's politics reflected its demographics; Norwood Park was a conservative stronghold. "It was," Ohlson noted, "the only Republican ward in Mayor Daley's Chicago. Police, firefighters, teachers, and other city employees had to live in Chicago, and our ward was filled with them."

Howard Hanssen, a Chicago police officer, and his wife, Vivian, lived in a modest two-story white bungalow in Norwood Park at 6215 North Neva Avenue. Howard Hanssen was serving as a petty officer in the Navy during World War II when, on April 18, 1944, their son and only child, Robert Philip, was born.

Before joining the force, Howard Hanssen had worked for the Campbell Soup Company, mixing spices for the vats. In the Navy, stationed at Great Lakes, Illinois, he had traded one police uniform for another. "He was a shore patrolman and traveled the trains, bringing back prisoners and AWOLs," Vivian Hanssen recalled.

The Hanssens on Howard's side were Danish or German, Vivian Hanssen thought. "Most likely Danish because of the double 's.' I was never sure which and I don't think he was sure. He came from a part that went back and forth." Vivian Baer Hanssen's own family background was German.

An intelligent and articulate woman, Vivian Hanssen was eighty-eight years old, widowed, and living in Venice, Florida, when her son was arrested as a Russian spy. Devastated by the news, she could offer no explanation for his actions. "He had a normal childhood. He was never in any trouble. Maybe a few things he wasn't happy about that I didn't know. But I don't want to talk about that.

"He had a pretty strict dad," she added. "I was the lenient one. He never showed any problems with me."

But Howard Hanssen, by several accounts, was more than strict; he was a stern disciplinarian, verbally and sometimes even physically abusive toward his son. Once, his father rolled him up in an old Navy mattress so he could not move. Trapped, with his arms pinned, Robert became frightened and began to cry. According to another account, Hanssen's father would spin him around until he became so dizzy he threw up, a bizarre punishment apparently designed to toughen him up. For much the same reason, his father, when Hanssen was a teenager, even secretly arranged for his son to fail his driving test. As a Chicago cop, Howard Hanssen could have managed this without any great difficulty.

*   *   *

When Hanssen was arrested, his wife, Bonnie, immediately called Plato Cacheris, the celebrated Washington defense attorney, and asked him to represent her husband. Cacheris agreed. He was used to high-profile cases; he had represented Aldrich Ames, the CIA spy, and Monica Lewinsky, among others. Cacheris asked Dr. David L. Charney, a Washington psychiatrist, to evaluate Hanssen, who talked at length to him about his father. Charney spent more than thirty hours with Hanssen, visiting him in jail in the months after his arrest.

"If I had to pick one core psychological reason for his spying, I would target the experience he had in his relations with his father," Charney said. "Hanssen's father seemed to be fundamentally impatient with him." His father, Charney concluded, was "borderline abusive." Among the various punishments he imposed on his son, "he forced him to sit with his legs spread in some fashion. I'm not implying a sexual element to the abuse. But he was forced to sit in that position and it was humiliating."

Jack Hoschouer, Hanssen's closest friend, said Howard constantly put his son down, and frequently complained that he would never be a success in life.

These accounts might be discounted as efforts to explain away Hanssen's espionage by apportioning some of the blame to his dead father. In American society, people who commit crimes often seek to paint themselves as victims. Whether Hanssen's treatment by his stern father was linked to his later betrayal of his country can be debated, but the relationship was without doubt a troubled one.

Jack's mother, Jeanette Hoschouer, said she had a clear memory of several encounters with Howard Hanssen, in which he openly and repeatedly bad-mouthed his son. She remembers running into Howard at the Jewel grocery store in Norwood Park. "He would say, 'Oh, my son, my son, is he ever going to amount to anything?' Always something belittling about Bob. No matter what Bob did, it wasn't right. I've never seen a father like that. He would never have a kind word to say about his only child."

Aside from putting down his son, Howard Hanssen's chief interest seemed to be betting on the horses. He spent almost all of his free time at the track. Even family vacations were planned around a day at the races in whatever city they were visiting.

People tend to edit out the bad experiences in the past and remember the good times. Hanssen knew his father was deeply disappointed in him. But in later life he preferred to cling to happier memories: his father taking him fishing, teaching him to shoot, building things together with Lincoln Logs. He remembered how he had tried to please his father by bringing him solutions to algebra problems.

As a boy, Bob Hanssen attended Norwood Park Grammar School and went on to Taft High School. It was there, in chemistry lab in his sophomore year, that he and Jack Hoschouer met, beginning their life-long friendship. Jack, whose family owned a printing business, had grown up next door to Norwood Park in Edison Park.

Hanssen's high school years sounded fairly normal. "We liked to look at girls, go out; we sometimes dated the same girls," Hoschouer recalled. It was all casual, he said. "Bob did not have a particular girlfriend."

Auto racing also captured their imagination. Trying to emulate their hero, Stirling Moss, the legendary British racing driver, the two teens ran their own version of the Grand Prix on the back streets of Chicago. "We broke a few traffic laws," Hoschouer said, "but we never got caught. We found some real curvy streets and saw how fast we could go. Testing our cornering skills." These antics usually took place in a Corvair that belonged to Hoschouer's mother.

In 1962, at age eighteen, Hanssen graduated from Taft. His photograph in the *Aerie,* the high school yearbook, reveals a crew-cut young man, wearing a tie, looking perhaps slightly younger than his age. Near his picture, he listed only three extracurricular activities—the Radio Club, the Honor Club, and Teacher's Helper—far fewer than many other students.* For his motto, he chose: "Science is the light of life."

Hanssen won a scholarship to Knox College, a small liberal arts school in Galesburg, Illinois. Hoschouer went off to St. Olaf College in Northfield, Minnesota. Although the two friends were separated geographically, they remained in close touch. "We spent our vacations almost every minute together," Hoschouer recalled. "He came up to St. Olaf once to see me and I went to Knox once."

At Knox, Hanssen majored in chemistry and math but also studied Russian. Momcilo Rosic, Hanssen's Russian teacher, was an anti-Communist Yugoslav. "I taught him only language, a requirement," he said. "Three or four hours per week, probably four.

"I think Hanssen took one year of Russian; he was a chem major, and Knox recommended that people in science should take French, Russian, or German. I am a strong anti-Communist; my students knew that. It was the Cold War; it was a struggle between two systems." Rosic said he was surprised that Hanssen chose to spy for Moscow. "He was certainly not influenced by me."

Nor was he influenced by his father, at least initially, in his choice of a career. Howard Hanssen wanted his son to become a doctor. Instead, after graduating from college in 1966 with a bachelor's degree in chemistry, he returned to Chicago and studied dentistry at Northwestern University for three years. The choice may have been calculated. "I think he went to dental school because his father wanted him to go to medical school," Hoschouer said.

Hanssen himself later claimed that he, too, wanted to enter medical school, but lacked the grades. In any event, cavities and bicuspids held little fascination for Hanssen. "After college I went to dental school," he

---

*Hanssen was a ham radio operator, an interest reflected in his membership in the Radio Club. Taft High School, like all Chicago schools at the time, did not use the traditional A through F grading system. Instead, it ranked students as S (Superior), E (Excellent), G (Good), F (Fair), or U (Unsatisfactory). To be admitted into the Honor Club, Hanssen had to have grades of E or above.

wrote years later to the editor of his high school alumni bulletin, "didn't like spit all that much (though I was in the 98th national percentile on my Dental Board exam), and decided to get an MBA and a CPA and go into law enforcement."*

In one of Howard Hanssen's encounters with Jeanette Hoschouer at Jewel's grocery, he complained about his son's tuition bills at dental school: "He's not going to amount to anything; I'm spending all this money on dental school."

In 1966, when Hanssen was studying dentistry, Hoschouer was taking graduate courses at the University of Hawaii. Jack's fiancée, Ayako Matsuda, was a nurse at the nearby Northwestern Memorial Hospital and lived in the nurses' residence. "Bob came over periodically to make sure I was okay," she recalled. "I'd feed him sandwiches, sometimes a grilled steak.

"He was so thoughtful. He knew I had to learn how to drive. He started to teach me. He took me onto the Kennedy Expressway, but I think my driving unnerved him. There were no more lessons after that.

"As a student at the dental school, he got a complimentary membership at the Playboy Club; all the first-year dental students did. He was so excited he called me up and said, 'Do you want to see what the Playboy Club is like?' And we rushed over there. And Bob was so innocent, he said, 'See those little things like bunny tails, you're not supposed to touch them.' "

While he was in dental school at Northwestern, Bob Hanssen met Bernadette Wauck, known as Bonnie, who came from a large and staunchly Catholic family in Chicago. There were eight children in all, four girls and four boys. One of her brothers, John Paul, became an Opus Dei priest and a professor at the Pontifical University of the Holy Cross in Rome, an Opus Dei institution; before entering the priesthood, he was a speechwriter for Robert P. Casey, the Democratic governor of Pennsylvania, who was an outspoken opponent of abortion. Bonnie Hanssen's uncle, Robert Hagarty, was a monsignor.†

---

*Letter to Geraldine Bloom from Robert P. Hanssen, May 2, 1999, in Taft Alumni Newsletter, Winter 2000.
†In later years, Hanssen had his own webpage, with photos of Bonnie's brother being installed as a priest in Rome. Because her brother was the last born of her siblings, he was known drolly within the family as "John Paul the Eighth," a sobriquet with a papal sound to it.

Bonnie Wauck was the daughter of Dr. Leroy A. Wauck, a Chicagoan, Navy veteran, and distinguished clinical psychologist who taught in Milwaukee at Marquette University, a Jesuit institution, and later for twenty years at Chicago's Loyola University.

Leroy Wauck, whose grandparents emigrated from Poland, was trained by the Jesuits in high school and seriously considered becoming a priest. He entered a seminary and studied there for two years until deciding it was not his calling. Before studying for the priesthood, he had dated Frances Hagarty, whose family roots were in Ireland, and they were married in 1944. Bonnie, their second daughter, was born two years later.

Except for the years in Wauwatosa, Wisconsin, when her father taught at Marquette, Bonnie grew up in Park Ridge, an upscale suburb of Chicago where Hillary Rodham Clinton also came of age. The Waucks lived at 609 Vine, in an old Dutch Colonial on a pleasant, tree-shaded street.

Bonnie, Frances Wauck recalled, was "a normal child, nothing extraordinary, a good kid, an average student, not a brilliant student." She went to the Mary Seat of Wisdom parish school. The Waucks, her mother said, were a close-knit family. "We all swam—summers on a lake in Wisconsin."

Leroy Wauck had once worked at the Chicago State Hospital, a psychiatric institution, and some of the children, including Bonnie, held summer jobs there. It was at the hospital that Bonnie encountered a tall dental student from Northwestern who worked there on weekends, sometimes even interviewing patients as though he were a psychiatrist. Bonnie was a sociology major at the time at Loyola, where all but one of her brothers and sisters went, taking advantage of the free tuition for children of faculty members.

When she brought Bob Hanssen home to meet her parents, they both liked him. "He was tall, dark, and handsome," her mother said. "He seemed to adore my daughter, he had good credentials in education—that was important to us—and treated her like a queen. That was enough for me."

They dated for about a year, and after Bonnie graduated from college, they were married in Park Ridge on August 9, 1968, at Mary Seat of Wisdom church. Leroy walked his daughter down the aisle. Bonnie Hanssen was twenty-one; her husband was three years older.

The young couple moved into an apartment on Chicago's north side. Bonnie taught grade school while Bob, who had by now abandoned dentistry, continued at Northwestern in his accounting classes.

But within a week of their wedding, Bonnie Hanssen received a highly disturbing phone call from a woman who said she was Bob's girlfriend and had just had sex with him. Bonnie might have married Bob, she said, but he belonged to the caller. When Bonnie confronted her new husband, he admitted he had seen the woman, but insisted there had only been some hugs and kisses. Bonnie tried to put the phone call out of her mind; she comforted herself by recalling what had occurred at a party at the state hospital. As Bonnie recounted it to family members, the woman was there and jumped onto Bob's lap; he had stood up and dumped her unceremoniously on the floor. Still, it was not a phone call that a wife would ever forget.

Having married into a rigorously Catholic family, it was almost inevitable that Hanssen would join the church. Before converting to Catholicism, however, he discussed the move with his mother, with whom he had always remained close. "It was shortly after they were married," Vivian Hanssen said. "He was friends with a monsignor who was a member of Bonnie's family; he has since died. He [Bob] asked me if it would hurt if he changed religions. I said no, I thought it was good for families to have the same religion." After joining the church, Hanssen became, to all appearances, ultra-religious, a devout, zealous Catholic, and like his wife and in-laws a member of Opus Dei.

Hanssen graduated from Northwestern in 1971 with an MBA in accounting and information systems. Afterward, he worked for a year as a junior associate at an accounting firm in Chicago. In 1973, he became a CPA.

But Hanssen, even at this early stage, hoped to get into intelligence work. He applied for a job at the National Security Agency, the nation's code-breaking and electronic eavesdropping arm. The NSA did not hire Hanssen, and he then sought work in law enforcement.

At the time, his father's career as a police officer was coming to an end. First a sergeant and later a lieutenant on the Chicago police force, Howard Hanssen had been for several years the district commander in Norwood Park, at the police station closest to the Hanssen home. Later, he was assigned to the notorious Chicago police "red squad," which engaged in illegal domestic surveillance of suspected Communists, leftists, political activists, and others deemed dangerous by Mayor Richard Daley's police force. In the early 1970s, the red squad fell into disrepute, as its activities and "subversive" targets—including the League of Women Voters and church groups—became known.*

Bill Houghton, a senior FBI analyst, had worked with Hanssen and knew him well. "He always spoke incredibly highly about his father. At one time after his father died he brought up his father's badge and held it like it was an icon. He used to talk about his father a lot. He would talk about his dad once a week. He always referred to his father in glowing, positive terms. He appeared to me to worship his father."

Hanssen told Houghton about his father's work on the Chicago red squad in the 1950s and 1960s. "Bob was proud of all the wiretapping and the break-ins and all the stuff that the squad did back then. In the early seventies the Chicago PD was starting to look into these things. He told me the squad was under his dad's supervision by then and a lot of the material that was collected had been gathered illegally.

"He said his dad took full responsibility for it. He told me there was a mysterious fire that broke out in the room that contained the file cabinets, and only the cabinets that contained the material from the red squad were destroyed; the cabinets right next to it were not burned. He told me the authorities were not amused by this incident. His father retired but there was a serious cloud over him. And Bob expressed great anguish about it. 'These liberal pinko bastards got away with everything and here they are trying to blame it on my dad.' He was very angry and bitter over a system that would allow his father to take the heat, while a lot of these pinko liberals got away with it."

Was Robert Hanssen angry that his father was wrongfully blamed, or because his father had in fact burned the files and was condemned instead of being secretly applauded inside the department? Houghton said Bob Hanssen was clear on the point. "He said his father had instigated the fire to destroy the evidence. Exactly."†

It was in July 1972 that Howard Hanssen retired. He did not, according to Jack Hoschouer, want his son to follow in his footsteps as a

---

*In 1982, the city of Chicago entered into a consent decree with the federal government, forbidding any further domestic spying by the police.

†Vivian Hanssen said she knew nothing of any fire. Her husband, she insisted, had retired "with a very good record. There was never anything like that." But she also said she never knew that Howard Hanssen had worked on the red squad. "I thought he worked on gangsters."

cop, but Hanssen did exactly that, joining the department in October, three months after his father had left the force.

The ambivalence of Hanssen's relationship with his father was underscored by his decision to join the police force. On the face of it, Hanssen appeared to be duplicating his father's career, perhaps trying to win his approval. In fact, his motive was just the opposite, in Jack Hoschouer's view: "His father made fun of him because he was only a cop; he put him down. He wanted his son to be more. He may have tried to emulate his father, but I think he did it to spite his father."

Yet Howard Hanssen must have harbored some internal pride in his son's decision, because of the symbolic act that followed. "His father sent him his gun when Bob joined the Chicago force," Hoschouer said. But the gesture resulted in some complications. "The postal service found the gun and intercepted it, and Bob had to go identify himself and pick it up someplace."

Robert Hanssen did not start out, like most rookies, as a beat cop. Instead, he was assigned to C-5, a secretive intelligence unit that investigated police corruption. As might be imagined, the unit was highly unpopular with the rank-and-file officers. It was an elite group that paralleled the internal affairs division but was separate from it.

Mitchell Ware, who was deputy police superintendent when Hanssen was on the force, supervised C-5. The unit's members ran sting operations, he said, and sometimes posed as drug dealers to snare crooked cops on the take. Chicago has traditionally had a high level of tolerance for municipal corruption; it is possible that the Daley machine decided to make a show of cleaning up the police force before the federal authorities moved in and did it for them.

Pat Camden, a spokesperson for the Chicago Police Department, said he assumes that Howard Hanssen advised his son not to go into C-5, whose members were regarded as finks. "If it was my son," Camden said, "I would be more concerned about his becoming a policeman first. Hanssen must have had total disregard for his father. In the unit you had qualified policemen, but he never made a street stop. How can you work in C-5 if you've never walked a beat?"

By May 1973, Hanssen was listed in VCD, the vice control division. "That was just a cover because C-5 was so secret," Camden explained. "He was never really in VCD."

At some point while working for the Chicago police, Hanssen was sent to a secret counterintelligence school to learn how to install bugs and other high-tech surveillance equipment. Ernie Rizzo, a Chicago private investigator, said he met Hanssen at the school, which was a storefront disguised as a television repair shop.

Robert Hanssen's three years as a cop were for the most part uneventful. He did receive one commendation. In June 1975, while waiting to testify in a case at the criminal courts building, Hanssen spotted a man running out of a courtroom. He was Donald Jackson, a prisoner with a long arrest record and a habit of trying to escape from the courthouse. There were hundreds of people in the halls as Hanssen and a burglary detective pursued the man through corridors and stairwells. Hanssen caught the culprit as he fled down a fire escape outside a second-floor window.

But Hanssen had set his sights higher than Richard Daley's police department. If the NSA would not have him, perhaps the FBI would. He applied to the bureau and was accepted. On January 12, 1976, at age thirty-one, he was sworn in as a special agent of the FBI.

"On Second Thought,
Give the Money to Mother Teresa"

After training at the FBI Academy in Quantico, Virginia, Hanssen was assigned to the Indianapolis field office, where he worked white-collar crime at the bureau's resident agency in Gary. The growing family, with two children, lived in nearby Munster.

All was far from harmonious when Hanssen's parents came to visit. According to Aya Hoschouer, who had married Jack in 1967, Bonnie Hanssen had confided to her that she finally confronted her father-in-law about the way he continued to treat Bob. "Early in their marriage when his parents would come to dinner, Bob would not come downstairs, he would get sick to his stomach and could not face his father at the table. Bonnie finally said, 'If you are under this roof, if you cannot be respectful to Bob, then you are not welcome to come.' "

In August 1978, Hanssen was transferred to the New York City field office. Now with three young children, Bob and Bonnie left the Midwest and moved into a house in Scarsdale, in Westchester County. In time, the Hanssens would have six children, three boys and three girls.

Although a transfer to the Big Apple might have seemed a welcome move up the bureau's career ladder, many agents shunned assignments to New York because of the high cost of living. Very few FBI agents could afford to live in the city itself. For most, the job meant a long commute by car or train from the suburbs, or being jammed into crowded subways, riding in from Queens. Scarsdale is an affluent community. The Hanssens bought a relatively modest house, and Bonnie joked to her mother that she lived "in the Scarsdale slums." Still, it was an expensive suburb, beyond the means of a young FBI agent with a growing family.

Nor was Hanssen's new job inspiring; he worked at first as an accountant in the criminal division. In March 1979, however, he was moved into the intelligence division. Now, for the first time, Hanssen was in the business of counterintelligence. But he was not, then or later, a street agent. Others might be assigned to the more glamorous job of surveillance and actually catching Russian spies; Hanssen was always in the back room.

His job was to help create a new, classified national counterintelligence database for the FBI. Much of the input came from New York, a major center of Soviet intelligence activity. In the city, the KGB operated from the Soviet Mission to the United Nations. In addition, there were Russian and other eastern bloc intelligence officers working in the secretariat of the UN itself. Both the Soviet mission and UN headquarters were thus prime targets for the FBI's counterintelligence agents in New York. The automated database Hanssen worked on contained information about hundreds of foreign officials, including intelligence officers. Its contents were classified up to the level of SECRET.*

In effect, Hanssen was compiling a who's who of Soviet intelligence. The data was not limited to the KGB and its known officers. Although the KGB, the Komitet Gosudarstvennoi Bezopasnosti, or Committee for State Security, was the best-known Soviet spy agency, its rival, the GRU, the Soviet military intelligence agency, was equally active in the United States. The GRU—the initials stood for Glavnoye Razvedyvatelnoye Upravlenie—was also a major target of the FBI.

The KGB and the GRU employed different covers overseas to conceal their espionage, a fact that Hanssen would quickly have realized. The KGB, for example, used Tass, the Soviet wire service, whose correspondents often doubled as spies. The GRU favored Amtorg, the Soviet commercial trading agency.

Although the FBI, when it finally closed in on Hanssen, initially believed his spying for the KGB had begun in 1985, it soon learned the

---

*Presidents since Harry S Truman in 1951 have issued executive orders allowing documents to be classified CONFIDENTIAL, SECRET, or TOP SECRET, depending on how much damage their disclosure might cause. But, in addition, there are code words for various categories of sensitive data that are, in effect, *above* TOP SECRET.

truth. He had in fact begun his career of betrayal in New York in 1979, almost immediately after he was transferred into the FBI's counterintelligence arm. And he had begun as a spy not for the KGB but for the GRU.

In 1979, Hanssen had walked into the Amtorg office in Manhattan and offered his services to the GRU. Interviewed by a government commission after pleading guilty to espionage, Hanssen claimed that his motive was money. "I wanted to get a little money and to get out of it," he said. The commission, headed by former FBI director William H. Webster, said in its report that Hanssen asserted he had spied because of "the pressure of supporting a growing family in New York City on an inadequate Bureau salary."*

The information Hanssen turned over to the GRU was sensational, one of the most guarded secrets of both the FBI and the Central Intelligence Agency. Hanssen gave away no less than the identity of TOPHAT—the most important U.S. intelligence source inside the GRU.

From his access to the FBI's files, Hanssen was able to identify TOPHAT as the bureau's code name for Dimitri Fedorovich Polyakov. At the time, Polyakov had been passing secrets to the United States for seventeen years. He was considered by Washington as an agent of supreme importance.

Hanssen had a chilling reason for his action; he wanted to turn in Polyakov to the GRU before the Russian might learn *his* identity and reveal it to the FBI. He had to be well aware that his information would probably result in TOPHAT's execution—that was the whole point. As the Webster panel put it, "Hanssen disclosed Top Hat's identity because he feared that the Soviet officer might be a threat to him."†

Hanssen passed three batches of secrets to the GRU. In his first approach, he disclosed that the FBI was bugging a Soviet residential complex. He also turned over a list of suspected Soviet intelligence officers. In a letter to the GRU complaining that his first payment was too low, he even revealed he was an FBI agent. He communicated with the GRU through encoded radio transmissions and through one-time pads, an un-

---

*"A Review of FBI Security Programs," Commission for Review of FBI Security Programs, U.S. Department of Justice, March 2002, p. 7. The Webster commission was created in response to Hanssen's arrest.
†Webster commission, p. 8.

breakable cipher system favored by the Russians. But of the various secrets Hanssen passed to the GRU, none compared to his betrayal of TOPHAT.

John F. Mabey, an FBI counterintelligence agent in New York, had recruited Polyakov in January 1962 at a clandestine meeting at midnight at Grant's Tomb. A few months before, Polyakov had let it be known he wanted to talk, but then said he had changed his mind. The FBI agent, an astute, wiry man who had joined the bureau right out of Notre Dame, kept after Polyakov. Finally, the Russian agreed to meet at Grant's Tomb. In that cinematic setting, at the dark, deserted resting place of the eighteenth president of the United States, John Mabey, then thirty-eight, had landed one of the biggest recruitments of the Cold War.

It was Mabey who chose the name TOPHAT.* Polyakov said he was willing to spy for America because he felt his talents had gone unrecognized by the GRU. He provided Mabey with the names of four Americans who were spying for the Soviet Union.†

When TOPHAT was posted overseas, the CIA took over handling him. TOPHAT, previously known as BOURBON by the CIA, was given a new code name by the intelligence agency: GTBEEP.

In 1973, Polyakov turned up in India as a Soviet military attaché. Polyakov would go fishing on the banks of the Yamuna River in New Delhi. He would seem to pay little attention to a heavyset, dark-haired man with a fishing pole who joined him on the riverbank. But the big man was Waldimir "Scotty" Skotzko, a veteran case officer whom the CIA had dispatched to India to handle the agency's most important asset.

In 1977, as they fished on the riverbank, TOPHAT reported that he had been ordered back to Moscow, news that alarmed Skotzko. What will happen to you if your work for us is discovered? he asked, knowing the answer.

---

*As far as Mabey could recall, he derived the name from Top Cat, a rakish alley cat who wore a little hat and was the hero of a Saturday morning Hanna-Barbera cartoon popular on television in the 1960s.
†They were Jack E. Dunlap, an Army sergeant working at the National Security Agency; Nelson C. "Bulldog" Drummond, a Navy yeoman; William H. Whalen, an Army lieutenant colonel assigned to the Joint Chiefs of Staff; and Herbert W. Boeckenhaupt, an Air Force sergeant who betrayed the secrets of the Strategic Air Command. Dunlap committed suicide; the others were arrested, convicted, and given long prison sentences.

"Bratskaya mogila," was Polyakov's grim reply. An unmarked grave.

In Moscow, Polyakov used a high speed "burst" transmitter given to him by the CIA to radio messages from a streetcar traveling past the American embassy. He was also given a clock for his apartment in Moscow that lit up in response to a radio signal to inform him that a dead drop where he had left documents had been cleared by the CIA.

In 1979, TOPHAT was posted back to New Delhi again, promoted by this time to the rank of lieutenant general. Over the years, Polyakov provided extremely valuable political-military information to the CIA, including data on Soviet strategic missiles, nuclear strategy, and chemical and biological weapons. In all, the material Polyakov stole for the CIA filled more than twenty-seven file drawers at Langley.

In 1980, General Polyakov returned to Moscow for the last time. Retired and surrounded by his family in Moscow, TOPHAT appeared to have escaped the fate that he predicted would await him if his spying was discovered. He was unaware that in New York, Robert Hanssen had already betrayed him to the GRU. But the Russians, for reasons still uncertain, took no action against him at that time.

Five years later, on April 16, 1985, Aldrich H. Ames, a CIA clandestine officer, walked into the Soviet embassy in Washington and left a letter with the KGB, offering information and asking for $50,000. A month later, he returned to the embassy and met with a senior KGB officer who was almost certainly Viktor I. Cherkashin, the embassy's chief of counterintelligence. Two days after that, he was handed $50,000. Then, on June 13, at Chadwicks restaurant in Georgetown, Ames handed over the names of virtually every CIA intelligence source in the Soviet Union, sending ten to their execution and many others to prison. For this he was eventually paid $2.7 million by the KGB and promised another $1.9 million, for a total of $4.6 million.

Among the names provided to the Russians by Ames were Valery Martynov and Sergei Motorin, the two secret FBI sources inside the Soviet embassy in Washington. But Ames also turned over the name of General Dimitri Fedorovich Polyakov of the GRU.

TOPHAT's son, a Soviet diplomat who had also been sent to New Delhi, was recalled from there in 1986 after only a year. At the CIA's headquarters in Langley, Virginia, when the directorate of operations (or DO) learned that the son had been recalled short of tour, it realized for the first time that TOPHAT might be in trouble. But it did not know why. That same year, as the CIA later learned, TOPHAT was arrested, although the Soviets did not reveal that fact until 1990. Later, Moscow said that Polyakov had been executed on March 15, 1988.*

The CIA could not imagine what had gone wrong. Then, with the arrest and debriefing of Aldrich Ames in 1994, Langley thought the mystery was solved. In 2001, the realization that Hanssen had betrayed TOPHAT in 1979, six years *before* Ames had done so, stunned the CIA and the FBI. And it created a new puzzle.

Counterintelligence has been aptly called a "wilderness of mirrors," and the news that Hanssen had given away Polyakov long before Ames raised intriguing questions. Why had the Soviets not moved immediately against Polyakov in 1979? A number of answers were possible. The KGB and the GRU were bitter competitors who barely spoke to each other (somewhat like the CIA and the FBI until coordination between the two agencies improved somewhat in the post-Ames era). The KGB looked down on the GRU as "the boots," or *sapogi,* a term of derision used by KGB officers among themselves when talking about their military rivals; the expression implied that the boot-wearing military men lacked subtlety and were their intellectual inferiors.

Against this background, the GRU may have wished to conceal from the KGB the embarrassing fact that one of its generals had been fingered as a CIA spy. And the GRU also may have wanted to conceal from the KGB the fact that it was running a mole inside the FBI.

Even if the GRU did share the information about Polyakov with the KGB, it is possible that the Russians did not act right away because they preferred to place the GRU general under surveillance to see where the trail might lead. Or Moscow may have wanted further confirmation, which it eventually got from Aldrich Ames. There is, of course, a more ominous possibility, that the Soviets might have used TOPHAT to feed disinformation back to the West, either having turned him or utilizing him for that purpose without his knowledge.

*   *   *

None of this was known to the CIA, the FBI, or to Bonnie Hanssen when she happened upon her husband in the basement of their home in

---

*General Polyakov was arrested on July 4, 1986, interrogated for twenty months, and shot.

Scarsdale writing a letter. Startled, he hastily tried to conceal the letter from her.

Bonnie Hanssen's first thought was that her husband was having an affair. He had stopped going to communion around that time, and she had noticed it; perhaps he was seeing another woman. She confronted him with her suspicion. It was nothing like that, Hanssen assured her. Then what was it?

Finally, Hanssen admitted to his wife that he was selling secrets to the Soviets.* He insisted, falsely, that he had not given them anything of significance; he was running a scam. But he also admitted that the Russians had paid him $30,000.

Dismayed at the news, Bonnie Hanssen insisted they see a priest. Because both Bonnie and her husband were members of Opus Dei— Bob had joined in 1978—they chose to see a priest from that organization. Founded in Spain in 1928, Opus Dei, which means God's Work, was approved by the Vatican in 1950 and given special status by Pope John Paul II in 1982 as a "personal prelature," independent to some extent of local dioceses. The organization claims three thousand members in the United States and eighty-four thousand worldwide.

Typically, Opus Dei priests do not operate from churches but from what the group calls "study centers" in a number of cities. Together, the Hanssens in the fall of 1980 went to one of these, the Crawford Center, later called the Overlook Study Center, at 99 Overlook Circle in nearby New Rochelle.

There the couple with the unusual problem consulted Robert P. Bucciarelli, a genial Opus Dei priest from New Canaan, Connecticut, who was a graduate of Harvard College and a theologian fluent in three languages. Father Bob, a somewhat short, dark-haired cleric, was also an enthusiastic tennis player with a serving motion that tended to disconcert his opponents.

That the Hanssens went to see Father Bucciarelli was not a random choice. Bonnie Hanssen already knew him from her involvement in Opus Dei. In October 1980, Father Bucciarelli had moved to New

---

*On the night of Hanssen's arrest on February 18, 2001, the FBI spoke to Bonnie Hanssen at her house and then escorted her to a hotel in Tysons Corner, in northern Virginia, and questioned her at length. She cooperated with the FBI and revealed to agents the encounter with her husband in the basement. It was the first time that the FBI learned that Hanssen's spying had begun not in 1985 but in 1979.

Rochelle from Chicago, the city where the first Opus Dei center in the United States was established. Bonnie's mother had known him in Chicago.

Now Hanssen had something to confess. He had, he told the priest, turned over information to the Soviets, and had received $30,000 in exchange.

Father Bucciarelli, contacted by the author, declined to discuss any details of the visit by the Hanssens, although he confirmed, obliquely, that it had taken place. "I really don't remember when he came to see me," he said. Roman Catholic priests are forbidden by canon law from disclosing what is revealed in a confession. However, a visit by a couple might be considered a consultation, rather than a sacramental confession, so the legal status of the Hanssens' visit was unclear.*

After listening to the Hanssens, Father Bucciarelli recommended that the FBI man turn himself in to the authorities. The next day, however, the priest telephoned the Hanssens and asked them to come back again.

At this next visit, according to the account later given to the FBI by Mrs. Hanssen, Father Bob said he had been pondering the problem and had second thoughts. The matter could be resolved, he said, if, instead of surrendering to the authorities, Hanssen gave the Soviet money to a worthy charity.

Plato Cacheris, Hanssen's lawyer after his arrest for espionage, confirmed the account of the couple's visit to Father Bucciarelli. "The priest told him he should turn himself in, then called Hanssen and said he could give the money to the church. He [Hanssen] told Bonnie he gave a certain amount each month to Mother Teresa."

Hanssen also told his wife that he would not sell any more secrets to the Russians, that he was done spying. "He said he would stop," Cacheris said. "She believed him."

There is, of course, a wonderful irony if Moscow's money was laundered in this fashion and in fact ended up with Mother Teresa through

---

*Congress has not recognized privileges for priests, lawyers, psychiatrists, and other professionals, but the United States Supreme Court, in *United States* v. *Nixon,* the famous Watergate tapes decision, declared that generally, "an attorney or a priest may not be required to disclose what has been revealed in professional confidence." By 1963, all fifty states had laws recognizing a confidentiality privilege for the clergy, but the laws varied a great deal and it was not always clear whether a priest or a person confessing was the holder of the privilege.

the Solomon-like intervention of Father Bob, the Harvard priest with the disconcerting tennis serve.

Although Hanssen insisted to Bonnie that he had given the money to Mother Teresa, there is no easy way to confirm that he actually did so. Sister Mary Dominga, director of the eastern region of Mother Teresa's Missionaries of Charity, declined to discuss contributions to the charity.

"We don't fund-raise, we don't ask for money," she said. "We depend on divine providence."

5

Headquarters

Jim Ohlson had joined the FBI in 1972, after serving with the 101st Airborne Division in Vietnam and earning a master's degree in math at the University of Pittsburgh. The bureau sent him to the defense language school in Monterey to learn Arabic, then to New York to work on Middle East counterterrorism investigations, "concentrating on Palestinian matters."*

After five years, Ohlson was promoted to the budget unit at FBI headquarters in Washington. The unit, with only four special agents and two clerks, was part of the bureau's intelligence division.† Small and unglamorous it might have been, but in any bureaucracy the people who work on the budget know everything, and this was true in the FBI.

In January 1981, a newcomer arrived at the unit from New York. Supervisory Special Agent Robert Hanssen, like Ohlson, was doing his first tour at headquarters. Because Hanssen was a CPA, the budget unit was a logical place for him to be assigned. He commuted to work from a house the Hanssens bought on Whitecedar Court in Vienna, Virginia.

"When I first met him," Ohlson recalled, "I asked where are you from? Chicago. What high school? Taft. My gosh, I was there. And it turned out we were just one class apart. A week or so later I brought in

---

*New York was considered so important an office that it was headed by an assistant director of the FBI. Ohlson's squad served under Assistant Director John Malone, known behind his back as "Cement Head" because, as one former colleague gently put it, "he was not exactly a rocket scientist."
†In 1993, the FBI's intelligence division was renamed the National Security Division (NSD).

the yearbook to show the secretaries and Bob and have a good laugh over our old pictures.

"We hit it off instantly," Ohlson said. Aside from their friendship, he respected Hanssen's technical ability. Ohlson was leaving the budget unit that spring, but before going he managed to wangle approval to buy a Texas Instruments programmable calculator. "We had no desktop computers yet, that was the closest thing to one. I was glad to hand it over to Bob. He put a financial program on it."

At the time, Joseph L. Tierney, a gray-haired Irishman from Long Island, was chief of CI-3, the counterintelligence support section for the division. As such, Tierney supervised both the budget unit and the bureau's Soviet analytical unit. Tierney, too, was impressed with Hanssen. "He was a very bright guy, and his assignment was very broad. He had an ability to explain technical stuff to people like myself who needed to know it."

It was almost inevitable, therefore, that within the budget unit Hanssen was detailed to the bureau's secret and highly sensitive Dedicated Technical Program. The name was deliberately vague, designed to mask the fact that it was the FBI's system for developing and refining bugs, wiretaps, and even more exotic spy gadgetry used against foreign embassies and other counterintelligence targets. "He worked on DTP, which paid for everything technical, chiefly electronic surveillance," Tierney confirmed.

"The program paid for R and D and acquisition of equipment. DTP would make the proposal and spend the money when it came through." In some instances, Hanssen would learn where a bug or other device was to be planted. "He would not necessarily know where it was going. But if it was a custom-made device for one installation, he would probably know where it was going in."

When the bureau's technical experts came up with suggestions for more sophisticated bugging devices, they would have to go to Hanssen. "They're always trying to make transmitters consume less power, make them smaller and better disguised," Tierney said. "He's taking the ideas and running them by the execs in the division; have the engineers gone gaga? Is this something we really need or is it marginal?"

As a result of his position, Hanssen knew the full array of the FBI's surveillance equipment, from miniature video cameras that could be concealed in a wall or ceiling, to tiny transmitters able to broadcast room conversations, even whispers. "He would have a pretty good grip on what were the strengths and inadequacies of our technical capacity," Tierney said. "He knew what we were dreaming of having and didn't have yet."

Hanssen, in short, was emerging as the FBI's Wizard of Oz. But unlike L. Frank Baum's fictional wizard, Hanssen was both real and capable. He not only had an overview of the bureau's ability to bug and tap its counterintelligence targets, he served as a watchman over the entire program. "He would monitor what had been approved two years before," Tierney said. "To see if the gadgets had been bought. He spent a lot of time on encrypted radio gear that we used internally."

The encrypted radios were a vital tool for the counterintelligence agents. When the FBI places a Russian intelligence officer under surveillance, it is well aware that the KGB (and now its successor, the SVR) monitors the airwaves to see if there is unusual radio traffic in an area—a tip-off that the FBI might be tailing one of their people. The encryption at least makes it more difficult for the Russians to be sure that the traffic is the FBI's.

Tierney appreciated Hanssen's skills and came to rely on him. "He was a geek, but fairly polished. He was a ham radio operator. He was not a degreed electrical engineer. The people in the engineering section, in TSD, the Technical Services Division, kind of resented it because he knew so much. If they were giving us a snow job he could tell us."

Although Hanssen's technical skills were recognized, he remained an aloof and rather remote figure, an outsider to most of his coworkers. That was certainly how Hanssen seemed to Dick Alu, a former FBI agent who worked with him in the budget unit for two years.

"Your typical FBI agent would be a used-car salesman whom you trusted—if that's possible. An agent to be effective has to be able to sell himself. You had to have good interpersonal skills. Bob did not have good interpersonal skills. Bob was the odd man out. Bob did not socialize after work. 'Hey, want to go out for a couple of pops?' Bob was not that type."

Partly it was his appearance, and the way he dressed. Under J. Edgar Hoover, FBI agents were required to wear white shirts and conventional business attire. "But after 1972," Alu said, "when Hoover died and he didn't roll the stone back after three days, the dress code changed dramatically. Not for Bob; he still wore the white shirt, the dark clothes."

Among at least some of Hanssen's fellow agents, his somber mien and conservative attire earned him the nickname "Dr. Death" and "Dr. Doom." Or, Alu said, "some people called him 'the mortician.'"

"He kind of lived in the shadows," said John F. Lewis, Jr., a former assistant FBI director in charge of the intelligence division. "If there was a shadow in the room, he'd be sitting in it. He was very, very bright. He was good at analytical work; his problem was he didn't work well with others. He was the last person in the world to say let's have a drink with."

Like Lewis, Phillip A. Parker, who was chief of the division's Soviet section in 1982 when Hanssen worked in the budget unit, remembered him as "a lurker," always hovering at the side of any gathering.

Donald E. Stukey, Parker's successor, considered Hanssen irksome. "When I was chief of the Soviet section, he'd come in once in a while. He had an annoying habit, if you were conducting a meeting in your office, he would stand in the doorway until you finally said, 'What do you want?'"

One veteran FBI counterintelligence officer, Edward J. Curran, knew Hanssen both in New York and at headquarters. "I found him to be very reclusive; his demeanor was somewhat uncomfortable. He was very thoughtful, very reserved, very quiet. Very poor in groups, always liked to get you aside in a corner. He's kind of in your space. You'd just try to get away from the guy. He's the kind of guy, you see him in the hall at headquarters, you'd turn the other way and try to escape."

Hanssen's boss, Joe Tierney, thought this view of Hanssen, which was shared by many in the division, was overdrawn, and he liked him. "He was more colorless in dress than the average agent, but not gloomy. He was a very bright guy. He was seriously religious." He remembered Hanssen as tall and gaunt, with pale skin. "He had kind of a nervous smile, sort of self-conscious. He smiled a lot."

Hanssen's ability to explain technical matters to his superiors, the quality that Tierney had admired, may have been helped by some coaching from Dick Alu. "This guy was extremely bright, one of the smartest people I'd ever run into," Alu said. "We were trying to come up with management techniques to measure how effective we were, to justify our programs to Congress. Bob came up with terminology and I'd say to Bob, 'I understand, you understand what you're talking about, but you got to present it to the management here who might not understand the terms you are using.'"

Alu told Hanssen, "You've got to use words like 'Dick and Jane carried a pail of water up the hill.' I could just see the wry expression on his face. He just didn't suffer fools gladly. Why should I have to reduce myself to this level? I said, 'You gotta be able to communicate with people. You communicate with whatever level they are.' "

Hanssen's friends in the bureau were few in number. To many, he came across as arrogant, someone who did not bother to conceal the fact that he thought himself brighter than his coworkers. The colleagues he did get to know well were those he apparently considered his intellectual equals.

In the bureau, Hanssen made no secret of his conservative political views. He talked about religion to anyone who would listen. He was vehemently antiabortion, and to all appearances a strong anti-Communist. He had no use for gays and lesbians.

Directly across the hall from Hanssen's office on the fourth floor were the division's analytical units. Paul Moore, who became one of Hanssen's closest friends in the bureau, worked in CI-3B, one of the two analytical units. A large, thoughtful, and soft-spoken man, Moore spoke Mandarin and was the FBI's foremost China analyst. In appearance and manner, he could easily be mistaken for an academic who had wandered into the Hoover building by accident.

Like Hanssen, Moore had grown up in Chicago and was educated by the Jesuits in high school. His father taught chemistry at Loyola University, where Bonnie Hanssen's father taught psychology. Moore was teaching a course on China at Georgetown University and still working on his Ph.D. when the FBI, desperate for a Chinese-language translator, tapped him in 1975.

Moore met Hanssen in 1981 when he joined the budget unit; their Chicago and Catholic ties helped to cement their friendship, but personal computers, then relatively new to the world, were even more important. "I finished my doctorate in 1981," Moore said, "and my wife, Janice, to congratulate me, says, 'OK, I will buy you a computer.' " Moore had heard that Hanssen was a computer guru. "I went to Bob Hanssen and said, 'What do you think I should get?' He said, 'You need to get an Apple, it would be just right for you.' So my wife paid for an Apple II+.

"Bob says there's a user's group, Washington Apple Pi; he introduced me to that. We met the first Saturday of every month in Bethesda. Bob was at those meetings. They had speakers, special interest groups you could go to.

"The people I hung out with were adults playing adventure games. Bob was always showing me things you could do in the computers, with jump cables, expansion card slots. Bob was definitely part of the pocket protector group.

"We were computer buddies. I remember on a Saturday morning at the Washington Apple Pi group—this particular meeting was in Constitution Hall—and a guy took his mouse and double-clicked and a folder opened up. The whole place, including Bob, stood up and cheered. It was the first meeting where they introduced the Mac.

"One day I got a chip that would increase memory from one to four meg, and I got this kit and I'm sweating blood trying to do it; you needed a special wrench to get into the computer. There were a lot of warnings about static electricity—don't touch this or that. Bob has his wrench going and I'm reading the instructions and Bob is working on it. Bob already had the motherboard out. The last step was to cut a wire. Bob takes the pliers and snips off the capacitor. When we turned on the power it took longer, it booted up slower, because it had more memory. And I'm saying 'Ohmigod, we did something wrong.' But it worked. He was fearless, and very competent."

Hanssen's technical talents continued to advance his status inside headquarters. He not only knew all of the FBI's technical surveillance secrets, he became one of the bureau's experts on the use of polygraphs.

Understanding lie detectors was, of course, an area of special interest to someone who had secretly been spying for the Soviets and might contemplate doing so again. Clearly Hanssen would not have welcomed a requirement that he take a polygraph himself; no doubt he explored ways to beat the machine in case that ever happened. Moreover, he was particularly well placed within the bureau to subtly discourage broader use of the polygraph.

Although the FBI had traditionally resisted lie detectors, in the early 1980s it was considering their wider use. At the time, the FBI administered polygraphs only in internal investigations of employees suspected of wrongdoing, and to agents or analysts who were detailed temporarily to the CIA or the NSA.* The FBI did not want other agen-

---

*During this period, two FBI analysts were polygraphed before being assigned to other agencies. Tierney and two other managers took the tests as well, he said, "as a leadership gesture. We were not going to subject our own people to it without doing it ourselves." But Tierney's action was an exception to the bureau's general practice at the time.

cies giving lie detector tests to its employees. "The bureau said, 'We'll do it,' " Paul Moore recalled. " 'We don't want our people being put through who knows what.' " And at the time, applicants for employment in the FBI were not given polygraphs.

Nor were agents assigned to particularly sensitive counterintelligence cases given polygraphs. A decade later that policy was changed. The FBI agents working on the Aldrich Ames case in the 1990s, for example, were given lie detector tests.

Polygraphs are notoriously unreliable, and for that reason evidence developed from lie detectors is not allowed in court. In contrast to the FBI, the CIA has an almost religious faith in the polygraph. The fact that Aldrich Ames, the CIA's most damaging mole, passed his polygraph tests (with a little advice from the KGB) did nothing to discourage that faith. Many CIA employees *think* that polygraphs work and are frightened of them, which makes their use at least partially effective. The agency's clandestine officers are supposed to be routinely polygraphed every five years, or when posted overseas.

As the bureau debated whether to expand its use of polygraphs, it brought in Dr. John A. Podlesny, a Ph.D. psychologist from the University of Utah, to study the problem at the FBI Academy in Quantico, Virginia. The intelligence division's liaison with the professor, Joe Tierney recalled, was Robert Hanssen.*

The result, according to one former FBI man, is that "Hanssen influenced the bureau not to use polygraphs." Academic studies about polygraphs tend to be abstruse, complicated documents, full of acronyms and jargon and not easily understood by those outside the polygraph fraternity. To FBI officials, Hanssen seemed particularly adept at explaining what it all meant. In Hanssen's interpretation, the data from the study meant that polygraphs had limited value, perhaps useful to a degree only in a specific investigation. Hanssen, Tierney said, described "two different scenarios. One where there is a focused investigation and the polygrapher knows a lot about the subject and the case and the areas where possible deception might occur. But it's different in a general, screening polygraph. It's a grind; everybody understands that most of the people they are polygraphing are good

---

*Podlesny, who remained with the FBI, confirmed that he had written the classified study of polygraphs for the bureau in the early 1980s. He said he did not remember Robert Hanssen.

law-abiding citizens." The work was so boring and unproductive, Tierney added, "You couldn't ask people to do it [screening polygraphs] for more than three years; they'd go crazy."

As Hanssen explained it, Tierney said, in all polygraphs "the likelihood of a false negative—the polygrapher says I see no indication of deception and the polygrapher is wrong—is higher than the likelihood of a false positive, where the polygrapher says the guy is lying and the polygrapher is wrong."

Put simply, Hanssen was reporting that polygraphs did not work very well because people could fool the machine. As a result, more subjects could get away with lying than could tell the truth but be wrongly accused of deception.

"There was a lot of loose talk about how to beat the polygraph: take two aspirin, clamp your toes together, think of people in a movie, or pinch yourself," Tierney recalled. "I have no idea whether any of it worked." But because of Hanssen's expertise about polygraphs, "he would have been in a pretty good position—better than others—to beat it, if it is possible, if he'd been given one."

Not that there was much danger he would ever be wired to the machine. "Hanssen knew the bureau's thinking, and that culturally it was unlikely to happen. There has been some speculation that if he had known he would have to take a polygraph, he would not have done what he did."

During Hanssen's time in the budget unit, he was at the nerve center of the intelligence division and its foreign counterintelligence activities. The unit managed the FBI's portion of the National Foreign Intelligence Program (NFIP), the program that accounts for about two-thirds of the nation's overall intelligence spending.* It was Hanssen's unit that prepared the division's budget figures for Congress. As a result, he had access to the full range of the FBI's intelligence and counterintelligence (CI) operations.

"In the budget unit," said David Major, a longtime FBI counterintelligence agent, "Hanssen knew what worked, what we were spending money on, and what we were going to spend money on. If he had been

---

*The National Foreign Intelligence Program includes the budget for the FBI, CIA, NSA, the Defense Intelligence Agency (DIA), and the National Reconnaissance Office (NRO). The other one-third of the intelligence budget goes for tactical intelligence under the control of the Defense Department in the TIARA (Tactical Intelligence and Related Activities) program.

a street agent he would only know what was going on in his squad. But Bob understood the totality. He was one of the few people placed to know everything. Very few people know everything; maybe thirty people out of hundreds."

Hanssen's access, in sum, was virtually unlimited. Major was blunt: "He knew all the secrets."

6

The Year of the Spy

In August 1983, after two years in the budget unit, Hanssen was transferred across the hall to the Soviet analytical unit, formally designated CI-3A but known in-house as the "A" unit.

Now he would be concentrating exclusively on the FBI's principal target, the Soviet Union. The analytical unit studied the espionage activities, methods, and agents of the KGB and the GRU in the United States. In short, in his new job, Hanssen would be analyzing who Moscow's spies were and how they operated here.

Hanssen's new boss was Thomas E. Burns, Jr., an astute New Yorker from Queens who went to Catholic schools and joined the FBI in 1964 right out of St. John's University law school. He and Hanssen got on well and sometimes lunched together in the bureau's cafeteria. Below Burns, the unit chief, were two supervisory special agents— Hanssen was one—and about eighteen analysts.

The A unit provided support for the FBI's Soviet operational section, which from headquarters supervised the counterintelligence efforts of the Washington and New York field offices as well as the other field offices around the country.* Once again, Hanssen was in the back room, watching from afar as others performed the more exciting work of trailing and occasionally catching Moscow's spies.

---

*The FBI's intelligence division was divided into operational sections, such as the Soviet (now Eurasian) section responsible for counterintelligence operations, and the analytical sections. As the names implied, the operational sections supervised operations; the analytical sections analyzed.

But in his new assignment, Hanssen learned about the FBI's operations using double agents. These were usually Americans, often someone in the military, who pretended to volunteer to spy for Moscow. The double agent, known in intelligence parlance as a DA, would pass along classified documents, most of them genuine, known in the trade as "feed." The feed would be cleared at a high level after officials decided that the documents would not cause irredeemable harm to national security; the purpose of the exercise was to convince the KGB or the GRU that the double agent was genuine.

"We were looking at feed," Burns said, "but mostly at the product, the tasking of the DA by the hostile service." By studying the information the Soviets asked the double agent to obtain, the unit could learn what the Russians were after, and what, by inference, they already knew.

Since Soviet intelligence played the same game, running doubles against the United States, Hanssen's unit would also try to determine whether any Soviet "walk-ins" to the FBI were genuine or fake. "We did reviews of the bona fides of volunteers and recruitments," Burns said.

The analysts studied material flowing in from defectors and received data from the Soviet operational section. "For example, a new Soviet might arrive at their embassy and based on his slot, it would be suspected he was an IO [intelligence officer]. We would look at reports on a new IO or suspected IO, looking for clues to establish whether he was in fact an IO."

But as important as these tasks were, the unit had another crucial mission: to pinpoint penetrations by Soviet intelligence inside the United States government. "If we identified a Soviet as an intelligence officer," Burns said, "the operational section would take a closer look at him, which in turn could lead to identifying a penetration. Or we might find an operation had been compromised. We would pass that along to the operational section, which would conduct the investigation. A penetration would be one possible explanation for the compromise."

The best way to find a mole, of course, was to recruit someone in the opposition intelligence service who could reveal the name. "A recruited agent gives away people right up front, to protect themselves," Burns pointed out.

Recruiting KGB agents was the responsibility not of the analysts but of the Soviet operational section of division 5, the intelligence division. "The highest purpose of a bureau recruitment would be to try to identify penetrations in the U.S. government," Burns added. This dovetailed nicely with the goal of the analytical unit. "The primary goal of our unit was to find where the Soviets were getting their information."

There was enormous excitement in 1983 in the intelligence division and in the Soviet analytical unit, because the FBI, unknown to Moscow, had recruited two KGB officers inside the Soviet embassy in Washington.

Lieutenant Colonel Valery Martynov had arrived in the capital in November 1980 with his wife, Natalya. A big man, over six feet tall and 190 pounds, he did not fit the stereotype of the glum Russian agent; he was jovial, with a friendly, cheerful manner, and spoke fluent English. He and his wife lived in Alexandria, Virginia, with their two children, a twelve-year-old son in junior high school and a daughter of five.

Martynov was a Line X officer, which meant that his job was to collect scientific and technical secrets for the KGB's Directorate T. In 1982, a CIA officer spotted Martynov at a technical meeting. A former CIA man recalled how the dance began. "Martynov showed up at a meeting, one in a series, and our guy chatted with him. Martynov missed the next meeting, but at one of the subsequent meetings he was there. The agency officer came back and said, 'This guy is different. This is a very unusual Russian.' "

At that point, COURTSHIP, a joint FBI-CIA unit created to recruit Soviets, moved in and took over. The operation was successful. Before very long, Martynov agreed to work for U.S. intelligence. The FBI gave him the code name PIMENTA; the CIA called him GTGENTILE. As his contact, the CIA assigned one of its most experienced case officers, Rodney W. Carlson. A tall, thin man with dark hair and a Lincolnesque face, Carlson in Moscow had handled the CIA's most celebrated spy, Colonel Oleg Penkovsky of the GRU. For the FBI, Martynov's case agent was Jim Holt, a white-haired Virginian and a veteran counterintelligence specialist. Over a period of three years, they met with Martynov more than fifty times, on the average of once every three weeks, in safe houses and other locations. His motives for spying for the FBI were not clear, although he was paid for his information and told that a much larger amount was being held in escrow for him in the United States should he ever decide to defect.

One intelligence officer who read the file on the case discounted money as Martynov's primary motive. Rather, he thought, "it was the excitement, and the idea of doing something really secret. You can't believe what you are told about motivation anyway, because people don't understand their own motivation. Martynov was intrigued by the game. He did not think spying for the Americans was wrong. Because he did not regard us as an enemy."

In a separate, parallel operation that also began in 1982, the FBI recruited Sergei Motorin, a young KGB major from Archangel, a port city in Russia's far north, who had arrived in Washington in 1980. Motorin was a Line PR officer, which meant he collected political intelligence. Sandy-haired, with a small mustache, Motorin, like Martynov, was a big man, a six-foot-two tennis player. He lived in an apartment in Arlington with his wife, Olga, and their two young girls.

But Motorin had a wandering eye; the FBI knew he was seeing a prostitute and had a mistress at the Soviet embassy as well, the wife of a diplomat. "He got into a wreck in his car with the hooker in the car," said a former FBI agent. "The insurance adjustor tipped us off. That's how it all started."

FBI counterintelligence agents in the Washington field office began keeping closer track of the KGB officer. Soon afterward, they watched Motorin walk into a store in downtown Washington and trade his operational allowance of vodka and Cuban cigars for stereo equipment. The vodka and cigars were supposed to be used to help recruit American agents for the KGB. The major was not only cheating on his wife, he had now committed an indiscretion that could get him into serious trouble with his superiors.

It was time for a chat. With the leverage it now had over Motorin, the FBI did not have too much difficulty in persuading him to listen, although it took several months and constant pressure to recruit him.

In April 1983, the FBI met with Motorin for the first time in a safe house, an apartment in Crystal City in northern Virginia. He was given the code name MEGAS. To the CIA, Motorin was GTGAUZE.

Joseph K. Eddleman, Jr., Motorin's FBI case officer, rented the safe house. Dale Pugh, one of the FBI agents handling Motorin, was given $4,000 and told to buy furniture for the apartment so the neighbors would not wonder why it was empty. Pugh loved the hamburgers at Ollie's Trolley across the street; he was disappointed when, to preserve security, they moved to another safe house in Alexandria, off King Street, and alternated between there and a third safe house across the river in Paper Mill Court in Washington, in the Georgetown high-rent district. In all, there were seventy-five meetings with Motorin over two years.

Communication is the most delicate part of any spy operation; the FBI could hardly just pick up the phone and call Motorin at the embassy to arrange a meeting. To contact "Sam Olson," the operational name Motorin chose for himself, the bureau gave him a special phone number, which was a beeper carried by FBI agent Mike Morton. "The number was just for Motorin," a bureau source said, "so if it rang, Mike knew it was Motorin." The arrangement was secure. "Motorin would beep him from a pay phone and Mike would call him right back at the pay phone."

Motorin provided the FBI with the name of every KGB agent in the Soviet embassy. But more important, the FBI man said, "he revealed the tasking he had received from Moscow Center, what they were told were priorities. But that was a joke; they were afraid of doing anything aggressively. Because they didn't want to be caught and thrown out of Washington. They loved being in Washington."

The KGB expected its officers in the capital to be alert. "Motorin told us once if they could send something to Moscow Center twenty-four hours before it appeared in *The Washington Post,* they were heroes."

The FBI was paying Motorin two hundred dollars a week and putting five hundred dollars a week into his escrow account. The bureau also bought him a tennis racket and a two-thousand-dollar diamond ring that he had picked out to give to his mistress in the embassy. "But he never gave it to her," the FBI man said. "We kept it. A big ugly diamond that really stuck out. It might have raised questions. We talked him out of it."

To preserve security, the FBI set up separate special rooms for the agents handling Motorin and Martynov. The room for the squad working the Martynov case was on the ninth floor of the Washington field office, then in a remote section of the capital on the Anacostia River with the unappealing name of Buzzard's Point. Another special room was set aside on the eleventh floor, the building's top floor, for the agents handling Motorin. Both rooms were locked and soundproofed.

Despite these elaborate precautions, word circulated within the tight, closed world of the intelligence division that the bureau had acquired sources inside the Soviet embassy.

And Hanssen, in the Soviet analytical unit, read the reports of the debriefings of the two KGB agents. "We got the product," Burns said. Although the FBI documents referred to Martynov and Motorin by their code names, it would not have been all that difficult for an insider to learn their true names. For example, by comparing the biographical information the FBI routinely compiled on Soviet diplomats in the Washington embassy with internal references in the debriefings of the two sources, their identities might become clear.

"Although it would be compartmented," Burns conceded, "the analysts might know the identities of sources. Hanssen probably would have learned of Martynov and Motorin's identity by name."

He did. Jim Ohlson, who kept up his friendship with Hanssen over the years, believes Hanssen learned their identities in subtle ways. "Even when he was in the budget unit he often talked to people in the Soviet analytical unit," he said. "In the analytical unit, he would have learned some clues. Sometimes the bureau would list an active source as inactive as a ploy to protect the source's identity. Hanssen could have detected this and put it together with other bits of information.

"Then there was the Hengemuhle incident." Joseph F. Hengemuhle was one of two top FBI counterintelligence agents working against the Soviets in New York; he was transferred to headquarters in the early 1980s to be chief of the Soviet section. But he came reluctantly, saying he would only stay until the bureau got a Soviet recruitment. His vow became known among his counterintelligence colleagues. After more than a year, Hengemuhle returned to the field in New York.

Hanssen remarked to Ohlson: "Hengemuhle's gone back. He must have gotten his recruitment." And in fact the bureau had gotten two.

Robert Hanssen, as he worked in the Soviet analytical unit, was a man with an enormous secret; he was himself a Soviet penetration of the FBI. One might assume that Hanssen would have been frightened that the two KGB sources would somehow learn his identity, or learn at least that an FBI man had sold secrets to the Russians, and reveal that to the bureau. But not to worry: it was to the GRU that Hanssen had betrayed TOPHAT, and the FBI's KGB sources in the embassy could not be expected to learn that, or indeed to know anything about a GRU asset. As long as he did not pass secrets to the KGB, his own secret was safe.

Hanssen knew that for his past sins, Martynov and Motorin could not betray him. But he could betray them.

*   *   *

Life was pleasant on Whitecedar Court, although the Hanssens, now with two more young boys, lived frugally with their five children. To all appearances they were a typical American family. They seemed so normal, in fact, that more than one acquaintance compared them to June and Ward Cleaver, the stereotyped suburban couple in the classic 1950s TV show *Leave It to Beaver.*

Vienna, Virginia, where the Hanssens lived, was a leafy bedroom community of well-kept lawns and watchful neighbors. Once a year, Bob and Bonnie and the children drove down to Florida to visit his parents. When Hanssen's father left the police force, he and his wife could not really afford the old neighborhood in Chicago anymore. After one big snowstorm, Howard developed bursitis in both shoulders. That did it; Howard and Vivian Hanssen retired to Venice, Florida. Bonnie's parents remained in Park Ridge, even after her father retired from the university.

Friends did notice how little Bob Hanssen seemed to spend, how careful he was about parting with his money. "They had three mortgages and drove used cars," said one. "The Hanssens never spent money, never went out to eat, except McDonald's on the way to Florida to see his parents."

To supplement her husband's FBI salary, Bonnie Hanssen taught religion and church history at Oakcrest, an Opus Dei Catholic school, which the couple's girls could attend with low tuition. The boys went to the Heights, another Opus Dei school in Potomac, Maryland.

Occasionally the Ohlsons, or Paul Moore and his wife, were invited for dinner. "When he lived out in Vienna we had dinner in each other's homes," Moore said. "He had this houseful of kids."

Hanssen seldom missed a day going to mass. Sometimes he would duck in for the noon mass at the chapel in the Catholic Information Center in downtown Washington, not far from FBI headquarters. The mass there was celebrated by the center's director, Father C. John McCloskey, an Opus Dei priest who knew both the Hanssens.

And once a month, Hanssen would go to the "evenings of recollection" at the Opus Dei Tenley Study Center on Garrison Street, just off upper Wisconsin Avenue in northwest Washington. The modern, red-brick building, formerly the high school of the Heights, houses a

Catholic youth center "dedicated to the character development of young men," its brochure explains, to help them become "committed to live by Christian principles."

The evenings of recollection were men-only events. According to Frank Byrne, the center's administrator, "Typically a priest delivers a meditation, talking for half an hour, perhaps on some point of doctrine, then the men repair to the living room for readings, perhaps the works of Ronald Knox,* then they return to the chapel and the priest gives the benediction." Sometimes guest speakers were invited as well. Twice, Hanssen persuaded Paul Moore to talk at the Tenley Center about his work for the FBI.

One night on the way to the Tenley Center, Hanssen had a serious automobile accident. "Some young guy made a left turn in front of him," Moore said. "Bob was badly hurt. I think his elbow was broken. He ended up with a very awkward cast, with his left arm out at an angle, and a rod sticking out. He couldn't drive.

"I lived in Arlington. I called him up and said, 'How are you getting into work?' He said, 'The car is wrecked, we have only the one car.' But he thought that God would provide."

A more secular solution ensued; Moore offered to drive Hanssen to headquarters. "It turned out I picked up not only Bob but his two girls in their high school outfits, saddle shoes and tartan skirts, and drove down Chain Bridge Road into Georgetown. At the time Oakcrest, the girls' school, was on MacArthur Boulevard. We dropped them off, and then we went downtown to the bureau."

And at work, Hanssen was gaining access to more and more sensitive material. In the analytical unit, Hanssen now sat on the FBI's foreign counterintelligence technical committee, which coordinated all of the division's electronic surveillance operations.

By late summer of 1985, Hanssen's headquarters time was coming to a close. For the FBI, it was an eventful year; an astonishing number of espionage cases were wrapped up by the bureau with a series of arrests, so many that the news media dubbed 1985 the Year of the Spy.

---

*Ronald Knox, the English author and theologian, was an Anglican who converted to the Catholic Church and served as chaplain of Oxford University in the years before World War II. Although known for his translation of the Bible, he also wrote popular detective stories.

The extraordinary series of spy cases had actually begun the previous year with the arrest in October of Richard Miller, the first FBI agent ever to be charged, and later convicted, of espionage. Miller, seriously overweight and bumbling, was working as a counterintelligence agent in the Los Angeles FBI office when he began an affair with Svetlana Ogorodnikov, a Soviet émigré woman whom he was supposed to be watching. Instead, she persuaded him to spy for the KGB, promising him $65,000 and a Burberry trench coat.*

Officials at FBI headquarters, greatly embarrassed by Miller's arrest, closely followed developments in the case, nowhere more so than in the intelligence division. Richard Miller's first trial opened August 5, 1985, a little more than six weeks before Robert Hanssen was to report to New York for a second tour in the city.

So Hanssen was well aware of the Miller case, and of the highly publicized arrest by the FBI a few months earlier, on May 20, 1985, of John A. Walker, Jr., the former Navy chief warrant officer who headed a family ring of Navy spies. Walker, who sold U.S. codes to the KGB, had spied for eighteen years.†

On August 1, 1985, as Hanssen also knew, Vitaly Yurchenko, a senior KGB official, had defected to the CIA in Rome, and information he provided led the FBI to place a former CIA officer, Edward Lee Howard, under surveillance. But Howard, aided by skills he had learned in the CIA, escaped into the New Mexico desert on September 21 and turned up in Moscow, a fugitive on espionage charges.

On the day that Howard escaped from the FBI, Hanssen was beginning his new assignment in New York, this time as a supervisor of a counterintelligence squad.

The march of espionage cases continued in rapid succession as Hanssen settled into his new job. On November 21, Jonathan Jay Pol-

---

*Miller's first trial ended in a hung jury on November 6, 1985. Convicted in a second trial, he was sentenced to life in July 1986. His conviction was overturned in April 1989 by a federal appeals court because the trial judge had allowed testimony about lie detector tests that Miller had failed. Finally, in October 1990, Miller was found guilty in a third trial, and sentenced in February 1991 to a prison term of twenty years.
†Walker pleaded guilty and was sentenced on November 6, 1986, to life in prison. His son, Michael, drew twenty-five years, and his brother Arthur and friend Jerry A. Whitworth were sentenced to life. All had served in the Navy.

lard, a U.S. naval intelligence analyst, was arrested as a spy for Israel.*
Only one day later FBI agents arrested Larry Wu-Tai Chin, a former
CIA broadcasting analyst who had passed secrets to Chinese intelli-
gence for thirty-three years, for which he received about $140,000.†
Three days after that, on November 25, Ronald W. Pelton, a former
NSA employee who sold that agency's secrets to the Soviets, was ar-
rested as a result of clues provided by Vitaly Yurchenko.‡

Sometime before leaving Washington, in the months that Hanssen
worked in the Soviet analytical unit, the decision to resume his career as
a spy that had been forming within him became final. He knew by then
of the arrests of Richard Miller and of the Walkers, the defection of Vitaly Yurchenko, the escape of Edward Lee Howard, and the fact that his
counterintelligence colleagues were working overtime to close in on
more spies. In the single year 1985, in fact, eleven persons were arrested for espionage and fourteen persons were convicted.

None of this deterred Hanssen in the least. His mind was made up.
This time, he decided, he would play in the majors. Despite the risks, he
would volunteer his services to a different branch of Soviet intelligence: the KGB.

---

*Pollard had spied for the Israelis during 1984 and 1985. He pleaded guilty in June
1986 and was sentenced to life on March 4, 1987.
†Chin was convicted in February 1986 and committed suicide on February 21, 1986,
by tying a plastic bag over his head while he was in jail awaiting sentencing.
‡Pelton was convicted of espionage in 1986 and sentenced to life in prison.

7

"Soon, I Will Send a Box of Documents"

The tiny CIA camera, disguised as a cigarette lighter, was like something straight out of a James Bond movie, a gadget that Q might have handed over solemnly to a nonchalant 007. Only this one was real.

In a San Francisco hotel room in 1981, Boris Yuzhin, a KGB officer assigned to the Soviet consulate in that city, met with a veteran CIA officer and an agency technician. The officer gave the miniature camera to Yuzhin, whose cover was that of a correspondent for Tass, the Soviet news agency.

The CIA camera, known as a tropel, was tube-shaped, with the lens at the opposite end from the flint. The specially designed lens was not much bigger than a dime. Yuzhin smoked, so a cigarette lighter would not be expected to arouse suspicion. The device actually worked, if only briefly, as a lighter.*

The CIA technician took over and demonstrated how Yuzhin was to use the camera to photograph documents in the Soviet consulate. The special film would allow him to take ninety pictures.

The Russian had been recruited by the FBI. The bureau brought in the CIA officer who gave Yuzhin the spy camera as a result of a then-unusual level of cooperation between the two agencies on an unrelated case. A CIA source in Indonesia, code name GTJOGGER, had revealed that a former agency officer, David H. Barnett, had sold CIA secrets to the KGB. The CIA turned over GTJOGGER's leads to the FBI,

---

*The CIA camera contained but a small amount of flammable fluid, so it was designed to be used only sparingly as a cigarette lighter.

which investigated and arrested Barnett, the first CIA officer ever to be charged with espionage. As payback for the CIA's help in the case, the FBI invited the agency to work with it on a case, and the CIA chose Yuzhin.*

Boris Yuzhin had first come to the United States six years earlier as a student at the University of California, Berkeley. He was then already working for the KGB. The FBI approached Yuzhin on a pretext, with the help of a woman he knew, and discovered that he admired American society. He soon began volunteering information to the bureau. The FBI assigned Bill Smits, who spoke Russian, as Yuzhin's case agent. In the San Francisco field office, Smits, who favored elegant three-piece suits, was known as the Count. He was earning a doctorate in public administration at Golden Gate University while handling Boris Yuzhin.

"He cooperated because he hated the KGB, the politics," Smits said. "He had no use for it. He saw it for what it was." Yuzhin's FBI code name was RAMPAIGE. The CIA called him CKTWINE.

Yuzhin went back to Moscow, but returned to San Francisco in 1978. His cover as a Tass correspondent was designed to mask his true position as a KGB Line PR officer assigned to collect political intelligence. A CIA officer explained why Yuzhin continued to spy for the United States. "He had been treated well, but he was considered a country boy from an inferior background. In the KGB you got promoted because of who you knew, not what you did. Yuzhin didn't have a protector. Even though he was a lieutenant colonel by the time he went back to San Francisco, he felt he was a quota bumpkin. They pushed a few along in a sort of equal opportunity program."

Yuzhin revealed to American intelligence the existence of the KGB's Group North, an elite unit of senior Soviet intelligence officers who specialized in recruiting American and Canadian targets worldwide. The KGB group was a kind of spy SWAT team with authority to travel anywhere on its missions.

Yuzhin also gave the FBI and the CIA leads that helped Norway to

---

*GTJOGGER was Vladimir M. Piguzov, a lieutenant colonel in the KGB. He was one of ten persons later executed after he was betrayed to Moscow by Aldrich Ames. David Barnett was sentenced to eighteen years in federal prison and served a little over nine years.

identify and arrest Arne Treholt, a high-level Soviet spy in that country's diplomatic corps.* Bill Smits continued as his FBI case agent.

Yuzhin photographed several hundred documents and cables from Moscow with the CIA's trick camera. When all ninety frames were shot, he would exchange the exposed film for a new roll. He was also given a small camera by the FBI; once, when using it, Yuzhin managed to take pictures of his own reflection on the documents, not a good idea had the film fallen into the wrong hands.

Some months later, Yuzhin committed a blunder that nearly cost him his life: he lost the cigarette lighter. He looked all over, but to no avail. Yuzhin, frantic, contacted his FBI handler for help. "I searched his car that night thinking he might have dropped it between the seats," Bill Smits said. "We damn near tore the car apart." No lighter. Yuzhin thought maybe he had dropped it at a friend's apartment. The FBI entered the apartment, searched it, and found nothing.

In the meantime, a janitor in the Soviet consulate had found the lighter by a pool table. Trying to light a flame, he took four pictures of himself. He turned the lighter in, and the KGB immediately recognized what it was. Yuzhin and another Soviet at the consulate, Igor S. Samsonov, were the prime suspects; both were smokers and shared an office.

In 1982, Yuzhin returned to Moscow, still under suspicion and closely watched. The KGB stationed its agents in the crawl space between the ceiling of the Yuzhins' apartment and the floor of the apartment above. The KGB had the Yuzhins under total surveillance, including their bedroom, twenty-four hours a day.

But without real evidence that the lighter was Yuzhin's, the KGB did not arrest him. The CIA hoped to stay in communication with Yuzhin, but he was wary now. "When he returned to Moscow," a CIA man said, "Yuzhin would only agree to give a 'sign of life,' such as a chalk mark. No meetings, no dead drops." For the moment, at least, Yuzhin seemed out of danger.

But he was not, because Hanssen had learned his identity, along with the true names of Martynov and Motorin.

---

*In 1984, Norwegian police arrested Treholt at the Oslo airport as he was about to leave for Vienna to meet his KGB control. He carried a briefcase containing sixty-six classified documents. Treholt was convicted and sentenced to twenty years.

*   *   *

For the Hanssens, his new assignment in New York City meant pulling up stakes again, selling their four-bedroom house on Whitecedar Court, buying a new one, enrolling the children in new schools. They sold their house in Vienna for $175,000. But they paid almost as much for a smaller, three-bedroom, two-story house in Yorktown Heights, in Westchester County again but farther north of the city and an hour-and-a-half commute from his office.

But Hanssen had already decided how to supplement his FBI salary, then about $46,000; it had, after all, worked before. As he arranged the details of moving himself and his family to New York, he was back in Washington on Tuesday, October 1, 1985.

From somewhere in Prince George's County, Maryland, he dropped a letter in a mailbox. Three days later, it was received by Viktor M. Degtyar, a KGB Line PR officer, at his home in Alexandria, Virginia.

When Degtyar opened the letter, he found another envelope inside, marked DO NOT OPEN. TAKE THIS ENVELOPE UNOPENED TO VICTOR I. CHERKASHIN. At that time, Viktor Cherkashin was the KGB's chief of counterintelligence, or Line KR, at the Soviet embassy. Less than four months earlier, it was Cherkashin who had accepted Aldrich Ames as a walk-in to the KGB, a decision that launched Ames's nine years of spying as the most damaging mole in the history of the CIA.

Inside the inner envelope of the letter to Degtyar was an unsigned typed letter to Cherkashin from Robert Hanssen. The KGB, not knowing his identity, gave him the simple code name "B." The letter said:

Dear Mr. Cherkashin:

Soon, I will send a box of documents to Mr. Degtyar. They are from certain of the most sensitive and highly compartmented projects of the U.S. intelligence community. All are originals to aid in verifying their authenticity. Please recognize for our long-term interests that there are a limited number of persons with this array of clearances. As a collection they point to me. I trust that an officer of your experience will handle them appropriately. I believe they are sufficient to justify a $100,000 payment to me. I must warn of certain risks to my security of which you may not be aware. Your service has recently suffered some setbacks. I warn that Mr. Boris Yuzhin (line PR, SF), Mr. Sergey Motorin (Line PR, Wash.) and Mr. Valeriy Martynov (Line X, Wash.) have been recruited by our "Special Services."

Having betrayed the three FBI sources and, as far as Hanssen knew, sent them to their doom, he described a classified intelligence collection program. In addition, "to further support my bona fides," as Hanssen put it, he included information about recent Soviet defectors to U.S. intelligence.

He added:

> Details regarding payment and future contact will be sent to you personally. . . . [M]y identity and actual position in the community must be left unstated to ensure my security. I am open to commo [communication] suggestions but want no specialized tradecraft. I will add 6, (you subtract 6) from stated months, days and times in both directions of our future communications.

Hanssen had no way of knowing that less than four months earlier, Aldrich Ames had already given up Martynov, Motorin, and Yuzhin to the KGB.* The fact that Ames had been down that path before him, and for the same reason, did not alter Hanssen's intent. At the very least, his betrayal provided important confirmation to the Soviets of the information they had already received from Aldrich Ames.

On June 13, 1985, Ames had wrapped up between five and seven pounds of cable traffic and other secret documents in plastic bags in his fourth-floor office at CIA headquarters. He took the elevator down, used his laminated ID card to get through the turnstiles that block every exit, and walked to his car in the parking lot. No guard asked to look inside the plastic bags; the CIA, as Ames knew, did not examine packages being carried out of the building.

Ames drove across the river to Chadwicks, a Washington saloon and restaurant under the K Street Freeway on the Georgetown water-

---

*Yuzhin was also given up by Edward Lee Howard, who did not know his name but told the KGB he was a Tass correspondent working in San Francisco, which was as good as naming him.

front. There he met Sergei D. Chuvakhin, a diplomat listed as a first secretary of the Soviet embassy. The KGB was using Chuvakhin as a cutout, or intermediary; Ames in turn was ostensibly developing Chuvakhin as an agency source.

At lunch, Ames handed Chuvakhin the plastic bags containing Langley's most precious secrets—the names of more than ten of the most important Soviet sources working for the CIA and FBI, including the three that Hanssen would betray four months later. Ames knew that many of them would die.

Long after, when he pleaded guilty to espionage in federal court, Ames described that day: "I did something which is still not entirely explicable even to me: without preconditions, or any demand for payment, I volunteered to the KGB information identifying virtually all Soviet agents of the CIA and other American and foreign services known to me. To my enduring surprise, the KGB replied that it had set aside for me two million dollars in gratitude for the information."* His decision to betray the CIA's agents, Ames later said, "was like the leap into the dark."

Hanssen, in betraying the three FBI sources, was not merely establishing his credibility with the KGB. He was also protecting himself against what in his letter he had called "certain risks to my security." The danger to Hanssen was that one or more of the three FBI sources might learn of his existence from their vantage point inside the KGB and reveal it to the FBI. The best way to eliminate that possibility was to kill them.

As Hanssen had promised, his first package of documents arrived in the mail at Viktor Degtyar's house in Alexandria ten days after the KGB man had received his letter. Inside were a large batch of classified intelligence documents, although not all were originals as he had said in his letter.

At 8:35 A.M. the next morning, October 16, FBI agents routinely watching the Soviet embassy from their lookout post across the street saw Degtyar arrive for work. He was carrying a large black canvas bag which the KGB man did not normally have with him. This was duly noted and recorded, but of course the FBI agents on surveillance duty

---

*Statement of Aldrich Hazen Ames in United States district court, Alexandria, Virginia, April 28, 1994. Ames was sentenced to life in prison with no possibility of parole.

had no way to guess what was in the bag. The contents could just as easily have been books, a change of clothes, or Degtyar's lunch.

A week later, this time from New York City, Hanssen mailed another letter to Degtyar's house. Perhaps not wanting his wife to surprise him again, Hanssen seldom wrote to the KGB in his den at home; he composed most of his letters on a laptop in his car.

In the message to Degtyar, Hanssen, the consummate professional, was not *asking* the KGB for instructions on where they wanted to leave the $100,000 he had asked for, or where he was to stash documents in the future, or how to signal the Russians—he was *telling* them.

The letter crisply laid out his plan:

DROP LOCATION   Please leave your package for me under the corner (nearest the street) of the wooden foot bridge located just west of the entrance to Nottoway Park.

PACKAGE PREPARATION   Use a green or brown plastic trash bag and trash to cover a waterproofed package.

SIGNAL LOCATION   Signal site will be the pictorial "pedestrian-crossing" signpost just west of the main Nottoway Park entrance on Old Courthouse Road. (The sign is the one nearest the bridge just mentioned.)

SIGNALS   My signal to you: One vertical mark of white adhesive tape meaning I am ready to receive your package.

Your signal to me: One horizontal mark of white adhesive tape meaning drop filled.

My signal to you: One vertical mark of white adhesive tape meaning I have received your package. (Remove old tape before leaving signal.)

After enclosing a schedule of dates and times for the signals and dead drops, Hanssen said he would acknowledge receipt of the money with his next package of documents.

The KGB gave the dead drop site in Nottoway Park the appropriate, if unimaginative, code name PARK. It was to become Hanssen's favorite drop site; over the next four years he used it seventeen times.

On Saturday, November 2, less than a week after receiving Hanssen's letter, the KGB loaded the PARK dead drop with $50,000 in cash, half of what he had requested. Because Hanssen's motives for spying for Moscow were complex, varied, and enigmatic, among those who knew him in the intelligence community it became the accepted wisdom after his arrest that he had not acted for money alone, or even primarily. While that may well be true, it should be noted that $50,000—and he was to receive a great deal more—was an amount greater than his annual FBI salary at the time. Hard cash was certainly not an insignificant factor in his mix of motives, as Hanssen himself later told his FBI debriefers and the Webster commission.

Along with the money, the KGB countered with their own arrangements for future contacts with Hanssen. In the spy trade, this schedule of meetings, drops, and dates is known as a communication plan.

Six days later, on November 8, Cherkashin was given another letter from Hanssen, who did not, then or later, reveal his identity to the Russians. Once again the letter was mailed to Degtyar's home in Alexandria. It was full of flattery for Cherkashin, praising "your courage and perseverance" in the face of what Hanssen said he assumed were the usual "bureaucratic obstacles." He went on in the same vein:

> I would not have contacted you if it were not reported that you were held in esteem within your organization, an organization I have studied for years. I did expect some communication plan in your response. I viewed the postal delivery as a necessary risk and do not wish to trust again that channel with valuable material. I did this only because I had to so you would take my offer seriously, that there be no misunderstanding as to my long-term value, and to obtain appropriate security for our relationship from the start.

Hanssen was using old-fashioned spycraft. As he well knew, even in the high-tech age of computers, the KGB and for that matter the CIA, perhaps surprisingly, clung to traditional methods of contacting agents and exchanging documents and money. Since both sides rightly assumed that their telephones were tapped, the use of signal sites and dead drops offered a measure of security that spies found attractive. Typically, the intelligence officer or agent would contact each other by leaving a signal, a piece of tape on a telephone pole or perhaps a chalk mark on a mailbox, to indicate that a drop had been loaded or cleared. Usually these signals were placed in such a way and at a height that someone driving by could see them without getting out of a car.

True, using hiding places to stash documents or money carried a small risk that children playing in a park might discover the secret, or someone's dog might snuffle into a dead drop. However, that slight danger was offset by the fact that the use of these established methods meant that an officer and his agent would not be caught together with incriminating material, as could happen in a personal meeting.

But the computer-savvy Hanssen hoped to drag the KGB into the age of cyberspace. He suggested they contact each other on a computer "bulletin board," using "appropriate encryption." Hanssen must have realized there was little chance of changing the ways of the KGB, for he wrote that, in the meantime, "Let us use the same site again. Same timing. Same signals." Hanssen proposed that the next exchange at a dead drop take place on March 3, 1986.*

Hanssen was not going to fuss over the money with his new paymasters. "Thank you for the 50,000," he wrote. "As far as the funds are concerned, I have little need or utility for more than the 100,000. It merely provides a difficulty since I can not spend it, store it or invest it easily without triping [sic] 'drug money' warning bells.

"Perhaps some diamonds as security to my children and some good will so that when the time comes, you will accept by [sic] senior services as a guest lecturer."

Even at this early stage, sixteen years before he was caught, Hanssen was aware that despite all of his professional precautions, the day might come when he was discovered and would have to flee. "Eventually," he wrote, "I would appreciate an escape plan. (Nothing lasts forever.)"

In the same letter, Hanssen made clear that he had access to communications intelligence and the supersecret collection methods of the National Security Agency. He warned the KGB of a "new technique" used by the NSA, which he described in detail.

Having already betrayed Martynov, Motorin, and Yuzhin and, as far as he knew, ensuring that they would be shot, Hanssen wanted to make

---

*In his letter to Cherkashin, Hanssen asked that the next meeting occur on September 9, which—under the coefficient of six that he established in his first letter to the KGB whereby to determine the true date, the KGB would subtract six months from September and six days from the date—meant that the exchange would actually take place the following March 3.

certain that the KGB believed he was a genuine mole whose information could be trusted. Referring to the three FBI sources, he wrote:

> I can not provide documentary substantiating evidence without arousing suspicion at this time. Nevertheless, it is from my own knowledge as a member of the community. . . . I have seen video tapes of debriefings and physically saw the last, though we were not introduced. The names were provided to me as part of my duties as one of the few who needed to know. You have some avenues of inquiry. Substantial funds were provided in excess of what could have been skimmed from their agents.* The active one has always (in the past) used a concealment device—a bag with bank notes sewn in the base during home leaves.

This last reference surely helped to identify and send Valery Martynov to his death, because logically it was Martynov who would be the "active one." Sergei Motorin had by then returned to Moscow and Yuzhin had gone back in 1982. And only the FBI and Martynov knew that he concealed the money he was paid by the bureau in the bottom of his travel bag. That fact was classified SECRET.

In the event, only Boris Yuzhin escaped the executioner. He was one of the lucky ones, if serving time in the Soviet gulag can be called that. Arrested in December 1986, he was sentenced to fifteen years for high treason. On February 7, 1992, after six years under harsh conditions in Soviet prisons, Yuzhin was one of ten political prisoners released from the notorious Perm-35 prison camp in the Urals under a general amnesty granted by Boris Yeltsin, then president of Russia. He later emigrated to the United States with his family.

Sergei Motorin had returned to Moscow on normal rotation in January 1985. After being identified to the KGB by Ames in June and Hanssen in October, he was arrested by December. A Soviet court that heard the evidence against Motorin said he had received $20,000 from the FBI, and it cited his purchase of a water bed as proof of his Western decadence.

---

*What Hanssen was saying here to the KGB was, Look, you don't have to take my word for it; we paid these sources to spy, so take a look and you may discover they have more money than they could have misappropriated from the KGB funds they were allotted to pay agents they had recruited in the United States.

From Moscow, Motorin had telephoned his woman friend in Washington several times. The calls continued through the late winter. The conversations were recorded and the FBI and the CIA read the transcripts. Later, the FBI concluded that Motorin was already under control and had been forced by the KGB to make the telephone calls, in an effort to deceive U.S. intelligence into thinking he had not been detected. But in February 1987, the last telephone contact took place. That month, he was executed.

Valery Martynov was lured back to Moscow on November 6, 1985, in a ploy that apparently did not arouse his suspicion. The key was Vitaly Yurchenko. The celebrated KGB defector had changed his mind about remaining in America and slipped away from his young CIA escort in a Georgetown restaurant; he then surfaced at a press conference at the Soviet embassy, claiming he had been kidnapped by the CIA, which no one believed. Martynov was ordered to escort Vitaly Yurchenko on the flight home.

Martynov told his wife, Natalya, and his two young children that he would be back in Washington soon. Shortly after Martynov flew back to Moscow, Natalya received a note from her husband saying he had reinjured a bad knee while carrying his luggage and had been hospitalized. He asked her and their son and daughter to come back to Moscow. As soon as their plane had landed, Natalya realized that her husband was in trouble. She was taken to Moscow's grim Lefortovo prison for interrogation. At first she thought her husband might be suspected of bringing in tape recorders or other electronic equipment and selling them. It was only then that she was told he had been charged with high treason.

Questioned repeatedly by the KGB, she was allowed to see her husband only four times during the next two years. The last time, knowing he had been sentenced to death, she brought her son with her.

Hanssen's letter, revealing precisely how Martynov had concealed the FBI's cash in his suitcase, reached Viktor Cherkashin on November 8, 1985. Martynov, with Vitaly Yurchenko, had left Washington only two days earlier on an Aeroflot jet to Moscow. If the KGB entertained any lingering doubts that Martynov had become a mole for U.S. intelligence, Hanssen's letter certainly removed them. There could no longer be any question.

On May 28, 1987, Lieutenant Colonel Valery Martynov was executed by a firing squad. He was forty-one.

8

"For Sale, Dodge Diplomat, Needs Engine Work"

While Hanssen continued in New York to funnel sensitive secrets to the Russians, in his day job he spied on them.

As a squad supervisor on his second tour in the city, Hanssen spent most of his time in a highly secret FBI wiretap installation on Manhattan's east side, a few blocks north of Grand Central Terminal. It was code-named POCKETWATCH.

Hanssen's squad was collecting electronic intelligence on Soviet commercial operations in the United States. Its primary target was Amtorg, the Soviet trading agency. For Hanssen, the wheel had come full circle; it was to Amtorg that he had volunteered in his first venture into espionage six years earlier, when he spied for the GRU.

The FBI agents under Hanssen operated discreetly out of a building near the Amtorg office.* Their targets also included Aeroflot, the Soviet airline, and other commercial offices. The agents were, in bureau short-hand, operating "offsite," meaning they were not working downtown at the FBI's large New York field office at 26 Federal Plaza, known irreverently as "the anthill."

At Hanssen's uptown shop, FBI agents and translators with earphones clamped to their heads listened in on what the Soviets were saying, at the same time recording all the conversations on tape for future

---

*Hanssen's squad was close by because of budget constraints. With the technology available at the time it was too costly to run the phone lines used for wiretaps over many blocks. "In those days, if you moved out of the area of a central telephone office, it was expensive," one FBI man recalled.

reference. They were, in the language of the agents, engaged in "over-hears" and analysis of the take. Amtorg encouraged Soviet exports, stimulating sales of Belarus tractors, for example. But the FBI was not interested in tractors; it was looking for intelligence officers.

Once again, Hanssen was toiling in a backwater, not at the center of the game. "Hanssen was a supervisor, but he had a nondescript squad," said Ed Curran, who worked counterintelligence in the city for a dozen years. "Amtorg is not like the Soviet mission or the UN, where the action was. At Amtorg, maybe you had a few IOs in there for cover, but they never did much. If you have forty or fifty Soviets in Amtorg, what you're looking for is two or three who are GRU or co-opted by them.

"I had illegals and KR [KGB counterintelligence], a hot trigger; you're always doing something. What Hanssen was doing was certainly not as important as a KGB squad, working against hostile, aggressive intelligence officers."

Hanssen's POCKETWATCH wiretap operation was a subunit of a separate, much larger eavesdropping installation, code-named MEGAHUT, also on the east side of Manhattan, not far from the UN. This was the bureau's central counterintelligence surveillance site for the entire city, with telephone lines running to the Soviet Mission to the United Nations on East Sixty-seventh Street, and as far north as the Russian apartment complex in Riverdale, along the Hudson River in the upper reaches of the Bronx.*

In every city where the Soviets had a diplomatic presence, there was such a central facility for the bureau's wiretappers. In Washington, it was known among the field agents as the Hole, and in San Francisco the Farm (not to be confused with the CIA's training base near Williamsburg, Virginia, with the same name). The technicians from MEGAHUT had set up the smaller office that Hanssen supervised.

It was one of the multiple contradictions of Hanssen's personality

---

*"Riverdale was the main target for MEGAHUT," said one FBI man. "We worked with NSA. Before they built Riverdale, they lived in hotels, the Excelsior, the Esplanade on the west side, and it was easy for us to go after them. We could be next door or on the floor above. We could talk to the manager, the neighbors. Then in the late seventies they [the Soviets] rounded them up and put them all in one complex in Riverdale." As secret as MEGAHUT was, at least some New Yorkers were aware that the FBI had a clandestine hideaway in their midst, even if the exact purpose remained mysterious. "Everybody in the neighborhood knew," the FBI man said. "We had 'No Parking' signs. That was the giveaway; the bureau really likes its cars."

that he appears to have worked hard simultaneously for both the KGB and the FBI. James Ohlson, who remained friendly with Hanssen after they had met at headquarters and discovered their Chicago roots, recalled a major counterintelligence breakthrough that Hanssen achieved, on his own time, to solve a troublesome problem for the bureau.

Ohlson was at headquarters in the FBI's information systems unit, developing computer programs for counterintelligence and counterterrorism. Hanssen, in New York, helped Ohlson develop a computer program that greatly improved the FBI's ability to track Soviet diplomats.

Until then, the bureau agents watching the Soviet Mission to the United Nations would write down when employees entered and left the mission, the date and time, their names if known, and whether they were alone or accompanied. But the system was cumbersome; if the FBI agents needed to check on the time and date that a Russian IO had left the mission, it might take two days of painstaking searches through the handwritten sheets to get the answer.

Hanssen wrote a software program on his Mac at home that allowed the agent in the observation post to record the date, time, name, place, and whether it was an entry or exit. Then, with one click of a mouse, the five fields were entered into the database. Each day the data would be downloaded from the laptop of the agent on surveillance duty to the New York field office. From there, it was relayed to Washington.*

Normally a program of this kind would be designed by the FBI's computer experts, but they recognized the usefulness of Hanssen's work and adopted the program he wrote. It was then used by FBI agents watching not only the Soviet mission but Amtorg and other Soviet offices as well. Hanssen had once again proven his skill with computers.

Listening in on the Russians at Amtorg, the FBI agents working for Hanssen would sometimes hear them exchanging jokes. Hanssen instructed his squad to collect them. Ohlson learned this when he visited Hanssen in New York in 1986. "The idea was it would shed light on what the Russians were thinking. I remember one he told me. Two Russian women are talking. One asks the other, 'Do you like sex or New Year's better?' The other answers, 'Obviously New Year's—because it comes more often.' "

---

*Today, the surveillance data is downloaded directly to Washington from the laptop, one of Hanssen's curious legacies.

*   *   *

After seven months in New York, Hanssen was ready to sell more FBI secrets to the Soviets. On June 30, 1986, he sent another letter through the KGB's Viktor Degtyar, warning that the NSA had discovered a vulnerability in Soviet satellite transmissions and was exploiting the loophole. That information was classified TOP SECRET/SCI.

Always alert to threats to his own security, Hanssen was worried about a reference to Viktor Cherkashin that he had seen in the debriefing of a Soviet defector, Victor Gundarev. Gundarev, the chief of counterintelligence and security for the KGB "residentura," its station in Athens, had defected to the CIA five months earlier, in February.* David Forden, the CIA station chief, had arranged to spirit Gundarev out of Greece to the United States.

In his letter Hanssen explained his concern to the KGB:

> I apologize for the delay since our break in communications. I wanted to determine if there was any cause for concern over security. I have only seen one item which has given me pause. When the FBI was first given access to Victor Petrovich Gundarev, they asked . . . if Gundarev knew Viktor Cherkashin. I thought this unusual. I had seen no report indicating that Viktor Cherkashin was handling an important agent, and heretofore he was looked at with the usual lethargy awarded Line Chiefs. The question came to mind, are they [the FBI] somehow able to monitor funds, ie., to know that Viktor Cherkashin received a large amount of money for an agent? I am unaware of any such ability, but I might not know that type of source reporting.

---

*Three years later, the author became personally involved in the fallout from the affair when Victor Gundarev called to complain about his treatment by the CIA. Gundarev, given a new identity and resettled in the United States by the CIA, said the agency had stalled in providing green cards for himself and his family and had tapped his telephone. He was so disillusioned, he said, he was thinking of redefecting. I wrote an op-ed piece for *The New York Times,* later expanded into a magazine article for the newspaper, warning that the agency might have another Yurchenko case on its hands. As a result of the publicity and Gundarev's complaints, the CIA instituted certain reforms in its defector program. See "Another Soviet Defector Threatens to Go Back," *The New York Times,* July 9, 1989, Section 4, p. 27, and "It's Cold Coming Out," *The New York Times Magazine,* September 17, 1989, p. 36ff.

In some way, Hanssen had managed to see a classified report of the debriefing of Gundarev dated March 4, 1986, only three weeks after Gundarev had been whisked out of Athens. The FBI report noted that the bureau's agents had shown Gundarev a photo of Cherkashin and asked if he knew him. Hanssen was clearly worried that the FBI was somehow on to the money trail from Moscow—which could lead straight to him. How Hanssen, relegated to wiretapping Amtorg in New York, had been able to read a report from headquarters on the debriefing of a KGB defector was not clear, but he had.

With Hanssen working in Manhattan, his access to drop sites around Washington was limited to those times when he either visited headquarters on FBI business or could slip out of New York on his own time. Communications with the KGB and exchanges of documents and money were obviously more difficult with Hanssen away from the capital.

In the same letter, he proposed an elaborate new scheme to resume contact with the Soviets. "If you wish to continue our discussions, please have someone run an advertisement in the Washington Times during the week of 1/12/87 or 1/19/87, for sale, 'Dodge Diplomat, 1971, needs engine work, $1000.'

"Give a phone number and time-of-day in the advertisement where I can call," Hanssen instructed. "I will call and leave a phone number where a recorded message can be left for me in one hour. I will say, 'Hello, my name is Ramon. I am calling about the car you offered for sale in the Times.' You will respond, 'I'm sorry, but the man with the car is not here, can I get your number.' The number will be in Area Code 212. I will not specify that Area Code on the line."

Hanssen had now revealed he was in New York, but provided no other clues to his identity.

On July 14—the KGB subtracted six months from Hanssen's dates—an ad ran for four days in the classified pages of *The Washington Times:* "DODGE – '71, DIPLOMAT, NEEDS ENGINE WORK, $1000. Phone (703) 451-9780 (CALL NEXT Mon., Wed., Fri. 1 P.M.)"

The number given in the ad was that of a pay telephone near a shopping center in northern Virginia. On Monday, July 21, Hanssen called the pay phone. The call was answered by Aleksandr K. Fefelov, a KGB officer working out of the Soviet embassy in Washington. Hanssen gave the number 628-8047. As arranged, he did not include the New York area code.

An hour later, Fefelov telephoned the New York number and told Hanssen that the KGB had loaded dead drop PARK. But two weeks after the phone conversation, Hanssen sent another note to Degtyar saying that he had not found the package at the dead drop and would call the pay phone again on August 18.

Spies make mistakes; as it turned out, the KGB agent who had stashed the package put it under the wrong corner of the wooden foot-bridge. When the KGB realized what had happened, it corrected its mistake.

On August 18, Fefelov was waiting by the phone. Hanssen called and the conversation was recorded by the KGB. Fourteen years later, this tape fell into the hands of the FBI when it obtained the KGB file on Robert Hanssen:

HANSSEN*: Tomorrow morning?
FEFELOV: Uh, yeah, and the car is still available for you and as we have agreed last time, I prepared all the papers and I left them on the same table. You didn't find them because I put them in another corner of the table.
HANSSEN: I see.
FEFELOV: You shouldn't worry, everything is okay. The papers are with me now.
HANSSEN: Good.
FEFELOV: I believe under these circumstances, mmmm, it's not necessary to make any changes concerning the place and the time. Our company is reliable, and we are ready to give you a substantial discount which will be enclosed in the papers. Now, about the date of our meeting. I suggest that our meeting will be, will take place without delay on February thirteenth, one three, one P.M. Okay? February thirteenth.
HANSSEN: . . . February second?
FEFELOV: Thirteenth. One three.
HANSSEN: One three.
FEFELOV: Yes. Thirteenth. One P.M.

---

*The KGB tape did not indicate Hanssen's or Fefelov's names; they are included here for the sake of clarity. A transcript of the conversation appears in the FBI affidavit seeking a court warrant for Hanssen's arrest, a document made public when the FBI announced the arrest on February 20, 2001.

HANSSEN: Let me see if I can do that. Hold on.

FEFELOV: Okay. Yeah. [pause]

HANSSEN: [whispering] [unintelligible]

FEFELOV: Hello? Okay. [pause]

HANSSEN: [whispering] Six . . . Six . . . [pause] That should be fine.

FEFELOV: Okay. We will confirm you, that the papers are waiting for you with the same horizontal tape in the same place as we did it at the first time.

HANSSEN: Very good.

FEFELOV: You see. After you receive the papers, you will send the letter confirming it and signing it, as usual. Okay?

HANSSEN: Excellent.

FEFELOV: I hope you remember the address. Is . . . if everything is okay?

HANSSEN: I believe it should be fine and thank you very much.

FEFELOV: Heh-heh. Not at all. Not at all. Nice job. For both of us. Uh, have a nice evening, sir.

HANSSEN: Do svidaniya.

FEFELOV: Bye-bye.

As a trained KGB operative, Fefelov was talking as cryptically as possible, to preserve security in case anyone overheard their conversation. He was trying to sound like an American businessman, with double-talk about "our company," papers, a meeting, "a substantial discount," and so on. Hanssen realized this but could not resist saying good-bye in Russian—spoiling the whole effect. One can almost visualize Fefelov shaking his head in despair, sighing, and then, determined to carry on like a good soldier, saying "Bye-bye" in English.

The KGB then put back the package containing $10,000 in cash in the PARK dead drop. Included with the money was a letter that proposed two more drop sites and a new accommodation address, a place to which it was felt Hanssen could safely send letters, code-named NANCY. The accommodation address was the home in Alexandria of Boris M. Malakhov, who was listed as second secretary of the Soviet embassy and was about to replace Degtyar as the embassy's press secretary. In fact, his true job was that of a KGB Line PR officer. As an additional measure of security, Hanssen was told to misspell Malakhov's name as

"Malkow." The package also contained a plan to enable Hanssen in an emergency to contact the KGB in Vienna, Austria.

Hanssen retrieved the money on August 19, the morning after the taped phone conversation.* He sent a letter to Degtyar the same day with a return address of Ramon Garcia, 125 Main St., Falls Church, VA, a fictitious street number. Inside the envelope was a handwritten note: "RECEIVED $10,000. RAMON."

In using the name "Ramon Garcia" with the KGB, Hanssen was trying to send a subtle message to the Russians. He hoped that the last three letters of Garcia would mislead the KGB into thinking that he worked at the CIA. But the hint was so subtle, there is no evidence that the Russians ever understood it.†

Hanssen's complicated communication plan, involving the ad for a mythical used Dodge, had worked. For the next year, however, he stayed below the radar and did not contact the KGB again. He had, after all, over a seven-year period revealed TOPHAT to the GRU, betrayed Valery Martynov, Sergei Motorin, and Boris Yuzhin to the KGB, and warned the Russians how the NSA was intercepting their satellite communications. He could afford to rest a bit.

---

*That the exchange went off as scheduled was a small miracle. The beginning of the conversation was not recovered by the FBI and parts of the tape were unintelligible. Near the start of the tape was the phrase "tomorrow morning," so Hanssen must have understood that is when he was to go to the drop. But Fefelov set the time and date as February 13 at 1 P.M. In his first letter to the KGB in 1985 Hanssen seemed to propose that in future communications the sender would add six to the month, date, and time, and the recipient would subtract. If Hanssen subtracted six from the month, date, and time, as he and the Russians had apparently agreed, the exchange would have taken place on August 7 at 7 A.M., an impossibility, since it was already August 18. Conversely, if he added six, the exchange would have occurred on August 19, at 7 P.M. In order to get it right and show up at 7 A.M. the next day, "tomorrow morning," August 19, Hanssen would have had to add six to the month and date but *subtract* six from the time. Somehow he must have figured out what Fefelov meant, because he got the money.

†When Hanssen was debriefed by the FBI after his guilty plea, he disclosed his attempt to send the KGB this subliminal, albeit false, coded message.

9

Anybody Here Seen a Mole?

Washington, which was built on a swamp, can be ghastly in the dog days of summer. Yet in the first week of August 1987, Robert Hanssen voluntarily returned to FBI headquarters. He had a facile explanation for his colleagues about why he had come back from New York short of tour.

Jim Ohlson recalled the circumstances. "Normally he would have stayed longer and returned as a GS-15 at higher pay. But he came back as a GS-14, because he said he wanted his children to attend an Opus Dei school, the Heights. Of course, in retrospect, we can speculate he may also have wanted to be back at headquarters, where he had more valuable access for the Russians."

Hanssen was reassigned to his old shop, the Soviet analytical unit on the fourth floor, again as a supervisory special agent. Now he was once more in charge of the team of analysts studying the modus operandi of Soviet intelligence agents in the United States.

The Hanssens bought their modest house in Vienna on Talisman Drive and settled in again to the familiar northern Virginia suburb. By now they had six children. To most of the neighbors, Hanssen seemed the perfect father, shepherding his flock to church every Sunday, keeping the lawn well trimmed.

And at headquarters, he resumed his friendship with Paul Moore, the bureau's China expert. As an analyst, Moore understood how his colleagues in the Soviet unit went about their work. "They are looking for anomalies, possible penetrations. They have read all the defector debriefings. And they might see something and say, Well, this is strange, isn't it? A typical thing would be it takes X amount of time to go from lieutenant to major in the KGB. Why was this one promoted early? Was anybody else promoted who worked in Washington at a certain time period? Maybe a bunch of secrets were passed to the KGB.

"It was the same with medals," Moore explained. If the FBI learned that certain KGB officers had received medals, that could be another tip-off that someone was passing documents to Moscow; such awards were often given for the successful handling of an American source.

"The people in the analytical unit were specialized," Moore added. "Some might look at Line X, the S&T officers, some specialized in illegals, and so on." It was exacting work, and about to get more so.

Very soon after Hanssen's return from New York, he was assigned to prepare a highly sensitive study, classified TOP SECRET. The FBI had lost its two assets in the Soviet embassy in Washington to the KGB executioners; the CIA's sources in Moscow were being rolled up, imprisoned, or shot.

The situation was intolerable, and it gave Hanssen's assignment a special urgency. He was to examine past penetrations of the FBI; he would carefully analyze every allegation about a possible traitor in the bureau ever recorded in the FBI's voluminous counterintelligence files.* The goal was to help the bureau's operational side pinpoint and arrest the mole, if one existed.

No more delicious assignment could have been handed to Hanssen. Since he controlled the mole study, he would make sure to deflect any analysis that might even remotely point in his own direction.

There was an enormous amount of material to sift through. Over a period of several years, Soviets recruited by U.S. intelligence, and defectors who came over to the West, often talked about gossip they had heard, or tidbits of information they possessed, that might point to the existence of a mole inside the FBI. Reviewing every report from every source containing such allegations would be a lengthy and painstaking task.

Hanssen assigned the research to the FBI's two top Soviet analysts, Jim Milburn and Bob King. The two sat on each side of Hanssen, all in the same cubicle, as they prepared the study.

---

*Although the initial affidavit in the Hanssen case referred to the study in broad terms as looking for penetrations in "the United States Intelligence Community," the indictment of Hanssen made clear that it was a detailed study specifically of whether "the Soviet intelligence services had penetrated the FBI."

James P. Milburn was not a name known outside of the closed world of intelligence, but he enjoyed immense respect within the FBI for his knowledge of Soviet intelligence and his analytical skills. If the bureau had a complex problem involving the KGB, it would more often than not turn to Milburn.

Red-haired and freckled, powerfully built and about six feet tall, Milburn liked to play basketball on his lunch hour in the bureau gym. "He would get into games with guys from records and fingerprinting," Paul Moore said. "He's a thirtysomething going up against these young guys from the ident division. He got injured a lot, he got some bad injuries doing that sort of stuff."

Bob King was a veteran foreign counterintelligence (FCI) analyst. He had come to the bureau from the CIA, a relatively rare progression that led to some good-natured needling in the Hoover building. "I used to accuse him of being a CIA penetration of the FBI," Moore said. In his previous work at the CIA, King had also been a Soviet analyst. Dark-haired and bespectacled, he was a heavy smoker who quit cold turkey when his doctors got after him. Milburn and King were both friendly, accessible types, Moore said.

"Oddly, both Hanssen and Milburn had kidney stones. They each had these big clear plastic water pitchers on their desks, they were supposed to be drinking a lot of water. One afternoon I found them both lying on the floor to get relief from these attacks." Moore could not resist a gibe at the sight of his two prone colleagues. "It's more expensive at the Harrington Hotel," he cracked, "but you'd have more privacy."

The two analysts assigned to the mole study, and Hanssen himself, had the advantage over the others in the unit. Most analysts looked at specific targets, such as the various KGB lines, and did not know much outside their own specialized areas, Moore explained. "But a few people did 'all source,' and that was Milburn, King, and Hanssen." Within the Soviet analytical unit, in other words, Hanssen was one of the very few entitled to know all the FBI's sources and secrets.

Or as David Major, the former FBI counterintelligence official, put it, "He was at the center of the hourglass, he saw everything."

*   *   *

The penetration problem had begun long before, with UNSUB DICK.

The story was a secret buried so deep within the FBI that it is revealed here for the first time.* UNSUB DICK—the UNSUB stood for "unknown subject"—was the first suspected KGB mole inside the FBI. Any history of penetrations of the bureau must start with him. The study by Hanssen, Milburn, and King would certainly have focused on this long-secret case.

The search for the penetration began early in 1962 when Aleksei Isidorovich Kulak, a KGB officer undercover at the United Nations, walked into the FBI office on East Sixty-ninth Street in Manhattan and offered his services as a spy. He said he was discontent with his lack of progress in his KGB career. The FBI gave him the code name FEDORA; the CIA called him SCOTCH.

Kulak, then thirty-nine, married and accompanied by his wife in New York, was a short, stocky man whose name meant "wealthy farmer" in Russian. "We called him Fatso," said an FBI man who worked the case. Kulak specialized in collecting scientific and technical secrets. He had a doctorate in chemistry and had worked as a radiological chemist in a Moscow laboratory. At the UN, he was a consultant to a committee on the effects of atomic radiation.

By walking into the FBI's office in Manhattan, Kulak had taken a big risk; the KGB might have had the building under surveillance. The FBI agents who met with FEDORA challenged him on this point. "We said aren't you worried they may be watching the FBI building?" one of the agents recalled. "He said he was not worried because all of our [KGB] people are out covering a meeting with your guy, 'Dick.' "

Uh-oh. This was the first time that the FBI had heard the name "Dick." FEDORA was clearly saying that the FBI harbored a mole. But he said he did not know the man's true identity.

FEDORA's revelation touched off an intense, long-running secret mole hunt within the FBI. "It went on for years; it drove us crazy," the FBI man said.

Not long after, another KGB officer in New York, Valentin Lysov, also warned U.S. intelligence of a mole in the FBI. Lysov approached the CIA and said he was in trouble, about to be recalled to Moscow, and needed money. The KGB man said there was a penetration in the FBI

---

*When the author asked David Major about UNSUB DICK, he declined to discuss it and replied: "You make my hair stand on end when you say that name. How do you know about UNSUB DICK?"

and told the CIA it had just twenty-four hours to meet his terms. Since Lysov was still on U.S. soil, the CIA turned the case over to the FBI. The bureau already knew that Lysov was in hot water; FEDORA had tipped off the FBI that Lysov got drunk in a bar and lost his wallet, and was being sent home on a pretext of attending a meeting.

When Lysov flew first-class to Copenhagen the next day, en route to Moscow, an FBI counterintelligence agent sat next to him. On the plane, the FBI man pressed the Russian about the alleged mole in the FBI. Lysov was vague and would provide no details. But he promised to return in six months with more information. He never did.

That still left the FBI with a problem; how to identify UNSUB DICK? Perhaps, the bureau's counterintelligence agents reasoned, a technique used by both sides could lead to the answer. Just as the bureau tried to recruit officers of the KGB, the Russians targeted the FBI's agents in New York. "We know they tried to make contacts, put people in bars near our office. FEDORA told us that."

The ongoing recruitment game, the FBI concluded, might be turned to its advantage in the search for UNSUB DICK. The FBI decided to dangle one of its agents to the KGB. He would hint that he needed money and might be amenable to recruitment.

One of the bureau's watchers, a street agent assigned to surveillance of the Soviet Mission, was chosen for the operation, code-named VALBEL. According to a former FBI man, the agent showed up at the apartment of Boris Ivanov, the KGB resident in New York, and rang the bell. "Ivanov slammed the door, but not before the agent said he would meet them at such-and-such time and place. In fact, a Line KR Soviet showed up. We ran the operation for six months; there were three or four meetings. We hoped we could tell from their questions who DICK was."

If, for example, the KGB asked for information about a specific FBI counterintelligence operation, it would mean they had learned about it already, which could narrow the list of suspects in the bureau who knew of that activity. Conversely, if the KGB did not ask certain questions, it might be because the mole had already provided the answers. VALBEL was a long shot. "We were trying to get them to show their hand," the former FBI agent said, "but they never asked the right questions." The KGB, wary of the dangle, did not bite.

The search for UNSUB DICK was complicated by the fact that there was intense controversy over whether FEDORA was a true agent in place for the FBI or a KGB plant. J. Edgar Hoover had total faith in FEDORA, although some of his counterintelligence agents who knew the case were skeptical. And the skeptics reasoned that if FEDORA was a plant, then perhaps there was no UNSUB DICK and the supposed mole was a phantom who did not really exist.

Although some in the FBI continued to have their doubts about Aleksei Kulak, he provided a good deal of useful information to the bureau, including the names of KGB officers and which U.S. military weapons and defense plants Moscow wanted him to collect data about. KGB walk-ins do not turn up every day; over a sixteen-year period during two tours in New York, the FBI paid him approximately $100,000. Kulak/FEDORA returned to Moscow for the last time in 1977.*

James J. Angleton, the CIA's controversial counterintelligence chief, considered FEDORA a fake, but then Angleton was a true believer in only one KGB defector, Anatoly M. Golitsin, who had come over in 1961 in Helsinki. All others were suspect to Angleton, most especially a later defector, Yuri I. Nosenko, who was imprisoned and brutally treated by the CIA in an effort to break his story. Nosenko never wavered, and in the end was rehabilitated by the CIA.† Angleton's suspicion, fueled by Golitsin, that the CIA was deeply penetrated led him on a destructive mole hunt for more than a decade that paralyzed the agency's Soviet operations and destroyed the careers of many loyal CIA officers. Finally, in 1974, Angleton was fired by CIA director William E. Colby.

In the FBI, the frustrating search for UNSUB DICK went on for years, but was never resolved. "We never found him," a former FBI official admitted. "Some people think they figured out who he was, but he is dead." In the files of the FBI, however, UNSUB DICK is still an open case.

The bureau fared only slightly better in another episode. Several years ago, the FBI closed in on a suspected mole, and again the entire affair was handled quietly and out of public view. A former FBI counterintelligence official recalled how the case had involved stolen documents and a phone booth in suburban Maryland.

---

*By then a news story in *The New York Times* reported that the FBI had recruited a Soviet KGB source in the United States, and later a book revealed the code name FEDORA. Those who doubted Kulak wondered why he was never arrested. The CIA eventually learned that Kulak had died, of natural causes, about 1983.

†Angleton argued that FEDORA/Kulak was a plant because he had supposedly vouched for Nosenko. But a former senior FBI official said Kulak had simply reported overhearing a conversation by two colleagues who thought it was too bad that Nosenko had defected, an event they could have read about in *The New York Times*.

"We got a package addressed to Hoover or the bureau saying, in stilted English, that a bureau agent was selling documents and would be at a phone booth in Rockville at a certain time. Inside the package there were a couple of surveillance reports from the Washington field office. We checked and found they were missing from the files.

"We figured the Soviets were feeding him back; they thought he was a dangle. But he wasn't. Sullivan had Baltimore run the case since the agent was in WFO [the Washington field office]." Sullivan was William C. Sullivan, then the FBI's assistant director for intelligence. Because the suspect had to be someone working in the Washington field office, he asked the FBI field office in Baltimore to take over, to avoid the awkward possibility that one of the agents assigned to sur-veillance of the phone booth might be the mole.

At the appointed hour, the agents from Baltimore were discreetly in place, watching the phone booth. But the stakeout was disappointing. "The guilty agent spotted the surveillance all around, knew they were from Baltimore, and did not go to the phone booth. Later, he called a friend in the Baltimore office and said, 'You must have something going on, I saw your whole group out on the street.' They said, 'Yeah, we were all out there,' but they didn't realize it was *him*."

The comedy of errors ended when the agent in Baltimore remem-bered the phone call from his friend, the FBI man in Washington, and sheepishly came forward with the name. "Once we learned who had called Baltimore, we took a look at him. The guy liked to play the horses and was having marital troubles. And he had worked the case where the two documents were missing." Still, the bureau had no proof, and the agent denied everything. "He was eased out," the former FBI official said. "By now, he is long dead."

When Hanssen directed the mole study, only one bureau turncoat had actually been caught and convicted. That was Richard Miller, the FBI agent arrested in 1984. But the Miller case in Los Angeles could not explain why the FBI and the CIA were losing agents in Washington and Moscow.*

---

*Earl Edwin Pitts, the second FBI agent ever arrested for espionage, had approached the KGB in New York in 1987 and began five years of spying for Moscow in July, not long before Hanssen returned to headquarters and began searching for moles. But Pitts was not arrested until December 1996, so his career as a spy was not known at the time of Hanssen's study.

Not only UNSUB DICK but all allegations of moles in the bureau, however vague, were in a real sense open cases. "Counterintelligence never stops trying to identify leaks, even years later," said Paul Moore. "CI is still looking for a guy who sold a document from the Manhattan Project to the Russians for $750. He's probably dead by now, but eventually the FBI will identify him. It's relentless, and it's all about details."

In 1988, after months of intensive work, the research and writing were done. What made the finished product so extraordinarily sensitive was the fact that it specifically identified each Soviet recruitment and defector who had alleged that the FBI was penetrated, and it described the information they provided. Thus, if the study were to fall into the hands of the KGB, it could endanger the safety of any living sources who had been secretly recruited by the FBI. It was, in short, a bombshell.

When the study had been completed, classified TOP SECRET, reviewed, and approved by Hanssen, the volatile, critical nature of its contents was protected by a stern warning on the first page:

IN VIEW OF THE EXTREME SENSITIVITY OF THIS DOCUMENT THE UTMOST CAUTION MUST BE EXERCISED IN ITS HANDLING. THE CONTENTS INCLUDE A COMPREHENSIVE REVIEW OF SENSITIVE SOURCE ALLEGATIONS AND INVESTIGATIONS OF PENETRATION OF THE FBI BY THE SOVIET INTELLIGENCE SERVICES THE DISCLOSURE OF WHICH WOULD COMPROMISE HIGHLY SENSITIVE COUNTERINTELLIGENCE OPERATIONS AND METHODS. ACCESS SHOULD BE LIMITED TO A STRICT NEED-TO-KNOW BASIS.

Better than anyone else in the FBI, Robert Hanssen knew how valuable his mole study would be to the KGB. Whose need to know could be greater?

10

The Spy

One month after Hanssen returned to Washington he began his most intensive period of espionage, even as he directed the study to find the
penetration inside the FBI, whom he saw every morning in the mirror.

The Soviet spy agency had, in previous messages, urged Hanssen to
travel overseas to meet with them. When the KGB was fortunate
enough to have a major source inside U.S. intelligence, it made every
effort to meet the asset outside the country. Thus the CIA's Aldrich
Ames met the KGB in Bogotá, the NSA's Ronald Pelton went to Vienna, others journeyed to Mexico City or Zurich.

There was good reason for this pattern; the KGB knew it could operate much more freely in an environment where it had more control. In
Washington or New York, the FBI greatly outnumbered the KGB, and
the risks of surveillance were accordingly much higher. In the case of
Hanssen, there was another reason that the KGB was pressuring the spy
they called "B" to meet overseas. They wanted to get a good look at
him, learn or verify his identity, and assess their man firsthand. As
Hanssen knew, a face-to-face meeting might lead to his unmasking; he
would surely be secretly photographed by the KGB, for example.

Following the instructions he had received a year earlier, Hanssen
early in September 1987 sent a letter to the accommodation address
NANCY, the Alexandria home of Boris M. Malakhov. The handwritten
envelope was addressed to B. N. MALKOW, with a fictitious return address.

In the letter inside, Hanssen once again made it clear that he knew
too much about counterintelligence to play the game by the KGB's
rules. Hanssen's "Dear Friends" letter began: "No, I have decided. It

must be on my original terms or not at all. I will not meet abroad or here. . . . I will help you when I can, and in time we will develop methods of efficient communication."

He told them that unless he saw "an abort signal on our post from you" he would mail "a valuable package." He would be looking for the KGB's signal and cash at the designated dead drop at 7 A.M. on September 16, or, if anything went wrong, on the same weekday and time in the three weeks following.*

"If my terms are unacceptable," Hanssen added, "then place no signals and withdraw my contact." He closed by flattering Cherkashin, though not mentioning him by name. "Excellent work by him has ensured this channel is secure for now. My regards to him and to the professional way you have handled this matter. Sincerely, Ramon."

According to the FBI, the KGB never knew Hanssen's identity until his arrest became public on February 20, 2001. Hanssen sought to preserve his anonymity for obvious reasons of self-protection: an FBI or CIA mole inside the KGB could not easily betray him if his identity remained unknown. His true name does not appear in the detailed KGB file of the case that the FBI eventually obtained. This could be seen as evidence, although certainly not conclusive, that the KGB never learned his name.

"They didn't know who he was," David Major insisted. "And if they checked up on Hanssen to find out his identity, that might have been detected by us [the FBI]. He was once seen at a drop by the KGB and he saw them. They knew it was a bureau source from the material, and they didn't need to know more."

Some experienced counterintelligence agents, however, snort at the idea that the KGB would not, over a period of sixteen years, have discovered Hanssen's identity. Since he often drove his car to drop and signal sites, it would not have been difficult to write down or photograph his license plate and learn the owner from public motor vehicle records.†
Or the KGB might even have followed him to his home or office.

---

*Using the six coefficient, Hanssen actually wrote the time and date as 1 P.M. on March 22. The true dates are given here for clarity.

†The Russians could have done so any time up to July 1, 1994. On that date a new law protecting drivers' privacy took effect in Virginia, where Hanssen's cars were registered. Under the state law, the name and address of the owner of a license plate was no longer a matter of public record.

"The Russians always have countersurveillance which would have seen his car," said Ed Curran, who worked on many of the major Soviet espionage cases for the FBI. If a Soviet source tried to remain anonymous in dealing with the bureau, Curran said, "we would do everything we could to find the guy's identity."

Dick Alu, another veteran FBI counterintelligence agent, was equally emphatic. "Bullshit they didn't know his identity! He's driving his own vehicle. After the first year when it became obvious this was not an FBI double agent operation, they had to find out who the hell it was and I'm sure they did."

Whether or not the Russians ever succeeded in learning Hanssen's identity, they were clearly convinced of the value of his information. True to his word, Hanssen mailed a package received by Malakhov on September 14 that included National Security Council documents marked TOP SECRET. The next day, the KGB placed $10,000 in cash in the PARK dead drop in Nottoway Park.

Along with the money, the KGB also proposed two additional dead drop sites in northern Virginia. One, code-named AN, was in a park in the western part of Fairfax County, and another, code-named DEN, was at a location even farther away.

Hanssen did not like the two new drop sites. Two weeks later, he left a note for the KGB at his favorite drop in Nottoway Park. "My Friends: Thank you for the $10,000. I am not a young man, and the commitments on my time prevent using distant drops such as you suggest. I know in this I am moving you out of your set modes of doing business, but my experience tells me . . . we can be actually more secure in easier modes."

He then suggested using a parked car as a drop; if the Russians did not think that a good idea, he agreed to clear AN "this once." But he asked the KGB to find "a comfortable Vienna VA signal site to call me to an exchange any following Monday." He signed the letter "Ramon." With the letter, Hanssen left a classified document describing the U.S. national intelligence program for 1987.

In insisting on drops close to home, and often using the same drops many times, Hanssen was breaking all the traditional rules of spycraft. But he may not have done so merely for convenience; using hiding places nearby helped him to conceal his activities. It allowed him to exchange documents for cash on the way to or from work, avoiding longer absences that he might have to explain to his family. He could even tell his wife he was going to walk the dog.

As far as the increased risk was concerned, Hanssen may have been thinking "out of the box" in contrarian style. If the FBI knew that the KGB rarely used drops more than once, or avoided drops near a spy's residence, then he would do just the opposite. This doubtless is what he meant by saying that "my experience tells me" easier is better.

The KGB was not about to argue with their primo spy, who could, they realized, break off communication at any time if his feathers were sufficiently ruffled. In which case, the Washington residentura would have some major explaining to do to Moscow Center.

Soon after, the KGB meekly proposed a signal site on the post of a stop sign on Courthouse Road, not far from Hanssen's home in Vienna. And at the end of the month, the KGB deposited $100,000 into an escrow account created for "B" in a Moscow bank.

In the first week of November, Hanssen sent another letter to Malakhov with a return address of J. Baker in Chicago. He said he had an urgent package for the KGB, and asked for a signal so he could leave it the following Monday. In future contacts, Hanssen added, whenever he used "Chicago" in a return address, it meant he wanted an exchange the next Monday.

Hanssen had never liked dead drop AN to begin with, and in mid-November he sent a querulous letter to the KGB with a return address of "G. Robertson" in Houston. It read:

> Unable to locate AN based on your description at night. Recognize that I am dressed in business suit and can not slog around in inch deep mud. I suggest we use once again original site. I will place my urgent material there at next AN times. Replace it with your package. I will select some few sites good for me and pass them to you. Please give new constant conditions of recontact as address to write. Will not put substantive material through it. Only instructions as usual format.
>
> Ramon

Hanssen was risking his life, but he wasn't about to risk his shoes. On Monday, November 23, the KGB, properly chastised—and no doubt anxious to avoid any further irritation of their golden source—carried out an exchange at the PARK dead drop site, Hanssen's old favorite.

Among the documents passed by Hanssen that day was a cable, classified SECRET, that reported on a meeting the previous month of Jack Platt, a CIA officer, and Gennady Vasilenko, a KGB major. A tall, athletic man, the Russian was a world-class volleyball player who had been selected for the Soviet Olympic team in 1964 but was sidelined by a shoulder injury before he joined the KGB. Vasilenko had worked in Washington in the late 1970s and was now stationed in Guyana. Platt had become friendly with Vasilenko in Washington, where they spent years trying to recruit each other, with no success. Still, both the CIA and the FBI continued to hope that one day it might happen.

When Vasilenko was leaving Washington in 1981 to return to Moscow, Platt invited him and his family to come for a farewell drink. The KGB man asked his superiors for permission. "He was told not to go and came anyway," said Platt, who founded a private security firm after he retired from the agency. "I said then, 'When you come out I'll find you.'

"In March of eighty-four he went to Guyana. From there, he was making calls to the SMUN—the Soviet Mission to the United Nations. Instead of saying, 'Hey, guys, it's Gennady,' he was using his full name." Platt was convinced that Vasilenko, knowing the FBI was listening, was trying to indicate to Platt where he was.

In October 1987, Platt flew to Guyana, and with an FBI agent met with Vasilenko, once more trying to recruit the KGB man, who was happy to see his friend but again turned him down. Platt did not give up; he said he would return to Guyana and they arranged to meet there again in February, on Platt's birthday.

In the files of the CIA, Vasilenko was designated with the code name GTGLAZING. In addition, as is customary, the CIA and the FBI gave him a joint cryptonym, MONOLITE.*

A copy of Platt's October cable to CIA headquarters reporting on his encounter with Vasilenko in Guyana fell into Hanssen's hands, but he erroneously reported to the KGB that the Russian was working for American intelligence. By misinterpreting the cable and passing it to the KGB, Hanssen had placed yet another life at risk.

---

*The Vasilenko story is hinted at in the affidavit and indictment in the Hanssen case. But the affidavit, using only the first letter of his joint cryptonym, refers to the KGB man simply as "M," and it nowhere mentions him by name.

This was so because Vasilenko could not afford to report his encounter with Platt to Moscow headquarters. He had become entirely too friendly with Platt. When a KGB officer is pitched by the CIA, he is required to report it—and then is almost always recalled to Moscow to remove him from temptation. To avoid a recall, and perhaps to sidestep having to explain his actions to the KGB, Vasilenko never reported the meeting.

But Hanssen had. In January 1988, two months after Hanssen put Platt's cable in the dead drop, Vasilenko was told to go to Havana for a KGB meeting. There he was jumped by two KGB goons who broke his arm and accused him of treason. He was sent back to Moscow, thrown into Lefortovo prison, and interrogated for about six months. Finally, he was released for lack of evidence but fired from the KGB.*

Hanssen in the same November package also provided a summary of the secrets divulged to the CIA by Vitaly Yurchenko during his three-month interlude as a defector two years earlier. Since Aldrich Ames had been one of Yurchenko's debriefers, the KGB already knew what secrets the defector had revealed; still, it was nice to get the information from a second mole.

Also included in Hanssen's package was a technical document describing COINS-II, the internal Internet used by the U.S. intelligence community to exchange information.† In return, the KGB left $20,000 in cash for Hanssen and a letter of best regards from the KGB chief, Vladimir A. Kryuchkov. The Russians also assured Hanssen that another $100,000 had been deposited for him in a Moscow bank at 6 to 7 percent interest.

Early in February 1988, Hanssen and the KGB exchanged documents and money once more at the PARK drop site, which the KGB, perhaps in recognition of its frequent use, had now renamed PRIME.

---

*Jack Platt learned of Vasilenko's arrest in 1988 but did not know who had betrayed him. The arrest of Aldrich Ames in 1994 pointed to one possible answer. But Platt was dubious that Ames was responsible, since Ames was in Rome in 1987 and would not have been likely to see the cable from Guyana. After the collapse of the Soviet Union in 1991, Platt learned that Vasilenko had survived prison and the two went into business together. In a remarkable post–Cold War story, Vasilenko became Platt's partner in the Hamilton Trading Group, Inc., their private security company with offices in McLean, Virginia, and Moscow.
†The acronym stood for Community On-Line Intelligence System.

Hanssen's letter, in addition to acknowledging the $20,000, provided detailed information about Victor Sheymov, an important Soviet defector to whose file he had access. He promised "a full report" on Sheymov "as soon as possible."

The CIA had smuggled Sheymov out of Moscow in 1980—"exfiltrated" him, in the agency's jargon for clandestinely spiriting someone across a border to safety. Sheymov, a communications expert, had worked for the KGB's eighth chief directorate, the Soviet equivalent of the NSA. He was a troubleshooter for the directorate, traveling frequently in the Communist bloc to unravel problems involving the security of codes and ciphers.

Hanssen told the KGB that he could read the Sheymov file because a special project involving the defector was about to begin. At the time, Hanssen was reviewing the file to prepare to take part in a series of debriefings of Sheymov. After meeting Sheymov, Hanssen became a personal friend of the Russian and stayed in close touch with him. Their families often socialized together. Sheymov, of course, did not realize his good friend in the FBI was reporting back to the KGB about him.

In the same exchange, Hanssen also identified a KGB illegal in the United States, an officer operating without diplomatic cover, who had been recruited as a double agent by the FBI. Once again, Hanssen had placed a bureau source in great jeopardy.

In his package, Hanssen also included certain secret details about U.S. communications intelligence, describing just what Soviet traffic the NSA was unable to read. Along with several classified documents on paper, Hanssen for the first time enclosed a computer floppy disk on which he had downloaded additional secrets.

In return, the KGB gave Hanssen $25,000 in cash and another letter of thanks from Vladimir Kryuchkov, the KGB chairman, for the information about M—Gennady Vasilenko. The KGB asked for more information about M and about the FBI's operations in New York.

In March, Hanssen mailed three more computer disks to the KGB. Once during that month, when the Russians tried to clear the newly named PRIME drop site, they could not, because there were too many people in the park. When the exchange finally took place, Hanssen included a particularly sensitive TOP SECRET report entitled "The FBI's Double Agent Program." The document was a detailed description of the FBI's double agent operations worldwide over a ten-year period, including joint operations with other U.S. intelligence agencies. The report would have included everything learned by every American double agent over a decade. It would also have helped the KGB to weed out any fake walk-ins floated by the bureau to offer their services to the Russians.

The KGB's package contained another $25,000 in cash and a letter saying it had been unable to read some of the computer disks. The letter also asked Hanssen for information about codes, submarines, and the Strategic Defense Initiative (SDI), President Reagan's proposed antimissile system, better known as Star Wars.

Early in April, the KGB received a letter from "Jim Baker" with a note that said: "use 40 TRACK MODE. this letter is not a signal." Hanssen, the computer whiz, was explaining to the KGB that he had formatted the floppy disks in a mode that hid the data on specific tracks. The disk would appear blank to anyone who did not use the correct codes to decrypt it.

Two days later, Hanssen sent another note, with another disk, explaining in greater detail how to decrypt the computer disks. The new disk included more information about Victor Sheymov, as well as details about another KGB officer and about two Soviet FBI recruitments.

Hanssen also renewed his request to be paid in diamonds, a subject he had raised early on with the KGB, in 1985. All that spring of 1988, he continued to funnel secrets to the KGB.

It was on Monday, May 30, that the KGB got its only fleeting glimpse of Robert Hanssen. A KGB officer arrived at the PRIME dead drop at 9:03 P.M., three minutes after the time that the exchange was scheduled to take place. In the dark, the KGB officer saw a man remove the signal, get into his car, and drive away.

It was mid-July before Hanssen made contact again, with a letter grumbling about arrangements. A spy's life, he seemed to be saying, was not easy, so please shape up:

> I found the site empty. Possibly I had the time wrong. I work from memory. My recollection was for you to fill before 1:00 A.M. I believe Viktor Degtyar was in the church driveway off Rt. 123, but I did not know how he would react to an approach. My schedule was tight to make this at all. Because of my work, I had to synchronize explanations and flights while not leaving a pattern of absence or travel that could later be correlated with communication times. This is difficult and expen-

sive. I will call the number you gave me on 2/24, 2/26 or 2/28 at 1:00 A.M., EDST. Please plan filled signals. Empty sites bother me. I like to know before I commit myself as I'm sure you do also. Let's not use the original site so early at least until the seasons change. Some type of call-out signal to you when I have a package or when I can receive one would be useful. Also, please be specific about dates, e.g., 2/24. Scheduling is not simple for me because of frequent travel and wife. Any ambiguity multiplies the problems.

My security concerns may seem excessive. I believe experience has shown them to be necessary. I am much safer if you know little about me. Neither of us are children about these things. Over time, I can cut your losses rather than become one.

Ramon

P.S. Your "thank you" was deeply appreciated.

On July 18 the exchange took place at PRIME, and this time the KGB received a truly enormous haul of secrets—more than 530 pages of documents, including a CIA analysis, classified TOP SECRET, of Soviet intelligence-gathering aimed at U.S. nuclear weapons capabilities. The CIA report evaluated how much Moscow knew about America's early warning systems and about the nation's ability to retaliate against a massive nuclear attack.

Hanssen also turned over an even more highly classified 1987 document, prepared for the director of central intelligence, entitled "Compendium of Future Intelligence Requirements: Volume II." This was a wish list of what the CIA wanted to know about the military strength of the Soviet Union and other countries, which thus amounted to a road map of what the CIA did *not* know. Hanssen also passed to the KGB a March 1988 CIA study classified SECRET and entitled "The Soviet Counterintelligence Offensive: KGB Recruitment Operations Against CIA."

The study of recruitment efforts aimed at the CIA contained a warning notice that read: "Intelligence Sources or Methods Involved (WNINTEL). National Security Information. Unauthorized Disclosure Subject to Criminal Sanctions."

Finally, Hanssen turned over the pièce de résistance, the study of Soviet penetrations of the FBI that he had personally directed and prepared with the assistance of Jim Milburn and Bob King. The KGB could now enjoy the product of this intensive effort by the FBI's Soviet analytical unit. The study, classified TOP SECRET, identified the sources that had hinted at moles in the bureau, and exactly what each had said.

In exchange, the KGB gave Hanssen another $25,000 in cash, and asked for data on several fronts, including FBI surveillance techniques and recruitment operations. The Russians also proposed two new dead drops near Hanssen's home in Vienna. Both were under footbridges in parks, one designated BOB—were the Russians trying to tell him something?—and the other CHARLIE.

On the last day of July, Hanssen mailed the KGB another computer disk, this one with information about the bureau's technical surveillance operations, which of course Hanssen knew a great deal about, details of a new recruitment in New York City, and the identities of several other Soviets the FBI had targeted for recruitment attempts. The following month, the KGB informed Hanssen that another $50,000 had been placed in his Moscow bank account.

This extraordinary pace of spying continued through the rest of the year. The last Monday in September brought another exchange, this time at BOB. Hanssen hid a package with about three hundred pages of material, including FBI documents and a verbatim transcript of a meeting of the Counterintelligence Group.*

Perhaps sensing from the tone of Hanssen's letters that their superspy was a man who needed a great deal of stroking, the Russians left yet another letter from KGB chairman Kryuchkov expressing his deep gratitude. They also advised Hanssen that by way of thanks another $50,000 had been deposited in his escrow account.

But business is business. The letter also discussed communications procedures and security measures and once again pushed for a personal meeting. Ever hopeful, the KGB included a discussion of passports.

It also asked Hanssen to provide information about the CIA's secret wiretap operations in the Soviet Union, details about agent networks, intelligence sources of U.S. allies, various FBI programs, and past spy cases. Up to this point, much, although by no means all, of the information Hanssen provided was about the spy wars between U.S. and So-

---

*The Counterintelligence Group was an interagency task force created during the Reagan administration that met monthly. It was unrelated to the Counterintelligence Group in the Soviet division of the CIA, which was headed in 1983 by Aldrich Ames.

viet intelligence—recruitments, targets, double agents, and the like. But this time, Moscow asked for data about missile technology.

Hanssen obliged, with a Christmas present for the KGB. On Monday, December 26, 1988, after celebrating the holiday with his wife and children and exchanging gifts in the warmth of his home on Talisman Drive, Hanssen hid another sort of package at dead drop CHARLIE.

Included with a floppy disk and 356 pages of material were six recent National HUMINT Collection Plan (NHCP) documents. The acronym stands for human intelligence—information gathered by spies, as opposed to that collected by electronic or other technical means.

Since the KGB wanted to know about missiles, Hanssen was certain they would be interested in the highly secret U.S. assessment and projection of Moscow's nuclear missile arsenal, including the number, strength, and details of its ICBMs and warheads. He gave them a document entitled "Soviet Armed Forces and Capabilities for Conducting Strategic Nuclear War Until the End of the 1990s."

Hanssen's neighborhood in northern Virginia was festooned with Christmas lights. The carolers on his quiet street had serenaded Hanssen in the frosty air with "O, Little Town of Bethlehem" and the other songs of the season of peace on earth. But Hanssen was following another star, passing secrets in the night that dealt with the unimaginable destruction of his own country.

11

Hanssen's Gods

One of the intriguing questions about Robert Hanssen was how he reconciled his religion with his treachery. By all accounts from close friends and colleagues, he was not merely religious; he was devout.

Hanssen went to mass almost every day, often at Our Lady of Good Counsel before work, and on Sundays at St. John's, both near his home in northern Virginia. But to take Holy Communion, as Hanssen did, to become one with the body and blood of Christ, Catholics are required to go to confession to unburden themselves of any serious sins to a priest, who will ordinarily absolve them if they show genuine contrition. They will be told to do penance, usually in the form of prayer. This cycle of sin—which, after all, is part of the human condition—confession, and absolution, or forgiveness, is a familiar and basic element of the Catholic tradition.

Hanssen told at least two persons who visited him in prison that he regularly confessed his espionage over a period of more than two decades. It is possible he did so obliquely, of course, in vague or general terms. There is no question that he disclosed his spying outright to priests at least twice, and almost certainly more often.

But Hanssen was confident that his secret would hold; confession is an inviolable sacrament of the Roman Catholic Church. Under the church's canon law, a priest who reveals what is said in confession faces excommunication. The priests to whom Hanssen confessed were under no formal obligation to advise him to stop spying, or to turn himself in, although they were free to suggest those options.

According to Professor Chester Gillis of Georgetown University, a leading theologian, it is possible for a penitent to confess the same sin many times. "Technically you can go back as many times as you want and forgiveness is without end in the Catholic tradition. Provided the sacrament is valid and there is true contrition on the part of the penitent, then if it is a repetitive act and the person asks for forgiveness again, he or she will be granted forgiveness again.

"This can be as simple as masturbation in pubescent youths, to murder. The gravity of the offense doesn't really matter.* If Hanssen confessed to espionage he would get absolution. If he said he intends to continue doing it, the priest has the right to refuse absolution. It would be rare.

"The priest might or might not ask about the details. The priest might not probe too deeply. For some people the sacrament takes place face-to-face. So the priest knows who it is, but he would never break the bond."

Superficially, Hanssen's religion might appear to have made it easier for him to spy, since he could confess and be granted absolution for his crime. But in reality his religion may have made his espionage more difficult, since he surely knew he had sinned and could not easily escape his burden of guilt. "A person in a state of grace can receive the Eucharist," Gillis said. "If a person is in a state of sin, he is not in a state of grace. Being in a state of grace means you have confessed a serious sin and been given absolution. In a state of grace means you are in a proper relationship with God. But if Hanssen's conscience was finely honed, he may have realized internally he was not in a state of grace. He might have felt he was juridically, but not internally."

After Hanssen, a twenty-four-year-old Lutheran, married into Bonnie Wauck's family, he become a convert to Catholicism. The family was deeply involved with the church. Not only was Bonnie's brother John Paul a priest of Opus Dei, but her uncle Robert Hagarty, her mother's brother, was a monsignor, and both her parents were active, as Bonnie was, in "the work," as Opus Dei was sometimes called by its members. Another of Bonnie's brothers, Mark A. Wauck, although an FBI agent, found time to translate the entire New Testament from the

---

*Professor Gillis pointed out that, contrary to popular opinion, absolution is not contingent on performance of the penance, because in the sacrament of reconciliation, the formal name for confession, forgiveness is granted before the person does the actual penance.

original Greek, a volume approved by the National Conference of Catholic Bishops.*

Surrounded as he was by vigorously enthusiastic Catholics, Hanssen's decision to become a convert was, if the term may be used, predestined. But he was strongly influenced, he told at least one close friend, by long conversations with his father-in-law, Professor Leroy Wauck, who later invited and accompanied Hanssen to his first Catholic retreat at Shelburn, Indiana.

Once Hanssen had converted, he became, to all appearances, a true believer who wore his faith on his sleeve and never lost an opportunity to urge people to go to mass or, if they were lapsed Catholics, to return to the fold. He also persuaded many of his friends to attend one or more Opus Dei "evenings of recollection" at the Tenley Study Center in Washington.

"He always tried to get me to church," said James Bamford, the author of two bestselling books about the National Security Agency who met Hanssen while working as an investigative journalist for ABC News. "One night he took me to an Opus Dei meeting at Tenley. There were prayers and some priest got up and talked about how to support the bishop. The priest talked about other church-type stuff. I couldn't wait to leave. It was like being back in Sunday school. I'm Catholic but I've gotten away from it. He really wanted to get me back in the church."

Similarly, Hanssen persuaded Tom Burns, a fellow Catholic and his boss during his first tour in the FBI's Soviet analytical unit, to accompany him to Opus Dei meetings. "At Hanssen's invitation, I spoke at Opus Dei at Tenley. They get people in to speak on various subjects. I had done a paper for the Army War College on terrorism in Western Europe. At Bob's invitation I spoke on that subject at the Opus Dei meeting. I did not join Opus Dei. I just didn't have the luxury of the time."

The Hanssens attended church at St. Catherine of Siena Catholic Church in Great Falls, Virginia, for a while. Burns was a member of the parish and Hanssen, first as a visitor, had been impressed with Father Jerome Fasano, the charismatic priest who was the pastor at the time. "That's why Hanssen came to St. Catherine's," Burns said.

But the Hanssens had problems at the church. In 1997, Father Franklyn M. McAfee became the new pastor. Reviewing the membership the following year, he noticed, as he wrote to Hanssen, that there

---

*New Testament: St. Paul Catholic Edition, translated by Mark A. Wauck (Staten Island, N.Y.: Society of St. Paul Alba House, 2000).

had been "no activity financially." The family was invited, politely but firmly, to return to their own parish.* Bonnie Hanssen wrote back for the family, asking to rejoin.

"They were reinstated," McAfee said. "They still didn't give anything. When they came back they made a pledge to the building fund, which they didn't have to do, and didn't act on that." Bonnie's letter also pledged to give St. Catherine a minimum of forty dollars a month. "They did not keep the commitment," McAfee said. The Hanssens, nevertheless, were not disinvited by the church a second time, and attended mass there some Sundays.

Father C. John McCloskey III, the Opus Dei priest and director of the Catholic Information Center in downtown Washington, knew Bonnie Hanssen well, through her involvement in Opus Dei. But he also got to know Hanssen when the FBI man, often accompanied by his oldest son, Jack, would occasionally go to noon mass at the center's chapel.

Normally, Father McCloskey celebrated the mass and heard confessions before and afterward. "He would take Holy Communion," McCloskey said. "If he did confession, I would not know because I would not see him. I hear confession in a confessional which preserves anonymity."

McCloskey had an unusual background for a priest. He had worked for five years on Wall Street, then decided to leave the stock market for the seminary. "I was a lay member of Opus Dei for many years," he said. "A small percentage are called to the priesthood." McCloskey was ordained in Spain in 1981, then did pastoral work in New York, Princeton, and Washington before becoming director of the Catholic center that brought him into contact with Hanssen.

He had strong feelings about Hanssen's espionage and did not hesitate to express them. "You cannot be a good Catholic and also be a traitor. It's one thing to commit an act of treason, confess it, repent it, and change your life. But to continually act in a traitorous sort of way is inconceivable. It is moral schizophrenia to try to live a life dedicated to God and at the same time compartmentalizing your life to that extent. The whole point of Christianity and Catholicism is *not* to lead a double life, but to be transparent.

---

*Because Hanssen lived outside the geographic boundary lines of the parish, McAfee could insist they contribute at least a minimal amount to the church. Persons who lived inside the parish lines were not subject to financial requirements.

"I'm not a psychologist or a psychiatrist. I'm a Catholic priest, but I have a lot of experience dealing with souls. There must be some deep psychological trauma, there is something radically wrong. To be able to conceal that from his friends and family, in addition to the moral flaw, there must be some deep hurts and problems."

Hanssen was able to carry this compartmentalization to extraordinary lengths. Often, to his friends and colleagues, he denounced the Soviets, to whom he was selling his soul and his secrets, as "godless." David Major, for one, remembered Hanssen using precisely that term. "He used to say to me the Soviets will lose because they are run by godless Communists. He said, 'You've got to have Christ in your life or you're never going to get anywhere.' "

Hanssen carpooled with his friend Paul Moore after he returned to Washington in 1987 to rejoin the Soviet analytical unit and direct the mole study. "One day," Moore recalled, "with just the two of us in my yellow Mercedes, we drove past the White House and somebody came on NPR talking about the implied social contract that is the basis of morality. He reached over and turned off the radio. 'That's enough of that,' he said. 'The basis of morality is not an implied social contract. It's God's law.'

"He made it clear he would be pleased if I became a more active Catholic, but he never said 'Let's go to church.' When I had trouble one time, he said, 'Have you ever thought about trying to bring God into the equation?' He said, 'Look, I know these guys in McLean who run a retreat center. Father Dan.' He gave me the phone number the next day.

"I asked him about Opus Dei. He said it is a lay group of people within the church who were married but potentially some of them would take vows. There are some lay people who take a vow of chastity. There are various vows in the church, and seven steps to priesthood. The purpose of Opus Dei, he said, is to help people lead holier lives, to make Catholic faith a more living faith. It has its own priests assigned to it."

Hanssen was repeating to Moore the fairly standard Opus Dei description of its goals. But he also told Moore something he had not revealed to others. "He said he had a disagreement with them over finances. They like to review your finances and say, 'Contribute this amount.' He said he didn't have that amount to give." In retrospect, Moore thought the exchange ironic: "He was probably already working for the Russians."

For the most part, however, Hanssen extolled the virtues of Opus Dei, a group that has often been criticized as too secretive, too conservative, too powerful within the Vatican, and too intrusive in the life of its members.

One somewhat disenchanted Opus Dei member who had been active at the same Tenley Center in Washington as Hanssen recalled that the organization had strong ties to the Reagan administration. "Half of the Reagan White House would come to the meetings at Tenley House," he said. "Opus Dei is very strong on recruiting people, and once they have you they don't let go. They're all over you. 'Do you have a problem getting to church? We'll drive you.' The members will not say much about it to outsiders. They are strict and conventional Catholics, and therefore comfortable with Pope John Paul II."

Hanssen was always encouraging his friends to learn more about Opus Dei. He gave his FBI colleague Jim Ohlson a copy of *The Way,* a book by the founder of Opus Dei, Josemaria Escriva de Balaguer. The slim paperback volume is a collection of homilies to guide the faithful on their way along the path of life. For example, the first teaching admonishes: "1. Don't let your life be sterile. Be useful. Blaze a trail. Shine forth with the light of your faith and of your love."*

Josemaria Escriva, whose movement so captured Hanssen's imagination, was a Spanish priest who founded Opus Dei in Madrid in 1928. The organization has always had strong roots in Spain; under dictator Franco, ten Opus Dei members served at various times as cabinet ministers. After Escriva's death in 1975 at the age of seventy-three, his supporters urged his beatification, the first step toward sainthood.

In order to reach that initial plateau on the way to canonization, a miracle had to be attributed to Escriva and approved by various papal bodies. A year after Escriva's death, a Carmelite nun was reportedly cured of a rare disease after her family prayed for Escriva's intercession with God. The miracle was officially accepted and Pope John Paul II, clad in golden robes, beatified Escriva in 1992 before some three hundred thousand people in St. Peter's Square. He then became known as Blessed Josemaria.

But this elevation did not take place without considerable controversy. Critics of Opus Dei complained that the beatification process had been speeded up, and that Opus Dei had helped to elect Cardinal Karol Wojtyla as Pope John Paul II in 1978 and exercised undue influence in

---

*Josemaria Escriva de Balaguer, *The Way* (New York: Scepter, 1979), p. 21.

the Vatican. It was John Paul II who elevated Opus Dei to the unusual status of a "personal prelature" in 1982. And early in 2002, he announced that Escriva would be made a saint in October.

The critics also see Opus Dei as an elitist organization that seeks to recruit talented young people who will rise in their professions and exercise influence in society. The Opus Dei schools, in the critics' view, play a key role in the recruitment process.

Officials of Opus Dei deny these various criticisms and claim that their influence in Rome is exaggerated. They point out that in the College of Cardinals, the body that chooses a new pope, only one of the 179 members, Juan Luis Cipriani Thorne, the archbishop of Lima, Peru, is a member of Opus Dei. "That is not a very big voting bloc," said Brian Finnerty, the Opus Dei communications director.

Like Hanssen, about 70 percent of the organization's eighty-four thousand members worldwide are married or about to be, and are known as supernumeraries. The rest are men and women who commit themselves to celibacy and are called numeraries, if they live in residences in Opus Dei centers, or associates, if they live with their families or on their own.

People who seek to become members must apply in writing and go through a six-month period of familiarization with Opus Dei. Before they are accepted, they must enter into an oral contract to commit to the organization's aims of holiness and to accept its jurisdiction in religious matters. All members are expected to perform small acts of penance during the day. Some of the celibate members, as a form of penance, wear a chain around their thigh known as a cilice.* "The cilice is designed to be uncomfortable but not harmful to a person's health," Finnerty said. "It does not break the skin."

Louis Freeh, who was FBI director when the bureau closed in on Hanssen and arrested him, attended the same church as did Hanssen, St. Catherine of Siena, and Freeh's son went to the Heights, the Opus Dei school, with the Hanssen boys. However, Freeh was not himself a member of Opus Dei, according to Finnerty.†

---

*The word literally means a hair shirt worn by monks or nuns in medieval times and made from Cilican goat hair. Cilicia was an ancient region of Asia Minor.

†Published reports that Freeh might belong to Opus Dei may have stemmed from confusion over the fact that his brother, John Freeh, had in the past been a celibate member of Opus Dei and director of the Tenley Opus Dei center in Washington and the Opus Dei center in Pittsburgh.

Was Hanssen's religion, his constant preoccupation with God, a genuine expression of deep faith, or part of his cover as a Russian spy? Although some counterintelligence officials think Hanssen's religion was a convenient cloak, those who knew him well disagree. True, his denunciation of "godless Communism" helped to throw off suspicion that he was on the payroll of the godless Communists. But Hanssen spent far too much time in his devotions, at church and with Opus Dei, and in long discussions about religion with his friends, for it all to have been a complete sham.

Ron Mlotek, who became a good friend of Hanssen's when they worked together at the State Department in the 1990s, had no doubt at all that the FBI man's faith was authentic. "The first time I set foot in his office to welcome him I saw he had two open Bibles lying on his desk and a crucifix on the wall. That launched us into a deep conversation about our respective faiths." And it was the beginning of their friendship.

Mlotek, the chief legal counsel of the Office of Foreign Missions, said they became friends "because Bob was a strongly religious Catholic who felt a kinship with an Orthodox Jew.

"Bob's basic argument is that all Catholics are Jews. Because Jews are our elder brothers. They worship a Jew. The Last Supper was a Passover seder. But Catholics are more fulfilled because of their belief in the resurrection. Those were his arguments. He never said 'Ron, become a Catholic,' but he did say, 'It would be good for you.' I went with him to Opus Dei meetings. He thought the fact that I was Orthodox was a common link." Mlotek added: "We had these conversations all the time—about the differences between the two religions, and about philosophy."

Jack Hoschouer, Hanssen's closest friend, also believed that he was genuinely devout. "His religion is real," he said. "When you find out where the money is, I think you'll find a whole bunch of Catholic charities got big contributions. That's only speculation. He often said, 'Evil is well-funded. The forces of good are underfunded.' He may have wanted to do something that would give him money for that reason."

Be that as it may, the stark contrast between Hanssen's militant Catholicism and his simultaneous service to the Soviets was so seemingly irreconcilable as to baffle his most intimate friends and family members. Even Father McCloskey, who was strongly critical of

Hanssen's betrayal of his country, considered him truly pious. So did Tom Burns, his former boss at the FBI.

"I believe he was seriously religious and a serious spy," Burns said. "Maybe a diagnosis would find him totally bipolar, able to segment different parts of his life. Parts that to all appearances were a contradiction."

Although Mlotek did not doubt Hanssen's faith, he thought he had answered the wrong calling. "He should have been a priest," Mlotek said. "I think everyone would have been better off. The whole world would have been better off."

12

Diamonds Are a Spy's Best Friend

Because Hanssen had suggested a few diamonds might be welcome, the KGB obliged with one in September 1988. Along with the third personal letter of thanks from KGB chairman Kryuchkov, which Hanssen fished out from under a bridge in Idylwood Park in northern Virginia, was a diamond worth $24,720.

A few months later, at Christmas, he received a second diamond valued at $17,748. For Hanssen, diamonds had the virtue of being small and therefore easily concealed. The cash that kept rolling in from Moscow was getting to be bulky and more difficult to hide, especially in a house that he shared with a wife and six children.

At the end of January, soon after the inauguration of the first President Bush, Hanssen left an emergency call-out signal for the KGB in the middle of downtown Washington, just above Dupont Circle at Connecticut Avenue and Q Street. The signal alerted the KGB to clear BOB, the drop in Idylwood Park, and it did so immediately. Hanssen had left a package there with a copy of a cable and a note reading: "Send to the Center right away. This might be useful."

Hanssen's choice of language was revealing, for it made clear how much he sought to ingratiate himself with his unseen colleagues in the KGB. Perhaps as much or more than the money and diamonds, their respect and approval was plainly important to him. "This might be useful" had the ring of an overeager subordinate trying to make brownie points with his boss. Hanssen was signaling that he was not only the KGB's man in Washington but always prepared and ever alert to their needs, a blend of Boy Scout and James Bond.

As spring came to the capital, Hanssen placed another signal for the Russians at a prearranged location, this time farther north on Connecticut Avenue at Taft Bridge, a heavily traveled span famously guarded by two pairs of stone lions. In the exchange that followed at dead drop CHARLIE, near his home, Hanssen left two packages. One contained a TOP SECRET/SCI document from the office of the Director of Central Intelligence that provided guidance for the next decade for MASINT, the most arcane and exotic form of the various types of intelligence collected by the CIA and other U.S. spy agencies.

Although the term is little known to the public, MASINT, which stands for measurement and signature intelligence, applies to a wide variety of data scooped up by satellites and by secret sensors around the globe and under the seas. MASINT includes, for example, satellites equipped with gamma ray trackers and X-ray spectrometers to measure radioactive fallout from a nuclear explosion, as well as infrared sensors to detect antiballistic missile tests. It includes powerful phased array radars, such as COBRA DANE at Shemya, Alaska, which was built to watch for a possible Soviet missile attack and measure Soviet missile test launches. And MASINT includes as well the hundreds of hydrophones planted on the ocean floor in a program called SOSUS to measure the distinctive acoustic signature of Soviet (now Russian) submarines.

The document passed to the KGB by Hanssen was significant because it reflected the consensus of the intelligence community on the secret operations and goals of the MASINT program. The report was crammed with specifics and highly technical information.* Hanssen must have been unusually nervous about transmitting it to the KGB, because for the first and only time he asked that it be returned. Typically there would be numbered copies of a highly classified report of this nature; Hanssen would have a difficult time explaining why the copy he had removed had vanished if he did not get it back.

Hanssen's second package contained another computer disk and more than five hundred pages of documents, many of them classified. In return, the KGB package was generous; it held $18,000 in cash and a third diamond, worth $11,700.

---

*The MASINT document passed by Hanssen, dated November 1988, was entitled "DCI Guidance for the National MASINT Intelligence Program (FY 1991–FY 2000)." It was prepared for the director of central intelligence by the intelligence community's Measurement and Signature Intelligence (MASINT) Committee.

He had now received diamonds valued at a total of $54,168, and the KGB began to fret about whether Hanssen was concealing the gems or flashing them around. The Russians asked what security precautions he was taking to avoid suspicions about the diamonds. Not to worry, Hanssen told the KGB; if anyone asked, he would say the diamonds came from his grandmother.

But on reflection Hanssen himself decided the gems were risky, or that cash was more practical, because only two months later he returned the first and third diamonds, valued at a total of $35,920, and asked for cash instead, which he received the following Christmas Day.

Although Hanssen was unaware of it, the fact that he was paid in diamonds was the first clue obtained by the FBI about an unknown spy that ultimately fit him. According to John F. Lewis, Jr., the former assistant FBI director in charge of the intelligence division, the bureau learned of a "diamond connection" years before it suspected Hanssen.

"We had heard from a defector that somebody was being paid in diamonds," Lewis said. "At least ten years ago or more." That information, while tantalizing, was also frustrating, because the defector, who may have heard corridor gossip at KGB headquarters, had no information about who was receiving the gems, or even in which agency the spy worked.

Four days after receiving the MASINT report, the KGB tried to return it, but for some reason Hanssen failed to retrieve the document the first time it was placed in a dead drop for him. A second attempt also failed, but on the third try, in late May, he got it back.

In Moscow, meanwhile, the KGB officers who had been handling the Hanssen case were recognized in a formal ceremony in April. Among the medals handed out at headquarters were the coveted Order of the Red Banner, as well as the Order of the Red Star and the Medal for Excellent Service.

For Hanssen, there was still the problem of what to do with the cash flowing in from Moscow. Depositing the money in banks or investing it in the market was risky, since to do so would leave a paper trail of unexplained, unreported income.

So when he returned the two diamonds for cash in May, he included a floppy disk on which he broached the idea of the KGB setting up a bank account in Switzerland for him and transferring bonds into it. The traditional secrecy of Swiss banking laws, Hanssen knew, would mask the source of the funds as well as the identity of the account holder.

A few months later, the KGB turned down Hanssen's idea of establishing a Swiss bank account. At some point, however, he went ahead and opened two bank accounts in Switzerland on his own, one at Credit Suisse and the other at Bank Leu. How much money passed through the accounts is not clear, but only a small amount remained in Switzerland at the time of his arrest.

*   *   *

Bill Houghton, who worked for Hanssen in the Soviet analytical unit during these years, liked him but remembered some odd conversations they had. "We would occasionally travel on business; we went out to Los Alamos once. He told amusing stories. He always used to kid. If we were waiting in an airport he'd say, 'That guy's walking funny. My dad always said to me, Always beware of people walking funny. If you see people walking funny they aren't normal.'

"Most people thought him very aloof. We got along because we were both interested in some of the same things. He would talk to me about computers, about codes. In Los Alamos, he said, 'Bill, you know how someone builds a nuclear weapon?' I said, 'No, I don't.' 'It's quite simple,' he said. For the next hour he outlined on a paper napkin how one builds a nuclear weapon. He was a sort of renaissance man.

"We were talking about careers one day and he said, 'Bill, have you ever been to an autopsy? It's fascinating, you should go some time.' He said, 'I did an autopsy, it's not gruesome at all. The first time I sliced off the skull and removed the brain—to hold a person's brain in your hand is such an awesome feeling. To think, a few days ago that was a sentient being and now you're actually holding it in your hand.' " Houghton was somewhat taken aback by the conversation. But he was used to Hanssen saying strange things, and he enjoyed their mutual interest in technical matters.

"Bob was really into shortwave. He would buy expensive equipment and bring it into the office. Apparently his friend Jack had given him an early GPS system and he thought it was really neat. I think I met Jack once. He talked about Jack a lot."

*   *   *

In August, Hanssen passed five rolls of film on which there were copies of highly sensitive documents. He was assured that $50,000 more had been placed in his escrow account in a Moscow bank.

It was on September 25, 1989, that Hanssen disclosed to the KGB the largest U.S. intelligence project of all. He had learned some of the details years before, in the early 1980s. When the Soviets began construction of a new embassy in Washington, the FBI had decided to launch its own secret construction project. To listen in on the Russians, the FBI built an elaborate tunnel beneath the embassy, manned around the clock by NSA technicians with the latest in sophisticated electronic eavesdropping equipment.

When Hanssen was still in New York and spying for the GRU, he had no need to know about the tunnel project. But that changed after he was assigned to headquarters in 1981. The hundreds of millions of dollars spent in building and maintaining the tunnel was for years a huge item in the FBI's budget, and Hanssen, working in the budget unit—and on the Dedicated Technical Program in particular—knew there was an expensive, long-term technical project.

Why had Hanssen waited perhaps as long as eight years to reveal this huge secret? The explanation he gave to debriefers after his arrest was that his information was fragmentary. "He was aware early on, from his budget office days," said one intelligence official, "but he didn't have the details, the description of what it was. He knew the funding, but it wasn't until much later he got the details."

Hanssen revealed the tunnel to the KGB in an exchange carried out at DORIS, a dead drop in Canterbury Park in Springfield, Virginia. Hanssen left eighty pages of documents under a footbridge in the park. One, classified TOP SECRET/SCI, was obliquely described by the government as "a program of enormous value, expense, and importance to the United States."

This was the embassy tunnel, although the government's affidavit does not say that, since the FBI has never admitted to the existence of the tunnel. The project was so sensitive and so secret that even today most FBI officials will not discuss it or even acknowledge it was ever built. "What tunnel?" is the typical response to inquiries about it.

On the September day in 1989 that Hanssen betrayed this multimillion-dollar secret, he received another $30,000 in cash. And the KGB for the first time put its message to Hanssen on a computer disk.

Alas, the Russians were proving to be technically challenged; in October, Hanssen, now calling himself "G. Robertson, 1408 Ingeborg Ct., McLean VA," wrote back, saying: "The disk is clean. I tried all methods—completely demagnetized."

On Halloween, the KGB, undoubtedly grateful for the electrifying news that a tunnel had been dug under their embassy, placed $55,000 in dead drop ELLIS, under the footbridge in Foxstone Park, and assured Hanssen that another $50,000 had been deposited for him in Moscow. The package also included a computer disk—this one readable—with yet another letter conveying regards from KGB chief Vladimir Kryuchkov.

On Christmas Day of 1989, Hanssen closed out his successful year of espionage with an exchange at dead drop BOB, in Idylwood Park. It had been a less successful year for the Soviets, whose empire was crumbling. That fall, one after another, the Communist regimes of Eastern Europe were toppled. The Berlin Wall came down in November, and East Germany opened its borders to the West. So it was unsurprising that the document that Hanssen passed to the Russians, classified SE-CRET and dated November 1989, was a National Intelligence Estimate (NIE) entitled "The Soviet System in Crisis: Prospects for the Next Two Years."

He also provided Moscow with the identities of three new FBI sources within the KGB and other Soviet agencies, which meant that he had now betrayed six FBI sources—Martynov, Motorin, Yuzhin, and the three new ones. In addition, he passed along information about four defectors.

In the same exchange, the KGB gave Hanssen another $38,000 in cash as payment for the two diamonds he had returned, plus a little extra for October. The package for Hanssen also included two computer disks with Christmas greetings from the KGB.

One wonders what he told his family as an excuse to leave home on Christmas Day. Perhaps he invented some errand and drove to the park.

It had been a fine year, and it was nice that the KGB reimbursed him for the two diamonds. But he had expected no less; he was entirely too important an agent to be trifled with by the Russians. As he returned home with $38,000 in cash to his wife and children, his dog, and his Christmas tree with its bright lights, he undoubtedly felt a glow of satisfaction. Perhaps he thought he really was the perfect spy.

But he did not know that seven months before, on that same day in May that he had returned the two diamonds to the KGB, the information he had passed would ultimately, if indirectly, lead to his downfall. On that day he told the KGB about a secret FBI investigation of a State Department official suspected of espionage. His name was Felix Bloch.

13

Let's Play MONOPOLY

Robert Hanssen had recently joined the FBI and was working in his first office in Gary, Indiana, when on August 23, 1977, a brief story about a construction project appeared in *The Washington Post.* The news was not really important enough for page one. Readers would have had to browse through to page two of the Metro section to come across the headline WORK BEGINS ON NEW SOVIET EMBASSY.

"Bulldozers have started clearing trees and dense patches of weeds from an upper Northwest site at Wisconsin Avenue and Calvert Street," the newspaper reported. The story was little more than three hundred words long.

But for a small group of FBI counterintelligence officials, it was big news indeed. Soon, the dump trucks, bulldozers, cement mixers, and heavy equipment of the George Hyman Construction Company would be in noisy full swing, roaring and rumbling onto Wisconsin Avenue and Tunlaw Road, behind the embassy, where a 165-unit apartment building was also being built to house the Soviet diplomats and their families. All the noise of construction and the comings and goings of the trucks would provide perfect cover for what the FBI had in mind.

With the work under way above ground, the bureau began construction of its own secret project underneath the embassy, an elaborate tunnel for electronic eavesdropping. The FBI bought a town house nearby with a basement that would become the entrance to the tunnel. It hired its own contractor and started the digging, which went on for years at a cost said to have reached hundreds of millions of dollars. The FBI gave the highly classified, ultrasecret project a code name: MONOPOLY.

To an extent, the tunnel project was the FBI's answer to what the intelligence agencies considered a huge mistake by the State Department. The new embassy was going up on Mount Alto, the second highest point in Washington. From there, the technical experts warned, the Russians would have a direct line of sight and a superb vantage point for listening in on the White House, the State Department, the Pentagon, and the CIA. The location was ideal for eavesdropping on radio communications, and for capturing telephone calls carried by microwave, the technology then widely used, since those conversations could not be intercepted without a direct line of sight.

"We were absolutely beside ourselves," said Dick Alu, a former FBI counterintelligence agent. "They [the State Department] never bothered to consult the intelligence community, the FBI or NSA."

The Soviets had been pressing for years for a bigger embassy that would also allow them to consolidate in one place half a dozen offices scattered around town. The State Department approved the Wisconsin Avenue site, in a northwest residential neighborhood on a hill high above Georgetown.

The Soviet embassy at the time was on Sixteenth Street in downtown Washington, in an ornate beaux-arts mansion built by the widow of George M. Pullman, the inventor who designed the railroad sleeping cars that bear his name. All sorts of powerful antennae sprouted from the roof of the embassy. Even before the decision was made to allow the new embassy to go up on Mount Alto, the FBI was concerned about the Soviets eavesdropping from the Sixteenth Street location on nearby U.S. government offices, including the White House.

The two construction projects—the embassy and the tunnel—proceeded apace, one visible, the other secret. When the $70 million Soviet embassy complex was completed a decade later, it included not only the eight-story chancery building faced in white marble and the nine-story apartment building, but an eight-classroom school, a playground, a gymnasium, an Olympic-sized swimming pool, a four-hundred-seat auditorium, an underground parking garage, and a large reception hall.

Meanwhile, work by a Soviet contractor on a new American embassy in Moscow had begun in 1979. That the Russians would try to plant microphones during the construction should not have come as an enormous surprise, given the long history of Soviet efforts to bug the American embassy. In Moscow in 1945, for example, the Soviets had presented to Ambassador Averell Harriman a carved replica of the Great Seal of the

United States. The hollow wooden seal had decorated the wall of four U.S. ambassadors before the listening device it concealed was discovered by the embassy's electronic sweepers in the early 1950s.*

It was no ordinary bug. Peter Karlow, a CIA officer in charge of the agency's technical staff, recalled the problems the experts faced. "We found it and we didn't know how it worked," Karlow said. "There was a passive device inside the seal, like a tadpole, with a little tail. The Soviets had a microwave signal beamed at the embassy that caused the receptors inside the seal to resonate. It had no current, no batteries, and an infinite life expectancy." The CIA's unsuccessful attempt to copy the bug was code-named EASY CHAIR.†

Construction of the new American embassy in Moscow was halted in 1985, when it was discovered that the building was riddled with literally thousands of tiny bugs; the structure had, in effect, been turned into a giant radio transmitter by the KGB. The Russians had delivered huge slabs of precast concrete with the bugs already embedded within. By the time the bugs were found, $22 million had already been spent on construction.

It was worse than that. A former FBI official remembered his dismay at what he saw when he inspected the New Office Building, or NOB, as the bugged embassy was called. Not only were there bugs, but the construction was such that KGB agents could secretly gain access to the building as well as run wires and microphones into it.

"I found it had large hollow structural support columns at each corner," he said. "The columns had a strong exterior, but inside they were filled with dirt and broken bricks. The concern was the KGB could go in underground, take out all the bricks, drain all the fill, and climb up into the building.

"Then they would have to get out of the columns. Perhaps there was some kind of a panel or door to allow access inside the building. All

---

*The embarrassing discovery was kept secret by the United States for almost a decade. But in May 1960, after the Soviets shot down the CIA's U-2 spy plane 1,200 miles inside their territory, Washington tried to counter international criticism by revealing the Soviet eavesdropping device. Henry Cabot Lodge, the U.S. ambassador to the United Nations, opened up and displayed the Great Seal and its tiny transmitter at the UN Security Council.

†Unknown to the CIA, British intelligence was able to replicate the Soviet bug, which MI5, the British internal security service, code-named SATYR.

they had to do was to remove the junk, go into the pillars, and go up, and have free run of the embassy."

Finding the tiny transmitters embedded in the embassy's walls had not been easy. Security experts from Washington were sent to Moscow with special X-ray equipment. They were trained rock climbers who had to hang off the side of the building as they went from floor to floor in weather that was sometimes forty degrees below zero.

The discovery of the bugs caused a great uproar in Congress. President Reagan wanted to raze the entire structure and start over with American construction workers. After years of debate, it was finally decided to demolish the top four floors, down to the floor slab of the sixth floor. Four new, bug-proof stories and a penthouse would be constructed, and any sensitive business would be conducted in the new part; any microphones below that level would not matter. The project was called Top Hat, which may have struck Hanssen as ironic, since at the outset of his career as a spy he had betrayed the agent code-named TOPHAT, helping to send him to his death.

The new floors were built by three hundred American construction workers flown in for that purpose, and special precautions were taken to make sure that this time there were no transmitters. No outsiders were allowed on the construction site, and security was tight. But while all this was going on, an incident took place that was not reassuring. In April 1997, an AWOL Russian soldier somehow managed to slip into the residence of the acting American ambassador and spend the night. He was discovered the next day, taking a shower.

Meanwhile, U.S. intelligence found that the Soviets had also built tunnels leading into and under the new American embassy in Moscow. The way this was learned was not publicized. "Satellites told us there were tunnels under the new embassy," one former intelligence official revealed. "There were air pockets; the heat varies when there are tunnels, and they were detected."

In Washington, the FBI's own tunnelers were hard at work. A major concern was disposing of the enormous amount of displaced dirt, but that was made much easier by the construction going on all around the site. The FBI's dump trucks would have blended in with the rest.

By 1980, the Russians and their families began moving into the apartments, the $12 million first phase of the project. But the Hyman company did not find the Soviets easy to deal with and chose not to bid on the rest of the work. "The Soviets would make an agreement and overnight change their mind," recalled Benny Pasquariello, who had supervised the building of the apartments as vice president of Hyman. "It was just not fun to work with them.

"They inspected everything, and there were a lot of delays because of that. The Soviets were constantly looking for bugs. Concrete was poured on site and they watched when we poured. They said to me a lot of times, 'We do not want to live in a glass house.' "

When the Hyman company pulled out, the $44.4 million second phase of the project, including construction of the embassy building, went to the Whiting-Turner Contracting Company of Baltimore.

All the while, the FBI was monitoring the construction. The bureau had people on site posing as construction workers and subcontractors. In addition, some of the real construction workers agreed to cooperate with the FBI after they were approached by the bureau with an appeal to their patriotism. These co-opted workers planted many of the bugs in the embassy itself. In an apartment house across Tunlaw Road, the FBI maintained twenty-four-hour surveillance of the construction site.

Below ground, there were problems with MONOPOLY from the start. Water leaked into the tunnel, and even with a set of blueprints of the embassy complex, the tunnel builders could not always be sure of the precise location of their targets. "The problem was, you didn't know where you were going to come up," one FBI man said. "We had the plans, but you don't know what a room is used for. It might end up being a Xerox room or a storage room. What you want is a coffee room where people talk. Or a secure room where they think no one can hear them."

Nor was the tunnel universally popular in the FBI's intelligence division. "We were concerned because a lot of our budget was going for that purpose," said one former senior FBI official. "We were pretty upset."

NSA provided and manned the sophisticated eavesdropping equipment that was brought into the tunnel as sections were completed. The tunnel, it was hoped, would offer technical advantages. Presumably, the NSA was able to tap into telephone cables from the tunnel. It is said to have experimented with exotic laser beam technology as well.

But some of the sophisticated equipment did not work, and the technicians spent a lot of time trying to figure out why. Soviet countermeasures were a likely explanation, since the Russians assumed all along that U.S. intelligence would attempt to bug their embassy.

At least the tunnel was spacious enough; those who have been inside say a person could easily stand up. It had sturdy walls and lights. It was not, in other words, some dark and dank passageway like a tourist might expect to crawl through in an underground cave.

Although the obvious purpose of the tunnel was to glean what is called positive intelligence by listening in to what the Soviets were saying, there was another, subtler goal. With luck, the NSA and FBI wiretappers might have been able to discover what the Soviets were overhearing in their own electronic eavesdropping efforts against American targets.

The Soviets, of course, did everything they could to foil the planting of any bugs. John Carl Warnecke, Sr., the architect who helped to design the Wisconsin Avenue embassy, said that the Russians had X-rayed "each inch of steel the night before it was put up." They also took all the window frames apart, inspected them, and reassembled them on site. The Russians insisted that the building's marble facing be cut two inches thick because they did not want a layer of epoxy glue, in which a bug could be hidden, between two thin marble slabs.

As the embassy buildings went up, the intelligence services on both sides kept a close eye on each other, Warnecke recounted. "Before lunch the KGB would come into our office in Washington, and I said to my staff, 'Tell them everything we're doing.' After lunch the FBI or the CIA would come in and say, 'What did they ask?' "

Warnecke, eighty-two and still practicing his profession in San Francisco, was amused after the Hanssen case broke to read about the FBI's tunnel, because, he said, the Russians have their own network of tunnels beneath the embassy complex. "We designed and connected tunnels to all the buildings for utilities and other things," he said. "We designed the underground passages at the request of the Soviets. I designed the Hart Senate Office Building, so I'm familiar with tunnels."

The FBI tunnel was dug so secretly that even the architect of the Soviet embassy and the builders were perplexed about how it could have been managed. Warnecke said he had not known about the FBI's tunnel. "I wonder how the hell they did it. To get all that dirt out, somebody would have spotted it."

But H. Russell Hanna, Jr., who worked on the planning and landscaping stage of the embassy project, speculated how it might have been managed. "There was a two- or three-story underground parking garage that had to be excavated," he said. "After the workers left the site at 4 P.M., someone else could have come in and started digging. The dirt could have been put on the stockpile and taken off the next day by the construction company, unbeknownst to them. The stockpile is not measured. The trucks are counted, but not the dirt. And underground tunneling doesn't have to be noisy, so it could have been done that way."

Benny Pasquariello, the Hyman official, firmly believed the FBI could not have dug it "without our knowledge." Asked if dirt from the tunnel could have been mingled with other dirt and trucked out without his company being aware of it, Pasquariello replied: "That's a possibility." But he remained skeptical.

Homer Willis, the supervisor on the site for Hyman, insisted the tunnel must have been dug at a later date. "I walked the job every day; somebody digging a tunnel under what we were building in my opinion didn't happen. Could I be wrong? Sure, but I don't think so."

According to Willis, the Russians tried to gather intelligence on the construction site. "They would come in around 3 P.M. every day. They would have three kinds of vodka and sit around and try to pump us for information."

Because the Soviets had built tunnels under the American embassy in Moscow, they tried to guard against that happening to them in Washington. During the construction of the embassy and related buildings by Whiting-Turner, the Soviets drilled holes thirty or forty feet deep and lowered sensors into the holes attached to a monitoring device. By that time either the FBI tunnel was already largely completed or the sensors failed to detect the burrowing underground.

Having built the American embassy in Moscow with corner pillars that would have allowed the KGB to insert agents and wires straight up into the building, the Soviets were not about to permit the same design on Mount Alto. One senior intelligence official described how the Russians avoided this trap. "When they built the concrete columns they were staggered"—he held up his hands to illustrate—"so you couldn't drill up vertically. You couldn't go straight up the columns because you would hit the floor above. I assumed they built it that way because they did it to us in Moscow."

In 1987, Soviet diplomats took reporters and photographers on a press tour of the Wisconsin Avenue complex, pointing to various places where they claimed transmitters had been discovered. One of the diplomats, Vacheslav Z. Borovikov, the embassy security chief, brandished a two-foot piece of pipe that he said had concealed a transmitter inside a marble column.

By that time work on the new Soviet embassy had been completed, but under an agreement between the two countries, the ambassador and his staff could not occupy the chancery building in Washington until the dispute over the bugging of the new American embassy in Moscow was resolved. As a result, the Russians did not move into their new embassy until 1994, three years after the collapse of the Soviet Union. By that time, there was no longer a Soviet embassy; it had become the embassy of Russia.

Of course, back in the early 1980s, after the Soviets and their families had moved into the apartments, the FBI tunnel may have produced some information from electronic eavesdropping on the apartments. But one veteran FBI counterintelligence official doubted that conversations overheard in the apartments were of much value. "The residential, that would be mostly for assessment: does he drink, does he get along with his wife, is he unhappy? In other words, for assessing recruitment possibilities. And accountability—where they are, maybe someone saying 'I have to leave early in the morning,' or 'I gotta go.' I can't imagine that it was ever very productive."

In 1989, Hanssen betrayed MONOPOLY. The FBI's tunnel was compromised from that time forward. Since the Russians did not occupy the embassy until 1994, they had five years to put countermeasures in place, and to build a secure room, like "the bubble" in the U.S. embassy in Moscow, for sensitive conversations.

Although the Russians might have been tempted to use their knowledge of the tunnel to disseminate disinformation—deliberately misleading their listeners with false data—most U.S. intelligence officials discount that possibility as too complicated a game. Unless it was done flawlessly, phony conversations might tip off U.S. intelligence to the fact that the Soviets knew about the tunnel, which in turn could point to the fact that somebody might have told them about it.

"There was no disinformation," said John F. Lewis, Jr., former assistant director of the FBI in charge of the intelligence division. Asked whether the tunnel had ever produced useful information, he replied:

"There was no information of any kind. I don't remember receiving *any* intelligence." Lewis's frank view was echoed by other former FBI officials.*

Perhaps it was fitting that a spy tunnel was betrayed by a mole, a creature that burrows underground. But the tunnel under the Soviet embassy was not the first to be compromised in exactly that manner.

Until it was revealed that Hanssen had told the KGB about the tunnel in Washington, the most famous spy tunnel was the one built by the CIA in Berlin at the height of the Cold War. What happened then was startlingly similar to what happened to the tunnel in Washington. In 1954, Allen W. Dulles, the legendary CIA director, approved the Berlin project, a joint effort with Britain's MI6, and gave it the code name OPERATION GOLD. Starting in an Army warehouse in West Berlin, the tunnel extended three hundred yards into Communist East Berlin. For a year, the technicians in the tunnel were able to tap into the cables that carried Soviet military and diplomatic communications.

Unfortunately for the CIA and MI6, one of those who helped plan OPERATION GOLD for the British was George Blake, an MI6 agent secretly spying for the Soviets. He had apparently switched sides for ideological reasons while he was in a North Korean prison camp, before he had joined British intelligence. Blake told the KGB everything about the tunnel; it was compromised from the start, and as a result produced very little of value. The Soviets ended the charade in April 1956 when they broke into the tunnel and trumpeted the news to the world.

Blake, in turn, was betrayed by a Polish defector. He was arrested in 1961 and sentenced to forty-two years in prison for giving away the identities of dozens, perhaps hundreds, of agents.†

---

*Some FBI agents who had been directly involved in the project defended it and insisted the tunnel had produced worthwhile data. The fact remained that the tunnel was compromised by Hanssen before the Soviets ever moved into the embassy, a reality that, in retrospect, made the project of dubious value. According to a senior former FBI official, "The tunnel was never completed." Some of the NSA's eavesdropping equipment failed to work as it was supposed to, he said, and may not even have been installed in the tunnel.

†In 1966, Blake escaped from Wormwood Scrubs prison to Moscow, where he took a Russian wife, Ida; fathered a son, Mischa; and was given a dacha by the KGB. In 1989, Blake asserted what Western intelligence had long suspected—that he had betrayed OPERATION GOLD.

*   *   *

The FBI, unaware that its own tunnel had been compromised, gave very hush-hush VIP tours of the installation to show it off to a select group of senior government leaders, including high-ranking officials of the CIA, a few members of the Senate and House intelligence committees, and visitors from MI6, the British secret intelligence service, and MI5, the British internal security service.

The tunnel proved to be a work in progress. Some digging went on for years because the passageway was expanded from its original length. There were, of course, suspicions within the FBI that the tunnel might have been compromised, if only because it was producing so little of value. But in the absence of hard evidence, the tunnel and its staff of technicians kept going. The project, like so many government programs, had taken on a life of its own.

A former senior CIA official, who had been given a tour of the tunnel, thought it had been abandoned a few years after the fall of the Soviet Union, "because the Cold War was over, and why risk damaging relations with President Yeltsin, and our new friends the Russians?"

Even before the Soviet Union collapsed, an extraordinary event took place in Moscow in the battle of the bugs. The setting was the office of Vadim V. Bakatin, a reformer who briefly headed the KGB late in 1991 after the failed coup against Soviet leader Mikhail Gorbachev. Robert S. Strauss, the U.S. ambassador, called on the KGB chief. Bakatin, in an unprecedented act, and to promote a friendlier atmosphere between the two countries, went over to his office safe and pulled out and handed to Strauss the blueprints of the new American embassy, showing the precise location of the KGB's bugs. He also gave Strauss a suitcase full of transmitters, saying, "These are the instruments that were used."

Despite the collapse of the Soviet Union a few months later, and with it the end of the Cold War, the tunnel under the embassy in Washington, now the embassy of Russia, remained in the FBI budget as late as the mid-1990s, even though it was producing virtually nothing useful. Still, there was the upkeep on the town house, and funds had to be allocated to pay the rather large electric bills and maintain the equipment.

When the tunnel surfaced, so to speak, in the days after Hanssen's arrest in 2001, the Russians issued the usual diplomatic protest, summoning an American diplomat to the foreign ministry in Moscow. In a statement, the ministry declared: "If these reports prove true, this will be a flagrant case of the violation of generally recognized standards of international law concerning foreign diplomatic missions."

Russia's ambassador to Washington, Yuri V. Ushakov, seemed a good deal more laid-back. "If we find it," he told a reporter, "perhaps we can use it as a sauna."

What does one do with a used tunnel? In the 1990s, even the project's champions in the FBI realized that its time had passed. But when senior counterintelligence officials met to consider the fate of the tunnel, a major argument broke out.

"The question," said one former FBI counterintelligence agent, "was, Should we fill it up? There was this big fight over whether to fill it full of concrete." John Lewis, for one, argued against it. What if it turns out to be the same old Russia, Lewis asked; suppose the Cold War comes back? The tunnel, Lewis argued, might yet prove useful in the future. At the time, of course, neither Lewis nor his colleagues knew that Hanssen had already betrayed the tunnel.

In the end, a compromise was reached. The tunnel was sealed up at the town house end, but not filled. "Of course you'd want to seal it up," the former FBI man explained. "How would you like to be living in the house and suddenly the Russians walk in?"

14

"A Contagious Disease Is Suspected"

A few months before Hanssen betrayed the tunnel under the Soviet embassy, he had also disclosed to the KGB the FBI's investigation of Felix Bloch, an American diplomat who had returned to the State Department after seven years in Austria.

It was in 1981 that Bloch began his secret Saturday morning visits in Vienna to Tina Jirousek, a prostitute specializing in sadomasochistic sex. At the time, Bloch was an economic officer in the American embassy on the Boltzmanngasse, a rising star in the State Department's foreign service who was promoted to deputy chief of mission two years later.

Bloch was one of the first to telephone Jirousek after she advertised in the *Kurier,* giving her measurements and her address and phone in the Lassallestrasse, near the Prater and its famous giant Ferris wheel, depicted in the film *The Third Man.**

Bloch would come to see her on Saturday mornings for a couple of hours, she recalled. She would always be dressed in leather costume and boots, with a whip. "He came every week, or almost every week,

---

*I found Jirousek working as a waitress in a coffee shop in Vienna a decade ago when I followed Bloch's trail through Europe for an article I wrote for *The New York Times Magazine.* She was thirty-four and out of the life by then, but she agreed to talk over lunch the next day. She was an intelligent, attractive woman with feather-cut blond hair, very clear green eyes, and a pug nose. At lunch, she wore an expensive but tasteful brown silk dress. Only her three-inch gold spiked heels suggested her former profession.

for seven years. He did not want regular sex. He only wanted to be beaten and humiliated." She would beat him, she said, "sometimes with my hands and sometimes with a whip."

For these services, Bloch paid her about $200 a week, or $10,000 a year, she said, which would add up to some $70,000 over seven years. She knew he was an American diplomat and had the impression that he was frustrated in his career and felt he deserved to be the ambassador. "He's complicated and it is hard to get to know him, he has a contact problem with people. It was very difficult to begin a conversation with him."

Bloch's preference for kinky sex would be of no relevance but for the fact that the FBI suspected he might be selling secrets to the KGB to pay for his weekly visits to Tina Jirousek, and perhaps others before her, when he was stationed in East Germany in the 1970s. The FBI brought Jirousek to Washington and put her up at a Ramada Inn in northern Virginia while she testified twice to a federal grand jury investigating Bloch.

Although Bloch could not easily have afforded to pay for his Saturday morning visits on his foreign service salary, he came from a moneyed background, so the investigators' theory that he might have sold secrets for sex was plausible but not necessarily persuasive.

Felix Stephen Bloch was born in Vienna in 1935. His parents were Jewish and got out with Felix and his twin sister in 1939, a year after the Nazis marched into Austria. The family settled in Manhattan, where his father prospered in the paper export business. Bloch and his sister were raised as Presbyterians.

He joined the State Department in 1958 as an intelligence specialist. A year later he married Lucille Stephenson, whom he had met in Italy when they were both graduate students in Bologna. Diplomatic postings followed in Düsseldorf, Caracas, West and East Berlin, and Singapore.

Bloch was sent to West Berlin in 1970. In the fall of 1974, the United States established diplomatic relations with East Germany and Bloch was assigned to East Berlin. The Blochs, by now with two daughters, moved to Pankow, a suburb of East Berlin. Bloch traveled to Leipzig several times. It was a period that the FBI scrutinized with special care as it delved into Bloch's past.

Unlike many foreign service officers who try to keep the CIA at arm's length, Bloch cooperated with the intelligence agency during his tour in Singapore. "Bloch was always courteous and helpful," recalled David T. Samson, who served in the Singapore station in the mid-1970s, when Bloch was in the embassy. "I even got him involved in an operation. The East German news agency had a correspondent there who obviously worked closely with the KGB. I introduced Bloch to him in September 1975 so that Bloch could develop this guy. Bloch was willing to do that for us."

In 1980, Bloch was sent to his native Vienna, where he was in his element. A tall, bald, compact man with an almost military bearing, Bloch seemed the perfect diplomat in Vienna, fluent in German and close to a number of Austrian officials, although he chafed under two successive ambassadors who were political appointees. He and his wife had a spacious house in Oberdöbling, one of Vienna's best neighborhoods. An opera and art lover, he collected the paintings of Gustav Klimt.

When Vice President George Bush visited Vienna in 1983, Bloch was the official in charge of the visit. He met Bush at the airport, and the photo album the Blochs carefully kept contained several pictures of a smiling Vice President Bush and Felix Bloch.

But while Bloch lived stylishly as second in command of the American embassy, as he glided through the endless round of diplomatic cocktail parties and receptions, there was another man present in Vienna, dispatched there as an illegal by the KGB, who moved in an entirely different world. He called himself Reino Gikman, although that was surely not his true name. Following standard KGB procedure for illegals, he had acquired the birth certificate in Finland of the real Reino Gikman, who was probably long dead, and stepped into his skin.

After spending time in Germany to build his cover, he came to Vienna in 1979, lived obscurely in a hotel for five years, and then moved into a modest gingerbread cottage in Hietzing with a widow named Helga Höbart. Supposedly a computer salesman for IBM, which he was not, "Gikman" was a regular at Kern's, a *Gasthaus* in the Wallnerstrasse, heavy on pork schnitzels and beef, where many people who worked in the nearby government offices ate lunch.

The FBI suspected that Gikman was Bloch's KGB control in Vienna, but neither the FBI nor the Austrian federal police were able to establish that the two had ever met there. Bloch told me that he had never known Gikman in Vienna but had met him in three other European cities, where he knew him as "Pierre Bart."*

Around 1986, Gikman was said to have been spotted by Austrian military counterintelligence entering the back door of the Soviet embassy in Vienna. This information made its way to the CIA, which opened a file on Reino Gikman and began tracking his activities.

In July 1987, Felix Bloch returned to the United States and a job at the State Department. Two years later, on April 27, 1989, U.S. intelligence overheard a telephone call between Reino Gikman and Bloch. The FBI opened a file on Bloch the next day. Because Bloch was now back on U.S. soil, the case was handed off by the CIA to the bureau.

The next month, Bloch flew to Paris and checked into the Hôtel Pullman St.-Honoré, a small, elegant right-bank hotel. Early on the evening of May 14, he strolled down the rue du Faubourg-St.-Honoré, a street lined with some of the world's most expensive shops, carrying a black airline-type bag with a shoulder strap. He stopped to look in the shop windows, perhaps studying the reflections in the glass to see if he was being followed.

And he was. At the request of the FBI, agents of the Direction de la Surveillance du Territoire (DST), the French counterintelligence service, were on him. At the Hôtel Meurice, across from the Jardins des Tuileries, he walked through the ornate, chandeliered lobby to a small bar in the rear. Gikman, the man he said he knew as "Pierre Bart," was waiting for him there.

The KGB illegal was a big, heavyset man, close to six feet, with dark hair, a beard, and a mustache. Gikman/Bart and Bloch had whiskies, then moved downstairs to the hotel's opulent Restaurant le Meurice, a place of dark-paneled wood, red walls, and hovering waiters. The French counterintelligence agents were close by. The DST secretly photographed the pair, both in the bar and in the restaurant.

Bloch placed his bag under the table. The two men chatted over wine and dinner. It was an expensive meal, but Gikman picked up the check. Bloch was first to leave the restaurant. When Gikman/Bart left,

---

*I interviewed Bloch for fourteen hours for the magazine article and was the only writer to speak with him about his life and alleged spying and his relationship with Reino Gikman. Contacted for this book, he declined to comment on the government's disclosure that the FBI investigation of him had been revealed to the KGB by Robert Hanssen.

he was carrying the bag. Soon afterward, the DST videotaped him entering his budget-priced hotel, the Saphir, near the Gare de Lyon.

Eight months later, I sat in Bloch's apartment in the Kalorama section of Washington. His little white dog, Mephisto, kept trying to jump into my lap. By that time, Bloch had been questioned intensively by the FBI. He had denied passing any documents to the Soviets or receiving any money. He had also checked Mephisto's collar, looking for FBI bugs, but did not detect any.

I asked him about the man he had dined with in Paris. "He was someone I knew as a stamp collector," he said. "I knew him as Pierre Bart. I don't know the name Gikman." And what was in the bag that he had left under the table in Paris? "Stamps were in the bag. Albums and pages of stamps."

That, at least, is also what Bloch told the FBI. Bloch, to be sure, had an extensive stamp collection in red leather albums, which he pulled from a bookcase and spent some time enthusiastically showing to me. He had, he said, been collecting stamps since childhood.

On May 22, 1989, eight days after Bloch met Gikman/Bart in Paris, Robert Hanssen told the KGB that the FBI was investigating Bloch and Reino Gikman.

Something very interesting happened after that. Although Moscow now knew that the FBI was on the case, and despite the risks, it permitted Gikman to meet again with Bloch in Brussels six days later, on May 28. Bloch was then in Belgium on official State Department business.

A few days later, early in June, Reino Gikman disappeared from Vienna. Helga Höbart was devastated. The friendly Finn had suddenly vanished from their house and from the *Hofräte-Stammtisch,* the bureaucrats' table, at Kern's. Gikman, pulled out of Vienna by the KGB, had gone to ground in Moscow.

Then, just after 6 A.M. on June 22, Bloch received a telephone call at his apartment in Washington from a man who identified himself as "Ferdinand Paul." But the person who called him, Bloch told me, was Pierre Bart. The FBI was listening.

The man told Bloch that he was calling "in behalf of Pierre" who "cannot see you in the near future" because "he is sick." The caller added, pointedly: "A contagious disease is suspected." The man then told Bloch: "I am worried about you. You have to take care of yourself."

Bloch said he hoped the disease was not serious. He wished the caller well and hung up.

To the listening FBI agents, the telephone call was clearly a warning to Bloch that his contacts with the KGB had been discovered. Worse yet, it meant that someone inside U.S. intelligence might have tipped off the Russians. When Bloch arrived at the State Department that day, he was summoned to the office of Ambassador Robert E. Lamb, the assistant secretary for diplomatic security.

Three FBI agents were waiting for Bloch. They questioned him for two and a half hours, confronting him with the surveillance photographs of both Bloch and Gikman taken in the restaurant in Paris.

The questioning went nowhere. Bloch denied to the agents that he had sold secrets to the Soviets or had ever met Gikman in Vienna. According to Bloch, "After a while they said, 'This is a lot of bullshit. Tell us the truth.' 'You can accept it or not,' I said." Bloch surrendered his black diplomatic passport and his blue regular passport. His building pass was revoked and he was placed on administrative leave.

The agents followed Bloch home. The next day he was questioned again for several hours. He turned over the key to his apartment to the FBI, which removed a briefcase, address books, photo albums, slides, checkbooks, files, and bank and investment records. For the next six months, he was never to be without close surveillance by FBI agents, working in three shifts round the clock.

None of this was yet known to the public. But James Bamford, working on the ABC News investigative team in Washington, learned of the FBI probe.*

On July 21, John F. McWethy, the State Department correspondent for ABC News, broke the sensational story that Bloch, a State Department official, was under investigation by the FBI as a suspected Soviet spy. Within minutes, the State Department confirmed the ABC account, naming Bloch as the subject of an FBI inquiry into "illegal activities" involving "a foreign intelligence service." A security breach "has occurred," the department added. The statement was highly unusual, since Bloch had not been charged with a crime.

For weeks thereafter, Bloch became the center of a media circus. On television night after night he appeared on the evening news, sometimes walking Mephisto, trailed by reporters, cameramen, and FBI agents. As he passed by, children greeted him as "Mr. Spy."

---

*Bamford said in an interview for this book that Hanssen was not the source. Although he later came to know Hanssen well, he said he had not met him until 1993 or 1994.

Bloch was in excellent physical shape; he had always walked for exercise and he led the reporters and the counterspies on some memorable treks in the heat, including a twenty-two-mile hike in early August that left one female FBI agent with bleeding feet.

When Bloch drove from his apartment, the press cars following the FBI cars following Bloch's car were reportedly being followed by Soviet cars. The FBI quietly put a stop to that; the Russians dropped out of the caravan.

The bureau, hoping to overhear something useful, had bugged Bloch's silver-gray Mercedes when he took it to the dealer for servicing in suburban Maryland. But Bloch had assumed his phones were tapped, his car and apartment bugged. His conversations with his wife in the Mercedes were unexceptional.

The FBI was utterly frustrated. Clearly, someone had tipped off the KGB, and that in turn had led to the cryptic warning telephone call to Bloch. But lacking evidence, and with Bloch sticking to his story about simply giving stamps to Pierre Bart, the FBI was stymied. There was no basis to make an arrest.

Early in December, Bloch was in New York shopping at Macy's with his usual FBI entourage. He went uptown to have lunch at the Waldorf Grill, then to his parents' apartment. His mother, who was watching his back, was the first to notice. She looked out at the street. "There's no one there," she told him. It was true; that afternoon the FBI surveillance suddenly ended. There no longer seemed any point.

Hanssen, from his vantage inside the Soviet analytical unit, had continued to funnel information about the Bloch case to the KGB. In August, he had provided a floppy disk with additional details about the FBI investigation.

More than a decade later, in November 2000, he revisited the Bloch case in a long letter to the KGB. In the letter, he attacked a fellow FBI counterintelligence agent and cited Bloch as an example of why he had refused to meet the KGB overseas. That might reveal his identity, he wrote, but his anonymity was "my best protection against betrayal by someone like me working from whatever motivation, a Bloch or a Philby."*

---

*Harold A. R. "Kim" Philby was the high-ranking British MI6 officer who for years secretly spied for the Russians and even rose to become head of the Soviet counterintelligence section of British intelligence. He eventually escaped to Moscow and died there in 1988.

Hanssen knew that in May 1989 Donald E. Stukey, a veteran FBI counterintelligence agent, had been sent to Paris to work with the DST in covering the meeting of Bloch and the KGB illegal at the Hôtel Meurice. Stukey was an experienced and well-respected FBI agent. As a former chief of the Soviet section for seven years, he had outranked Hanssen and found him annoying. Now Hanssen, without mentioning Stukey by name, unleashed a vituperative attack on him in his message to Moscow. Although the letter covered a number of matters, it read in part:

> Bloch was such a shnook. . . . I almost hated protecting him, but then he was your friend, and there was your illegal I wanted to protect. If our guy sent to Paris had balls or brains both would have been dead meat. Fortunately for you he had neither. He was your good luck of the draw. He was the kind who progressed by always checking with those above and tying them to his mistakes. The French said, "Should we take them down?" He went all wet. He'd never made a decision before, why start then. It was that close. His kindred spirits promoted him. Things are the same the world over, eh?

After Hanssen's arrest in 2001, the letter was among the material made public by the FBI. Stukey, who retired from the bureau in 1996, was not amused at Hanssen's abusive description of him as someone unable to make decisions. "I've never been accused up to now of being unable to make decisions," he said.

Bloch was not arrested in Paris for good reason, Stukey added. "It was early in the investigation, so we weren't ready to move in. And we didn't want them [the French] to. The French did not have a case against Bloch, he had not broken their laws, so they had no cause to arrest him in any event.

"We were case-building then. At that time, we didn't even know if a crime was being committed. To say we were going to make an arrest was patently absurd. Either he [Hanssen] was trying to impress his Soviet handlers or he did not understand the situation. We were working closely with the Department of Justice and trying to wrap this up in the U.S. We thought it was U.S. classified information he was passing. We don't make arrests without the authority of the Justice Department. We did not have authority from the internal security section of the Justice Department to make an arrest."

The FBI was determined to find the source of the tip-off to the KGB, the person who had told the Russians about the Bloch investigation so they in turn could warn him. The failure to make a case against Felix Bloch was a constant, nagging reminder to the FBI of an enormous unsolved problem. It stuck in the bureau's craw and would not go away.

Beyond any other episode, the Bloch case made it apparent that someone on the inside, with access to highly sensitive files, had alerted the KGB. That source had to be found. For more than a decade the FBI and the CIA worked to uncover the penetration. They had Robert Hanssen's mole study, of course, to provide the necessary historical background.

There were several false starts, and the bureau went down the wrong trail for three years, mistakenly suspecting an innocent CIA officer. But, as events would make clear, the compromise of the Bloch case eventually led to the arrest of Robert Hanssen. It was the unexplained tip-off to the KGB and the subsequent warning telephone call to Bloch that drove the mole hunt for a decade to its ultimate, dramatic conclusion.

Felix Bloch was dismissed by the State Department and deprived of his pension of more than $50,000 a year. He was never arrested for espionage, never indicted or charged. He moved to Chapel Hill, North Carolina, where he worked for a while bagging groceries. He was arrested twice for shoplifting food, the first time at the grocery where he worked. Bloch had wheeled a cart filled with chicken noodle soup, coffee, frozen catfish, and other items out to his Mercedes without bothering to pay.

There are a number of retired foreign service officers living in the area, and because Bloch had never been charged with espionage, he was asked to one of their Foreign Service Day reunions and came. But after his first shoplifting arrest he was not invited back. His wife filed for divorce.

He spent one night in jail after his first arrest, but in both cases was sentenced to perform community service. He volunteered at the local Red Cross chapter, where he put in long hours and impressed the director. By 2001, when Robert Hanssen was apprehended, Bloch was working as a city bus driver, wearing a blue uniform.

Transit officials in Chapel Hill said he was a good bus driver.

15

"Oh My God, Look What He Leaves Lying Around!"

It was Jeanne Beglis, Bonnie Hanssen's sister, who noticed the money, thousands of dollars in bills, just sitting there on Bob Hanssen's dresser. Beglis immediately pointed out the huge wad of cash to her sister.

"Oh my God, look what he leaves lying around!" Bonnie Hanssen exclaimed.

It was the summer of 1990, and Hanssen by that year had received almost half a million dollars from the KGB, so it was perhaps not surprising that he was getting a little casual about where he left his money. He was normally more careful, hiding much of the cash in a box under his bed.

Despite the startling amount of cash on the dresser in her bedroom, Bonnie Hanssen maintained later that she had suspected nothing. Perhaps another woman would have had questions, family members conceded. But not sweet, naïve, religious Bonnie, they said, whose main focus, as her family and friends saw her, was to be a good mother and an old-fashioned housewife. Her husband handled the family's money, paid the bills, wrote the checks, prepared the taxes. "She batted out six kids and had at least three miscarriages," said one family friend. "Taking care of the children and her husband was Bonnie's life."

She knew, it was true, that a decade earlier her husband had taken money from the Soviets, but she had insisted he see Father Bucciarelli, and after that he had promised to stop. She loved her husband, and surely this good man, who went to mass almost every day, would not deceive her.

Still, the incident bothered Jeanne Beglis. She never suspected Bob Hanssen was a spy, but she did tell her husband about all the cash she had seen on the dresser. Jeanne, a child psychologist, and her husband, George, an architect and building contractor, lived across the street from the Hanssens on Talisman Drive.

When the Hanssens returned from New York in 1987, Jeanne noticed that a house on the block was up for sale and told Bonnie about it, which is how the Hanssens came to live on the same street. It was nice for the two couples to be so near each other; most of the rest of the Wauck family was in Chicago or scattered elsewhere, and the two sisters and their children were often back and forth in each other's houses.

Jeanne Beglis regarded her brother-in-law as an enigma. As close as the families were, she never felt she really knew him. Yet Jeanne was fond of Bob. She thought Hanssen a sweet man, goofy but harmless, a big, tall, lumbering, socially awkward guy.

When the Hanssens had lived in New York, before they moved to Talisman Drive, he would call up sometimes and say he would be in Washington and ask to stay with them. He would sit in their living room on those trips, with a big grin, and have absolutely nothing to say. Jeanne would comment privately to George, "For God's sake, the man cannot make conversation. He doesn't know how."

Bonnie Hanssen was not that way. She was known among her siblings as plainspoken. Bonnie would tell you exactly what she thought. Bonnie was volatile and impulsive, and she had quite a temper when angry; get her going and she could fly off the handle. Bob was very different. To Jeanne Beglis, her brother-in-law seemed a dreamer, with an odd fantasy life that could sometimes be glimpsed in sudden, disconnected comments he would make. Not that he ever talked much, but when he did he was always saying bizarre things. After the 2000 presidential election, for example—a few months before he was arrested—he remarked, with a wild-eyed look and a cackle, "Let's take everybody out who voted for Gore and shoot them."

It was only a joke, of course, but family members recall that during the Cold War years Hanssen would come up with a lot of crazy schemes to go after the Soviets. Some involved computers. "He'd bore you to death with computer talk—computers were his whole world," said one.

At the Hanssen dinner table, another family member said, Bob forbade certain topics of discussion. "The family is so strict that they could not even discuss homosexuality. When the 'don't ask, don't tell' policy for gays in the military came up during the Clinton years, it was proscribed from family conversation."

But all that money Bob seemed to have to spend was a frequent topic of discussion among his in-laws for years. The Hanssens had put in all new carpeting when they moved into the house, and an expensive new front door. Where was he getting the money? From the banks and the mortgage lenders, it seemed. He refinanced his house more than once, and frequently restructured his debts and took out loans. "There were always explanations," a family member said.

Bonnie told Jeanne that after Hanssen's car accident, he had received $40,000 for his broken wrist from the insurance company. And although he may have told his wife that, it was not true. The actual amount he received was much smaller.

Not long after the Hanssens moved into their split-level house on Talisman Drive in 1987, they decided to remodel. The major addition on the back of the house was designed by George Beglis, who also supervised the construction. The work expanded the house greatly, adding a large deck in the rear, and below it an extra family room, big enough for a Ping-Pong table for the kids. All told, the remodeling cost about $70,000, but in this instance, despite the cost, it did not create gossip among the relatives because the Hanssens, when they moved back from New York, had sold their house in Yorktown Heights at a substantial profit. And Hanssen told his family that most of the cost of the remodeling had come from the fictional $40,000 insurance settlement.

It was in 1990, not long after Jeanne Beglis had spotted the cash on Hanssen's dresser, that she remembered telling her brother Mark Wauck about it. But Wauck, like Hanssen an FBI counterintelligence agent, later told investigators that he had heard a different version of the incident.

Mark Wauck, with a law degree from Loyola University of Chicago, had joined the FBI in 1978, two years after his brother-in-law. He was assigned to the intelligence division and sent to New York City, a prime counterintelligence playing field, in the early 1980s. He was there for three years, but these years did not overlap with Hanssen's two tours in New York. In 1986, he was transferred to the Chicago field office, where he was still assigned when Hanssen was arrested fifteen years later.

Within the family, there were sharply conflicting versions of the story about the money. In August 1990, Mark, his wife, and their children visited Washington from Chicago. Mark was on business, attending a two-week conference on Soviet and Eastern European affairs at the State Department. The Beglises had invited Mark and his wife, Mary Ellen, to dinner during their visit. Mary Ellen Wauck recalled Jeanne Beglis telling her in the kitchen before dinner that one day, not too long before, Bonnie Hanssen had come running across the street to her house, alarmed that she had found $5,000 in cash on Bob's dresser.

But Jeanne Beglis remembered only seeing money on the dresser, and Bonnie's exclamation about it. Bonnie had been looking for something she wanted to give her, perhaps an article of clothing, and that was how they happened to be in the bedroom. Jeanne believed it was her brother Mark whom she had told about the money. In interviews with government investigators, she said she did not recall Bonnie running across the street or being upset at the discovery. Jeanne Beglis did think the amount was $5,000; the money had a paper band around it, like banks use, and the total may have been printed on the wraparound band.

Memories and details may differ after ten years. The bottom line, however, was that both Jeanne Beglis and Mary Ellen Wauck agreed that a large amount of cold cash had been left lying on the dresser of the Hanssen bedroom.

Mary Ellen Wauck recalled telling her husband about the money after they returned to Chicago that August. It was a troubling piece of information, because Special Agent Mark Wauck knew something that other family members did not. He remembered a conversation with Bonnie in 1985, when she had told him of a remark that Hanssen had made to her: "Maybe I'll retire in Poland," he had said.

It was the same year that Hanssen had begun spying for the KGB, although no one knew that at the time. The remark about Poland, then a Soviet satellite, had a special resonance for Mark, since he was studying the language in anticipation of working Polish counterintelligence cases, which in fact he did when he returned to Chicago in 1986. The comment struck him as not something any FBI agent ought to go around saying, let alone someone working in counterintelligence. But by itself, it was not enough to act upon. Now, however, he had also been told about the large amount of cash that Hanssen had left on the dresser.

And there was something else, a third element. As an FBI counterintelligence agent, Wauck had heard that the bureau was actively looking for a mole inside U.S. intelligence.

For Special Agent Mark Wauck—a straight arrow, a man who

translated the Bible, a lawyer—the three pieces of information he now possessed posed a terrible dilemma. It was clear to him that his brother-in-law had more money than his FBI salary could possibly provide. Perhaps there was some innocent explanation. But there was another, more ominous possibility, one that Wauck hoped could not be true.

It was hard for him to believe. Wauck knew Hanssen well. For years, the two FBI agents had exchanged e-mails grousing about this or that bureau policy. But that sort of grumbling was common in any bureaucracy, and the two men, after all, were in-laws who could exchange private complaints. Now, however, if Wauck did not report what he knew to the FBI, he himself might be failing in his responsibilities to the bureau and to the country.

On the other hand, if he did report his suspicions to the bureau, he might damage the career of his sister's husband, placing him under a cloud even though he might well be innocent of any wrongdoing. And in that case, if it somehow got back to Hanssen that his brother-in-law had reported him as a possible spy, it would destroy Mark Wauck's standing within the family.

If Hanssen was in fact innocent, Wauck might even be harming his own FBI career by speaking out. He did not want to seem a nutcase, making wild allegations. He expected that the bureau would be skeptical of his information; the traditional attitude of the FBI at the time was that we don't have moles; we don't hire those kinds of people. And to think the unthinkable, if Robert Hanssen *was* a spy, he might well be dooming his brother-in-law to life in prison.*

It was not only that. His sister would be left alone, her husband probably behind bars for the rest of his life. His six nephews and nieces would, for all practical purposes, be deprived of a father. Even for someone who had not translated the Gospels, Mark Wauck faced a choice of biblical dimensions.

He agonized over it for weeks. Unlike his parents, his sister Bonnie, his brother Greg, and his brother-in-law, he was not a member of Opus Dei, but he was a good Catholic, and a man of strong conscience. In the end, he knew what he had to do.

---

*At the time there was no death penalty for espionage. The Supreme Court had outlawed capital punishment in 1972, then restored it to the states in 1976. But there was no federal death penalty for espionage from 1972 until 1994, when Congress, in the wake of the Aldrich Ames case, restored the penalty if certain criteria were met.

Sometime in September, he went to a supervisor in Chicago. There was the stack of money on the dresser, thousands of dollars; Bob Hanssen's remark about maybe retiring in Poland; and Mark Wauck's knowledge that the bureau was actively looking for a mole. Wauck later told investigators that he related all this to the supervisor and said he was concerned that his brother-in-law might be involved in espionage.

Soon, Wauck believed, there would surely be major repercussions inside the FBI. He was confident the bureau would act swiftly to determine if Bob Hanssen was a spy, a Soviet mole. Hanssen would be investigated. If it somehow became known within the family that he had turned in his own sister's husband, he might become a pariah.

Wauck waited as the weeks, then months, went by.

And nothing happened. To Special Agent Mark Wauck, it was as though he had tossed a paper airplane into the Grand Canyon and watched the wind take it in long, slow spirals until it disappeared from view. He could not even be sure that his report ever got out of Chicago.

Mark Wauck was not the only family member to harbor suspicions about Hanssen. Greg Wauck, later a postal inspector in Philadelphia, was living in Chicago at the time. As he recalled, he had heard from his sister Jeanne about the money and that Bonnie Hanssen had been upset. He was sufficiently concerned that he called his brother Mark and asked: "Do you think this guy is fooling around with the Russians?" Mark, who may already have warned the bureau by that time, changed the subject.

Several months after Hanssen's arrest, Mark and Mary Ellen Wauck were questioned by lawyers from the Department of Justice at the Marriott hotel at Chicago's O'Hare Airport. The lawyers, acting for the inspector general's office of the Justice Department, were conducting the internal probe of the FBI's handling of the Hanssen case for Attorney General John Ashcroft. Mary Ellen Wauck repeated her recollection that, as the story was related to her, Bonnie Hanssen had run across the street to tell Jeanne about the money.

Mark Wauck was interviewed for hours, both by the FBI and by the department's lawyers. According to the account that he gave, the superior to whom he had reported his suspicions was Special Agent Jim Lyle, the supervisor of the Russian counterintelligence squad in Chicago. He said he had asked Lyle to accompany him to a small interview room so that they could meet privately.

Wauck knew Lyle; they had worked on the same KGB squad in New York and had commuted into the city together. A reddish-haired Southerner, born and raised in eastern Tennessee, Lyle was a respected counterintelligence specialist who, after New York, had been a supervisor in the GRU unit at FBI headquarters and then was transferred to Chicago. Like Bob Hanssen, Lyle was a great admirer of General Patton and collected photographs and books of the World War II soldier. Wauck believed that Lyle, despite what he considered his gruff, military manner, would act on his warning.

Wauck told the Justice Department lawyers that in his meeting with Lyle he ran through the three elements that concerned him: the cash in the bedroom, his brother-in-law's comment about retiring in Poland, and the fact that there was an ongoing mole hunt.

"Do you know what you're talking about?" he said Lyle asked. Wauck claimed he replied, "Yes, I'm talking about espionage."

Wauck said Lyle questioned him closely about the money. Couldn't there be innocent, alternative sources of money that would just as easily explain it?

Wauck said he had suggested some possibilities. He knew the Hanssens had sometimes received financial help from Bob's parents; when they needed a car, Howard would buy it for them. Wauck admitted he could not prove the money had not come from Howard Hanssen, or was not cash that his brother-in-law had raised for Opus Dei or other charitable or religious purposes.

Wauck told investigators that Lyle seemed skeptical, which did not surprise him, given the enormity of what he was suggesting. After about half an hour, Wauck related, Lyle said he had done the right thing by coming forward; the matter would be handled in an appropriate fashion. Wauck did not put his suspicions in writing, nor was he asked to do so.

Jim Lyle also told his version of their conversation to the FBI, but it differed in many significant details from Wauck's story. In an interview with the author early in 2002, Lyle agreed that Wauck had spoken to him about some unexplained money that Hanssen had possessed. On virtually every other point, however, he disputed Wauck's version of their conversation.

"He was telling me something about Bonnie along the lines of, it could have related to Bonnie had a question about something Bob had done or was doing, and it may have been something about money; she may have found some money in a drawer, Bob had some money and she didn't know where it came from.

"I don't remember what I said. I know there was a question about Bonnie and money. Also that Bonnie had raised a question about somebody; Bonnie was concerned Bob had a relationship with somebody, but not with the Russians. I don't remember any remark about Russians, or speculation that it involved espionage.

"It was some questions Bonnie had about Bob and some things she didn't understand about Bob. My thought was, 'What is this to me?' " According to Lyle, the discussion seemed to him to involve marital problems between Bob and Bonnie Hanssen.

Lyle said he did not even recall the conversation until the FBI interviewed him about it after questioning Wauck. "When I learned that Bob Hanssen was a spy for the Russians I was as surprised as anyone," Lyle said. He also insisted that the conversation had taken place not in 1990 but in 1992. By that year Wauck had transferred to Lyle's squad, which is how he said he placed the date. Their talk, he added, took place not in an interview room but by Wauck's desk along the window of the squad room. "He was sitting in his chair, and I was leaning against the window." The conversation, Lyle said, had not taken half an hour. "It lasted two, three minutes at the most."

Lyle said he wondered, "Was Bonnie Hanssen making some allegation to Mark about misconduct? It was not specific, and almost as though he was just asking my opinion about it. My reaction was, 'I dunno, Mark, if she's got questions about something he was doing, why doesn't she ask him?' He didn't say this was something that had to be investigated. I never gave it another thought. I didn't document it, I didn't write it up, I didn't it report to anybody.

"He did not approach me in any formal sense to allege that he suspected or Bonnie suspected that he was spying for the Russians. In retrospect do I think he was talking about espionage? You bet. But we now know that she [Bonnie] already knew about espionage, so why would she be asking about money?"

Did he recall that Wauck said Hanssen had made a remark about retiring in Poland? "I don't remember anything about Poland. But if he said it, I would have said, 'What is he, nuts?' "

And did Wauck say he knew the FBI was looking for a mole? "If he said that to me, I would have said, 'What mole hunt?' I didn't know anything about a mole hunt."

Still, Lyle confirmed a key element of Wauck's story. "There was an issue about money. Bonnie didn't know where Bob got some money." But, he said, "I walked away thinking, What was that about?"

After Chicago, Lyle returned to Washington in 1998 and was detailed to the CIA. A year later he was named chief of the Russian espionage unit at FBI headquarters. In 2000, he went back to the CIA as chief of the Counterespionage Group, the agency's main unit in charge of catching Russian spies. As head of the CEG, he also was in charge of the Special Investigations Unit, which has the responsibility for ferreting out moles inside U.S. intelligence.*

Did Wauck's warning ever reach FBI headquarters? Lyle's statement that he never passed Wauck's concerns on to Washington was supported by his superiors at headquarters at the time. The senior FBI officials to whom such a report would have gone all agreed that it never reached headquarters. Robert B. Wade, the longtime deputy chief of the Soviet section, held that position in 1990 and 1992. "A report like that would go to the section and probably go to me," Wade said. "I was the operational guy. If it didn't go to me, I would be asked about it." And did he recall any such report about Hanssen? "No, nothing," he said.

Donald E. Stukey—the same FBI agent who had gone to Paris on the Bloch case—was head of the Soviet section in 1990, and he, too, said he had never heard that an FBI agent had reported concerns about Robert Hanssen. Raymond A. Mislock, Jr., who succeeded Stukey and served for three years, said no such information had ever reached him.

The incident of the money on the dresser was not the only time that Wauck had been surprised at Hanssen's apparent easy access to cash. Around 1993, on one of Mark Wauck's visits to Washington, Mark and Bob and the Hanssen boys had gone to Andrews Air Force Base for the air show held there every spring. The thousands of visitors watched as the Air Force's Thunderbirds gave their spectacular aerial demonstration, roaring overhead in tight formation. But it was a bright day and the boys had forgotten their sunglasses. To the amazement of Mark Wauck, Bob Hanssen went to a booth and bought everyone expensive Ray-Bans. The boys looked cool, but it was one more troubling incident;

---

*In 2002, Lyle retired from the FBI.

Mark Wauck was astonished that Hanssen could casually spend that kind of money.*

FBI officials, who preferred to rely on Lyle's version, asked why, if Wauck felt his concerns had been ignored by Lyle, did he not take it to the next level, which would have been Michael J. Waguespack, then the assistant special agent in charge (the ASAC) for counterintelligence in the Chicago office? But Wauck told investigators that he assumed his information had gone up the line. As the months turned into years and he heard nothing further from the FBI, he thought no news was good news; he was mistaken and Bob was innocent. And yet, he could hardly forget what he had done and why.

For eleven years, until Hanssen's arrest, Mark Wauck lived with his secret. When the news broke, he urged his superiors in the FBI to disclose that he had raised questions early on about his brother-in-law. He sent an e-mail to the new FBI director, Robert S. Mueller III, urging disclosure. Sooner or later it would become known, he argued to his superiors; better to put it out up front. He was overruled.

Wauck's story, despite the fact that Lyle disputed many key aspects of his account, was an embarrassment to the FBI, which knew that sooner or later it would leak out, as it did. An FBI agent had told a superior years earlier about his brother-in-law's unexplained cash, and his concerns were not followed up. The bureau's only public comment was to confirm that a conversation had taken place, that it had been evaluated but did not result in the discovery of Hanssen's espionage.

Privately, however, some bureau officials sought to discredit Wauck's account, hinting that some of what he claimed to have said to Lyle might have been an effort to portray himself in a favorable light after the fact. Perhaps, they implied, Wauck wanted plaudits as someone who had suspected Hanssen, and at the same time had also sought to protect himself and avoid any inference that he had failed to come forward with his suspicions.

"Wauck was not a guy who fit in with the squad," said one FBI agent. "He fancied himself an intellectual of sorts. He always thought

---

*Today, Ray-Ban sunglasses can cost well over one hundred dollars, for the Aviator model, for example, but even in 1990 a pair cost up to fifty-five dollars. Hanssen reportedly bought a pair for himself as well as for the three boys. Had Hanssen bought only four pairs, he could easily have spent over two hundred dollars.

he was smarter than anyone else." That view of Wauck, remarkably similar in tone to how Hanssen himself had been perceived by his fellow agents, may have contributed to the bureau's lack of interest in Wauck's concerns about his brother-in-law. Because Wauck was another outsider, his words may have been discounted.

But Wauck's story could hardly be ignored after Hanssen's arrest. It was investigated extensively. At the end of August 2001, the FBI sent two agents to the Beglis's home. They questioned Jeanne Beglis closely about the cash she had seen on the dresser and how that information had been relayed to her brother.

The FBI also questioned the Beglises about Hanssen's remark about retiring in Poland. The agents asked whether Hanssen owned real estate in Germany, Poland, or the former Soviet Union, and whether he owned jewelry or a BMW.

In November, at George Beglis's office in Vienna, Virginia, Jeanne Beglis and her husband gave a deposition to the Justice Department inquiry. One of the department's lawyers who questioned the Beglises seemed skeptical that Bonnie Hanssen had failed to connect the dots. Given Hanssen's earlier spying in 1979, he asked, if you saw all that money, wouldn't you say to your husband, "Hey, what's this?"

The differences in the recollections of Jeanne Beglis and Mary Ellen Wauck about Bonnie's reaction to seeing the money, whether or not she had been alarmed and run across the street, was not unimportant, because it went to the question of whether or not Bonnie Hanssen suspected that her husband had gone back into the spy business.

But Bonnie Hanssen, who was also questioned at length by the FBI, said she did not even remember the whole incident. And if I did find money, Bonnie told family members, he would have lied to me about it anyway.

Bonnie Hanssen told her sister Jeanne that she did not remember her husband talking about retiring in Poland. She had never suspected anything about his spying, she said. But Bonnie Hanssen never revealed to her sister that she knew Hanssen had spied for the Russians in 1979.

She would not have been upset about seeing the cash, Bonnie told her brother Greg, because by then Bob had put her on a cash budget. Perhaps he thought she had used their credit cards too often, but whatever the reason, she was to use cash, which he provided, for the family's purchases. The Hanssen home, it would appear, was not a bastion of women's lib; for all the enormous, overdue changes in American society wrought by the women's movement, it seems barely to have touched the house on Talisman Drive. Bob made the decisions about money, and Bonnie was complaisant.

Both the FBI and the Justice Department were, for good reason, attempting to find out the truth about Mark Wauck's conversation with Jim Lyle, to unravel the details of what was actually said and why it had not been acted upon. The truth was elusive, since there were no witnesses to the conversation. But Mark Wauck had tried to raise a flag about the cash in his brother-in-law's bedroom; no one disputes that much.

Perhaps, as Lyle contends, Wauck had failed to make his concerns clear enough. But if his warning about the unexplained money had been followed up, Robert Philip Hanssen, the most damaging mole in the history of the FBI, might have been caught a decade sooner.

16

"Life Is Becoming Too Fast"

As the spring of 1990 approached, Hanssen was on a roll. Early in March, he passed to Moscow secret data about four Soviets who were FBI or CIA sources—a KGB officer, a Soviet illegal, and two defectors.* That raised to ten the number of sources whom he had identified, including the three who were executed.

Before Hanssen's espionage career came to an end with his arrest, he had betrayed an astonishing fifty human sources or recruitment targets. In addition to those who were executed, a number of others were imprisoned after he provided their names to the Russians.

In the packet of secrets he passed in March he also gave the KGB the latest secret analysis of Soviet strategic nuclear capabilities, dated only a month earlier. The Russians in turn left $40,000 for Hanssen, which meant he had now received well over $400,000 from the KGB. Along with the cash, Moscow gave him a wish list of a wide variety of secret information they hoped he could steal.

In May, Hanssen turned over more than two hundred pages of documents. He also informed the KGB that he was about to be promoted and would be traveling for a year. The Russians gave him another

---

*The four were described this way in the FBI's affidavit. The term *defector* is ambiguous because it normally means an intelligence officer who escapes from his country and asks for political asylum from another government. But in this instance—since the KGB would know who had left the Soviet Union and gone over to the West—it might refer to a defector or agent in place, someone who remains on the job but provides information to U.S. intelligence.

$35,000 and asked that along with any "especially hot" material he include "guidance" on what the KGB might use and act upon without pointing back to him and endangering his security.

Certainly the KGB did not want to risk losing such a valuable source, but at the same time the request may have had the dual purpose of flattering Hanssen and making him feel in control. The operatives in the first chief directorate, the KGB's foreign intelligence arm, showed a keen insight into Hanssen's psyche; they may not have known his name, but they knew their man.

A few weeks later, with Hanssen about to be out of pocket for a year and with the prospect that their contacts might dwindle, the KGB left a long letter for him under the footbridge in Foxstone Park.

Dear Friend:

Congratulations on Your promotion. We wish You all the very best in Your life and career. . . . Your friendship and understanding are very important to us. . . . We don't see any problem for the system of our future communications in regard to this new circumstances of Yours. Though we can't but regret that our contacts may be not so regular as before, like You said.

We believe our current commo plan . . . covers ruther [*sic*] flexibly Your needs: You may have a contact with us anytime You want after staying away as long as You have to. So, do Your new job, make Your trips, take Your time. The commo plan we have will still be working. We'll keep covering the active call out signal site no matter how long it's needed. And we'll be in a ready-to-go mode to come over to the drop next in turn whenever You are ready: that is when You are back home and decide to communicate.

All You'll have to do is to put Your call out signal, just as now. And You have two addresses to use to recontact us only if the signal sites for some reason don't work or can't be used. . . . But in any case be sure: You may have a contact anytime because the active call out site is always covered according to the schedule no matter how long you've been away. . . .

Thank You and good luck.

Sincerely,
Your friends.

Hoping to enlarge its network in America, and knowing that Hanssen might find it difficult to pass many secrets while he was busy on the road, the KGB also asked him to "give us some good leads to possible recruitments" among "interesting people in the right places."

Hanssen, as he had told the Soviets, was promoted in June. He joined the FBI's inspection staff, which meant he would be traveling around the country and overseas to scrutinize the bureau's field offices. The mole would now be checking up to make sure that everything in the field was completely secure and running according to the rule book.

For Hanssen, it was a necessary career move. It is not easy to get promoted in the FBI. Those who remain street agents cannot rise above a GS-13 in pay grade. To become a GS-15, agents must normally pass three hurdles: they have to put in time at headquarters, run a squad in the field, and get certified as an inspector. Hanssen had met the first two requirements and now was about to embark on the third.

"People don't realize how difficult it is to become even a fourteen," said David Major. "The bureau has about a hundred and seventy members of the Senior Executive Service [SES], and it has three hundred fifty GS-15s. Out of almost twenty-eight thousand employees."

In the culture of the FBI, doing time as an inspector is an obligatory sentence to a kind of motel purgatory. Some lucky agents are able to combine their inspection chores with assignment to a field office.

"We called that 'rent-a-goon,' as opposed to being a full-time goon," said Dick Alu, who had worked with Hanssen in the budget unit. "It is a real pressure cooker," Alu said, recalling his own stint in the inspection division.

"You are unloved by the people you are seeing, and the chief inspector is evaluating you. Our symbol in the inspection division was a rat with a long tail and an oversized *schwanz*. Most people had nicknames. That sort of humor was our only relief. We worked from six in the morning to ten at night. My weight went up, my cholesterol went up, another year and I'd probably have been dead."

Some time in that summer of 1990, Hanssen gave his friend Jack Hoschouer an expensive Rolex watch. "I said no; he kept pressing it on me," Hoschouer said. "I tried to give him money, he wouldn't take it. He said he had bought it for himself but Bonnie thought it was clunky and ugly and insisted he take it back. So he gave it to me instead.

"I wore the watch and Bonnie said, 'Oh, you've got a watch just like the one I made Bob take back.' "

"I told him he's crazy to do this. He had said he was in debt. I gave him four hundred dollars and he gave it back to me and it went back and forth and finally I just gave up and kept the money. I said, I don't understand this, but he's my friend and he wants to do this."

Hoschouer said he puzzled over the gift but thought back on what Hanssen used to say about his father. "His father, as a policeman, knew where to get things wholesale. He always said that about his father. And since he was a cop people gave him good deals on stuff. Essentially, I thought that's what happened here."

But Hanssen had bought a second Rolex for himself. Bill Houghton, who had befriended Hanssen when they worked together in the Soviet analytical unit, remembered his fascination with Rolexes. Around 1993, Houghton said, Hanssen had mentioned the sidewalk peddlers outside FBI headquarters. "People sell fake designer watches outside the building. He said, 'Bill, you ever look at these? Look at these, they're pretty good.' He shows me a fake Rolex that he picked up for like twenty bucks. He said, 'I've been talking to this guy and one way you can tell if it's real is it breaks the second hand into five parts. If you see a Rolex that clicks second to second, it's a fake. This guy can get me one for one hundred bucks that breaks it into five parts, and looks real.'

"Later he said, 'I've got a Rolex.' I said, 'That's amazing.' I turned it over and it had all the stamps on the back. It was a real Rolex, no fake. I said, 'Bob, this is a real one.' He said, 'Yep, I thought I owed it to myself.' At the time they cost about $7,500.

"He told me he came from money, Bonnie had money, his dad left him money, and he told me he bought his house in New York for two hundred fifty thousand dollars and sold it for five hundred thousand dollars. A day or two later he had another Rolex in his hand. He said, 'Bill, I want you to have this.' It was one of the twenty-dollar fakes. 'I don't need a fake one, I've got a real one.' So I said, 'All right, I'll take it.' Then he told me he bought a ladies' Rolex for Bonnie as well."

But by the summer of 1990, Hanssen could afford to give a real Rolex to Jack; the KGB had already paid him more than $450,000. The Russians heard from Hanssen again that August when he mailed them a floppy disk that contained a variety of classified data. The following month the KGB gave Hanssen another $40,000 in cash, and in a message assured him that some of his material had gone "to the very top," presumably to the Kremlin and Soviet leader Mikhail S. Gorbachev.

That may have been so, but again, the words were also designed to flatter and stroke their man in Washington.

Hanssen did not contact the KGB again until February 1991, when he left an emergency call-out signal. In a message at CHARLIE, he revealed that the FBI's chief of counterintelligence in New York had told him that the bureau had recruited a certain number of Soviet sources, presumably at the Soviet mission to the UN. And in passing, he remarked that the $40,000 he had received was "too generous."

In the exchange the KGB left $10,000 in cash for Hanssen and a floppy disk pinpointing two new sites. One, code-named GRACE, was located under a footbridge in Washington's Rock Creek Park. The cash pushed Hanssen over the half-million-dollar mark in KGB income.

On April 15, although the KGB surely understood that Hanssen would not be paying income tax on his money from Moscow, it passed along another $10,000 and a poem that, in effect, urged him to stop and smell the roses. The message was addressed as usual to "Dear Friend." It began, "Time is flying. As a poet said:

> *"What's our life,*
> *If full of care*
> *You have no time*
> *To stop and stare?"*

The rest of the letter from the KGB was positively chatty:

You've managed to slow down the speed of Your running life to send us a message. And we appreciate it.

We hope You're O'K [*sic*] and Your family is fine too. We are sure You're doing great at Your job. As before, we'll keep staying alert to respond to any call from You whenever You need it.

We acknowledge receiving one disk through CHARLIE. One disk of mystery and intrigue. Thank you.

Not much a business letter this time. Just formalities. We consider Site-9 cancelled. And we are sure You remember: our next contact is due at ELLIS.

Frankly, we are looking forward to JUNE. Every new season brings new expectations.

Enclosed in our today's package please find $10,000. Thank You for Your friendship and help.

We attach some information requests. We hope You'll be able to assist us on them.

Take care and good luck.

Sincerely,
Your friends.

By early July 1991, Hanssen's tour in the inspection division was over. He would spend the next six months at headquarters, in the Soviet operations section, as a program manager in the unit that tried to counter Soviet efforts, in particular by the KGB's Line X, to steal U.S. scientific and technical secrets.

As soon as Hanssen was back at headquarters, he immediately left a floppy disk with almost three hundred pages of documents for the KGB. "I returned, grabbed the first thing I could lay my hands on," he explained in his letter. "I was in a hurry so that you would not worry, because June has passed, they held me there longer."

He had at least five years until he could retire, Hanssen noted, adding: "Maybe I will hang in there for that long." He also passed along a report on a joint FBI-CIA operation and classified documents dealing with human intelligence plans and nuclear proliferation. He walked away from the drop with another $12,000 in cash in his pocket and a KGB disk that praised "Your superb sense of humor and Your sharp-as-a-razor mind. We highly appreciate both."

Having shamelessly flattered Hanssen once more, his handlers adopted a smarmy, deferential tone: "If our natural wish to capitalize on Your information confronts in any way Your security interests we definitely cut down our thirst for profit and choose Your security. The same goes with any other aspect of Your case. That's why we say Your security goes first. . . . We are sure You remember our next contact is due at 'FLO.' "

In that next exchange, in August, Hanssen actually suggested that the Soviets could learn something from a thorough study of how Mayor Richard J. Daley, whose autocratic style Hanssen greatly admired, had governed Chicago. Since the Soviet Union was only four months away from collapse, perhaps he was on to something. Still, it seemed a reach to think that a system once run by Joseph Stalin could pick up any pointers from Dick Daley.

On August 19, the same day Hanssen suggested that the Kremlin study Mayor Daley's leadership style, a group of plotters in Moscow, among them Vladimir Kryuchkov, the KGB chief, staged an attempted coup against Gorbachev. Russia's president, Boris Yeltsin, astride a tank, led the countercoup that restored Gorbachev to power. Several of the Soviet republics, including Russia, declared their independence.

This time, the KGB flattered Hanssen for his political advice. They wrote: "[T]he magical history tour to Chicago was mysteriously well timed. Have You ever thought of foretelling the things? After Your retirement for instance in some sort of Your own 'Cristall [sic] Ball and Intelligence Agency' (CBIA)? There are always so many people in this world eager to get a glimpse of the future."

Hanssen came away from that exchange with another $20,000. Finally, in October, along with providing a new secret document on the double agent program, Hanssen got around to responding to the KGB's request that he suggest others who might be recruited to spy.

He gave them the name of Jack Hoschouer, his closest friend, the man who was like a brother to him. Hoschouer, Hanssen wrote, was an "old friend" and a military officer who had recently been told he would not be promoted.

Hoschouer's Army career had begun in the late 1960s, after his two years of graduate courses at the University of Hawaii. The Vietnam war was in full swing and Hoschouer, who was in the ROTC, was called to active duty as an infantry officer in November 1968. He was sent to Vietnam as an adviser to a South Vietnamese battalion in 1970, and a year later was a captain in command of an air infantry company in the 1st Cavalry Division.

After Vietnam, he served with the special forces in Germany for three years, returning there in 1989 as a military attaché in the American embassy in Bonn. Although he had been promoted to lieutenant colonel in 1985, it was clear that he would not be advancing any further than bird colonel, which Hanssen knew when he gave his name to the Russians.

According to Hoschouer, the KGB did not follow up on Hanssen's suggestion. "I was not contacted," he said. "If the Russians pitched me, I was too dumb to realize it. If they wanted to approach me, I had a lot of official contacts with the Soviets in Bonn and it would have been easy to do." But he could remember nothing that even remotely resembled a pitch.

Hoschouer retired from the Army in 1994. What was his reaction to learning seven years later that his closest friend had offered him up as a morsel to the KGB? "I still don't know," he said. "I was disappointed I'd been passed over for promotion, in ninety-one, I think, that was true. Maybe he thought in some twisted way he was trying to help me out. My own feeling is he was under so much stress from his own situation, he wanted somebody he could talk to."

Did Hanssen really think that if the Russians ever managed to recruit Hoschouer, they could pal around as spies together, just as they had broken a few traffic laws as teenagers in a Corvair on the back streets of Chicago?

Even if Hoschouer had agreed to become a spy, he pointed out, "I would not have been able to discuss it with him, since he was in the FBI." Moreover, the KGB is careful not to tell one spy about another. Aldrich Ames worked for the KGB during some of the same years as Hanssen did, but there is no evidence that either was aware of the other's role.

By the time of the October exchange between Hanssen and the KGB, the Soviet Union was teetering on the edge of disaster. The political upheavals in Moscow had directly affected the KGB. Kryuchkov, who had sent all those nice letters to Hanssen, was sitting in prison, which must have been somewhat unnerving to the FBI man. The KGB's first chief directorate (FCD), its foreign intelligence arm at Yasenevo, had been split off and declared an independent agency. After the final collapse of the Soviet Union, it would be rechristened the SVR.

Hanssen's handlers were anxious to assure him that despite all these seismic events, he could rely on business as usual. The spies had survived, and were now actually more independent.

"There have been many important developments in our country lately," the Russians acknowledged to Hanssen. "So many that we'd like to reassure You once again. Like we said: we've done all in order that none of those events ever affects Your security and our ability to maintain the operation with You. And of course there can be no doubt of our commitment to Your friendship and cooperation which are too important to us to loose [sic]. . . ."

The spies in the *les* (forest), as the officers in the first chief directorate often called their organization, were obviously deeply worried that Hanssen would decide, in light of the instability in Moscow, to disappear forever, as suddenly as he had appeared in 1985. The genie might vanish back into the bottle and be permanently beyond their reach.

But in the meantime, there was work to be done. The Russians provided new communications plans and asked Hanssen for a broad variety of classified information. They also requested a specific current document that analyzed Soviet knowledge of U.S. reconnaissance satellites. "It's fun to read about the life in the Universe to understand better what's going on on our own planet," they wrote.

Gently, they also asked about some pages that seemed to be missing from Hanssen's hastily assembled July package. "Sometimes it happens, we understand," the Russians said. "Life is becoming too fast."

On December 12, the KGB received a letter from Hanssen postmarked in Washington but with a bogus return address of "J. Baker, Box 1101, Houston, TX." In it, Hanssen alerted the Russians to a new electronic eavesdropping gadget that was about to be targeted against them. "DEVICE APPROVED . . . COMING SOON," he warned.

Four days later, Hanssen and the KGB carried out an exchange at BOB, in Idylwood Park. Hanssen turned over a classified research paper from the CIA's Counterintelligence Center dated November 1990 entitled "The KGB's First Chief Directorate: Structure, Functions, and Methods."

He also passed to the Russians a budget summary from the office of the Director of Central Intelligence, stamped SECRET, that revealed the scope of the FBI's foreign counterintelligence programs. And on the twenty-sixth floppy disk that he passed to the KGB, he said he was embarrassed about the pages missing from his July package.

Hanssen was about to be promoted again; this time he would be chief of the new National Security Threat List unit at headquarters. At NSTL, he would be working on the FBI's efforts to counter economic espionage. He had received "an increase in salary and authority," Hanssen wrote. That was the good news. The bad news was that this moved him "at least temporarily out of direct responsibility." He added that "a new mission for my new group has not been fully defined" but "I hope to adjust to that. . . . As General Patton said . . . 'let's get this over with so we can go kick the shit out of the purple-pissing Japanese.'"* Hanssen often quoted Patton, whom he admired almost as much as Mayor Daley.

---

*The quote is close to a line in one version of the fiery speech General George S. Patton, Jr., made to his men in England in 1944 just before the Normandy invasion. The FBI's affidavit in the Hanssen case delicately omits the expletives that Hanssen attributed to Patton. But the full text, including the remarkable urological reference, later became very important, as will be seen.

The technically minded Hanssen also proposed a new communications system to replace the cumbersome dead drops, the plastic bags squirreled away under footbridges, and all that unpleasant slogging around in the dark in the mud. As Hanssen outlined it, he would set up an office somewhere in Washington that would not be tapped or bugged by the FBI, since the bureau would be unaware of it. There, he and the KGB could communicate directly by computer, using special equipment with advanced encryption technology.

From the drop in Idylwood Park, Hanssen extracted $12,000 in cash and a KGB floppy disk that contained communications plans and asked for information about various classified matters.

But Hanssen did not reply. What the KGB had feared all along now happened. Their apprehension was always there in the background; it could be sensed between the lines of their warm and fuzzy letters to Hanssen. It was the fear that one day he would simply disappear.

As often as the Russians might drive by the emergency call-out site near Dupont Circle, there were no chalk marks, no sign that their man was ready for another exchange of money and secrets. As often as they checked their mail at the accommodation addresses in Alexandria, there was no word from "Ramon Garcia," no more letters from "Jim Baker" or "G. Robertson."

Robert Hanssen had gone to ground.

In less than two weeks, the Soviet Union would be no more. Defectors from the KGB were already knocking at the door of the CIA, and their numbers were likely to increase. Even though Hanssen had been careful to conceal his name, perhaps one of the defectors might know something that would lead to him. He may even have wished he had not quoted General Patton, or talked about Chicago, or provided other clues that might point to his identity.

Throughout the intelligence community there was a sense of victory, tinged with relief; the Soviet Union was history. At the CIA, Milt Bearden, the chief of the Soviet division, presided over his office's annual Christmas gathering. The celebrants sported buttons with a hammer and sickle and star against a white background, and in big letters three words: "The party's over!" All in all, it did not seem a good time to be spying for the Russians.

But there was another reason that Hanssen broke off all contact in December 1991. More than a decade earlier, he had consulted Father Bucciarelli when he promised Bonnie that he would stop spying. This time, on a trip to Indianapolis, Hanssen had gone to see a second priest, who also urged him to stop betraying his country.

And so, weighing the dangers of being caught that flowed from the imminent collapse of the Soviet empire, and armed with the importunings of the cleric in Indiana, Hanssen made his decision.

He would go into hibernation.

17

Play It Again, Sam

Joanna's 1819 Club on M Street in downtown Washington is the sort of place where businessmen slip in on their lunch hour or after work to ogle naked women gyrating to music under the bright lights. Compared to some strip clubs, it gets a fairly sedate crowd: patrons are more likely to be wearing suits and ties than bowling jackets and industrial caps.

Knowing her audience, Priscilla Sue Galey sometimes began her act dressed as a secretary, with a briefcase and glasses. In the anonymity of Joanna's, the customers could watch Priscilla Sue take it all off.

"They all pictured their secretaries coming into the office that way," Galey said. "A couple of the men told me that. But mostly it's ego building. We come and sit and talk to them, hug them. Maybe this is the only place they can get away from their wives. They often come to watch and talk to a particular girl."

In the fall of 1990, she said, while she was dancing at Joanna's, a tall man sent a waitress over to her with a ten-dollar tip. The patron had also asked the waitress to relay a compliment. "It was something like he had never expected to find such grace and beauty in a strip club."

Galey ran after the man as he was leaving and caught him at the door to thank him, more for his words than the money. A couple of weeks later, Robert Hanssen was back. This time, he gave her his business card, with the embossed gold seal of the FBI.

She was awed, and a little scared at first, to find out that her admirer was an FBI agent. But perhaps, she thought, since he was, he could do her a favor. Then thirty-two, Galey said she had lost track of her father and could only remember meeting him once.

"I asked him to find my father. He said he'd try, 'We have ways of doing that, we can find almost anybody.' He wrote down the name of my father, Jerry Roberts. He got my mother pregnant in the church parking lot and my grandfather ran him off with a shotgun, in Marion, Indiana."

She had last seen her father when she was eight, Galey said. "He came to the house only once, and played the piano with me, and he looked at me and said, 'She's mine.' " Then he was gone.

Hanssen never found Galey's father, but at their next meeting he had a surprise for her. He gave her a sapphire-and-diamond necklace.

To Galey, it was as though a fairy tale had come true. Guys who came to strip clubs did not give the dancers jewelry worth thousands of dollars—not, at least, without wanting something in return, and she insisted Hanssen never did. There was, she asserted, except for one time, no sex, no hugs, no kisses, no physical contact.

This was a very unusual man, Galey realized, something far outside her usual experience. She had married briefly at sixteen, acquiring the name Galey, dropped out of high school, and moved to Columbus, Ohio, where she began stripping. There, she won the title of stripper of the year in the old burlesque theater in Columbus. "Charlie Fox was his name, the owner, and he taught me how to do it. He was like a drillmaster, teaching me how to strip. 'You have to put on a show,' Charlie would say."

In 1980, with another stripper, she moved to Boston and danced at the Golden Banana under the stage name of Traci Starr. Four years later, she came to Washington and danced for a time at Archibald's on K Street, an area notable for its lobbyists and fat cats. Then she switched to Joanna's.

And the money was good. "At Joanna's, I could make two, three, four hundred a night—one night eight hundred—on tips. The eight hundred dollars on one night was with a whole bunch of Oriental men. I think they were Japanese. I lit my nipples on fire, and they were pushing all this money at me. It's a stripper's trick. You turn away from the audience. First you have to split the matches, wet them, then put them on your nipples, and light the matches and in the dark, it looks like your nipples are on fire. 'Oh,' the Japanese said, 'Ooh, oh, oh,' and all of them were pushing hundred-dollar bills at me. I'm still laughing about it."

Galey impressed Hanssen with more than her trim body and her stripper's skills. Although she never completed high school, she was obviously very intelligent, interested in art, in life, and intellectually curious. She also had a sense of humor. "Stripping isn't bad," she said, "once you get over the being naked part."

According to Galey, Hanssen was always trying to improve her spiritual life, continually urging her to go to church. He would ask, "What are you planning to do with the rest of your life? Are you getting any closer to God?" But, she said, although she passed a church every day on her way to Joanna's, "I felt it was hypocritical for me to go to church and then go down to the club and take my clothes off."

Once, Hanssen drove her to his church in northern Virginia, so she would know where it was, and he urged her to attend mass there. She did go to the church one Sunday, but only got as far as the parking lot. "I saw him and his family go in, and I just couldn't do it."

Hanssen also drove her by his house on Talisman Drive. "I think he was just proud to show me how he lived." She envied the placid suburban neighborhood and the ordinary family life it evoked, a stability she had not known. But he never told his wife about her, she said. "He couldn't explain a stripper."

The fact that Hanssen frequented strip clubs was a secret that none of his FBI colleagues and friends knew about, except for Jack Hoschouer, who would accompany him to the clubs when he was in town.

Hanssen befriended other strippers besides Galey. He knew Dep Mullins, a Vietnamese woman who danced as "Brooke" at Joanna's. They met in the summer of 1999 when Hanssen, accompanied by Hoschouer, visited the club. "I speak some Vietnamese," Hoschouer said. "We invited her over and we spoke a little. 'Dep' means beautiful in Viet. She was raised in Hawaii, grew up on Maui. We saw her again early in 2000." Both the FBI and the Justice Department investigated Hanssen's encounters with Mullins. There was no evidence, however, that Hanssen ever developed with other strippers the same close and lengthy relationship he enjoyed with Galey.

Often, when an FBI agent retired, his coworkers would give a farewell party for him at one of the strip clubs. The club favored by many FBI agents was the Good Guys, two blocks down from the Russian embassy.*

Paul Moore remembered a conversation with Hanssen at FBI headquarters around 1990, the same year he met Galey. "I've been to strip clubs twice, once at the Good Guys, where a bureau guy who was retiring got a plaque from the club, he'd been there so much. I told Bob about it and I said it was not too tawdry, it was a fairly joyful atmosphere. He said no, it was sinful. He said, 'You were paying women to tempt men.' It was just the kind of thing you would get from a priest."

Some weeks after Hanssen gave Galey the necklace, she mentioned to him that she needed to have a tooth fixed. Before long, Hanssen left an envelope for her at the club; inside she found $2,000 in hundred-dollar bills. By this time, Galey had almost convinced herself that Hanssen might be her long-lost father; it might explain his generosity. "I fantasized that he was my father, or an angel."

Hanssen's inspection duties that year were arduous, but he apparently had time to see Galey between trips, for they took long walks together, she said. "We walked to art galleries. To the National Gallery, to the Hirshhorn. He did offer to take me to the National Archives, but I was more interested in art than history. I like the old masters, Leonardo especially."

When they were out together, Hanssen had his own ideas of how Galey should dress. "We were going to one of the art galleries. I had on very high white heels. He said, 'You know your feet are going to hurt.' What he really was saying was, 'Please don't look like this.' We walked to a shoe store, picked out a new pair of regular blue or black pumps, and I wore them. He always wanted me to wear navy blue."

What was going on here? Hanssen may have been having some sort of midlife fling, except it wasn't much of a fling by Galey's account. More likely, it seemed he was living a weird combination of a James Bond fantasy—the spy with a pretty woman on his arm—and the *My Fair Lady* version of the Pygmalion myth, with himself in the role of Professor Higgins to Galey's Eliza Doolittle. He would uplift Galey, im-

---

*Russians from the embassy also patronized the Good Guys, often leaving unsteadily. From time to time, "FBI agents on surveillance would approach the Russians at the Good Guys," said one bureau counterintelligence agent. "Sometimes when the Russians were so drunk they didn't know where they were we would try to help them to their cars. The next day we'd call them and they'd say 'No, no, it was a mistake.'"

prove her mind, and help her into a spiritual realm that somehow was lacking at Joanna's. Or, on the other hand, as one observer suggested, "Maybe it was Opus Dei's idea of an affair."

Whatever Hanssen's motive, his involvement with Galey went on for more than a year, and he risked taking her to places where they could be seen together. "One time he took me to lunch at a cop club, a private club. He said they were policemen and FBI agents. You had to be buzzed in. It was in Washington somewhere. On the way to the club, I discovered he was carrying a gun. He said, 'I wonder if they'll make me check this.' "

It was en route to the same lunch that Hanssen made a remark that startled Galey. She had asked him a question about something—she did not recall what—"and he said, 'I could tell you, but I'd have to kill you.' You could see it was a joke. He was smiling." Still, Galey was unsettled by the remark.

Sometimes, Hanssen talked politics. "He explained Communism. He said it's not like America, where you have individual rights; in Russia, the government has control of everything. But the way he explained it, it didn't sound as bad as everyone made it out to be. It probably did have its good aspects. Because no one went hungry. It was like Communism is not all bad, but they did control every aspect of your life."

In April 1991, Hanssen told Galey he was going on a trip to Hong Kong. Galey had a genuine enthusiasm for anything Asian, not just because of the eight-hundred-dollar night and how the Japanese patrons had appreciated it when she set her nipples on fire, and she pleaded with Hanssen to bring her back a souvenir. To her amazement, he asked if she would like to go with him.

She said she could not afford the trip, but Hanssen asked her to walk with him to a travel office. There, he picked up his airline reservation, and before she knew it, he had handed her a round-trip ticket to Hong Kong. When she tried to hug him for the gift, he shrank back. "He said, 'Oh no, that is not necessary, it's not necessary,' and he smiled, like he didn't want to hurt my feelings." If she changed her mind about going, he said, she could turn in the ticket and keep the cash. "It was all magic," Galey remembered.

If she asked him where all the money was coming from, "he would explain it away by telling me it was his inheritance." Her time with Hanssen "was the most wonderful thing that ever happened to me. I really didn't want to question it too much. It might make it go away."

And so they flew to Hong Kong, on separate flights, and stayed at the same hotel in separate rooms for two weeks. They had breakfast together every morning and dinner at night. Once, they took the ferry to Kowloon, and Hanssen showed her around the streets and shopping malls. Galey was thrilled when they visited a sailing ship in the harbor. On most days, however, while Hanssen went about his inspection duties for the FBI, Galey shopped and went sight-seeing.

"Over cheesecake in Hong Kong, I said, 'Mr. Hanssen, you must have done something wrong in your life.' He thought for a while and said, 'Well, I changed some test scores in college.' That was it. I said, 'You never cheated on your wife, you never went out with the guys and did something crazy?' He said, 'No, I've never done any of that.' He lived a very sterile life as far as I could see.

"He was very straitlaced. He had compassion. You could see it, and you could tell that he was a good man."

She was baffled as to what Hanssen wanted. "I never met any man who didn't deep down want to screw me," she said, matter-of-factly. "I had to find out." She had wondered, she said, "if he was repressed because of his family and church." She had to know "if he really wanted sex."

So in Hong Kong, far from Talisman Drive, Galey made her move. "I had a lot of souvenirs and needed a bigger suitcase to get them home," she said. "I asked him to come to my room to see the souvenirs and see how big a suitcase I would need. He came to my room."

Galey was circumspect at first in describing what happened, but said that in the hotel room, she came on to him. What occurred next, she said, wasn't "finished." She regards sex, she added, as "meaning intercourse between two consenting persons that is finished," a definition almost Clintonian in its precision. "There was no consent," she said.

When asked to explain what all these elaborate semantics meant, she was more direct. "I was very drunk," she recalled. She had, she said, begun with oral sex. "And when I started, he said, 'Where in the world did you learn how to do that?' I thought, 'Oh my God, he's never even had a blow job.' I think he stopped me when I was ready for intercourse. I came up for that but he was not consenting, he did not want it. I never dreamed that he wouldn't. As I remember it, that's what happened. I felt a little bit ashamed, a lot of hurt. I knew what I did had never been done to him before."

On the trip, there was not much talk about Hanssen's work. "In

Hong Kong," Galey recalled, "he mentioned the Chinese mafia, and he mentioned the Russians, but he never went into any details."

Friends say Hanssen admired James Bond and liked the movies about the exploits of Agent 007. But he may also have fantasized that he was Humphrey Bogart, living a real-life romantic role in *Casablanca*. Whenever they were in a piano bar together, Galey added, there was one song that Hanssen would request. "In Hong Kong," she said, "he always asked for 'As Time Goes By.' "

Hanssen never took Galey into FBI headquarters, as far as is known, but he did take her to the bureau's training academy in Virginia, south of Washington. "He took me to Quantico after Hong Kong. He put a CIA badge on me so I would have entry to everywhere. He said, 'If anybody stops you, you're to say, "I'm working on the Eisenhower project, or something like that, and it's top secret, and I can't talk about it." ' It was like a big joke. I saw the library, the shooting range, the little town they set up for training agents. I didn't shoot in the shooting range, although I would have liked to. He didn't shoot either, although he bragged how good a shot he was."

It was in August 1991, a few months after their trip to Hong Kong, that Hanssen urged Galey to get a driver's license. She said she had not had one for five years, because there was no reason; she could not afford a car. Well, he asked, if you could afford a car, what would it be?

"Either an old Jaguar convertible, with the spoked rims," she replied, "or it has to be a Mercedes." Those are good choices, Hanssen said.

Galey got her license and at their next lunch, on August 5, at Jaimalito's, a Mexican restaurant in Georgetown, Hanssen had some surprises for her. First, he handed her an envelope. "It was an American Express card with my name on it. I never had a credit card. I thought that was wonderful. And then he handed me a pair of keys, and I knew they were nice keys, because they had the little leather holders on them, so they had to be to a nice car, and I was like, 'What are these for?'

"And he says, 'This is for your new car.' And he said, 'I looked for a Jaguar, but I got to thinking that the maintenance on that might be too much for you. It's a Mercedes, a champagne silver Mercedes, and it's being cleaned up, and when we're through eating, we'll go pick it up.' And I'm like, 'You bought me a Mercedes!' I couldn't finish eating, I couldn't even eat. I kept asking questions, and said, 'Do we have to eat, can't we just go?' "

Afterward, they drove out to Alexandria to pick up the car, a 1985 Mercedes-Benz 190E Sedan, for which Hanssen had paid the dealer $10,500 in cash. Galey could not believe it; she drove fifty miles out of her way when she went back to her apartment in Silver Spring, Maryland, just to be in the car.

Around the same time, Hanssen gave Galey an expensive laptop. She said Hanssen indicated that if she could learn how to use the computer it would help her out of the strip club and on the path to an office job. But Galey was not able to get the laptop to work, and decided that Hanssen had put in some kind of code to lock the computer and test her abilities. "My mother is good at computers and could not make it work. She couldn't boot it up, which led me to believe it was protected."

In retrospect, she wondered if the laptop was part of a plan that Hanssen had to enlist her to help him spy. "It became an obsession that I learn how to use computers. He wanted me to learn how to e-mail, to send him messages from afar. I used to think he was just trying to improve me. Now I think he wanted me as an asset. He was preparing me for something."

That Hanssen would risk having anyone else to assist him in his espionage for Moscow seems highly improbable. But Galey's speculation was not dismissed out of hand by the FBI, which interviewed her after Hanssen's arrest. "I think he was trying to develop her, Galey, into some kind of cutout," said one veteran counterintelligence expert. "He gave her the computer, he was trying to test her skills. Otherwise, and assuming there was no sex, why did he spend all that time with her?"

Toward the end of the year, Galey said, Hanssen told her that he wanted to send her to France to see "the incorrupt saint." Although he did not elaborate, "There is such a shrine in France. He was going to send me there. He always told me, miracles happen every day."*

Aside from the necklace, the trip to Hong Kong, the Mercedes, and the laptop, all big-ticket items, Hanssen had another, small present for Galey. "He gave me a video of *Casablanca* around the time he gave me the computer. He said it was a classic. I took it home for the holidays in

---

*In the Catholic Church, the bodies of some saints are considered "incorrupt" because they have not deteriorated or have done so only partially. These relics are often credited with miraculous cures of ill or disabled persons. The most famous example is Bernadette, the celebrated French nun whose body lies in a convent in Nevers, France.

1991." But before she left, they had dinner together at a club in Maryland. There was a piano bar, and once again, Galey said, Hanssen asked for "As Time Goes By."

A kiss is just a kiss. With the romantic melody playing in the background, Hanssen surprised Galey with an unexpected question. "That's the evening when he asked if he wasn't happily married, would I ever be interested in him? I was totally confused. I said, 'Of course I would be.' "

Galey said her confusion stemmed from the fact that up to that evening, Hanssen had always talked about how important his family was. "It was obvious his wife and kids were everything to him. He often spoke of his wife and children and how dedicated he was to them."

But as matters turned out, it was to be their last dinner together. The decision to go back to Columbus that Christmas turned into a disaster for Priscilla Sue Galey. Her life went rapidly downhill. She stayed for two months, longer than she had planned, ran up debts, and her car was wrecked in a collision with a city truck.

"The Mercedes was smashed. Totaled. In March of ninety-two. That's the day my life went really bad. My friends were smoking crack. There was no insurance. The guy who was supposed to pay my insurance on the car said he had smoked it, he spent the money on crack."

The laptop and the diamond-and-sapphire necklace were pawned for a fraction of their value. When the money ran out, she used the American Express card to buy Easter dresses for her nieces. But Hanssen had told her that the credit card, for which he paid the bills, was to be used strictly for expenses for the Mercedes or for emergencies. When he saw the dresses on the credit card statement, he flew to Columbus. There was an awkward encounter with Galey, "a very stiff meeting," as she put it, and he retrieved the card and left.

It was not only Galey's friends who were into drugs. She became hooked on crack, and turned to prostitution to support her habit. She was arrested in 1993, caught in a police sting, when a friend she was with sold crack to an undercover cop. Her mother, Linda Harris, called Hanssen on his direct line at the FBI to ask for help, but he refused. Galey pleaded guilty to avoid a longer sentence and spent a year in the state reformatory for women in Marysville, Ohio. Later, she had a child out of wedlock and fell deeper into her life on the streets of Columbus.

If she could visit Hanssen in prison, which she would like to do, she wants to ask him a question. "I just want to know, 'Why? What could

ever change you from this paragon of virtue? What could change you?'
In my eyes he was a god."

Still, Hanssen had helped her more than she ever dreamed any man
would. "He showed me a different way of living, a whole new me." She
felt this way even though their relationship had not lasted and she had
failed to better herself, as he had seemed to want, instead doing just the
opposite.

She was deeply disappointed at the news that Hanssen was a Russian spy. "It kind of hurts my feelings that he lied to me; he was the one
man who wasn't capable of lying, it didn't seem like, and I trusted him
so much. He gave me back my faith in men. I'm just disappointed, that's
all."

Galey shook her head. "Hell, I'm used to it. For him to make a magical world and then . . . I guess it's just, like, there goes my fairy tale
again."

18

"He Was Dragging Me by the Arm, Screaming at Me"

Kimberly Schaefer grew up in a working-class neighborhood in Ferndale, Maryland, south of Baltimore, and got a job at the FBI at age eighteen, right out of high school. She was assigned to the tour office, escorting visitors through the bureau's headquarters in Washington.

A bright and articulate woman, she was moved to the FBI's intelligence division in less than a year. In 1992, she married Michael Lichtenberg, then a sales representative for a steamship company. They bought a house in Ferndale, near her parents, and in a few years started a family.

In 1993, Kimberly Lichtenberg was working in the National Security Threat List unit in the intelligence division. The unit chief, Robert Hanssen, presided over an office of about ten people on the fourth floor. There were three or four FBI agents, a few support workers, a secretary, and a typist. Lichtenberg was an intelligence assistant to Supervisory Special Agent James A. Werth.

Hanssen could hardly have failed to notice that Kimberly Lichtenberg was tall and willowy, with long blond hair and striking, clear blue eyes. And by Lichtenberg's account, at least, he did more than look.

"I never really knew him until I was transferred into his unit," she said. "I'd heard things about him: 'Dr. Death.' As a female, I'd never want to be alone with him. I got weird vibes. He'd make sure he'd brush against me when he passed by. The same with other females in the office. I never, ever felt comfortable around him." Hanssen, she asserted, had brushed against her "many times."*

She added, "Hanssen considered women beneath him. He spoke down to them. But if he wanted to rub up against me he would. And the bureau is a boys' club."

In truth, Hanssen did not approve of women in law enforcement. That retrograde conviction was in tune with his conservative views in general. Women in the bureau, he would grumble, were dysfunctional for the organization. But to hold that opinion, he once complained, was not politically correct.

At about 3:30 P.M. on February 25, 1993, Hanssen summoned Lichtenberg, a secretary, and a typist to a meeting in his office. There had been some minor squabbling in the clerical ranks and Hanssen wanted to get to the bottom of it.

"The secretary had been complaining about the typist," Lichtenberg said. "Hanssen asked, 'Kim, are you having any problems with the typist?' I said no, I didn't. Hanssen said, 'Well, the secretary says you've been complaining.' I said, 'No, I've no problems with the typist.' "

Lichtenberg was getting nervous about missing her ride in the carpool. She lived near the Baltimore/Washington International Airport and if she did not show up for her ride she would have no way to get home. "I said, 'I have to leave to catch my van.' I turned and walked out. I thought the meeting was over. It was a little before four, when I usually leave. I was not being flippant. I was respectful."

After she left the meeting, she said, "I was heading for my pod area," where a friend and fellow FBI employee, Candy Curtis, was waiting for her.

She had just reached her cubicle, she said, about thirty feet from Hanssen's office, when he caught up with her.

"He yelled, 'Get back here!' I said, 'No, I need to get home, this doesn't involve me.'

"No sooner had I said that than he grabbed me by my left arm and spun me around. I lost my balance and fell to the ground. He never let

---

*Lichtenberg agreed to meet with the author to recount her story although she was still employed by the FBI in a sensitive position in the intelligence division, now the National Security Division. She expressed some concern that her criticism of how the bureau dealt with her case might cause problems in her job, but she was willing to speak out anyway.

go of my arm. He was dragging me by the arm, screaming at me. He continued to drag me back by my arm toward his office, screaming and yelling at me."

Lichtenberg, hoping for help, called out to Candy Curtis.

"He was yelling, 'I told you to get back in here.' When I yelled 'Candy!' he starts yelling, 'You're insubordinate!'"

Candy Curtis, Lichtenberg said, heard the commotion. "When she heard me call her name, she got up, walked out of the pod and saw everything. She saw me in a tug-of-war stance. She didn't see me fall to the ground, but she saw me trying to get up.

"I got back on my feet. He was still holding my arm and I hit him on the chest and broke free."

Curtis confirmed Lichtenberg's account. She had heard the commotion and saw most of what occurred, she said. "Definitely. I was there and did witness it. He was pulling her physically. She was still low down, crouched. It went on until he saw me. He had no idea I was there."

Once free of Hanssen, Lichtenberg fled with Candy Curtis. "We ran to the section chief, Nick Walsh. He said, 'Wait here.' He ran down to talk to Hanssen and came back and said, 'Do you want to receive medical attention?' I said, 'My van is probably going to leave me.' He said, 'You better go and come back in the morning.'"

Lichtenberg hurried to her car pool. "I had bruises on my arm and a bruise on my cheek." She was shaken and upset by the encounter.

"The people in the van were angry at first. They were waiting. Then they saw me. I cried all the way home."

Lichtenberg went to her parents' house. "I'm their only daughter. When my father saw the bruises, he started crying. My father was a crane operator, a big man, but he was crying.

"My parents and my husband took me to the emergency room at North Arundel Hospital. I was X-rayed. The tendons on my arm were stretched; they never fully came back to normal. I still can't sleep on my left side."

Michael Lichtenberg called Nick Walsh at the FBI. "I asked if my wife was going to be safe. He said, 'I can't guarantee her safety.' I said, 'Then transfer her. Get her out of there.'" As of now, he added, "She's not coming in."

The next day, Kimberly Lichtenberg said, "Two agents from division five came to the house and took a statement." Lichtenberg told them what had happened. She also told the agents that Hanssen had made her uncomfortable in various ways. He had a habit, she said to them, of walking up to her desk and staring down at her. When she asked if there was anything he wanted, or that she could help him with, he would answer "No," and walk away. Sometimes, she recounted to the FBI agents, Hanssen would come up to her and place a hand on her arm or shoulder and shake her slightly. When Hanssen did this, she told the agents, "He would say, 'I'm just trying to shake you up this morning.' "

In recalling her statement to the agents, Lichtenberg said that although Hanssen did not shake her in a "mean way" on these occasions, he should not have touched her at all. But she said she feared that if she complained, Hanssen, as her boss, could retaliate in various ways—he could block her promotion, for example—so she did not.

Michael Lichtenberg was worried about what Hanssen might do next, and said so to the two agents. "I told them I felt this guy was very unstable," he recalled. "I said, 'I can't believe nothing is being done with this guy. He has a gun. It isn't even being taken away from him.' "

The agents later typed Kimberly Lichtenberg's statement, and she approved and signed it. Candy Curtis also gave a statement to the internal FBI investigation in support of Lichtenberg's account.

Kimberly Lichtenberg said she sought to file an assault complaint with the police in Washington. "I wanted to file criminal charges but I wasn't able to," she contended. "The detective took notes. He talked to the bureau. He said they told him it was an inside matter."

After Hanssen attacked her, Kimberly Lichtenberg took a month-and-a-half leave from the FBI. "I had physical therapy for a few months. I also saw a psychotherapist, a woman who said, 'Kim, you've got to do something about this.' "

A year later, the Lichtenbergs filed a civil complaint in the District of Columbia Superior Court against Hanssen for "assault and battery, gross negligence," and "intentional infliction of emotional distress." They asked for $1,360,000 in damages.

Because Hanssen was a federal employee, the case was transferred to federal court in Washington. The Justice Department, defending Hanssen, moved to dismiss the complaint. In a statement filed with the court, John D. Bates, the chief of the civil division, found that "defendant Robert P. Hanssen was acting within the scope of his authority as an employee of the United States at the time of such alleged incidents."

In other words, the government was arguing in Hanssen's defense that because he was on duty at the time he dragged Lichtenberg down the hall, she and her husband had no cause of action.

Lichtenberg also filed a workers' compensation claim for her injuries. Her lawyer, Steve Huffines, represented her in both the lawsuit and her compensation hearing. Because the government said Hanssen was acting within the scope of his official duties, Huffines maintained, it would have been "a difficult standard to overcome. The only way to get action outside a claim of 'scope of employment' would be if he pulled a gun out and shot her."

In the end, the civil suit was dismissed by Judge Thomas Penfield Jackson after Huffines, apparently as the result of a clerical mixup, did not appear for a court date. Lichtenberg fared better in her compensation claim. She was awarded $16,000 for her injuries and continuing disability.

When she returned to work, she was transferred out of Hanssen's unit into a new job administering clearances and background checks for bureau employees. Even so, she could not avoid running into Hanssen. When that happened, "He smiled and would say hi, but he never apologized. I learned he was suspended for five days."

Lichtenberg got a letter of censure from the FBI. "It said what he did was wrong but that I had provoked him by leaving the meeting without being dismissed and I was insubordinate." Lichtenberg has asked that the letter be removed from her employment file.

Two years after the attack, Lichtenberg was working in the basement of the FBI in a SCIF. (The acronym, pronounced like a word, stands for Sensitive Compartmented Information Facility, a place where highly classified documents are kept.) The SCIF was specially enclosed so that its equipment would not give off electronic emanations.

"I was pregnant and Hanssen would come to the basement office where I was working, 1B045, where he signed in and got his mail." At the time, Hanssen had been assigned to duty at the State Department but would come to headquarters daily. "I went to see Joe McMahon, the section chief. 'You know they've put Hanssen down here?' The section chief said yes, he knew. 'Don't worry about it.'"

But Lichtenberg did worry. She talked to her supervisor. "My immediate boss wrote a two-page memo about the situation, but the bureaucracy did nothing." Hanssen continued to report to the basement office. "I ran into him five or six times a week. I was losing weight and my OB said, 'If they don't remove him, you will lose the baby.' "

"I went to Barbara Duffy, the FBI ombudsman. I told her the whole story. She called McMahon and said get him out of there." Hanssen then reported in to another office, on a different floor, and Lichtenberg, to her immense relief, seldom encountered him after that.

The last time she saw Hanssen was about three weeks before his arrest. "The elevator was coming up from the garage. I was on 1B, the floor where I work, so he had to be coming up from the garage. The elevator door opened and he was there. It was just him. He said, 'You getting on?' I said, 'No.' If there had been somebody else on the elevator I would have. I just didn't want to get on it with him."

On February 20, 2001, she was at work at FBI headquarters as usual. "I usually watch Channel 13, the local television news, in the morning. That morning for some reason or other I didn't. I came into work. I'm at my desk. My former unit chief came to me. I'd heard rumors of a spy case brewing. He said, 'They arrested him.' I said, 'Anybody I know?' He said, 'Oh yes, you know him. It's Bob Hanssen.' "

A few months before Hanssen was arrested, Michael Lichtenberg had taken a job at the FBI in the criminal division. As a result, he knew more about the structure and operations of the bureau than he did in 1993. He recalled the visit of the two FBI agents who had come to the house to interview his wife after Hanssen had manhandled her. "The two agents were from the intelligence division. They should have given it to the criminal division. I didn't know that at the time; now I know."

If Hanssen had been suspended and investigated by the FBI's Office of Professional Responsibility, he said, the outcome might have been different. Perhaps a clue pointing to Hanssen's espionage activities might have been turned up. "If they had pulled him and done a thirty-day OPR investigation," he said, "they might have found something. That's the sad part."

19

Hibernation

Although Hanssen had gone into his hibernation mode at the end of 1991 as the Soviet Union collapsed, he volunteered his services to the Russians again in 1993, a fact that the FBI learned to its surprise only when it debriefed him after he had pleaded guilty to espionage.

For most of the 1990s, Hanssen the spy was dormant, having abruptly cut off his contacts with the KGB. But in 1993 he revolunteered to the GRU, the Russian military intelligence arm for which he had spied in 1979, when he had received the $30,000 that he later told Bonnie Hanssen he had sent to Mother Teresa.

Hanssen explained to his FBI and CIA debriefers that his reemergence in 1993 was the result of overwhelming curiosity, to which he succumbed. It was a curiosity about what had happened to information he had previously passed to Moscow.

At least twice, Hanssen had provided the KGB with a complete roster of the FBI's double agent (DA) cases. Typically, in these operations, an American military enlisted man or officer under FBI control would offer secrets to Soviet military intelligence. One frequent goal would be to see what secrets the Russians asked the double agent to obtain. That in turn would indicate what Moscow did not know. Conversely, the questions that were not asked might suggest what the Russians already knew. It was these double agent operations that led to Hanssen's fleeting, risky attempt to recontact the GRU, because it was the GRU that the FBI had targeted in these cases.

"It was almost an academic curiosity," one senior intelligence official explained. "He had given up a lot of DA cases that the FBI and the military ran with the GRU as the target. They were joint ops. Hanssen sees them continue to operate and wonders why. Is the KGB not sharing his information with the GRU? Why are these cases still going on?" It was beginning to drive Hanssen up the wall; he had to know the answer.

"So he makes an approach to a GRU officer stationed in the Russian embassy in Washington. He has a package of documents with him that he was ready to give to the GRU guy. He approaches him early one morning in the garage of the apartment building where the GRU man lives and introduces himself. 'I am Ramon Garcia,' he says.

"The GRU man thinks it is a trap, gets into his car, and drives away. It apparently stunned Hanssen. He may have thought that all of Soviet intelligence would know by now about the famous Ramon Garcia."

Hanssen's risky move then took an astonishing turn. The Russians, convinced that the episode was a ploy by U.S. intelligence to entrap the GRU officer, lodged an official protest with the State Department. They even said that the unknown man who had approached their officer described himself as "a disaffected FBI agent."*

The FBI opened an investigation to try to determine the identity of the man who had, in Deep Throat fashion, approached the Russian spy in the parking garage. But there was very little to go on, and the case went nowhere. This was noted with relief and satisfaction by Hanssen, who closely followed the progress of the investigation in the FBI's internal computer system.

*   *   *

Hanssen was acting more and more like a man who had come loose from his moorings. There was his bizarre attack on Kimberly Lichtenberg in February, and the risky, Walter Mitty–like failed approach to the GRU. Hanssen's father died that same year, bringing to an end their difficult, complex relationship. And it was also in 1993 that Hanssen broke into Ray Mislock's computer.

Mislock, a tall Texan who commanded a Swift Boat in the Vietnam war, had joined the FBI in 1972 and two decades later had risen to chief of the former Soviet section, by then renamed the Eurasian section.

"One day I was sitting there in my office," Mislock recalled, "and

---

*Webster commission report, p. 12.

Hanssen comes in with a piece of paper in his hand. He said, 'You didn't believe me that the system was insecure.' He handed me the piece of paper and it was an exact copy of a document I had just written on my computer! I think it was a memo I was writing to the director. The memo was sensitive, and classified.

"I grabbed it out of his hand and ran down the hall to Pat Watson's office, the deputy assistant director for operations. He was angry." Together with Watson, Mislock marched into the office of Harry "Skip" Brandon, the official in charge of computer and security programs for the intelligence division.

"We had a very loud conversation," Mislock said. "We had a very animated conversation. I was really ripshit."

Brandon tried to calm Mislock down. "Okay," Brandon said, "we'll look into it."

Mislock was not appeased. "Having been told the system was secure, I wasn't going to accept that," he said. "I went into the counterespionage unit and disconnected all the computers from the LAN. That happened in a space of thirty minutes, and I was still steaming."

Hanssen was delighted to explain how he had hacked into the computer of the FBI's top official in charge of countering Russian espionage. "At some point we ended up in Hanssen's office and he gave a demonstration of how he did it," Mislock said. "After that, the computer people in the division worked to plug the vulnerability. I was not angry at Hanssen. I was angry at the people who had given me assurances that the system could not be hacked. At the time, people were appreciative he had done what he had done."

In retrospect, Mislock theorized that Hanssen had hacked into the FBI's computers for his own reasons. "He went in to look and see if there was anything to indicate he was being watched. He had to come up with a story to explain why he was in the system in case there was some tracking software he didn't know about." Hanssen may have been worried, Mislock believed, that he had left computer traces that might lead back to him.* "So he came forward and was the person who pointed to the vulnerability."

---

*His concern was well-founded. FBI computers are designed so every keystroke by a user can be reconstructed if necessary. But in 1993, the FBI was not investigating Hanssen or tracking his computer usage.

Everyone in the division knew what Hanssen had done, and there was considerable buzz about it. Once again, Hanssen had demonstrated his computer wizardry. By breaking into Ray Mislock's computer, he was dancing on the edge, but he had gotten away with it.

*   *   *

Around the same time, Hanssen was meeting regularly at an unmarked CIA installation in northern Virginia as the FBI member of a secret group dealing with nuclear proliferation. Through his work on the nuclear issue, he developed a close friendship with Barton A. Borrasca, the CIA's specialist on how Pakistan was financing its nuclear weapons program.

If Robert Hanssen could be said to have had a groupie in the U.S. intelligence world, it was Bart Borrasca, who became an unabashed admirer of the FBI agent. They had met in the early 1990s. At the time, Hanssen was no longer funneling secrets to the KGB. He was still working at FBI headquarters as chief of the threat list unit.

Borrasca, who had targeted ICBMs in the Air Force, joined the CIA in 1991 to work on nuclear proliferation. With the Soviet system crumbling, the agency had begun to focus on the proliferation issue in the post–Cold War era. During the Reagan administration, Borrasca had monitored NASA's space shuttle program in the Office of Management and Budget, then worked for Boeing's space systems division in Washington before moving to the CIA.

In April 1992, CIA director Robert M. Gates created the Nonproliferation Center (NPC) within the intelligence agency. It was headed for the next five years by Gordon C. Oehler, a career CIA officer. Borrasca moved over to the new center, which had the mission of monitoring and trying to control the spread of nuclear weapons in the world.

"Borrasca worked in the Transfer Networks Group at NPC," said one agency colleague. "They focused on unraveling all the shipping and financial networks used by proliferating countries. They were trying to figure out where to put pressure to stop that activity. They studied how countries were moving money and nuclear technology. Borrasca was the Pak guy; he was responsible for Pakistan."

The fact that Hanssen had worked on nuclear weapons issues was not disclosed after his arrest. As Oehler described the interagency committee on which he served as the FBI's member, "We had a community group which we called CNPC, the Community Nonproliferation Committee.* That was headed by Bob Walpole, who was my deputy. It was a community coordination mechanism, a group of people who got together once a month to talk about problems. They met in Rosslyn in an agency facility."

Hanssen regularly attended these meetings in the early 1990s. "Apparently, during this period Borrasca befriended Hanssen," said a CIA colleague of Borrasca who knew of the close friendship that had developed between the agency analyst and the FBI agent. "Borrasca used to go to Hanssen's house for dinner. He often talked about Hanssen."

At the CIA, Borrasca earned a reputation for unpredictable behavior, at least among some of his coworkers. "Bart went to the Paris air show with a group of CIA analysts," one CIA officer recalled. "Boeing had a chalet near Paris where they put up their executives at the air show. To impress his CIA colleagues, Borrasca goes up to the Boeing table and says, 'I have some CIA people with me, can we put them up at the chalet?'—thereby blowing the cover of the CIA officers, some of whom were undercover.

"At Paris, Borrasca became convinced that the Chinese were following him around. So he began following the Chinese delegates, taking their photographs. He had a very conspiratorial style."

Gordon Oehler put it more kindly. "Bart was a very sincere person who sometimes took off in the wrong direction. There was no ill intent on his part to do anything wrong. He had a lot of energy and sometimes it was hard to pull it back. He was a very hard worker."

At the CIA, according to one colleague, Borrasca had difficulty with sensitivity training designed to make employees aware of sexual harassment. "In sex harassment class, which everyone took, he once asked, 'What about the rights of the harasser?' "

Apparently, the sensitivity training did not make an indelible impression on Borrasca. "Once someone looked out the window and remarked, 'What a beautiful view.' Borrasca was looking the other way, staring at a secretary in the room, and he said, 'The view is pretty good here, too.' " Two or three times, the colleague said, female CIA employees complained of alleged sexual harassment by Borrasca.

---

*The word "community" has a benign ring to it that conjures up trim suburban lawns, town hall meetings, and church suppers. In the intelligence world, the word is commonly used to refer to the CIA, the FBI, the NSA, and various other spy agencies that together constitute "the intelligence community."

The CIA is divided into two main directorates. The spies, the clandestine officers, are in the directorate of operations (DO), and the analysts in the directorate of intelligence (DI). "Although Bart was an analyst," the CIA man said, "he was very heavily into anything to do with espionage, which may be why he was friendly with Bob Hanssen." There was another link that drew the two together: both were members of Opus Dei.

Borrasca held Hanssen in such high regard that he kept urging his boss in the Transfer Networks Group, Jack Duggan, to meet him. Finally the three went to lunch. Duggan, a six-foot, white-haired Boston Irishman, was unimpressed. He came back from lunch and remarked dryly: "Birds of a feather."

But it was in 1993 or 1994, the CIA man said, that Borrasca dropped a small bombshell. He reported to a CIA superior that "Hanssen said he was running an operation against President Clinton. They were using cameras, microphones, the whole bit." Borrasca implied that Hanssen was personally involved in the supposed FBI operation directed at the president, "because Borrasca said Hanssen talked about showing him an audio- or videotape from the surveillance."

The sensational allegation that the FBI was bugging and taping the Oval Office alarmed Borrasca's superior, who insisted he repeat it to Suzanne Spaulding, the CIA attorney assigned to the Nonproliferation Center. The CIA officer recalled Spaulding's alarm.

"She told Borrasca to cut off his relationship with Hanssen. 'Stop it! Stop it right away,' she said. 'This is totally outside your job responsibility.' Borrasca said, 'Please don't say anything about this that would ruin my relationship with Hanssen, it's very important to me.'"

Spaulding, a well-respected figure in the intelligence world, had served as a senior staff member of the Senate Intelligence Committee and was later executive director of National Commission on Terrorism, a panel established by Congress.

She recalled the meeting with Borrasca. "Bart spent a lot of time with the bureau, and I cautioned him we were not a law enforcement agency. I don't remember that story [about Clinton]." Asked whether a report that the FBI was bugging the president of the United States was something she would easily forget, she replied: "He maybe didn't say it that way. Or I didn't take it seriously."

Hanssen, however, told a similar story to his close friend Jack Hoschouer. The Clinton White House, he assured Hoschouer, was under electronic surveillance.

There is no doubt that Hanssen was interested in Clinton, whom he did not admire. More than twenty times, he searched the FBI's computerized case files for the names "Hillary Rodham Clinton," "Hillary," "Chelsea," and "Clinton."*

But several former high-level FBI counterintelligence officials said they doubted that the surveillance of Clinton had occurred. "We wouldn't wiretap the president," said one. "Maybe somebody working in the White House. Maybe [Borrasca] misunderstood what Hanssen said." If it was a criminal matter, he added, Hanssen, as an agent in the intelligence division, would not have been involved.

"We did have some trouble" with White House officials, the FBI man acknowledged. One senior presidential adviser had concealed certain questionable contacts, he said. And during the Clinton administration, the National Security Agency's handling of politically sensitive intercepts involving high administration officials led to a bureaucratic battle with the FBI. As one example, the FBI man said, the name of Secretary of Commerce Ron Brown, who died in a plane crash in the Balkans in 1996, turned up in a number of NSA electronic intercepts. "NSA was sending transcripts to the very people who were mentioned. Brown's name would appear in an NSA transcript and they would routinely send it to Brown at Commerce. The bureau and NSA fought over this practice."† But, he repeated, he knew of nothing to support Hanssen's story that President Clinton was a target of FBI electronic surveillance.

It was during this same period early in the Clinton administration that Bart Borrasca introduced James Bamford to Hanssen. Bamford was working at the time as an investigative reporter for ABC News, but he is best known as the author of two bestselling books about the NSA.‡

Bamford had known Borrasca, a native of Orchard Park, New York, a suburb of Buffalo, since childhood. "My family lived for a time out-

---

*Webster commission, p. 41n.
†Brown spent much of his time as commerce secretary battling probes into his private business dealings. At the time he perished in the plane crash, he was under investigation over charges that he received improper payments from former business partners. The inquiry was dropped after his death.
‡*The Puzzle Palace* (New York: Houghton Mifflin, 1982) and *Body of Secrets: Anatomy of the Ultra-Secret National Security Agency* (New York: Doubleday, 2001). Bamford declined to identify the person at the CIA who had introduced him to Hanssen. The fact that it was Borrasca was learned independently by the author.

side Buffalo, and I met him when I was about five years old. Years later, both of us ended up in Washington. I was working for ABC News. He was in the CIA. I would see him from time to time, and he said, 'I have this friend who works for the FBI.' "

A soft-spoken man with a gentle, low-key manner, Bamford was happy to add an FBI counterintelligence agent to his remarkable number of contacts in the spy world. Bamford, whose father served in the merchant marine, was a Navy veteran and had lived on a houseboat on the Potomac for a while. When Borrasca brought Hanssen around, Bamford was living on a sixty-foot cabin cruiser appropriately named the *Safehouse.*

Later Bamford took Bonnie and Bob Hanssen, and Adelia and Bart Borrasca, out on the *Safehouse* with its two-man crew. "On the cruise and other times, we talked about Felix Bloch, a common denominator." Bamford had dug up the Bloch story for ABC News in 1989 and Hanssen was a counterintelligence agent for the FBI, so they often traded views on the case. At the time, the great puzzle in the affair was how the KGB had known to warn Bloch that he was in danger. What Bamford did not then know, of course, was that Hanssen was a Russian spy, the very one who had tipped off the KGB to the fact that Bloch was under investigation by the FBI.

Borrasca piloted his own plane, a Beech Bonanza, and one time Bamford and Hanssen flew with the CIA man to a gun show in Virginia near Fredericksburg. Hanssen brought along his oldest son. "Hanssen seemed right at home at a gun show," Bamford said. "I did my best to hide my antigun feelings. He'd explain what various guns were. I'd ask what is this, what is that? He would tell me. He seemed to know his way around a gun show."

As the friendship between Hanssen and Bamford blossomed, they had lunch together several times, occasionally with Borrasca. Bamford remembered visiting Hanssen at his office at FBI headquarters. "He introduced me to a couple of agents who had worked on the Ames case." Later, when Hanssen was assigned to the State Department, he visited his office there. They would lunch in the State Department cafeteria or at a restaurant nearby.

Hanssen knew that Bamford, on a trip to Moscow, had interviewed Viktor Cherkashin for ABC in 1995. Hungry for details, Hanssen questioned Bamford closely about Cherkashin. What had he said? What was he like? Hanssen even asked to see a transcript of the interview. "I wouldn't show him the transcript," Bamford said, "because that was against network policy, but I did tell him what Cherkashin had told me."

There was good reason for Hanssen's curiosity. If Cherkashin ever defected to the West, he was in a position to destroy Hanssen, whose life was literally in the hands of the Russian spymaster he had never met. It was to Cherkashin that Hanssen had first volunteered his services back in 1985. And when Hanssen had learned in 1986 that KGB defector Victor Gundarev had been shown a photograph of Cherkashin, he fretted that perhaps the FBI was on to the fact that Cherkashin was handling a major source—himself.

Hanssen, Bamford recalled, was always working religion into their conversations. The FBI man would leave work sometimes to attend antiabortion rallies, Bamford said. When Hanssen finally persuaded him to attend an Opus Dei meeting, Bamford, as noted earlier, could hardly wait to escape.

In retrospect, Bamford thought Hanssen must have had his own reasons for wanting to be his friend. Bamford's contacts might somehow prove useful to Hanssen in his double life; the ABC man's access to Cherkashin was one obvious example.

But Hanssen also would sometimes urge Bamford to do news stories on certain topics. "Hanssen would say, 'You should do a story on the infiltration of U.S. society by the Russians.' Hanssen said Russian intelligence could come into the United States undercover as a TV crew to get secrets from a scientific lab, for example." "You ought to look into that," Hanssen would say.

In April 1996, when Bamford married his second wife, Bonnie and Bob Hanssen came to the wedding. In September 1996, Bart Borrasca died of cancer at the young age of forty-nine. Robert Hanssen and Jim Bamford were pallbearers at his funeral mass.

With their mutual friend gone, Bamford saw less of Hanssen after that. "The relationship tapered off after 1997," Bamford said. "We just kind of drifted away." Bamford left ABC in 1998 to write his new book on the NSA. Three years later, he was in for a shock. "On February 20, I turned on my computer and went to the *Washington Post* website. It said there had been a big spy arrest. I saw Hanssen's name and said to myself, 'Good, he's made a great spy arrest.' And then I saw he was the guy arrested.

"I couldn't believe what my eyes were seeing. It was surreal. For three years my job at ABC was finding spies. And here, all along, he was one."

20

"There Has to Be Another"

In February 1994, the FBI arrested Aldrich Ames, Moscow's mole inside the Central Intelligence Agency. He had betrayed dozens of CIA agents in the Soviet Union, causing ten to be executed.

Ames had begun his spying in 1985, while chief of the Soviet counterintelligence branch of the CIA. Although the agent losses were quickly detected by the agency, it took nine years for the CIA to conclude that Ames was the traitor.

Late in 1986, Gardner R. "Gus" Hathaway, then the CIA's counterintelligence chief, appointed Jeanne R. Vertefeuille to head a special task force to find the penetration who was destroying the agency's Soviet assets. A short, gray-haired, grandmotherly woman with glasses, Vertefeuille was so unlikely-looking a counterspy that she might have been chosen by central casting for dramatic irony. But Vertefeuille had an encyclopedic knowledge of KGB cases, and it was her mole hunt unit that eventually pinpointed Ames as the spy.

It was not the first time that the intelligence agencies were obliged to search for moles. There had been a long series of secret FBI studies, some run jointly with the CIA, aimed at discovering penetrations in the two agencies. In the 1970s, for example, the FBI had received information suggesting that an unidentified CIA officer had volunteered information to the Russians. The bureau gave that investigation the code name TRAPDOOR. The case was closed and reopened several times over the years but never resolved.

When it was learned in 1986 that Valery Martynov and Sergei Motorin, the two FBI assets in the Soviet embassy in Washington, had been arrested in Moscow and were to be executed, the bureau formed a six-person team to try to learn how the two had been detected. James T. "Tim" Caruso, a counterintelligence supervisor at FBI headquarters, was appointed head of the task force. A tall, intense New Yorker with thinning red hair, Caruso named the task force ANLACE, after a tapered medieval dagger. Counterintelligence is painstaking work; fourteen years were to go by before it was understood that the two Soviet assets had been betrayed by both Ames and Hanssen.

Not until April 1991 did Jeanne Vertefeuille's group and the FBI join forces to try to discover why the agency had lost its network inside the Soviet Union. Jim Holt, who had been Martynov's case agent, and Jim Milburn—the pair were known as "Jim squared" inside the FBI—both worked on the joint team.

One member of Vertefeuille's task force was Sandy Grimes, who had come over to the mole hunt team from the CIA's Soviet division. She had once carpooled with Ames and was struck by how his personality had changed when he came back from Rome sporting expensive Italian suits and capped teeth. It was Grimes who ultimately zeroed in on Ames by comparing the deposits in his bank account to the dates of his lunches with Sergei D. Chuvakhin, a Soviet diplomat in Washington. Ames had official approval to meet the Russian, whom he was supposedly cultivating for the CIA; but Grimes discovered that either on the same day as or the day after each lunch with Chuvakhin, Ames deposited large sums of money in his bank account. She realized then that the mole had to be Ames.

Grimes's persuasive analysis moved the drama toward its final act. In the spring of 1993, the joint FBI-CIA mole hunt team produced a secret report code-named PLAYACTOR/SKYLIGHT. It estimated that thirty CIA Soviet operations had been sabotaged between 1985 and 1986 and described the efforts of the KGB to deflect the search for a Soviet spy in the CIA. The mole, the report added, must have worked in the CIA's Soviet division in counterintelligence.

The report amounted to a virtual description of Ames, whose name was included on a list of forty people in an appendix. The joint mole hunt team actually took a vote on who the mole was. At the CIA, according to R. Patrick Watson, the FBI's number two counterintelligence official at the time, "People sat around a table and voted who was the most likely candidate. Ames got more votes than anyone else."

In May 1993, the FBI opened its case on Ames. It was directed by

Robert M. "Bear" Bryant, the head of the Washington field office, and John Lewis, his deputy. Lewis chose Special Agent Leslie G. Wiser, Jr., to run the squad that placed Ames under surveillance. Both the case and Ames were code-named NIGHTMOVER. Nine months later, the FBI operation culminated in Ames's arrest.

In the highest councils of the CIA and the FBI, however, the arrest of Aldrich Ames in 1994 brought only a fleeting sense of relief. As the damage assessment of the Ames case proceeded, it quickly became apparent that his actions—the betrayal of the CIA's entire Soviet network—could not explain all of the puzzles still haunting the two agencies. There were a number of anomalies, as such unexplained events are known in the intelligence world, but the one that still loomed largest was the Felix Bloch case.

Somehow the KGB had been able to warn Bloch that he was in danger. And Aldrich Ames had not known about the FBI investigation of Bloch. He did not have access to the case. In the late spring of 1989, when someone had alerted the KGB to the FBI surveillance of Bloch, Ames was winding up a three-year tour in Rome. He did not return to the United States until July 20, 1989, a full month after the telephoned warning to Bloch.

Details are the essence of counterintelligence, and spycatchers must pay close attention to details if they are to prevail. The troublesome facts of the Bloch case could not be ignored.

After the arrest of Aldrich Ames, Senator Dennis DeConcini, the Arizona Democrat who was chairman of the Senate Intelligence Committee, held closed hearings on the case and personally interviewed Ames at length in his jail cell. During the hearings, he said, the FBI made it clear "there has to be another."

There were other anomalies besides the Bloch case. "There were a lot of things that Ames did not know about," one CIA man recalled years later. "One of the things was the tunnel. And one or two other bureau technical collection systems that had clearly been compromised."

One of these was an ingenious FBI operation code-named SPIDER-WEB.* The bureau did not have the manpower to trail every Russian intelligence officer in Washington around the clock, but it devised a

---

*Both SPIDERWEB and MONOPOLY, the tunnel under the Soviet embassy, were betrayed to the KGB by Hanssen, but of course this was not yet known in 1994.

scheme to track them electronically. During the 1980s, the FBI managed to plant devices in the cars used by the Soviets.

The gadgets planted in the cars were neither microphones nor homing devices. SPIDERWEB was something new entirely. When a car driven by an intelligence officer passed certain fixed points around the Washington area, the bugs would transmit a signal, rather like the E-ZPass or similar devices that are common today and used by commuters to drive through tollbooths.

Sometime prior to 1991, SPIDERWEB crashed. "The devices stopped working," said one FBI man. "We knew the operation was compromised because the Russians took all their cars into the garage and tore them apart. The bureau's theory was they found one and pulled all the cars apart and found all of them. In reality, we now know they had been tipped off."

In the 1980s, Jeanne Vertefeuille had not initially been given the resources she needed to run the CIA's search for the penetration; as time passed, the agency seemed to have other priorities. It was Paul J. Redmond, a senior CIA counterintelligence officer, who was credited with reviving the mole hunt that in 1994 resulted in the FBI's successful surveillance and arrest of Aldrich Ames. Within weeks of Ames's capture, Redmond had set up a Special Investigations Unit (SIU) as a follow-on to the mole hunt unit.

In May 1994, President Clinton, reacting to the Ames case, reshuffled the government's counterintelligence agencies. It had, after all, taken nine years for the CIA to catch up with Ames. Among other changes, Clinton's Presidential Decision Directive 24, in an unprecedented action, required that an FBI agent head a Counterespionage Group (CEG) within the CIA's Counterintelligence Center. It was not a popular move within the CIA, which thought it could do its own spy-catching.

And so, against the background of the Bloch mystery and the technical losses, the FBI and the CIA secretly launched a new mole hunt in 1994. To run it, in compliance with the Clinton directive, the FBI selected Ed Curran.

Then fifty, Curran had the right experience and background to try to discover the penetration. Tall, slim, and athletic, the father of four, he looked the part of an FBI man. He was a New York boy, born and raised in the Irish ghetto at 125th Street and Riverside Drive. His family moved to New Jersey, and Curran worked his way through college with his first FBI job, as a clerk in the Newark office. He got his degree in 1968 and became an FBI agent the same year. The bureau sent him to New York in 1972, and he began a full-time career as a counterspy. In the Soviet section at headquarters in the mid-1980s, he had worked on some of the most important cases—Pelton, Howard, and Yurchenko.

In August 1994, Curran came from the FBI to CIA headquarters in Langley, Virginia, and took over the Counterespionage Group (CEG). In that post, he also supervised the SIU, which was first located on the fourth floor of the new CIA headquarters building and then hidden undercover behind an unmarked door on the first floor of the adjoining older headquarters building. About seven CIA and three or four FBI specialists staffed the SIU. So secret was the mole hunt unit that very few of the 125 employees of the CIA's Counterespionage Group knew what it was doing or even where it was. Only a handful of CIA people were allowed into the SIU office, although dozens of FBI agents had free access.

The agency and the bureau had historically mixed like oil and water. In part, this was due to their different missions. The CIA's task was to collect intelligence; the FBI was ultimately a law-enforcement agency with responsibility for investigating crimes and arresting people, including spies. Conflicts were bound to arise.

"Whenever the CIA has a problem they circle the wagons," said one FBI counterintelligence agent. "And it's not just CIA. NSA had polygraphed a guy ten times, and he failed each time. A code clerk, he'd had sex with transvestites in Asian alleyways; his regular sex partner was a German shepherd. To wait as long as they did before calling in the FBI was outrageous. We never made a case against the code clerk."

As the SIU began its work, there were inevitable clashes of cultures and personalities. Redmond, a Harvard man from Massachusetts who could swear in Serbo-Croatian—he had served in Yugoslavia for the CIA, as well as in the Near East—and Curran, the street-smart New Yorker, did not get along. But the bureaucratic infighting was largely the result of the presidential order putting the FBI onto the CIA's turf.

The new mole hunt team got off to a rocky start. Only Diana Worthen, a midwesterner who had been Ames's intelligence assistant in Mexico City, was a holdover from Jeanne Vertefeuille's task force. She had good qualifications for the job—it was Worthen who was the first to raise the alarm about her old boss when she saw his affluent lifestyle and large house in Arlington, Virginia. But Worthen stayed with the new mole hunt unit less than two years.

Laine Bannerman, whose father had headed CIA security a generation earlier, was the first, albeit short-lived, head of the SIU. "She was very friendly, a DO person from the Russian side," Curran said, "but very protective of the CIA. She thought she was in charge and would decide what the FBI got. We had to resolve that right away. We immediately had conflicts. She's trying to protect the agency's jewels, and we're trying to investigate."

Soon, Mary Sommer, a CIA reports officer from the Central Eurasian (CE) division, was brought in to run the unit, although Bannerman remained a member. With all the bureaucratic clashes going on, Curran imported Jim Milburn from the FBI to work with the SIU. Milburn was one of the two analysts who had prepared the study of moles in the FBI that Robert Hanssen had directed in 1988.

Essentially, the mole hunt never ended, because the search for penetrations carried out under the cryptonyms TRAPDOOR, ANLACE, PLAYACTOR/SKYLIGHT, and NIGHTMOVER had now been taken over by the SIU. "There was no crypt," said Curran. "We didn't want people to know what we were doing."

Although there were only ten CIA and FBI specialists who composed the SIU, fifty or sixty FBI agents were assigned to the mole hunt at Buzzard's Point, then the location of the bureau's Washington field office. "They had desks and badges at CIA and could come and go as they pleased," Curran said.

In addition to those assigned to the field office and at the CIA, other agents at FBI headquarters were detailed to the search for the mole. They were based, and kept their files, in the "Black Vault," an oddly shaped secure room on the fourth floor directly across from the Soviet section where Hanssen had worked.*

In the FBI's New York City field office, meanwhile, a separate mole hunt was in progress. Cases had gone bad, and the bureau had source information hinting that there was a penetration in the New York office. Louis Freeh, the new FBI director, became convinced that agents in the

---

*According to David Major, "The vault was the off-limits office where they were looking for a penetration. Officially we didn't know what they were doing, but everybody knew." Robert Hanssen certainly was aware of what was going on in the Black Vault, a few feet from his own desk.

Big Apple were not pursuing the problem vigorously enough. Freeh abruptly transferred the bureau's New York counterintelligence chief and named Thomas J. Pickard, an accountant by training, to replace him. Pickard in turn brought Tim Caruso to New York as his deputy.

Soon a more intense mole hunt was under way. Robert Wade was dispatched from headquarters to work the case "off campus," in FBI parlance, which meant he operated quietly out of an apartment on the west side of Manhattan, with a team of three or four agents from headquarters and a like number carefully chosen from the New York field office.

According to Pickard, the mole hunters drew up a list of everyone, including special agents, who worked in counterintelligence and had access to the cases that had gone south. "About two hundred employees, special agents, support employees, were looked at," he said. One FBI agent in particular became the chief suspect, but nothing was ever proven against him.

As in most mole hunts, other innocent agents were caught up in the net. A. Jackson Lowe, the assistant counterintelligence chief in New York, was summoned to the airport at one point to meet a group of senior FBI officials from headquarters. The spy in the New York field office, they informed him, had met his Russian contact somewhere away from the Soviet Mission to the United Nations. Grimly, they informed Lowe that the suspect walked with a limp. The counterspies from headquarters had asked Lowe to come to the airport because they knew that his partner walked with a limp, the result of a degenerative bone disease. A man with a limp! It began to sound like something out of an Alfred Hitchcock movie. Lowe didn't know whether to laugh or cry. His partner, he said, was the field office liaison with the KGB. "He goes into the mission every six weeks," Lowe told the officials. "He wouldn't need to meet anyone outside the mission."

There was never any case made against Lowe's partner, a loyal agent, and the suspicions were soon dropped. But the man had tears in his eyes when Lowe later told him what had happened. "How could they even *think* I would do something like that?" he asked.

The sweeping New York mole hunt that began in 1993 found no moles. But about two years later, with the help of a Russian defector, the FBI did uncover the agent, no longer in New York, who had been the penetration. The bureau gave him the code name BLINDSWITCH.

He was Earl Edwin Pitts, an FBI counterintelligence agent who spied for the KGB in New York for five years, between 1987 and 1992, and was paid $124,000. He turned over to the Soviets details of FBI counterintelligence operations against the Russians. The Russian defector, Rollan G. Dzheikiya, told the FBI he had introduced Pitts to the KGB at the New York Public Library.

Dzheikiya had been the Communist Party chief at the mission, an unpopular job, since staffers were required to kick back a huge chunk of their salaries to the Party. After the Soviet Union collapsed, Dzheikiya stayed in New York, trying to make it on his own. He hoped to remain in the United States and needed a green card to become a permanent resident. So he was amenable to helping the FBI when the bureau, aware of his circumstances, came knocking at his door.

The bureau ran a sting against Pitts, with agents posing as Russians. He was arrested in December 1996, pleaded guilty, and was sentenced to twenty-seven years. He told investigators he began spying because he had become enraged at the FBI, in part because of his low pay and the high cost of living in New York.

*　　*　　*

In Washington, the secret joint effort of the FBI and the CIA, if it did not pick up the scent of Robert Hanssen, at least played a role in the unmasking both of Earl Pitts and of another spy, this one in the CIA.

Harold James Nicholson, the highest-ranking CIA officer ever charged with espionage, was arrested at Dulles Airport in November 1996 as he prepared to fly to Switzerland to meet his Russian handler. When Nicholson fell under suspicion, some two hundred FBI agents had been assigned to the case. The investigation of the CIA officer was at the root of some of the static between the two agencies. "A lot of people in SIU thought Nicholson was not the guy, we were picking on him," said one FBI man. "That's where Curran and Redmond got at odds with each other."

Handsome, smooth, friendly, and articulate, Nicholson did seem an unlikely spy. He had been CIA station chief in Romania, then deputy chief of station in Malaysia. But divorced, with three children and short of money, he asked the SVR *resident* in Kuala Lumpur for $25,000, eventually collecting $300,000 from the Russians. In return he gave Moscow the names of about three hundred graduates of the Farm, the CIA training base near Williamsburg, Virginia, and hundreds of documents, including a summary of the debriefing of Aldrich Ames after Ames had pleaded guilty to espionage. Nicholson, who liked to call himself Batman, agreed to cooperate with the government and was sentenced to twenty-three years in prison.

While the mole hunters were wrapping up these high-profile spy cases, the CIA and the FBI were slowly working their way through a bureaucratic maze known inside the CIA as "the A-to-Z list." The list was a direct fallout from the Ames case. The Counterespionage Group and CIA's Office of Security (OS) were reviewing a huge backlog of polygraph tests to make sure another mole was not lurking somewhere inside Langley. It was a tedious, time-consuming job.

"The A-to-Z list had about three hundred people who had SPRs," said one CIA official. "Significant Physiological Responses on the polygraph. Some of those on the list had nothing to do with CI. Some had contacts with foreign nationals. Several dozen were referred to the bureau, as required by law. The vast majority were sorted out by the Office of Security."

"Gradually, over several years we cleared most of it up," another CIA man said. There were two parallel efforts going on, he explained. "You had OS and the Counterespionage Group and the bureau working on the A-to-Z list. Simultaneously, SIU and the bureau were working on the new search for penetrations.

"There were people on the A-to-Z list whose careers were affected. Some people didn't get to go overseas. The agency's polygraphers got very tough because they had been criticized for having passed Ames. In the hysterical atmosphere after Ames, there were agency people referred to the bureau. And the bureau takes their time, but they were overwhelmed with the numbers." The job of sifting through the three hundred names on the CIA list took years. Even after Hanssen's arrest in 2001, several of the A-to-Z cases were still unresolved.

The same directive issued by President Clinton that established the Counterespionage Group also created a government-wide interagency panel to coordinate counterintelligence in the light of the Ames debacle. The National Counterintelligence Center, or NACIC, was housed at CIA headquarters, and its chief was Michael J. Waguespack, a senior FBI counterspy.

Robert Hanssen was particularly interested in the new center, perhaps because it would have afforded him access to counterintelligence information from all agencies of the government across the board, as well as information about counterintelligence activities overseas. Because NACIC was only a research and coordinating body, FBI agents involved in operational activities were not stampeding to join the new center. But Hanssen pressed Waguespack to get him transferred into NACIC.

"You'll have to take a polygraph," Hanssen was cautioned.

Hanssen had never had to take a lie detector test during his entire career in the FBI. No thanks, he replied; he had been reflecting further about the transfer and thought he might just as well remain at headquarters.

21

Mole Wars

Pete O'Donnell thought there was something odd about the Pitts case. O'Donnell was a veteran FBI counterspy who had worked for a dozen years in New York City on Squad 30, the unit that watched the KGB.

Earl Edwin Pitts, the FBI counterintelligence agent, had been arrested as a Russian spy in 1996. At headquarters, Special Agent Thomas K. Kimmel, Jr., was assigned to direct the damage assessment. Kimmel had little background in foreign counterintelligence, so he called in O'Donnell to help him.

At fifty-five, Kimmel was a tall, wiry man, with blond hair and blue eyes, handsome enough to be cast as the older cowhand in a Hollywood western. His consuming preoccupation, aside from his work, was to try to remove the stain on the family name. His grandfather was Rear Admiral Husband E. Kimmel, who with Army Lieutenant General Walter Short was officially blamed for the disaster when the Japanese attacked Pearl Harbor.

"I am the sixth graduate of the naval academy in my family," he said in an interview in the living room of his home in northern Virginia, where he sat near an oil portrait of his grandfather.*

In September 1997, the damage assessment team began work. Kimmel headed a group of four agents and four analysts. Their mission was

---

*Kimmel and his family have tried for years to clear the admiral's name and restore his rank, which reverted to two stars when he was relieved of his command in December 1941 after Pearl Harbor. In 2000, Congress passed a law requesting the president to nominate both Kimmel and Short to higher ranks.

to discover exactly what secrets Pitts had sold to the KGB, what programs might have been compromised, and how extensive the damage was to U.S. security.

As O'Donnell began examining the documents in the case, including the transcripts of the extensive FBI debriefings of the spy, it struck him that the way the Russians had run Pitts was peculiar. The KGB was not exploiting him. They were not asking for a lot of material or for specific documents. To O'Donnell, one obvious reason might be that the Russians had another source inside the FBI. If the KGB was already getting a plentiful supply of secrets from a mole in the bureau, it might explain its laid-back handling of Earl Pitts.

O'Donnell shared his suspicions with Kimmel, who agreed and demanded to see sensitive counterintelligence files that he hoped would support their theory. Kimmel soon found himself about as popular inside headquarters as the proverbial skunk at a garden party. In part, the root of the trouble was cultural.

Division 5, the intelligence division, by then renamed the National Security Division, was a cadre of specialists in counterintelligence. The spycatchers believed they knew their business, and although O'Donnell was an insider, Kimmel was not. At the time he was assigned to the Pitts damage assessment, Kimmel was working on the bureau's inspection staff, never an admired group to begin with.

From the start, there was friction between Kimmel and the managers of the intelligence division, including John Lewis, who had taken over as the assistant director in charge in February 1997, and Ed Curran, then the chief of the Russian section.

Lewis was a husky former captain in the Marines who had served in Vietnam, as well as on the staff of the National Security Council and in the CIA. Although soft-spoken, he left no doubt about who was in charge; he allowed Kimmel to have access to some files, but kept him on a tight leash.

To Lewis, it appeared that Kimmel was trying to expand his damage assessment in the Pitts case into a mole hunt. But that was not his brief; the bureau and the CIA already had the SIU and dozens of people trying to find the penetration. Kimmel, Lewis made clear, was to stick to his task.

Kimmel was asking to see case files, including raw files, that had nothing to do with Pitts. That raised Lewis's hackles. He did not want Kimmel and his team combing through the files of unresolved cases and learning the names of suspects. Some of the files, Lewis said, identified bureau agents who had been scrutinized in the New York mole hunt before Pitts was caught.

"Others related to sensitive source reporting from both the bureau and the agency on walk-ins around the world, [SVR] hallway gossip about penetrations. We had a walk-in to the Soviet embassy in Portugal where the guy flashed CIA creds. He, Kimmel, wanted everything in the world we had on penetrations to see if it in some way related to Pitts. But his job was to see what Pitts had compromised.

"We were not about to allow him to be privy to all of those files. My job as assistant director was to protect sources and methods. I was not about to open them up to someone who had no sensitivity nor complete understanding of highly classified information relating to penetration of the U.S. government. I was not going to open up our entire innermost secrets to someone who had never even worked this stuff." Kimmel, Lewis added, was "a good investigator" but "although well intentioned, he was very difficult to work with. He had confrontations with everyone."

Lewis did not disagree with Kimmel's theory that the KGB's handling of Pitts might suggest the existence of another penetration. "The fact that the Russians had not tasked Pitts—we knew that. It was common sense there might be somebody else."

Kimmel, for his part, strongly defended his study of the Pitts case. "My hypothesis was the greatest damage Pitts was doing was making it more complicated for FBI counterintelligence teams to uncover what turned out to be Ames. The Soviets could play one off against the other and confuse the trail. The great unknown was, are there more than Pitts?

"It was inconceivable to me that we are saying that the KGB's number one job is to penetrate the FBI and they have Pitts as a source and are not exploiting him to a greater degree. That doesn't make any sense to me. If the shoe was on the other foot and we had only one Soviet source, we would be falling all over ourselves to exploit every drop of blood from the guy."

On February 12, 1999, Kimmel met in a seventh-floor conference room at FBI headquarters with Louis Freeh, the director; Neil J. Gallagher, who had become the division chief some months after Lewis retired; and other FBI officials. Freeh asked Kimmel whether he thought there were other moles in the FBI, but Kimmel said he had not had access to enough information to form a judgment.

Freeh ordered Kimmel to investigate further and authorized him to see more files. But Kimmel was not shown all that he wanted to see because counterintelligence officials continued to restrict his access to sensitive cases.

The following month, Kimmel met with Freeh again. "I did not say definitely that I thought there was a mole in the FBI," Kimmel said. "But it was perfectly obvious I was concerned there was a mole in the FBI."

Looking back on these events, Kimmel said that when he prepared his study he was unaware that when the FBI interviewed Pitts in prison in June 1997, the convicted spy was asked whether he knew of any other moles inside the bureau. Pitts said he did not, but he also said he suspected Robert Hanssen because Hanssen had broken into the computer of another counterintelligence official. Bureau officials assumed this was a reference to the time in 1993 when Hanssen had hacked into Ray Mislock's computer. Since they already knew about that incident, and Hanssen had come forward and claimed to Mislock that he was simply trying to prove that the FBI computer network was vulnerable, the FBI discounted what Pitts said.

"The debriefings of Pitts are a foot high," Kimmel said. "If Hanssen's name is in any of that I missed it. All the debriefings were recorded. I don't know if it made it to the transcript. I read every word of every transcript and don't recall seeing Hanssen's name. That is not to say I couldn't have missed it. If I missed it, then shame on me. And in that case, everyone else on my team missed it, too."

Kimmel submitted his 250-page report in March 1999. He said that Robert Bryant, then FBI deputy director, had ordered him to confine his assessment to the Pitts case. The report went to the CIA and other intelligence agencies, and to the Senate intelligence committee. Kimmel prepared a shorter, 150-page version for internal use by the FBI. "Neither has anything about other penetrations," he said.

But in a separate short memo in April, Kimmel speculated that the bureau might harbor a mole. In May, the National Security Division issued a twenty-eight-page analysis of Kimmel's memo, concluding that he had not produced any real evidence to support his theory. Nevertheless, when news reports of Kimmel's study and his turf struggles with the intelligence division were published in *The New York Times* after Hanssen's arrest, it was one more blow to the bureau, already battered by a series of embarrassing mishaps in unrelated cases and by the fact that Hanssen had gone undetected for more than two decades.

The disclosures left the appearance that the bureau had fumbled the chance to catch a mole in its ranks two years earlier. FBI officials in turn argued that Kimmel had never produced any solid evidence, only "hunches" that proved correct but were not supported by hard facts. In effect, the FBI argued that Kimmel had simply lucked out.

"He was right," Neil Gallagher said. "But for the wrong reasons."

A happier moment … Robert Hanssen, at age seven in 1951, proudly holds up his catch with his father, Howard, a Chicago police officer. But the two already had a deeply troubled relationship.

"Science is the light of life...." Hanssen's future technical prowess was forecast by the motto he chose for his high school yearbook and his membership in the ham radio club.

Hanssen's high school classmate Jack Hoschouer became his lifelong friend.

Chicago, August 1968: A smiling Hanssen, twenty-four, and his bride, Bonnie Wauck, twenty-one. Standing behind them are his parents, Howard and Vivian Hanssen. Seated at left is Howard's mother, Louise.

October 1970: After dropping out of dental school, Hanssen switched to accounting at Northwestern University. Here, while a student, he poses with Bonnie, right, and her sister, Jeanne, in front of the Wauck family home in Park Ridge, a Chicago suburb.

Bob and Bonnie at a Wisconsin park in the early 1970s. In 1972, after working briefly as an accountant, Hanssen was hired as a police officer in Chicago and assigned to investigate corruption on the force. Four years later, he joined the FBI.

A pudgy Hanssen, now a special agent at FBI headquarters in Washington, D.C., relaxes on the deck of his Vienna, Virginia, home in the early 1980s. He had already begun his career as a Russian spy and betrayed vital secrets to Moscow.

The spymaster. Viktor Cherkashin, the KGB counterintelligence chief in Washington, was contacted by Hanssen in an unsigned letter when the FBI agent resumed spying in 1985. Cherkashin told the author that the KGB never learned Hanssen's identity.

After a two-year tour in New York City, where Hanssen wiretapped Soviet installations, the couple returned to Washington in 1987 and bought this house on Talisman Drive in Vienna.

Jack Hoschouer. He was unaware that Hanssen, his best friend, had offered him up to the KGB as a possible target for recruitment. But the Russians never approached him.

Bob and Bonnie Hanssen in Vienna, Virginia, in the late 1980s. It was his most active time as a Soviet spy.

Hanssen would leave a piece of white tape on this signpost near his home to signal the KGB that he had left secret documents at dead drop ELLIS, a hiding place under a footbridge in the park.

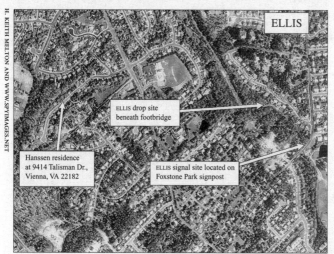

ELLIS

ELLIS drop site
beneath footbridge

Hanssen residence
at 9414 Talisman Dr.,
Vienna, VA 22182

ELLIS signal site located on
Foxstone Park signpost

A satellite view of dead drop ELLIS in Foxstone Park, the signal site, and the Hanssen house on Talisman Drive.

Dead drop LEWIS, used by Hanssen and the KGB to exchange documents and money, was beneath the wooden stage in this outdoor amphitheater in Arlington, Virginia.

The electric utility pole used as the signal site for dead drop LEWIS. Hanssen failed to pick up the last $50,000 the Russians left for him at LEWIS after rain washed the tape off the pole. The FBI recovered the money.

In 1989, Hanssen tipped off the KGB to one of the FBI's biggest secrets—the eavesdropping tunnel it had dug under the new Soviet embassy in Washington. The FBI wondered why the multimillion-dollar project produced so little of value.

© DAVID WISE

CYNTHIA KWITCHOFF/CI CENTRE

"He knew all the secrets...." David Major, a former senior counterintelligence agent who worked with Hanssen, said the FBI spy's job gave him access to the bureau's most sensitive operations.

Paul Moore, a former FBI analyst, befriended Hanssen.

CYNTHIA KWITCHOFF/CI CENTRE

© DAVID WISE

General Dimitri Fedorovich Polyakov, right, code name TOPHAT, in a top hat. Photo was taken aboard the *Queen Elizabeth* in 1962 as Polyakov and two unidentified Soviet companions were returning to Moscow. One of the most valuable FBI and CIA sources of the Cold War, Polyakov was betrayed first by Robert Hanssen, then by CIA turncoat Aldrich H. Ames, and later executed.

Lieutenant Colonel Valery Martynov of the KGB was secretly working for the FBI until Hanssen betrayed him. Lured back to Moscow, Martynov was executed.

Boris Yuzhin, a KGB officer secretly spying for the FBI, was luckier. Although imprisoned after Hanssen betrayed him, he was pardoned, and now lives in California.

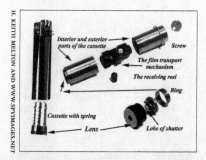

H. KEITH MELTON AND WWW.SPYIMAGES.NET

Interior and exterior parts of the cassette — Screw

The film transport mechanism

The receiving reel

Ring

Cassette with spring

Lens — Lobe of shutter

Major Sergei Motorin of the KGB, another FBI asset in Washington, was also betrayed by Hanssen. When he returned home, he, too, was executed.

Yuzhin fell under suspicion in the KGB when he lost this tiny camera, disguised as a cigarette lighter, which had been given to him by the CIA.

SEX, LIES, VIDEOTAPE, AND CASH

Hanssen and his friend Jack Hoschouer, left, in a rare photo together. Hanssen sent him nude pictures of Bonnie when Hoschouer served in the Army in Vietnam; later Hanssen insisted his friend watch him having sex with Bonnie, at first through a window, and then on closed-circuit television through a video camera Hanssen had hidden in the bedroom of his house.

FBI agent Mark Wauck, Bonnie Hanssen's brother, told an FBI supervisor in Chicago that a large amount of unexplained cash had been seen on Hanssen's dresser. This information was not relayed to FBI headquarters in Washington.

Bob and Bonnie Hanssen on the wedding day of their daughter Jane, 1995.

The stripper. Hanssen, infatuated with Priscilla Sue Galey, whom he had met in a Washington strip club, took her on a trip to Hong Kong and gave her expensive jewelry.

"You bought me a Mercedes!" Galey could not believe her good fortune when Hanssen gave her a silver Mercedes, for which he paid $10,500.

In 1993, Hanssen physically attacked Kimberly Lichtenberg, who worked in the headquarters unit he supervised. He received a mild reprimand, but there was no internal investigation of the agent who was arrested eight years later as the most damaging spy in the history of the FBI.

Hanssen in 1993 at a farewell party in Washington for an FBI colleague. At the time this photograph was taken, he had temporarily broken off contact with Moscow following the collapse of the Soviet Union.

Bonnie Hanssen in 1995. She told investigators she knew nothing of her husband's spying after 1980. When Hanssen was arrested, she cooperated with the FBI and, as a result, received a share of his pension.

When Tom Burns, who had been Hanssen's boss at the FBI, retired in 1995, Hanssen collected the money for his farewell dinner.

*You are cordially invited to
a farewell dinner
in honor of*

Thomas E. Burns, Jr.

on his retirement from

The Federal Bureau of Investigation

December 1, 1995

*Abrams/Chaffee Room, Ft. Myer Officers' Club
Arlington, Virginia*

Cocktails 6:00 p.m.   *$28 per person*
Dinner 7:00 pm   *Cash bar*

*Make checks payable to: Robert Hanssen
9414 Talisman Drive, Vienna, Virginia 22182
(202 647-5576)*

RSVP by November 22, 1995

Hanssen resumed spying for Russia in 1999 while assigned by the FBI to the State Department's Office of Foreign Missions. In this group photo of OFM, Hanssen, center, towers over a bespectacled Tom Burns, directly in front of him. Next to Burns, with beard and mustache, is Ron Mlotek, OFM's chief legal counsel, who formed a close friendship with the FBI agent.

Robert P. Hanssen
Senior Policy Advisor
Office of Foreign Missions

U.S. Department of State   202-647-5576 TEL
Washington, DC 20520   202-736-4391 FAX

Hanssen's State Department business card.

State Department official Felix Bloch, enjoying a Fourth of July garden party at the U.S. embassy in Vienna, was under surveillance as a suspected Soviet spy when Hanssen tipped off the KGB, which in turn warned Bloch he was in danger. The Bloch case triggered a new mole hunt that eventually led to Hanssen's downfall.

KGB illegal Reino Gikman, as "Pierre Bart," met with Bloch in Paris and later warned him of "a contagious disease," cryptic language that meant the FBI was investigating.

The FBI spy seems unworried at a family picnic in the late 1990s.

FBI agent Thomas K. Kimmel, Jr., thought there might be a mole in the FBI but lacked proof. The portrait in the background is of his grandfather Admiral Husband E. Kimmel, who the FBI man maintains was wrongly blamed for Pearl Harbor.

November 2000: A gloomy Hanssen at a family Thanksgiving gathering in Chicago. He was unaware that three weeks earlier the FBI had spirited a KGB file out of Moscow that conclusively pointed to him as the mole.

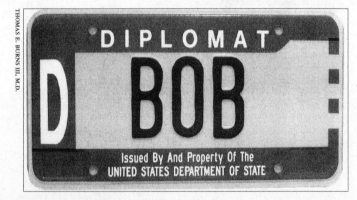

Hanssen was to be presented with this souvenir diplomatic license plate when he left the State Department in January 2001. But the gift was not ready at his going-away party and Hanssen never received it; he was arrested five weeks later.

A plastic bag that Hanssen had used to wrap documents he passed to the Russians was recovered by the FBI in the KGB file the bureau obtained from a former Russian spy. Two of Hanssen's fingerprints were identified on the bag, the final evidence the FBI needed to arrest him.

The FBI retrieved the $50,000 in hundred-dollar bills that the Russians had left for Hanssen at dead drop LEWIS before his arrest. The FBI man received more than $600,000 in cash and diamonds during twenty-two years as a Russian spy.

The last dead drop. Hanssen hid seven documents in dead drop ELLIS, under this footbridge in Foxstone Park, on the afternoon of February 18, 2001. Four minutes later, as he emerged from the woods, he was arrested.

AFTERMATH

For FBI director Louis J. Freeh, the Hanssen case was one of a series of debacles that afflicted the bureau. Less than three months after Hanssen's arrest, Freeh announced he was leaving the FBI before the end of his ten-year term.

Federal agents were taking no chances when Hanssen was brought into court in May 2001.

Celebrated Washington defense attorney Plato Cacheris, who represented Hanssen, worked out a plea bargain with prosecutors that avoided the death penalty.

Former FBI and CIA director William H. Webster headed the commission appointed after Hanssen's arrest that strongly criticized the FBI for "pervasive inattention to security."

U.S. Department of Justice

A Review of FBI Security Programs

Commission for Review of FBI Security Programs
March 2002

The Webster commission report called the Hanssen case "possibly the worst intelligence disaster in U.S. history."

Dr. David L. Charney, the psychiatrist who evaluated Hanssen extensively in prison, said a prime motive for his spying was to preserve his image in Bonnie's eyes as a good provider.

In May 1995, Robert Hanssen was dispatched to the State Department for what turned out to be six years as the FBI's senior represen-
tive to the Office of Foreign Missions. He settled into Room 2510C on
the second floor of the main State Department building.

Tom Burns was glad to see his old friend again. Burns, still with the
FBI, was the deputy assistant secretary of state for OFM. He had been
Hanssen's boss in the FBI's Soviet analytical unit more than a decade
earlier. Both had six children and were members of the same parish, St.
Catherine of Siena. Hanssen advertised his religion, Burns remem-
bered. At the State Department, "He had a crucifix and a picture of the
Blessed Mother on the wall of his office."

In his State Department post, Hanssen, acting for the FBI, monitored travel by foreign diplomats and plans by foreign countries to acquire additional property or build new embassies. Russian diplomats
and those from certain other countries were subject to restrictions on
travel beyond twenty-five miles from Washington.*

"If a travel request came in," Burns said, "Hanssen would clear it
with the Soviet section of the bureau. The same request would go via
OFM to the Defense Department, and they would also reply. Then we
would come back with an answer.

"Hanssen at the State Department was also on an interagency counterintelligence group. The interagency group consulted by phone and
fax, and sometimes there were meetings, usually at State."

Occasionally Burns would lunch with Hanssen. "He was frugal
with lunch," Burns recalled. "We would eat in the State Department
cafeteria. His choice for lunch would be a burger or a slice of pizza.
There was a whole array of stuff at the steam table, but he never chose
anything. He never spent a lot of money."

It was at State that Hanssen forged his friendship with Ron Mlotek,
the chief legal counsel at OFM. In part, that friendship flourished because of their mutual interest in religion. The two became close enough

---

*In 2001, nine countries were required to seek some type of travel approval. Three
countries, Russia, China, and Vietnam, had to file a request with OFM for their
diplomats to travel beyond twenty-five miles from the capital, but were then free to
go after forty-eight hours unless turned down. Six other countries, Cuba, Iran, Iraq,
Libya, North Korea, and Sudan, had to receive advance approval from OFM to travel
beyond the twenty-five-mile limit. Ukraine and the other former Soviet republics,
and the once-Communist countries of Eastern Europe, were no longer under any
travel restrictions.

22

Recontact

The State Department's Office of Foreign Missions was created by Congress in 1982 in the wake of the controversy surrounding the hilltop location of the Soviet embassy in Washington and the bugging of the American embassy in Moscow. It was time, Congress decided, to establish a watchdog over foreign embassies in Washington, one that could not only control where they were built but could also encourage reciprocity in how the Soviets and other nations treated U.S. missions in their countries.

It was not accidental that the first head of OFM, with the rank of ambassador, was James E. Nolan, Jr., who had been chief of the Soviet section in the FBI and then moved up to the number two counterintelligence position in the bureau. With Nolan in place, the Soviet diplomats were required to book all travel through OFM.

"I can't say they're overjoyed," Nolan said at the time. "They can't even buy a shuttle ticket to New York at the airport now. They can only go on with a prepaid ticket."

Under the law, OFM could require the Soviets to call the State Department if they needed a repairman at the embassy. This, of course, opened up all sorts of possibilities for U.S. intelligence agencies. Recalling the Watergate break-in, one insider said: "Nixon's plumbers had worked for the CIA. Now if you work for CIA, you may have to be a plumber."*

---

*The same rules prevailed in Moscow, where for years American officials had to call the foreign ministry for airline tickets, housekeepers, television repairs, and other services. The office they called was really part of the KGB.

that Mlotek invited Hanssen to the bar mitzvah of his son, Noah, in 1999. It was to take place at the Georgetown Synagogue, which Mlotek attended, as did Senator Joseph I. Lieberman, Al Gore's running mate in 2000.

The lights in the synagogue were on a timer, since Orthodox Jews are forbidden to touch anything electric on the Sabbath. On the appointed day, the timer failed and the lights went out. *Oh no,* Mlotek thought, *my son will have to stumble through his bar mitzvah in the dark.*

"Fortunately," Mlotek said, "Hanssen was one of the first guests to show up and quickly figured out how to fix the timer." He was, said Mlotek, the "shabbas goy," or Sabbath gentile.*

Some months later, Hanssen attended the wedding ceremony for Mlotek's second marriage. Noah had planned to videotape the wedding, but he got caught up helping out and talking to the guests, and Hanssen stepped in. Mlotek may have the only wedding video of a State Department official taken by a Russian spy. Hanssen, of course, is nowhere in it; he was behind the camera.

"In my family, we called him 'Machine Gun Bob,' because he had one," Mlotek said. "In his car trunk, with four hundred rounds of ammunition." Mlotek discovered this one day when Hanssen offered to drive him to the FBI. Mlotek was puzzled when Hanssen did not go down to the State Department garage to get his car. "I thought he had a parking permit for the basement. But we went across the street to the parking lot off Twenty-third Street in the old OSS buildings on Navy Hill."

"Bob, why do you park across the street?" Mlotek asked.

"I can't park in the basement because you have to leave the key in the car," Hanssen replied.

"Why can't you leave the key?"

Mlotek was in for a surprise. "He opened the trunk and there was this armory. The machine gun was a bureau gun he had checked out, and a nine-millimeter pistol. The ammunition was in waterproof bags. He said, 'I could drive my car into the Potomac River and come out shooting.' "

---

*The term originated in an earlier era, before there were electric timers, when Orthodox congregations had to make sure that a gentile, perhaps a retainer engaged for that purpose, or a janitor, was available to turn on the lights.

When Mlotek pressed Hanssen on why he drove around with a machine gun in his trunk, "He said his commute took him past the CIA, on Route 123. The day that Kansi killed the people there, he had driven by eight minutes earlier.* It haunted him. Ever since that day he felt this sense of guilt and powerlessness. This had such a profound effect he said he would get weapons and keep them with him. That maybe he could prevent it from happening again.

"A favorite quote of his, of both of us, was that civilizations collapse when good men do nothing."†

Sometimes, Hanssen talked to Mlotek about the clout his father enjoyed as a Chicago cop. "He told me about all the perks his father had. For example, if they were going to a movie and it was sold out, his father could get him in, often without having to pay. In high school, he took his prom date to a fancy Chicago restaurant and the maître d' recognized him as Captain Hanssen's son." (In fact, Howard Hanssen never rose above the rank of lieutenant.)

"Bob admired Mayor Daley. 'This is a guy who knew how to run things,' Bob would say. Bob was a neoconservative and a Republican. He was a great fan of Ronald Reagan, as I am. He abhorred Bill Clinton, whom he called the scum of the earth and someone corrupting the entire nation. He thought counterintelligence and counterterrorism had been degraded under Clinton, and he felt the bureau's counterintelligence people were incompetents."

Hanssen shared his conservative political views with Mlotek. He made no secret of his antipathy toward gays, for example. "Hanssen despised homosexuality and homosexuals in general," Mlotek recalled. "He was opposed to homosexuals in government not because they were security risks susceptible to blackmail, which is no longer true if they are out of the closet, but because of his belief that homosexuality was a great moral perversion, a gross abnormality."

---

*In January 1993, Mir Aimal Kansi, a twenty-eight-year-old Pakistani, walked along a line of cars waiting to turn left into the CIA headquarters and systematically gunned down the occupants with an AK-47 assault weapon, killing two CIA employees and wounding two other CIA workers and an agency contractor. Kansi was arrested by the FBI in Pakistan in 1997, brought to the United States, tried and convicted of murder in a Virginia court, and in January 1998 sentenced to death.

†The familiar quotation "The only thing necessary for the triumph of evil is for good men to do nothing," often attributed to Edmund Burke, the eighteenth-century British statesman, is probably a version of a similar idea expressed in his *Thoughts on the Cause of the Present Discontents* (1770).

Mlotek's duties at the State Department brought him into frequent contact with intelligence officials. Since Hanssen was an FBI counter-intelligence agent, they would often discuss espionage. "Driving through Georgetown, he showed me some famous espionage sites. He pointed out signal sites, such as the mailbox on which Aldrich Ames placed a chalk mark. He knew an enormous amount about cryptography and one-time pads. We talked about the great game between the United States and the Russians and how it was affected by the demise of the Soviet Union. He said that nothing had changed—the Communists were still there, they were regrouping and as active as ever. The KGB had only changed its name.

"His view was that Communism was the work of Satan. He said that all the time. He was a great expert on Communism. He had read Marx and many books on Marxist philosophy. The great fallacy of Communism, he said, was that they believed that man is perfectible by his own effort. He said that man can't be perfectible by his own effort because he is inherently sinful."

Despite his serious, somber manner in the FBI, Hanssen had yet another side that few colleagues ever saw. "He had a great sense of humor, a British sense of humor," Mlotek said. "It was subtle, refined humor. He was a huge aficionado of Monty Python, *Fawlty Towers,* and John Cleese. He had Monty Python tapes in his car and he knew them by heart."

*   *   *

In 1997, Hanssen, while still working at the State Department, requested access to the FBInet, the bureau's internal computer network. He could not gain entry to the FBI network on the State Department computers.

Nothing happened with Hanssen's request, so he turned to his friend Jim Ohlson for help. As Hanssen knew, Ohlson had just been appointed chief of FBI security. To put Hanssen on the FBInet would require a dedicated line linking the FBI and the State Department, with encryption at both ends. Bureaucracy being what it is, installing the special line would have taken some time to arrange. Ohlson called the computer support staff for the National Security Division and asked them to expedite matters. Hanssen got his dedicated computer and the access he wanted to the FBI network.

But about a month later, Hanssen's computer crashed and failed to boot up. He asked for an FBI technician to fix it, but again nothing happened. Once more, he turned to Ohlson for help.

Ohlson obliged. He again called the computer staff and told them to fix Hanssen's problem. Although Ohlson was not in charge of the computer staff, he was senior enough that they sent a technician who swapped out Hanssen's hard drive for one that worked. The failed hard drive was routinely sent to CART, the FBI's Computer Analysis Response Team at Quantico, which analyzes computer problems.

To their surprise, the CART techies found a password breaker on Hanssen's hard drive. A password breaker is a program that can be downloaded from the Internet and is used by hackers to attack webpages or other data that are password-protected. What was Hanssen doing with a password breaker?

As director of security, Ohlson called Hanssen in and demanded an explanation. He had gone to bat for his friend and was embarrassed by what had happened. And there were echoes of the episode four years earlier when Hanssen had broken into Ray Mislock's computer at headquarters.

Hanssen explained that he was trying to connect a color printer to his dedicated computer and could not, because he needed an administrative password to get into the control panel of the Windows operating system to make the necessary changes. FBI computers, however, are not designed to be fiddled with. The FBI does not want users changing the settings, so administrative passwords are put in to block people from making changes. Most of the printers at the bureau are black and white. To connect to a color printer meant changing the computer's internal settings. Hanssen said he had used the breaker to try to circumvent the password. Ohlson accepted this as a plausible enough explanation, but he warned Hanssen not to do it again. "A password breaker on your hard disk does not look good," he cautioned his friend.

After Hanssen's arrest, Ohlson remembered all this, which now took on a possibly more ominous meaning. For all he knew, Hanssen might have used the password breaker to access all sorts of bureau programs and files. Ohlson contacted his former office of security and reported the incident.*

---

*When FBInet began in the early 1990s, all the security protections were not in place. "Later on," Ohlson said, "the system had a server and agents were instructed to write sensitive documents to a protected segment of the server. With the password breaker he could get into the protected part."

By the summer of 1997, Hanssen was restive. Monitoring travel arrangements for foreign diplomats was dull work. At OFM, James Bond would have died of boredom. Hanssen had been stuck at the State Department for more than two years now, and there seemed no end to the dreary assignment.

Moreover, Hanssen needed money again; at least that was the explanation he offered to government debriefers after his arrest. At the time he resumed spying, he said, he was "running up credit card debt," had refinanced his house twice, and his mortgage payments had grown so steep that he "was losing money every month and the debt was growing." He claimed to have set a "financial goal" for himself of obtaining $100,000 from the Russians to pay down his debt.* It was time to get into the phone booth, change costume, and—faster than a speeding bullet—become Ramon Garcia.

On July 25, he went into the FBI's computers, typed in his user ID and password, and accessed the bureau's secret and highly sensitive case files. Hanssen was now logged into the FBI's Automated Case Support System (ACS), a collection of computerized databases of investigative files and their indexes. ACS had only existed for two years. Hanssen went immediately to the largest database in the system, known as the Electronic Case File. This is truly the bureau's inner sanctum, because it contains electronic messages and other documents from current, ongoing FBI investigations and indexes. It amounts to the FBI's own private Internet.

On this day, Hanssen typed in his own name. He was looking to see whether he was the subject of an FBI investigation. He found nothing. But the following year, on March 20, he went back into the computer and tried to find a reference to himself under DEAD DROP AND KGB. Over the next nine months, Hanssen searched eight times for various keywords. Among the different words he searched for were DEAD DROP AND RUSSIA, 9414 TALISMAN, and ROBERT P. HANSSEN.

In April 1999, he was at it again, entering his name and address, and even searching for WHITECEDAR COURT, where he had not lived since 1985, the first year he contacted the KGB. In August, he searched for FOXSTONE, the park that was the site of dead drop ELLIS. He was back into the ACS files nine more times that year, entering keywords that might point to him.

---

*Webster commission, p. 12.

By the fall of 1999, Hanssen, after eight years, was ready to resume his career as a Russian spy. Emboldened at having found nothing worrisome in the FBI computer files, he once more contacted the KGB—which had become the SVR after the fall of the Soviet Union. He proposed an exchange in Foxstone Park in mid-November.

The evidence suggests that Hanssen—except for his failed attempt to recontact the GRU in 1993—had been inactive during the eight years from 1991 to 1999. After his arrest, some intelligence officials speculated that Hanssen might not have been dormant during the entire period. But on October 6, Hanssen received a reply from the SVR which, from its content and almost ecstatic tone, clearly was welcoming him back after a long absence.

"It's good to know you are here," the SVR wrote. "Acknowledging your letter to V.K. we express our sincere joy on the occasion of resumption of contact with you.* We firmly guarantee you for a necessary financial help. Note, please, that since our last contact a sum set aside for you has risen and presents now about 800.000 dollars. This time you will find in a package 50.000 dollars. Now it is up to you to give a secure explanation of it."

Further evidence that Hanssen was being embraced after a long absence was provided by the growth of the escrow account and by the next sentence in the SVR's letter: "As to communication plan, we may have need of some time to work out a secure and reliable one." Here again, the language indicates that Hanssen had been long out of contact.

The SVR's message reviewed the signals, the strips of white adhesive tape that they and Hanssen were to use on the post by the park sign. Hanssen's tape was to be vertical, the SVR's horizontal, just as before. Then, in case he had become rusty from lack of practice, his handlers added: "After you will clear the drop don't forget to remove our tape that will mean for us—exchange is over."

The SVR also proposed a new signal site in one of Washington's most exclusive residential neighborhoods, an electric utility pole at the intersection of Foxhall Road and Whitehaven Parkway. In the same letter, the Russians also suggested it was time to move on from adhesive tape to thumbtacks, and they went into extraordinary detail about the

---

*"V.K." was not further identified. The FBI affidavit that quoted from the Hanssen file described him only as a "senior officer" of the SVR. He was, however, Vladimir A. Kirdyanov, ostensibly the first secretary of the Russian embassy at the time.

size and color, even telling Hanssen what drugstore chain carried the right ones:

> At any working day put a white thumb tack (1 cm in diameter, colored sets are sold at CVS) into the Northern side of the pole at the height of about 1.2 yards. The tack must be seen from a car going down Foxhall Road. This will mean for us that we shall retrieve your package from the DD [dead drop] Foxstone Park at the evening of the nex [sic] week's Tuesday (when it's getting dark).
>
> In case of a threatening situation of any kind put a yellow tack at the same place. This will mean that we shall refrain from any communication with you until further notice from your side (the white tack).

Apparently, five months went by before Hanssen heard from the Russians again, and judging by the letter he sent on March 14, 2000, he was becoming unglued.

"I have come about as close as I ever want to come to sacrificing myself to help you, and I get silence. I hate silence. . . . Conclusion: One might propose that I am either insanely brave or quite insane. I'd answer neither. I'd say, insanely loyal. Take your pick. There is insanity in all the answers.

"I have, however, come as close to the edge as I can without being truly insane. My security concerns have proven reality-based. I'd say, pin your hopes on 'insanely loyal' and go for it. Only I can lose."

On the same day, he went back into the FBI computer and searched for the keywords DEAD DROP AND SVR. Again, he found nothing. But clearly Hanssen had persuaded himself that time was running out on his career as a spy, as evidenced not only by his desperate words but also by his repeated searches in the FBI computer, which continued throughout the year.

The searches were dangerous, because at any time the computer systems operators might spot his excessive and highly suspicious usage by auditing the retrieval logs. FBI counterintelligence agents do not normally enter their own names and addresses in the ACS. They are expected to be the hunters, not the hunted.

Finally, in his letter to the SVR in March 2000, Hanssen added, dubiously, that he had made his decision to become a spy as a teenager, in-

spired by the autobiography of Kim Philby, the Soviet mole inside
British intelligence.

> I decided on this course when I was 14 years old. I'd read
> Philby's book. Now that is insane, eh! My only hesitations were
> my security concerns under uncertainty. I hate uncertainty. So
> far I have judged the edge correctly. Give me credit for that.
> Set the signal at my site any Tuesday evening. I will read
> your answer. Please, at least say goodbye. It's been a long time
> my dear friends, a long and lonely time.
>
> Ramon Garcia

Were Hanssen not a traitor to his country, the last words of his letter would be poignant. And his claim that Philby's memoir influenced
him to spy was bogus. Philby's book was not published until 1968,
when Hanssen was twenty-four.*

Half a dozen times during 2000, Hanssen continued to search the FBI
database for his name, as well as for TALISMAN DRIVE and, several times,
the keywords DEAD DROP. Once he entered SVR AND DEAD DROP NOT GRU.
And as he had done before, he searched DEAD DROP AND RUSSIA.

On June 8, Hanssen wrote the SVR a long letter in which he said,
"Enclosed, once again, is my rudimentary cipher." Hanssen was probably referring to a system of letter substitution that he had used in some
of his messages to Moscow. He apologized for reusing it many times—
repetition is a laxity that opens a window for code-breakers—but explained that he did so in case Moscow had lost the key, further evidence
that he had been in hibernation for some time.

Hanssen's dependence on the Russians, his apparent psychological
need for their approval, was obvious from his next sentence: "Thank
you for your note. It brought me great joy to see the signal at last."

He went on to say, however, that they required better and faster
ways of contacting each other. Hanssen now proposed that the Russians
leave the era of tape and thumbtacks behind and switch to a Palm VII
organizer. He owned a Palm III, he said, which wasn't a bad little hand-
held computer. But "the VII version comes with wireless internet capa-
bility built in. It can allow the rapid transmission of encrypted
messages, which if used on an infrequent basis, could be quite effec-

---

*Kim Philby, *My Silent War* (New York: Grove Press, 1968).

tive. . . . Such a device might even serve for rapid transmittal of substantial material in digital form."

If Hanssen sounded a little like a Palm Pilot salesman pitching a reluctant customer, it was at least consistent with his geeky, albeit knowledgeable, fascination with computers and the latest technology.

As his letter reflected, the tone of Hanssen's communications with the Russians had changed after he resumed spying in 1999. He was at once more desperate—"I am either insanely brave or quite insane"—and less deferential.

For example, he not only lectured the Russians about the need for wireless transmissions, he chided the SVR for bugging a State Department conference room without letting him know. If he had been told in time, he said, he could have warned Moscow that the operation had been detected by the FBI.

On December 8, 1999, the bureau's agents had arrested Stanislav Gusev outside the State Department. Gusev, who was listed as an "attaché" in the Russian embassy, had arrived in March. FBI counterintelligence agents had spotted Gusev hanging around the State Department. He was seen sometimes sitting on a bench, and at other times moving his car around the building, parking at different locations and taking care to feed the meters to avoid a ticket.

The FBI concluded that Gusev was conducting an electronic eavesdropping operation. A tiny battery-powered transmitter had been planted in a conference room on the seventh floor, the inner sanctum of the State Department. The bug was concealed inside a piece of molding about three feet above the floor, the sort of wooden strip that keeps chair backs from scuffing the wall.

The transmitter, the FBI said, had been "professionally introduced," which meant that the Russian spies had cut away a piece of the molding and then replaced it with an identical matching piece containing the bug. That suggested that the Russians, or a confederate on the inside, had access to the room more than once, to case and photograph it, and probably to take a paint chip so their technicians could match the color of the molding.

Gusev activated the bug by remote control, and it broadcast to a tape recorder in his car. The Russians used low-power batteries to make the bug more difficult to detect, but that also meant that its range was limited, and someone had to be outside the building to turn on the bug and record the signals.

Once the FBI realized what Gusev was up to, the State Department security staff, using sophisticated equipment borrowed from the CIA and other agencies, electronically swept the entire building, until finally, after months of searching, the device was found in the conference room just down the hall from Secretary of State Madeleine Albright's office. Although the room was assigned to the Bureau of Oceans and International Environmental Scientific Affairs, other officials also used it for meetings, some of them sensitive. As many as one hundred meetings may have been overheard and recorded, officials said.

When the FBI arrested Gusev, he had the remote control on his person. Since he had diplomatic immunity, he was turned over to his embassy but ordered expelled from the country.

The FBI, of course, wanted very much to know how the Russians managed to get the bug inside the building and how long it had been in place, broadcasting secrets. Several batteries were found inside the piece of molding, so the gadget might have been active for as long as four years, according to one intelligence source.

"The Gusev affair didn't help you any," Hanssen wrote to the Russians. "If I'd had better communications I could have prevented that.

"I was aware of the fact that microphones had been detected at the State Department. (Such matters are why I need rapid communications. It can save you much grief.) . . . I had knowledge weeks before of the existence of devices, but not the country placing them. . . . I only found out the gruesome details too late to warn you through available means including the colored stick-pin call.* (Which by the way I doubted would work because of your ominous silence.) Very frustrating."

He added:

"The U.S. can be errantly likened to a powerfully built but retarded child, potentially dangerous, but young, immature and easily manipulated. But don't be fooled by that appearance. It is also one which can turn ingenius [sic] quickly, like an idiot savant, once convinced of a goal. The purple-pissing Japanese (to quote General Patten [sic] once again) learned this to their dismay. . . ."

---

*The stilted language in some of the correspondence contained in the KGB/SVR file suggests that perhaps some of Hanssen's letters were translated from English into Russian and then back into English. The reference to "the colored stick-pin call" almost certainly means the yellow thumbtack that the SVR instructed Hanssen to use as an emergency signal. It would be very odd for a native English speaker such as Hanssen to call a thumbtack a "colored stick-pin."

Then, buttering up his handlers, Hanssen said he greatly appreciated the "highly professional" references in their messages to information they had exchanged in the past as a subtle way of reassuring him "that the channel remains unpirated. This is not lost on me." In other words, the prior references were a way to prove to Hanssen that the FBI was not running a sting against him—a favorite bureau tactic in spy cases—and that the messages he was receiving were really coming from Moscow.

Hanssen's mood was mercurial, because he switched in an instant from flattery to a Bogartian, tough-guy, don't-try-to-con-me stance. All that money the Russians said they had put in escrow for him, now $800,000, was a fable.

> [W]e do both know that money is not really "put away for you" except in some vague accounting sense. Never patronize at this level. It offends me, but then you are easily forgiven. But perhaps I shouldn't tease you. It just gets me in trouble.
>
> thank you again,
>
> Ramon.

After twenty-one years as a Russian spy, Hanssen was indeed about to get into trouble, but not in a way he expected.

23

BUCKLURE

The Safeway in the Georgetown section of Washington is only a few blocks down the hill from the Soviet (now Russian) embassy, and many of the residents of the embassy's apartment complex like to shop there. The store is also widely known as "the social Safeway" because it is popular with the upscale young professionals who live in the area.

In 1982, the produce section of the Safeway was the setting for an unlikely Cold War drama. Dimitri I. Yakushkin, the KGB *rezident* in Washington for the past seven years, was about to return home to Moscow. The FBI knew this, and the CI-2 squad that specialized in the KGB's Line PR political officers decided to approach him to see if he could be persuaded to defect.

A cold pitch, as it is known in the business, to a KGB *rezident,* especially an experienced spy like Yakushkin, had almost no chance of success, but nothing ventured, nothing gained. For a week, the squad, operating out of the Washington field office, was on Yakushkin, waiting for a moment when he was alone. It came in the Safeway.

Special Agent Dale H. Pugh sidled up to the KGB man who was in the produce section, carefully feeling the oranges for any soft spots. The Russian made a striking figure. He was six foot four, about 220 pounds, and wore a beret, which made him look like a cross between an artist in Montmartre and a Redskins linebacker. Yakushkin came from a prominent Russian family. Urbane and well-educated, fluent in English, he had been the KGB *rezident* at the Soviet Mission to the United Nations for six years before he was sent to Washington.

The KGB man had come shopping with his wife, Irina. In the store, they split up. Another FBI agent, Grover Gibson, was trailing her, keeping Pugh in his line of sight so that he could signal his partner if Mrs. Yakushkin suddenly decided to rejoin her husband. The FBI men were dressed in belted trench coats; they had not expected to end up in a supermarket, and Pugh felt conspicuous among the grocery shoppers.

Pugh introduced himself to Yakushkin, identified himself as an FBI agent, and gave a fake name that he often used operationally. Yakushkin asked to see his ID. Pugh, a rookie at the time, produced it, realizing with a sinking feeling that it wouldn't match the name he had given. Yakushkin, examining Pugh's credential, saw that right away, and smiled.

The FBI man tried to persuade Yakushkin to meet him somewhere so they could talk privately, but the KGB agent would have none of it. Finally Pugh, following instructions from his squad supervisor, James O. Stassinos, offered the Russian $20 million to defect to the United States.

"Young man," Yakushkin said, "I appreciate the offer. Twenty years ago I might have been interested." And with that, he walked away.

Yakushkin appeared more amused than offended by the encounter. But there was an unspoken subtext to the dialogue by the orange bin at the Georgetown Safeway. Yakushkin had a girlfriend from North Carolina the entire time he was in the United States. As he may have suspected, she was an FBI source. What he told her, and it was not much, she told the FBI.

Dale Pugh did not mention the woman when he made his pitch. Nor was it a question of coercion; Yakushkin was too big a figure in the KGB to worry about how the liaison would look in Moscow if the FBI revealed it. But the bureau hoped that Yakushkin liked his woman friend well enough that she might be an additional incentive for him to defect and remain in the United States. The FBI even asked the woman to give Yakushkin a copy of Graham Greene's novel *The Honorary Consul* in the hope that it might put ideas in his head.*

The novel, set in a provincial town in the north of Argentina, has the usual array of expatriate, tormented Greene characters. Charley Fortnum, the British honorary consul, is sixty-one and a drunk. He marries a twenty-year-old prostitute; when he is kidnapped by leftist revolutionaries who mistake him for the American ambassador, the British

---

*Graham Greene, *The Honorary Consul* (New York: Simon & Schuster, 1973).

government does not even consider him worth the ransom. After he is rescued by police, London rewards his years of service by dismissing him. The bureau may have thought that the theme of an older man in love with a younger woman, living in a foreign country and unappreciated by his government, might resonate with Yakushkin.

It was not the first time that the FBI had tried to romance Yakushkin. A previous attempt by FBI agent Ted Gardner had taken place in downtown Washington at the Mayflower Hotel a year earlier. Gardner, then in charge of the Washington field office, accompanied by Phillip Parker, his counterintelligence chief, waited in the lobby for Yakushkin, whom they knew was due at the hotel with his woman friend, either to drop her off or join her in her room. The pair arrived, but when they reached the elevators, a third, unknown person had joined them, so Gardner did not make the approach.

Neither money, sex, nor Graham Greene influenced Yakushkin. The KGB man went home as scheduled, and rose to become head of the American department of the spy agency's first chief directorate, its foreign intelligence arm. He was a mentor and protector of Vitaly Yurchenko, who had been security chief of the Washington embassy when Yakushkin was the *rezident*. Yurchenko was the high-level KGB man who defected in 1985, changed his mind, and returned to Moscow three months later.*

As a senior KGB agent and top official in the Washington residency, Yakushkin would have been a huge catch for the FBI. The bureau would never have paid anything like $20 million to get him, but the field agents might have dangled that enormous sum to play on his ego and show that they were serious. Had Yakushkin defected, his knowledge of Moscow's spying was so extensive that he could have shut down the KGB's operations in the United States.

The two attempts to recruit the top KGB man in Washington demonstrated that the FBI was not hesitant to use cash as a weapon to recruit Russians in the Cold War. At least in some circumstances, the bureau and the CIA hoped, money might be the bait to land the big one.

---

*Yurchenko was rumored to have been in some sort of trouble in 1985, and the CIA suspected that it was Yakushkin who sent Yurchenko to Rome that year, to get him out of Moscow. It was from Rome that Yurchenko defected to the CIA on August 1, 1985, only to redefect to Moscow on November 6. Dimitri Yakushkin retired in 1986 with the rank of major general. He died at the age of seventy-one in Moscow on August 9, 1994.

And so, in 1987, long before the arrest of Aldrich Ames in 1994, the FBI launched a joint operation with the CIA, aimed at buying Soviet intelligence officers with large amounts of cash. The program, designed by Robert Wade, the assistant chief of the FBI's Soviet section, was codenamed BUCKLURE by the FBI; the CIA called it RACKETEER.

"BUCKLURE was created to recruit Russians who could help us find a mole," one veteran FBI agent explained. With the help of the CIA, the bureau began logging the whereabouts of Soviet intelligence officers who had worked in the United States at a time when American assets were being lost in the Soviet Union, and who had then gone back to Moscow. Some had been reassigned abroad, others had retired. Many were KGB "American targets" officers, the Line KR spies who had been sent to the United States to try to recruit people, especially inside American intelligence.

Before long, BUCKLURE had compiled a list of ninety to one hundred potential recruits worldwide. "The list became very focused on those who we wanted, who would have the answers," a former senior FBI official said. All the approaches to the KGB officers were made outside Russia.

By the mid-1990s, however, despite the efforts of BUCKLURE and the arrests of the CIA's Jim Nicholson and the FBI's Earl Pitts, the Special Investigations Unit at the CIA, with the help of dozens of FBI agents, had not solved all of the anomalies still plaguing U.S. counterintelligence, including the tip-off to Felix Bloch and the troublesome technical compromises.

The trolling for SVR agents through BUCKLURE and RACKETEER was intensified. In the beginning, the going price for a KGB officer who could identify a mole was a million dollars.* It was hard cash, ready to be paid.

A CIA man involved in RACKETEER said the figure of a million dollars was based on actual experience. "Sometime in the early eighties," he said, "we offered a KGB officer in Latin America five hundred thousand dollars and he turned it down. So we upped it to a million. We jointly put a million bucks into a fiscal kitty. A million per guy."

When a likely prospect was located abroad, the FBI might ask the CIA to make the approach. The FBI man explained what might be said

---

*Over the years, and allowing for inflation, the $1 million bounty increased substantially.

to the Russian: "We know you are a good guy, you don't want to defect or work for us. But you give us the name of a penetration, we give you a million dollars. You don't have to defect, and nobody knows about this except the president of the United States and the two of us."

"We pitched a lot of people," another senior FBI man recalled. "The Russians got wind of what we were doing around nineteen ninety-six or ninety-seven. They knew we were trying to recruit people for a lot of money."

The bureau set its sights high; it did not hesitate to go after even the celebrated Viktor Cherkashin, the canny KGB chief of counterintelligence in the Washington residency, who, as the CIA and the bureau later learned to their sorrow, was the key player in the handling of both Aldrich Ames and Robert Hanssen.

The attempt to recruit Cherkashin was made by Ray Mislock, then the special agent in charge of counterintelligence for the FBI's Washington field office. Cherkashin had returned to Washington around 1997 to attend a conference. It was long after the collapse of the Soviet Union, and by this time senior KGB officers often fraternized with American intelligence officials, their former foes, at various international meetings.

Cherkashin had agreed to have dinner at the Old Angler's Inn in Potomac, Maryland, with Brent Scowcroft, who had been national security adviser to President Gerald Ford and the first President Bush. It was arranged beforehand that Mislock would show up as an unannounced added guest. At an opportune moment during dinner, Mislock let Cherkashin know what was on his mind. Relations are better, Mislock said; we would like to solve some unanswered questions. Cherkashin was noncommittal. The dinner was pleasant, the three men chatted amiably. But after dessert and coffee, by prearrangement, Scowcroft bowed out.

Now Mislock, as he had plotted, was alone with Cherkashin. He offered to drive the former KGB man back to his hotel in Tysons Corner, across the river in northern Virginia. In the car, Mislock pitched Cherkashin. He was explicit; the FBI man wanted to know the identity of the mole inside U.S. intelligence.

Mislock did not have to mention a million dollars—the KGB officer knew what was tacitly being offered. For Cherkashin, it could have been a very profitable ride back to his hotel.

But Cherkashin was a tough guy, a KGB veteran with a poker face that never betrayed his thoughts or emotions. Mislock got nowhere. At the hotel, he let Cherkashin out of the car and they bade each other a pleasant good night.

It did not end the bureau's continued interest in Viktor Cherkashin. "We gathered all the information we had on Cherkashin," a former senior FBI man said. "There was an event involving a bicycle that Cherkashin was riding through Rock Creek Park in the mid-1980s. We thought it might involve a penetration. Cherkashin may have been checking a signal site, getting ready to clear a drop, or perhaps meeting an individual. We reexamined those events, such as Cherkashin showing up in Rock Creek, in the post-Pitts, post-Ames time frame. The incident was being looked at very intently to see if it was a drop, a signal site, or even a brush pass."*

The FBI assigned Special Agent Mike Rochford to examine the Cherkashin file. He had been the case agent responsible for tracking Cherkashin in the early 1980s. He was also one of two agents who had interviewed Vitaly Yurchenko during his brief interlude as a defector. Rochford spoke Russian and knew a lot about the KGB. He was to play a central role in the unmasking of Robert Hanssen.

"Mike Rochford began an exhaustive reexamination of everything we had on Cherkashin," the FBI man said. "When code clerks had arrived, when the pouch was sent to Moscow, little things that might indicate something big going on." Then, as the mole hunters focused on particular possible suspects, they could turn to Rochford's study. "We would look to see if there was anything corresponding with the suspects' lives that would explain intense activity in the residency."

Just such wisps, strands, and tiny details are the tools of counterintelligence. Often, the microscopic attention to detail ends in frustration and turns up nothing. "The Cherkashin study did not lead directly to Hanssen," the FBI man said, "but it eliminated some suspicions."

*　　　*　　　*

---

*In a brush pass an intelligence officer and a source move closely by each other, usually in a crowd, and without stopping or seeming to recognize each other transfer a document or other material so quickly that an observer, even a few feet away, might not see it happen. Although normally accomplished on foot, it could be managed by two people riding bicycles.

At the end of July 2000, Hanssen retrieved a letter from the SVR. It sought to reassure him that the political changes in Russia "had not affected our resources," meaning that they still had plenty of money to pay him. After a number of upheavals in the Russian cabinet, Vladimir Putin, a former KGB officer, had been elected president six months earlier, in March. Once again, the SVR assured Hanssen that his "personal security" came first.

His handlers then asked for information on "human, electronic and technical penetrations in our residencies here and in other countries." Apparently the SVR knew about the active search for penetrations secretly being carried on at the CIA and the FBI, for the letter said: "We are very interested in getting . . . information on the work of a special group which serches [sic] 'mole' in CIA and FBI. We need this information especially to take necessary additional steps to ensure Your personal security. . . ." In effect, Moscow was asking Hanssen how close the mole hunters were getting to him.

Once more, the SVR pressed Hanssen to meet outside the United States, which he had consistently refused to do. In the meantime, it set the next exchange at LEWIS, in the Long Branch Nature Center, for November 21. And the SVR proposed to use dead drop ELLIS in Foxstone Park once a year, on February 18. It was a date that would prove fateful for Robert Hanssen.

The SVR also chided Hanssen for continuing to send letters to them through the mail. "You know very well our negative attitude toward this method," the Russians said. But a very brief note giving a date, time, and place would be all right if he needed an "urgent exchange."

Again rejecting Hanssen's pleas to deposit money in his Swiss bank accounts, the SVR argued that it was "very risky to transfer money in Zurich because now it is impossible to hide its origin." Then, seeking to reassure their mole that there would be no leaks at Moscow's end, the letter added that "an insignificant number of persons know about you, your information and our relationship."

On November 17, 2000, Hanssen wrote back, complaining that "For me breaks in communications are most difficult and stressful. Recent changes in U.S. law now attach the death penalty to my help to you as you know, so I do take some risk."

But, he assured Moscow, "I know far better than most what minefields are laid and the risks." The SVR, he said, might overestimate the

FBI's abilities, but still, an overconfident Russian intelligence officer might, "as we say, step in an occasional cowpie. (Message to the translator: Got a good word for cowpie in Russian?? Clue, don't blindly walk behind cows.)"

He added:

> No one answered my signal at Foxhall. Perhaps you occasionally give up on me. Giving up on me is a mistake. I have proven inveterately loyal and willing to take grave risks which even could cause my death, only remaining quiet in times of extreme uncertainty. So far my ship has successfully navigated the slings and arrows of outrageous fortune.
>
> I ask you to help me survive. . . .
>
> On meeting out of the country, it simply is not practical for me. I must answer too many questions from family, friends, and government plus it is a cardinal sign of a spy. You have made it that way because of your policy. Policies are constraints, constraints breed patterns. Patterns are noticed. Meeting in this country is not really that hard to manage, but I am loath to do so not because it is risky but because it involves revealing my identity. That insulation has been my best protection against betrayal by someone like me working from whatever motivation, a Bloch or a Philby.

Still pushing for money in a Swiss bank, Hanssen agreed that Switzerland offered no real security, "but insulated by laundering on both the in and out sides" it could be managed. Perhaps he could set up a corporation that would lend him mortgage money to conceal his SVR payments.

> Cash is hard to handle here because little business is ever really done in cash and repeated cash transactions into the banking system are more dangerous because of the difficulty in explaining them. That doesn't mean it isn't welcome enough to let that problem devolve on me. (We should all have such problems, eh?) How do you propose I get this money put away for me when I retire? (Come on; I can joke with you about it. I know money is not really put into an account at MOST Bank,

and that you are speaking figuratively of an accounting notation at best to be made real at some uncertain future. We do the same.

Want me to lecture in your 101 course in my old age? My college level Russian has sunk low through inattention all these years; I would be a novelty attraction, but I don't think a practical one except in extremis.)

So good luck. Wish me luck.

It was his last letter to the Sluzhba Vneshnei Razvedki. Unknown to Robert Hanssen, his luck had already run out.

24

The Wrong Man

In 1998, a year after Brian Kelley had returned to CIA headquarters from overseas, he was invited to join a supersecret counterespionage operation.

The agency, he was told, had snared a Russian intelligence agent who was ready to defect, to come to the West and solve at last the mystery of who had compromised the Felix Bloch case. It was an exciting assignment, particularly for Kelley, the counterintelligence officer who was first to discover the trail that led to Bloch.

To join the secret operation, Kelley was told he would have to submit to a lie detector test. Kelley had taken a routine polygraph a year earlier and had no objections to undergoing another. Once he was strapped to the machine, the examiners questioned him, probing his reaction to the possibility that the mole who had warned the KGB about Felix Bloch was soon to be unmasked.

Kelley was assured he had passed the polygraph test. But soon afterward, his superiors in the directorate of operations told him that the anticipated Russian defector had changed his mind and would not be coming to the United States after all; as a result, Kelley was no longer needed for the special operation.

The entire business was an elaborate ruse to deceive Kelley into taking a new polygraph, where he could be questioned about the betrayal of the Bloch case. There was no Russian defector, no secret operation.

Unbeknownst to Brian Kelley, he had emerged as the prime suspect in the secret FBI and CIA mole hunt that had begun after the arrest of

Aldrich Ames four years earlier. And, ironically, it was the Bloch case that had cast the dark shadow of suspicion on Kelley, an innocent CIA officer.

The FBI gave the effort to uncover the mole a new code name: GRAYSUIT.

As suspects emerged, they would be given cryptonyms as a subset of the word GRAY. Thus it was that in the innermost sanctum of the bureau's mole hunters, Brian Kelley became GRAY DECEIVER.

Kelley was well known in the counterintelligence world, for he had built his career as a specialist in illegals, the Russian spies sent to the West without benefit of diplomatic cover. Kelley had headed the illegals group at the CIA.

His was an arcane, difficult specialty, because illegals are rarely detected. They do not pose as diplomats and often steal the identities of long dead or living persons—they can be anybody.

It was Kelley who was credited with unmasking Reino Gikman, the KGB illegal who turned up in Vienna when Felix Bloch was deputy chief of mission. And it was Gikman, metamorphosing into "Pierre Bart," who dined in Paris with Bloch in mid-May 1989 and left with the airline bag that Bloch had placed under the table. It was Gikman as well who had called Bloch a month later to warn him of "a contagious disease."

Although Bloch was not arrested or charged with espionage, inside the CIA Brian Kelley was widely known and admired as the officer who had made the Bloch case. He received a medal at an awards ceremony, and among his colleagues he was given credit for his detective work. It was not his fault, after all, that an unknown mole inside American intelligence had warned the KGB so that it, in turn, could warn Bloch, to the great and continuing frustration of the FBI.

And it was precisely because Kelley had broken the Bloch case that he fell under suspicion. When the mole hunters hunt, they construct a matrix, matching the nature of the secrets believed to have been compromised with the names of the people who had access to those secrets. Then they attempt to winnow down the list, eliminating the names, for example, of those whose access might have occurred only after the suspected date that the information leaked.

Brian Kelley had joined the CIA after twenty years in the Air Force. He was persuaded to join the agency by Gus Hathaway, who as the CIA chief of counterintelligence had appointed the mole hunt team that eventually unmasked Aldrich Ames as a KGB spy.

At the agency, Kelley was a career officer in the directorate of operations. He had carved out his illegals specialty almost from the start. He worked counterintelligence cases in New York City in the early 1980s, and later was posted to Panama for a time, returning to headquarters at the end of 1997. Long divorced, he had a daughter who also worked at the CIA, and two sons.

Kelley was dedicated to his work. But he told friends he felt he was never fully accepted in the agency because he had been a military man, not a career CIA employee from the start. A former colleague described him as "balding, nondescript, very serious, not outgoing, not joking, always cautious, always protective."

When Kelley returned from Panama, he was assigned to review the Bloch case files, to go over them once again to make sure nothing had been missed. But he did not know that the task was a subterfuge, designed to keep him busy and cut off from other agency operations and secrets.

As Kelley reported to CIA headquarters each day in Langley, Virginia, his life was under microscopic examination a few miles away, across the Potomac in the Washington field office of the FBI. And the agent looking through that microscope was Mike Rochford, the FBI man who had run the Cherkashin study for the bureau that reexamined the file on the KGB counterintelligence officer, including the episode with the bicycle in Rock Creek Park.

Rochford, a tall, affable man, had a background that would turn out to be remarkably similar to Robert Hanssen's. He was born in Chicago, where his father had been a police officer for almost three decades. He was educated at Catholic schools in that city and joined the FBI in 1974. Hanssen had studied Russian in college; the bureau had sent Rochford to language school to learn Russian.

At the field office, Rochford was in charge of the squad assigned to find the suspected penetration inside American intelligence. The more he looked at Brian Kelley's career, the more convinced he became that Kelley, GRAY DECEIVER, was the mole.*

---

*Sometimes when the bureau's counterspies talked to each other about Kelley, they simply referred to him even more cryptically, in a sort of shorthand, as "GD."

In counterintelligence work, once a person falls under suspicion, the investigators may seize upon innocent events and circumstances that suddenly take on ominous meaning. During the era when James J. Angleton headed counterintelligence at the CIA, a score of loyal officers were shunted aside or even fired, their careers destroyed on the flimsiest of evidence. In one classic case, Peter Karlow, a CIA officer, actually fell under suspicion because his name began with the letter K. A defector had said the agency harbored a mole whose name began with that letter.*

Convinced that Kelley was their man, the FBI applied to the Foreign Intelligence Surveillance Court, the shadowy, little-known wiretap panel in the capital, and obtained permission to place the CIA man under intense scrutiny. His home was bugged and secretly searched, as was his garbage; his telephones were tapped, and his every move was carefully watched.

Once, for example, when Kelley traveled to New York and to Niagara Falls, the FBI was with him. The bureau was ready to pounce; the famed tourist attraction is on the Canadian border, and sometimes KGB agents were known to slip over the border to meet a contact. Kelley in fact was there on a trip for the CIA. But the bureau convinced itself that he was taking evasive action, known in the spy trade as "dry cleaning," to lose a tail.

"They had surveillance on him and we lost him at the border," a former FBI counterintelligence official said. "We thought he was cleaning himself."

In Panama, Kelley was seen brushing past what one agent called "an individual suspected of a connection to Russian intelligence. It was a very quick pass; there could have been a verbal exchange as well." But for all the bureau knew, the man may have been a source recruited by Kelley for the CIA; he was never asked about the contact.

The physical surveillance was carried out by "the Gs," FBI jargon for the SSG, the bureau's Special Surveillance Group. The Gs are a special team of surveillance experts, selected to look like ordinary citizens.

---

*Karlow, the principal suspect in Angleton's mole hunt, was fired by the CIA in 1963, fought for twenty-six years to clear his name, and eventually received a secret medal from the director of the CIA and close to half a million dollars from the agency under a "Mole Relief Act" passed by Congress. See David Wise, *Molehunt: The Secret Search for Traitors that Shattered the CIA* (New York: Random House, 1992).

A young mother with a baby in a stroller, joggers, street repair crews in hard hats, an old man with a cane, telephone linemen, white-haired grandmothers with shopping bags, young lovers necking in the park—all may be Gs on the job.* "The Gs were on him for a long time," one former FBI man said.

Try as it might, Rochford's squad, even with the benefit of the watchers and electronic eavesdropping, was not able to nail down the evidence to make a case against Kelley. It could not do so for the simple reason that he was totally innocent.

So the FBI decided to run another sting against him. Perhaps if Kelley could be duped into thinking the FBI was on to his supposed espionage, he would try to run. In November 1998, some time after the phony assignment that tricked Kelley into taking the lie detector test, a stranger appeared at the door of his home.

In a thick foreign accent, the man said the authorities now knew about his spying. The stranger handed him a piece of paper with an escape plan and told him to be at a nearby subway station the next evening. Then the man disappeared into the night. It was an obvious FBI sting that failed for two reasons—Kelley was not a spy, and he reported the incident to the FBI the next morning. He even gave a description of the foreigner so that a bureau artist could sketch the man.

But the FBI simply assumed that Kelley was too clever by half to fall for their sting. He was so cool and confident, Rochford believed, that inside the Washington field office Kelley became known as "the Iceman."

When the FBI secretly searched Kelley's home in Vienna, Virginia, agents found a map of Nottoway Park with what it regarded as suspicious markings. Soviet intelligence officers had been seen in the vicinity of the park, and the discovery of the map added to Rochford's and the bureau's conviction that the investigation was on the right track.†

The FBI, meanwhile, had quietly begun questioning certain CIA officers about Brian Kelley. In February 1999, bureau agents twice in-

---

*The Gs are civil servants, not FBI agents, and earn lower pay than the agents. But all are trained in surveillance, photography, and communications. They are chosen precisely because they do not resemble the public's concept of FBI agents.

†Since the FBI had not yet identified Hanssen as the mole, the bureau had no way of knowing when it discovered the map in Kelley's home that Hanssen had repeatedly used PARK/PRIME, the dead drop in Nottoway Park.

terviewed a woman who was a CIA officer and a friend of Kelley. As a participant in the agency's executive leadership program, she had recently developed a proposal to provide the services of a chaplain at CIA, an idea which the agency's director, George Tenet, is said to have supported. Soon after, she went on leave from the agency to work with a religious organization.

According to John Moustakas, a Washington attorney who later represented both Kelley and the female former CIA officer, the FBI agents asserted that the woman was trying to cover up for Kelley, and they claimed not to believe her initial statements to them.*

"They accused her of false statements and suggested she was a cutout for Kelley. In August different FBI agents confronted her at a mailboxes-type store. The agents were a little friendlier and took her to a diner and talked to her."

In the interim, Kelley had learned that some of his colleagues were being interrogated about him, and he asked the woman CIA officer if she had been approached. "She felt badly that, because she'd signed nondisclosure agreements, she told Brian she had not been questioned, which was not true. He thought it strange that she should not have been questioned, since a lot of other people were."

By this time, Moustakas added, the woman decided that, because her interrogators had accused her of lying and had made clear they felt she was at least complicit in spying, her CIA career was over. "She knew she could no longer be effective in covert work and resigned from the agency."

For a time, the CIA resisted the FBI's concentration on Kelley, arguing that, aside from the Bloch case, he would not have had access to some of the information the bureau believed to have been compromised. According to Moustakas, the bureau had an answer for that; he said FBI agents speculated that Kelley, single and a divorcé, might have obtained the information by seducing women employees of the agency.

Espionage is a very difficult crime to prove, and when the FBI's various stratagems had failed—the fake mole operation and the stranger at the door—it decided to confront Kelley. Sometimes in such

---

*Moustakas did not disclose the surnames of either of his clients to the author. He offered to make Kelley available to be interviewed for this book, but only on condition that Kelley's name not be used. That offer was declined. Kelley's identity was learned independently and his name and case discussed with the author by several current and former intelligence officials.

a setting suspects confess, often in the desperate if misguided hope that they will be "turned" and played back by the bureau against the Russians.

At 1 P.M. on August 18, 1999, Kelley was summoned to a meeting in a small conference room in the Counterintelligence Center (CIC) at CIA headquarters. Awaiting him there were two special agents of the FBI, Rudy Guerin and Doug Gregory. Guerin was one of the agents who, five years earlier, had arrested Aldrich Ames.

Gregory, who also worked at WFO, the Washington field office—although not on Rochford's mole hunting squad—was called in because he had earned a reputation as the best investigator in the FBI's New York division. In his late fifties, of medium height, with gray hair and glasses, he was known to be methodical and thorough.

"Gregory is a very serious, a very competent guy," one FBI colleague said. "WFO thought he was a great case agent; any hard case they turned over to Doug Gregory. No personality, difficult to get along with, and he had a real hard-on for the agency. They brought Gregory in when they were ready to do the interview with Kelley."

The two FBI men minced no words. From the start of the interview they accused Kelley of being a Russian spy. They knew all about his activities and even knew his SVR code name, they told him. For Kelley, it was a very frightening moment; by now, Congress had changed the law, and espionage carried the death penalty. Like a character in a Kafka novel, he had no way to prove he was innocent.

The FBI agents triumphantly pulled out a copy of the marked map of Nottoway Park that they had taken from his home. The FBI had stamped it SECRET.

The "spy map," the agents informed him, was proof that he was the long-sought Russian mole. The X marks and the times written on the map indicated when and where he had placed secret documents in dead drops.

"How do you explain this!" one of the agents shouted.

"Where did you get my jogging map?" Kelley countered.

Moustakas, a tough, stocky, no-nonsense former federal prosecutor, was indignant as he described the scene. According to Moustakas, the FBI agents told Kelley he would already be in jail if George Tenet, the director of the CIA, had not intervened. "They told Brian he was about to be arrested; the only reason he hadn't been is out of deference to Tenet. They said Tenet had prevailed upon them to give Brian one more chance to 'come clean.' It was ridiculous; anyone knows if he confessed he'd be arrested. My mother wouldn't fall for that."

The questioning went on for several hours, the agents urging Kelley, who had no lawyer present, to confess his capital crime. Kelley said he had nothing to confess.

The agents weren't buying it. Unless he admitted his espionage, they said, they would have to question members of his family, including, over Kelley's "imploring objections, his frail eighty-four-year-old mother," who was in a nursing home.

At the end of the interrogation, Moustakas said, Kelley was escorted out of CIA headquarters by a senior counterintelligence officer, who also took his badge. He was placed on administrative leave that was to last twenty-one months. In limbo, falsely accused as a spy and facing a possible death penalty, Kelley, having served his country for thirty-seven years, had nowhere to turn. He could only wait, and hope that he would eventually be cleared of the crime he knew he had not committed.

On that same afternoon in August, while Kelley was being confronted by Gregory and Guerin, his twenty-eight-year-old daughter, a CIA employee in the agency's personnel department, was escorted to a small windowless room with a table and four metal chairs. Two FBI agents, a man and a woman, were there. "Please sit down," one of the agents told her. "We have some bad news for you." Frightened, Kelley's daughter could not imagine what had happened.

"Your father is a spy," the FBI agent said. "He's working for the Russians."

The room seemed to spin. Kelley's daughter loved her father and had followed in his footsteps by joining the CIA. When the FBI man accused her father of espionage, it was as though her world had suddenly disintegrated. She began to shake and weep uncontrollably. She stood up and turned away from the agents, facing the wall, still sobbing.

After a few moments, she regained her composure and sat down. The interview continued. The male agent did the questioning while a younger female agent took notes.

The FBI man pulled out a copy of the jogging map and informed her it showed the location of dead drops. She denied her father could possibly be a spy, but that appeared to infuriate the agent.

He pounded the table. "Come on," he yelled, "we know what he did!"

Agents fanned out to find the other family members, and the same scene was repeated. Over the next forty-eight hours, Kelley's ex-wife, his two sons, and two sisters were all interrogated by the FBI.

In Connecticut, the agents warned Kelley's sister that if she did not cooperate they would question her ailing mother in the nursing home.

In Kentucky, the FBI caught up with Kelley's younger son at his office, flashed the map, which they said had come from his father's den, and explained that it proved he was a Russian spy. After an hour, the distraught son lurched past his staring coworkers and out into the rain to be alone. He wondered: could it possibly be true?

In Manhattan, the FBI located Kelley's oldest son, who was on a business trip and about to leave for a flight back to Washington. The agents escorted him to La Guardia Airport, questioning him as the car crawled through the rush-hour traffic.

As soon as he got home that evening, he called his father and drove to his house in Vienna. His father was waiting in the driveway.

"I just want to make sure you believe me," he said.

"You never have to worry about that," his son replied as they hugged.

In the end, after pleas by family members, the FBI did not in fact interview Kelley's mother in the nursing home. But several of his friends and colleagues were interviewed and sworn to silence.

As summer turned to fall, Kelley was having repeated problems with the telephones at his home. In October, a technician dispatched by the telephone company to investigate the trouble found a bug on the line.

All during 2000 and into 2001, Brian Kelley remained on leave, barred from Langley headquarters. The experience, Moustakas said, was "emotionally devastating to him and his family." Kelley told friends he never would have gotten through it all but for a parish priest in whom he confided, who took him under his wing and helped him cope.

Kelley and his children lived with uncertainty for eighteen months, until February 19, 2001, when he received a telephone call from an FBI agent asking to meet him at the bureau's office in Tysons Corner, in northern Virginia. At the office, Kelley was shown a heavily censored report of his interview at CIA headquarters in 1999. He was asked to read it and to make any corrections. That seemed to be the first hopeful sign; he was not told, however, that Robert Hanssen, the real mole, had been arrested the previous afternoon.

On the *Today* show the next morning, NBC News broke the story of Hanssen's arrest, and six hours later Louis Freeh, then the FBI director, held a press conference to make the official announcement. Kelley's nightmare was over, but not quite.

The FBI asked Kelley whether he would be willing to take yet another polygraph test to confirm that he was not a Russian spy, and he agreed. When the test was over, the operator told him he had shown no evidence of deception.

He was not immediately reinstated at the CIA, however, and was not allowed to return to work until May. In the meantime, he considered whether to sue the government or seek some other legal remedy for what had happened to him and his family. Having spent his life in the service of his country, first in the Air Force, then in the agency, he decided, for the moment at least, to soldier on. But he no longer worked on Russian illegals and was reassigned by the CIA to a different job.

What he did want was an apology, and a statement that he was officially cleared, but both were slow in coming. In late April, two months after Hanssen's arrest, Kelley and the female ex-CIA officer contacted James Woolsey, the former director of the CIA, at his Washington law firm, Shea & Gardner. Woolsey promised to help and referred them to his associate, John Moustakas.

In a letter to Freeh in June 2001, Moustakas pointed out that Kelley and his family had lived for eighteen months with "espionage accusations involving death penalty offenses" and was barred from work for twenty-one months, including opportunities for advancement in his career at the CIA. The experience, he wrote, "left indelible personal scars that will never fully heal and a cloud that will continue to mar his impressive career unless it is explicitly dispelled."

What Brian Kelley wanted, his lawyer wrote, was "an unequivocal statement . . . that the espionage activities leveled against him as early as February 1999 have proved to be unfounded and that he has been exonerated unconditionally. We believe that you are the correct government official to issue such a statement."

Freeh didn't.

Instead, he ducked and had his deputy director, Thomas J. Pickard, write back. Finding the penetration, Pickard wrote on June 14, was a top priority because the information lost "was extraordinarily sensitive and damaging to the national security." He added: "Given your background as an Assistant United States Attorney, I know that you understand the need to fully pursue this type of investigation. I do not doubt the necessity of the investigation, nor the integrity of the personnel who carried it out."

Pickard went on to throw Kelley a small bone. "I acknowledge and regret the impact of this investigation on the life of your client . . . and his family." But in view of the pending prosecution of Hanssen, the FBI could not discuss the matter, although the bureau would deal with "any concerns" his client had after the prosecution was concluded.

Moustakas was furious when he read the letter. The FBI had refused to declare that Kelley was innocent! He wrote back to Pickard in July. No one was doubting that the FBI had to investigate the losses, he agreed. But there was a big difference between pursuing leads and "accusations of espionage . . . the threat of arrest for capital crimes" and the treatment of his client's family, "including threats to interrogate his eighty-four-year-old mother.

"Under the circumstances it is simply not enough for the FBI to say that it 'regrets' the impact its investigation had. . . . That is the sort of thing an airline might say to a passenger whose flight had been delayed for a few hours. But my client was not merely inconvenienced; his life was turned upside down. . . . I do not accept your claimed inability to exonerate an innocent man because of the pending prosecution of a guilty one."

Moustakas added: "Why then is it so hard for the FBI to say, in point-blank fashion and just as a matter of honesty and fairness, that its suspicions about [Kelley] and its espionage accusations against him turned out to be totally unfounded and that . . . it was on the wrong track?"

As it happened, three days later, President Bush appointed Robert Mueller to replace Freeh. Perhaps that made it easier for the FBI to do what it should have done all along. The following month, on August 16, Neil J. Gallagher, the assistant director in charge of the National Security Division, wrote to Kelley.

"I sincerely regret the adverse impact that this investigation had on you and the members of your family," Gallagher wrote. "It was not the intent of the FBI to either discredit you or to cause you or your family any embarrassment. If this has occurred, I am sorry."

Gallagher assured Kelley he was no longer a suspect and that "the FBI has ceased its investigation of you." He offered to place the written exoneration in Kelley's CIA personnel file.

Kelley finally had the apology and declaration of innocence he had wanted. Neil Gallagher had done the right thing, and GRAY DECEIVER was found guiltless at last.

Moustakas said he was "generally pleased." He added, "The letter makes clear what everyone has known forever; that he's not a spy, that he never was a spy, and that the nightmare should be over." Moustakas's only objection was that "it happened way too late."

Some remarkable coincidences were apparent once the FBI realized that Robert Hanssen, not Brian Kelley, was the long-sought mole. Kelley had once lived on the same street as Hanssen, five houses away from the real spy. He jogged in Nottoway Park, the location of Hanssen's favorite dead drop, the one he had used seventeen times. The two men were about the same age and both worked in counterintelligence. Sometimes their paths crossed; they had once traveled to the same conference and another time had participated in a briefing of senior military officials. Kelley had on one occasion gone to Latin mass at the same church, St. Catherine, that Hanssen and his family had attended.

However, these coincidences, while intriguing in retrospect, were wholly irrelevant. Until the FBI zeroed in on Robert Hanssen, it did not know that the mole had lived on the same street as Kelley, or used Nottoway Park, or that the two men had once gone to the same Catholic church. The similarities simply had nothing to do with the FBI's erroneous belief that Brian Kelley was a traitor.

How could it have happened?

Partly it was bureaucratic blinders, the FBI's ingrained belief that the mole was more likely to be a CIA officer than one of its own. Partly, it was the nature of counterintelligence. Unmasking a mole is a difficult business. The job of the counterspies is to suspect everyone and trust no one. When they think they have a suspect, they may tend to seize on that person to the exclusion of all others. And once under scrutiny, Kelley's every move fueled the bureau's distrust.

"They will be very reluctant to let you go once you are under suspicion," said Paul Moore, the former FBI counterintelligence analyst. "The principle is, there are no coincidences. But there *are* coincidences in life."

As the mole hunters reassure one another that they are on the right track, they become caught up in a self-reinforcing mechanism, and belief gradually hardens into reality. In time, not only Rochford but almost the entire senior echelon of the FBI's counterintelligence managers became absolutely convinced that Kelley was their man.

In retrospect, a high-level FBI official strongly defended the FBI's three-year investigation of Brian Kelley, arguing that it acted on evidence that appeared valid at the time and only later proved wrong. "He fit all the descriptors in the matrix, had all the right accesses, was in right places at right times. He lived in northern Virginia, where we knew the Soviets were active. There was some stuff in his computer that was suspicious. He was discovered surreptitiously doing things that appeared to be espionage-related. He had some strange overseas travel and strange contacts." It ought not to be surprising, however, that a CIA officer might have unusual contacts. Brian Kelley, as the bureau finally admitted, was entirely innocent.

One who did not agree with the pursuit of Brian Kelley was Ed Curran, the FBI agent who headed the Counterespionage Group inside the CIA and supervised the Special Investigations Unit hunting for the mole. He maintained that he, for one, opposed the intense focus on Kelley. "I was very vocal that Kelley was not the guy," Curran said.

One source close to the mole investigation declared: "Rochford couldn't let go of this thing. WFO was totally in charge. They had a big success with Ames, they were walking on water, and nobody was going to get in their way. It was arrogance.

"Why weren't we looking at a dozen people? A lot of people fit the criteria; why weren't we looking at them?"

Even after it was over, there were some lingering questions about the Kelley case, at least for John Moustakas. He said that when the FBI had interviewed his other client—Kelley's friend and former colleague—she had been asked about diamonds, parks in northern Virginia, and other matters later associated with Robert Hanssen; that led him to think that perhaps the bureau knew about Hanssen much earlier than late 2000, as it stated publicly.*

Moustakas's conjecture was understandable. However, the FBI had learned about the KGB and diamonds years earlier; it gave that information the code name KARAT. "There was a 'diamond connection'; we heard from a defector that somebody was being paid in diamonds," said

---

*At his February 20, 2001, press conference announcing Hanssen's arrest, FBI director Freeh was asked when the investigation began. "I don't want to pinpoint the exact time," he replied. "I would say it was the latter part of last year."

John Lewis, the former chief of the FBI's National Security Division. "It goes back at least ten, fifteen years, maybe more. But source accounts were often vague as to which agency the mole was in. Sometimes it was the bureau, sometimes the CIA."

*   *   *

GRAYSUIT had looked very different—and with a far less certain outcome—at the start of 2000. The arrest of Robert Hanssen and the resulting vindication of Brian Kelley were still more than a year away. The hunt for the mole was not going well.

At the time, the FBI was still confident that Kelley, suspended from his job at the CIA, was Moscow's penetration. But the dawn of the new millennium had not brought the bureau any closer to gathering the proof it needed. The FBI had to face the fact: the case against GRAY DECEIVER had stalled.

25

GRAYDAY

For the FBI's mole hunters, as 2000 began, the failure to end their search with an arrest was as frustrating as it was intolerable.

The problem had to be solved, even if it cost millions of dollars. Brian Kelley, the FBI believed, might yet be flushed from his burrow with enough cash.

BUCKLURE was still an active program, although under a new code name. It was based on the premise and the hope that money might lead to the recruitment of a KGB or SVR officer who could identify the penetration. With luck, the operation could wrap up GRAYSUIT, the overall code name for the mole hunt.

At FBI headquarters and the Washington field office, the hunters focused on finding the right Russian source who could identify the mole, producing conclusive proof against Kelley. For security reasons, the effort was in the hands of a deliberately small number of persons, including Neil Gallagher, the senior counterintelligence official at headquarters; Sheila Horan, his deputy; Timothy Bereznay, the chief of the Eurasian section; and Mike Rochford, the unit chief for Russia.

Gallagher, a tall New Yorker who grew up in the South Bronx, joined the FBI in 1973 and spent much of his career in criminal work and counterterrorism. But he had worked as a counterspy in New York for five years and at headquarters in the early 1980s.

At the Washington field office, the effort was led by Tim Caruso, the special agent in charge (SAC) for counterintelligence, who was respected as one of the bureau's top counterspies and had been involved almost continuously in the search for penetrations. Caruso's number two was Leslie Wiser, who had won recognition in 1994, when he ran the innovative and successful surveillance that culminated in the arrest of Aldrich Ames.

The counterspies and the analysts who worked with them drew up a wish list of potential recruitments, many of whom at one time or another had been KGB or SVR American targets officers in Washington or New York. Some were still active at SVR headquarters in Moscow and could not, for the moment, be approached; others had turned up in various capitals abroad. Still others had retired to their dachas.

As the mole hunters studied the names on the list, they tried to correlate their presence in Washington, or the years they held management positions in the KGB, with known intelligence losses. In narrowing the list, they were helped by Yevgeny Toropov, a KGB officer in Ottawa, listed as first secretary of the Russian embassy, who was a secret source of U.S. intelligence.

The FBI counterspies began to focus more and more on one former KGB officer. When he was stationed in Washington, he had been of interest to the FBI. The Russian had gone into private business after he retired from intelligence work and was living in Moscow.

Mike Rochford had managed to make contact with him outside the United States on more than one occasion when the Russian had traveled abroad, and the former KGB man had seemed willing to talk further. But an approach in Moscow would be risky; CIA and FBI agents were closely watched in the Russian capital.

Then the counterspies hit on a possible solution. The FBI knew that the Russian was interested in expanding his business overseas. The bureau approached an executive of an American corporation who agreed to help by inviting the Russian to a fictional business meeting that would supposedly take place in New York in the late spring of 2000. The invitation would seem plausible because the company that issued it was in an industry related to the business that the Russian was in.

It was much easier in 2000 for a Russian citizen to travel to the West than in the days of the Soviet Union, when it was virtually impossible, except as part of an official delegation. Still, the former KGB officer had to provide a convincing explanation for his trip. The FBI, the secret sponsors of the sham meeting, arranged to have an invitation sent to the Russian on the company's letterhead.

"It was just to give him plausible cover to make the trip," one FBI official said. The invitation was the document that the ex-KGB spy needed to show to the authorities in Moscow to justify his travel to New York.

The Russian may have suspected that the FBI was behind the invitation, but there was no way he could be sure of that. "We invited him," the FBI official said, "but he did not know it was us."

And the ploy worked. The news was electrifying when it reached FBI headquarters. The Russian was coming. The plan was operational.

Mike Rochford, because of his experience and previous contacts with the former KGB man, was selected as the agent to make the approach in New York, and if successful, to negotiate the terms with the Russian.

Rochford was not only fluent in Russian but a man who might inspire confidence in his talks with the ex-KGB officer. His appearance helped. Although only in his mid-forties, he was gray-haired, with a gray mustache. A bit heavyset, calm, and soft-spoken, Rochford looked more like an English professor at an Ivy League college than a counterspy.

Rochford had started out at age twenty-three on CI-4, the KGB squad at the Washington field office, targeting Soviet counterintelligence officers for a decade. There followed three years in Nashville, where he acquired a taste for country music. Later, he moved up to a key counterespionage post at headquarters. He went back to Washington field in 1994 and for five years was in charge of the squad assigned to find the suspected penetration inside American intelligence.

Only Rochford was to meet the former KGB man. But a support team of half a dozen FBI agents accompanied Rochford to New York in April 2000. They included Les Wiser; Jim Milburn, the veteran FBI Russian analyst; Special Agent Debra Smith, now the squad supervisor for the mole hunt at the Washington field office; and special agents Ben Gessford and Gwen Fuller from the field office. The CIA also dispatched its own officers to work with the FBI agents.

The Russian, to the enormous excitement of the counterspies gathered in New York, indicated he was willing to deal—but slowly. Such matters were difficult, the Americans should understand, and would require extended discussions. He could not be expected to make a hasty decision. Still, it was not impossible that, providing various conditions were met, some accommodation could be reached of mutual interest.

But that was not the half of it. The Russian had a sensational secret, one he had kept from the KGB and the SVR, and from everyone else.

To Rochford's utter astonishment, he revealed that he had access to the crown jewel, the actual KGB file on the American mole.

But how could this be? The Russian had stayed on only briefly when the KGB's First Chief Directorate, its foreign intelligence arm, was renamed the SVR after the collapse of the Soviet Union in December 1991. Then he had left the government and retired. Surely there was no way he could get back into SVR headquarters, remove one of their most sensitive files, and stroll out with it unchallenged by armed guards.

The answer was soon apparent. Before he retired, and while he still had full access, he said, he had thoughtfully removed the file from Yasenevo, the Russian foreign intelligence headquarters, as insurance against a rainy day. He well understood its potential value. He had stashed it away and he was the only person in the world who knew where it was.

He did not have the file with him in New York, of course, but if the price was right . . .

The news was far beyond what GRAYSUIT's managers ever could have anticipated. The file! The actual mole file!

The Russian's revelation that he possessed the file meant that the bureau, no matter how high the cost, would have to strike a deal with him.

Mike Rochford knew something about how important real documents and files could be. In 1992, after being turned away by the CIA, Vasili Mitrokhin had defected to MI6, the British secret intelligence service, with an unprecedented trove of documents he had copied while working as the chief archivist inside the KGB. The British had whisked him to London and given him a new identity.* Rochford, often with Bob Wade, a veteran FBI counterspy, had flown to London a dozen times during a two-year period to debrief Mitrokhin about the materials. Mitrokhin's files revealed dozens of previously unknown KGB operations and unmasked two spies.

---

*Although detailed and valuable, Mitrokhin's notes did not go beyond 1984, the year that he retired, and did not, therefore, point to the current KGB mole that GRAYSUIT was trying to uncover. Mitrokhin turned over only a portion of his materials in his initial contacts with the British. MI6 is said to have then slipped into Mitrokhin's apartment in Moscow and made off with six large suitcases containing the rest of his cache. See Christopher Andrew and Vasili Mitrokhin, *The Sword and the Shield: The Mitrokhin Archive and the Secret History of the KGB* (New York: Basic Books, 1999).

Now, in a New York hotel room, Rochford began the negotiations to buy the file. For Rochford, aided by his support team, it was essential to establish a bond of trust with the Russian. "You don't just offer the money," said one experienced FBI counterintelligence agent. "That can be insulting. You have to give some thought about each individual. You have to build a personal relationship. Of course the money comes up."

As the talks proceeded, the Russian cautioned Rochford that the file did not contain the name of the mole, or reveal in which agency he worked, since he had never divulged either. But there were enough clues in the documents, the ex-KGB agent said, that he was confident the file would enable the bureau to identify "Ramon Garcia."

There were several secret meetings over the better part of a week between Rochford and the Russian, as they hammered out the agreement, including how many millions of dollars the FBI would have to pay for the file—after the bureau had a chance to examine it, of course.

That condition was one of the first hurdles to be overcome, and it was a major one, because the FBI insisted that the Russian relinquish the file before he was paid. The bureau was not about to buy a pig in a poke.

"He wanted the money up front," one FBI source said. "The guy said he could get a tape recording with the mole's voice, but he didn't know who he is. It sounded fishy. Is this guy trying to scam us? 'This is going to be a dynamite tape,' he says."

A tape recording! Now the FBI agents wanted to get their hands on the file more than ever. But the Russian had to be persuaded to turn over the file first, and to trust the U.S. government to keep its commitments if the file, upon analysis, proved to be what he said it was.

It was a delicate dance, because the thought must have crossed the mind of the former KGB officer that once the FBI had the file, it could walk away and leave him sitting in Moscow with no payment at all, duped by the Americans. "His concern," one FBI official recalled, "was that he not be squeezed like a lemon and just left."

The million-dollar bounty that BUCKLURE had offered more than a dozen years ago was now far too low. Aside from inflation to consider, there was the unique value of the product.

"He wanted a great deal of money without producing anything," the FBI official said. Both sides were wary. "It was like two scorpions. He wanted more and we wanted less."

Finally, after intense negotiations, Rochford and the Russian settled on a price, and it was huge: the FBI paid a whopping $7 million for the file on the mole.

A good-faith initial deposit was placed in escrow in a U.S. bank. There would be a series of payments into the account over the next several months.

Aside from the negotiations over price, there were a host of other questions to be settled. Arrangements would have to be made for the file to be physically handed over in Moscow. But the FBI is largely precluded from operating overseas; the CIA would have to be brought in to manage this part.

The ex-KGB officer would then need to get out of Russia, with as many family members as possible. He would surely be imprisoned or shot if the SVR discovered what he had done.

There were details to be worked out about his life in the United States. He would have to be given a new identity, his personal safety and that of his family guaranteed for life. It would not be enough to settle him into a seaside mansion in La Jolla or some other pleasant spot; he would have to feel certain he was beyond the reach of the SVR. True, the KGB reportedly gave up assassinations more than two decades ago, but defectors, even if they do not spend every moment looking over their shoulder for a hit man from Moscow, are never entirely free of concerns about their security.

Officials were extraordinarily tight-lipped about many of the details involved in acquiring the file and getting it out of Russia.* But when, as planned, the former KGB man returned to Moscow after the negotiations in New York, the CIA established contact with him. When all the arrangements were complete, it was to the CIA that the Russian turned over the file.

Early in November 2000, the file, carefully guarded every moment of its clandestine journey from Moscow, arrived at FBI headquarters in Washington. According to a senior bureau official, "It came in one package, which was actually several smaller packages, all of which would fit into a medium-sized suitcase." The file was able to fit into such a relatively small space because much of the material was on computer floppy disks.

---

*For example, the FBI declined to discuss the location of the meeting with the Russian source. A senior counterintelligence official would say only that it took place "in a city on the East Coast."

Everything was taken immediately to the FBI laboratory on the third floor. The first order of business was a forensic examination of the file. The documents were carefully dusted for fingerprints, but there were no useful prints on them or on the floppy disks. Then every document, envelope, and disk was photographed.

One of the packages came with a note that said, "Don't open this." The FBI counterintelligence agents were itching to open it and overwhelmed with curiosity, but they waited. In a few weeks, they knew, the Russian would come out of Moscow and explain the mystery package.

In the meantime, there was work to be done. There were translations needed; some of the material was in Russian. For example, the KGB man had managed to compile an inventory and description in Russian of every document—six thousand pages in all—that had been passed to Moscow by the mole; the list would have to be translated back into English.

The file included the letters exchanged by the Russians and the mole over the course of fifteen years, some on computer disks, and many of the titles of the documents he had given to the KGB. The actual documents that the mole had passed to the Russians were not included in the package from Moscow. But the detailed notes taken by the KGB man described the documents in sufficient detail so that the FBI could retrieve them from its own files, as well as from the files of the NSA and the CIA.

FBI analysts began a thorough examination of the file, searching for clues that would confirm the identity of the mole at last. The letters and the disks nowhere identified the mole by name or by organization; he was referred to as "Ramon" or "B" or "Ramon Garcia." But there were hints here and there: the KGB's source talked about new assignments and promotions on certain dates. GRAY DECEIVER, it was believed, would soon be arrested.

One of the packages contained the potential treasure that the Russian had first revealed in the meetings in New York, a tape recording of a conversation labeled July 21, 1986, between a KGB officer, Aleksandr K. Fefelov, and the unknown mole. The KGB officer, speaking from a pay phone, had taped part of the conversation.

Sometime in November, Michael Waguespack listened to the tape. Wags, as he was known, was a gray-haired, congenial Louisianan who grew up in the Cajun country near New Orleans and was regarded as one of the best counterintelligence agents in the bureau. He had worked espionage cases, including some major ones, for more than twenty years, in San Diego, Chicago, New York, and Washington. To hear the tape, Waguespack, with Mike Rochford and Tim Bereznay, went to one of the FBI lab's secluded rooms tucked away in the basement of headquarters.

As they settled back to listen, they were certain that they would, at last, hear the voice of Brian Kelley, GRAY DECEIVER. "This was the piece we needed to nail it down," Waguespack said.

No one expected to hear the voice that boomed out into the room.

"It was apparent to all three of us it was not him," Waguespack said.

The agents were stunned and chagrined at the unexpected turn of events. Three years lost; all that effort, and now, just as Rochford was sure that the mole was within his grasp, the shocking revelation, on a fourteen-year-old snippet of magnetic tape, that the bureau had been chasing the wrong man.

But if the voice on the tape was not Brian Kelley, then who was it?

Waguespack recalled his frustration. "I kept listening and I said, 'I know that voice. The inflection. I know that voice, but I can't put it with anybody. That voice sounds familiar.' We broke off that day still unsure.

"Bob King and the other analysts started to look at the material in the file. It had the Patton quote." Twice in the KGB file, the mole had quoted General Patton as saying to his troops, "Let's get this over with so we can kick the shit out of the purple-pissing Japanese." And suddenly King knew where he had heard those words. "King recalled that Hanssen had used that phrase, 'the purple-pissing,' when King worked for him in the Soviet analytical unit," Waguespack said. "He remembered it. He said, 'I think that is Bob Hanssen.'

"We went back and listened to the tape again and this time I realized it was Hanssen. I said, 'My God, that's him!' I went to Neil Gallagher and I said, 'Strap on, because here we go.' "

On November 22, Gallagher received his first briefing on the contents of the file. The mystery package had still not been opened, but the voice on the tape had been recognized and the documents analyzed.

It was, clearly, time to shift gears. "We thought we had Kelley," a senior FBI official admitted. Now everything had changed.

All the evidence made it plain that the mole was Robert Hanssen. Even aside from the voice on the tape, and the Patton quote, the analysis of the KGB file was persuasive. The mole's first letter to the KGB was dated October 1, 1985, and mailed from a Washington suburb. Although Hanssen had been assigned to New York by then, FBI records showed he was in Washington on that day. The mole had said in May 1990 that he would be going on more trips, and that was the year that Hanssen began his travels as an agent in the inspection division, including his jaunt to Hong Kong with Priscilla Sue Galey. In November 1991, Hanssen had been promoted to unit chief at higher pay; in December he told the Russians he had received a salary increase and more authority. There were the references to Chicago, Hanssen's birthplace, and the mole's admiration of Mayor Daley. There were many other clues that made it plain who the betrayer was, and that it was not the CIA's Brian Kelley.

Within the next forty-eight hours, GRAY DECEIVER was no longer the target of the investigation. Now there was a new code name: GRAYDAY.

There could no longer be any doubt about the identity of the mole. GRAYDAY was Robert Hanssen.

Within the small contingent of mole hunters, GRAY DECEIVER had often been referred to in shorthand as simply "GD." By designating Hanssen as GRAYDAY, the agents could still informally speak of the new target as "GD." That would give the impression that they were still talking about GRAY DECEIVER. The decision to keep the same initials was deliberate, so that even the official cryptonym, GRAYDAY, would be tightly held.

There was good reason for this. If Hanssen learned that the bureau had suddenly locked onto a new target in its search for the mole and given the suspect a new code name, there was always the risk that he might flee. He had, after all, asked for an escape plan in his first year as a spy for the KGB. In his briefcase, he carried a current passport.

By mid-December, the Russian was safely in the United States. Some members of his family had also gotten out. And the $7 million was his, to be paid out over a period of time.*

The FBI was now able to open the last package, the one that the source had cautioned not to unwrap.

The former KGB man explained the significance of the mystery package. Inside was an ordinary black plastic trash bag, of the kind

---

*"We were not going to hand him all the money at once," one official said, "and have it misspent and he turns around and says he is poor. Or compromise the security of himself and his family by spending a lot of money."

that suburban homeowners use to dispose of leaves or garbage. When Hanssen filled a dead drop, he would wrap the documents and disks in a plastic trash bag and tape it up to waterproof it and protect it from the elements. Then he would wrap the whole package in a second plastic bag.

The Russian said that under normal procedure, someone else had opened the bags. He would then receive a pile of documents that had been handled first by others. "Only once did they drop off the outer bag with the documents," an FBI official said. "When he removed the outer bag, he assumed that the only persons who had touched the inner bag were himself and Ramon. So he carefully put the inner bag in an envelope." The plastic bag was to prove one of the most vital items in the file that the Russian removed from Yasenevo.

When the package was opened, the bag inside was taken to the FBI lab and processed. Two latent fingerprints were found on the bag. They belonged to Robert Philip Hanssen. And they were the only identifiable prints in the entire file.

The plastic bag sealed GRAYDAY's fate. There had been no question for several weeks that the mole was indeed Bob Hanssen, but now the bureau had solid forensic evidence. It would have been difficult for even the most dexterous defense lawyer to explain what Hanssen's prints were doing on a plastic bag that had been reposited in a secret file inside the KGB in Moscow.

The FBI had followed a false trail for three years, stumbling in the dark, but now it had pulled off an impressive and unprecedented counterintelligence feat. There had been defectors and walk-ins over the years who had provided valuable information, but nothing had ever happened like this. The bureau had engineered the source's travel to New York and had managed to pull off the seemingly impossible—to extract a file on the most damaging mole in the history of the FBI from the most guarded building in Russia.

Gallagher put it this way: "The FBI was able to reach into the KGB back room and bring out what is usually the most difficult part of any espionage case, the evidence. Because the evidence is usually gone. In this case we were able to bring it out of Russia. We were proactive, it didn't just happen."

Although Gallagher would not talk about the money that the FBI had paid for the file, he indicated the source was happy with the outcome. "He was very satisfied with the financial arrangement. And a lot of security-related issues were taken care of. We have covered his financial security and his personal security and assisted him in the transition."

The CIA kept silent about its part in getting the file out of Moscow, but Gallagher credited the intelligence agency with playing an important role. Historically the two agencies, with different missions, have often clashed. It took six years before they formed the joint task force in 1991 that resulted, three years later, in the arrest for espionage of the CIA's Aldrich Ames.

"This was different from Ames; they worked with us on all aspects of the investigation," Gallagher said. "They handled a lot of the resettlement. They also worked with us on the recruitment effort and the success of the operation."

Among the intelligence agencies, "resettlement" is the term used to arrange for a new life and a new identity for defectors, such as the Russian who provided the mole file. The CIA's National Resettlement Operations Center (NROC) makes these arrangements from its secret location near Washington.*

The FBI was careful to say little about the KGB man. But officials confirmed that he lives somewhere in the United States and is well protected. And rich.

The SVR would have figured out fairly quickly who stole its file—certainly after Hanssen's arrest, if not before. FBI director Freeh, in announcing the arrest on February 20, 2001, disclosed that the FBI had obtained "original Russian documentation." By that time, the Russian source was long gone from Moscow. Since presumably only a limited number of KGB and SVR officers would have had access to such a sensitive file, the Russians could have ascertained who among them had suddenly left town—and had not been seen since. (Even months after Hanssen's arrest, some FBI officials still were clinging to the thought that it was possible, if not likely, that the SVR was still trying to figure out who had absconded with the file.)

---

*NROC has more than four hundred defectors on its rolls, and a total, with dependents, of about 1,800 people. Many are Russian, but the defectors include thirty nationalities. The CIA avoids the word "defector"; NROC instead prefers the term "resettlees" or "defector-hero." Some of the more valuable ones are supported for life.

One of the unanswered questions in all this is whether the SVR ever realized, until Hanssen was apprehended, that its file was missing.* Because the file obtained from the Russian ends in December 1991, it is possible that it had been archived around that time. And the SVR may have had no cause to search for the file because Hanssen did not contact the KGB again for eight years after the Soviet Union collapsed.

"Some of what we got was closed files, older files," Gallagher pointed out. "They may not have known they were missing if they had no reason to look for them."

But they know now, he said. "There is an empty space where the file should be."

*   *   *

Hanssen, still assigned to the Office of Foreign Missions at the State Department, was placed under surveillance. It had to be done cautiously, since he was, after all, a trained counterintelligence agent and might detect any watchers. But the surveillance was done by the Gs, the FBI's Special Surveillance Group, and they were good at their jobs.

It would be much easier to track Hanssen if he could be lured back to FBI headquarters, but the problem was how to do that without arousing his suspicions. Hanssen's interest in computers provided the answer. He prided himself on his computer skills, which were considerable, and the counterspies decided to exploit that fact and offer him a promotion and a job in computers.

Mike Waguespack called Hanssen in to headquarters in December. Hanssen seemed extremely tense at their meeting. Waguespack thought he knew the reason: *he's thinking this is it, and that's why I called him in.*

When Waguespack, a deputy assistant director of the National Security Division, offered Hanssen a cushy job in the Senior Executive Service, the elite corps of the federal government, at higher pay, he vis-

---

*In the mists that surround the world of counterintelligence, there are always questions that may never be answered. How did the Russian manage to make off with the file undetected? Did no one suspect him for eight years? By what great good fortune did he receive and save the plastic bag with the fingerprints of Robert Hanssen? For that matter, how did the FBI manage to find and recruit the one person in all of Russia who had the file it needed? It is possible to speculate infinitely about these mysteries, but the bottom line is the FBI got the file, learned in great detail what secrets had been lost to Moscow, and caught Hanssen.

ibly relaxed. Waguespack explained that Hanssen's new responsibility would be to ensure that as the bureau developed new computer programs they would be secure.

A few days later, Hanssen met with Gallagher, the division chief, for the final job interview. "I asked him to take the special assignment," Gallagher said. "It promoted him into SES. It recognized him for his computer expertise. We were playing on his ego." And Gallagher had one more inducement to throw in the pot. "Since he was approaching fifty-seven, the retirement age, I said we would extend him if he wanted to."

Hanssen was delighted. It was about time the bureau, even belatedly, was recognizing his brilliance. The senior levels of the intelligence division were finally taking notice. He would be back at headquarters after his long exile at State, with a parking spot in the FBI garage.

In the meantime, he could not neglect his other duties. On December 12, he was seen driving four times past Foxstone Park, the site of dead drop ELLIS. It was a significant moment because, for the first time, the bureau now knew that Hanssen was an active spy. It is much harder to prove the case against a spy who has gone dormant; now there was a chance that GRAYDAY could be caught in the act.

The day after Christmas, he cruised by the park again three times, looking for the taped signal. Late in the afternoon, he stopped his car for several seconds, studying the park sign, then drove off. Then, just before 9 P.M., he parked near the park entrance, walked over to the signal site, and swept the beam of his flashlight up and down the wooden posts near the sign. He must have found nothing, because he turned and walked away, raising his arms in exasperation. He got back in his car and drove to a nearby Tower Records store.

Half an hour later, he was back. He stopped his car again in front of the Foxstone Park sign for a few seconds and then drove off. Again, there was no signal from the Russians.

After New Year's, he had to wrap up his work at the State Department and get ready for the new job. On January 12, Tom Burns, his boss and former FBI colleague, presided over a going-away party for Hanssen. The affair was held at the China Garden restaurant, in the mall area of the Gannett Building, then the home of *USA Today,* just across the river in Arlington, Virginia.

His colleagues turned out to wish Hanssen well. "There were fifteen to twenty people there," Burns said. "As his superior, I made the usual perfunctory remarks—we'll miss you, don't be a stranger—and I thanked him for his efforts." He added wryly: "The full extent of which, of course, I didn't know."

There was no plaque. But the State Department office controls the distinctive red, white, and blue license plates issued to foreign diplomats, a familiar sight in the capital, and when a colleague left, he would traditionally be given a unique souvenir. "Usually what we would do would be to give a diplomatic license plate with his name on it, mounted on a wood background," Burns explained. "But it had not been struck yet at the firm where we have the plates done."

So Hanssen would have to wait a bit for the special license plate with the name BOB in big letters. It would not be ready for another month.

26

Sleeping Tiger

On January 15, 2001, Hanssen reported to Room 9930 at FBI head-quarters in his newly created position in the Information Resources Division. Gone were the days of sharing cubicles. "We gave him a nice office," Gallagher said.

Three times in January, he searched the FBI database again, looking for his name, for FOXSTONE, and for other indicators that he might be under investigation. But the mole hunters had made sure there was nothing there to be found.

Once the FBI was satisfied that the KGB file brought from Moscow was that of Robert Hanssen, it moved quickly to present the evidence to the Justice Department's Office of Intelligence and Policy Review. It asked that office to apply to the Foreign Intelligence Surveillance Court for permission to begin electronic eavesdropping on GRAYDAY, and secretly to enter and search his home, his office, his computers, and his cars.

Although Hanssen was unaware of it, he was under observation at all times in his ninth-floor FBI office. A tiny, concealed video camera had been secretly installed there before he moved in. The images were relayed by closed-circuit television to the FBI's Washington field office, where they were constantly monitored.

The FBI also tapped Hanssen's home and office telephones. But the bureau was foiled in its attempts to get inside his house to search it, download his home computers, and plant bugs to pick up room conversations. "We couldn't get into the house," one FBI agent said. "There were kids at home, someone [was] always in that house; she [Bonnie] didn't work that much."

However, the FBI found a fortuitous way to keep the Hanssen residence under round-the-clock surveillance. A house across the street was put up for sale in December 2000. Perry and Laura Hood, the owners, could hardly believe their good luck when a woman who called herself "Ann Manning" paid $362,500, all cash, on December 22, only twelve days after the place went on the market. She did not seem to care about the loose bathroom tiles or other problems that buyers fuss about; her only proviso was that the Hoods clear out within two weeks. One neighbor was curious when a telephone lineman let drop that he had installed eight lines for the new tenant; apparently Ms. Manning really liked to talk on the phone a lot. In the process, the installer had inadvertently managed to cut the phone lines briefly to other houses in the neighborhood.*

On the evenings of January 9, 23, and 26, the FBI watched Hanssen as he drove by the signal site at Foxstone Park, either slowing down or coming to a stop. Although his next exchange was set for February 18, he seemed desperate to pick up a signal from the Russians, the little white piece of tape that would indicate they were still there, but he saw nothing. Perhaps he was looking for a warning, a message in dead drop ELLIS that would confirm his worst fears, but the signal never came.

If the SVR ever realized that its file on the mole was missing, along with the former officer who had left Moscow and not returned, it never warned Hanssen that he was in trouble. But the Russians may not have known that the file was gone and that their prime source had been identified and his days were numbered.

Hanssen's precautions in never disclosing his name to Moscow had helped to protect him all these years, but that same secrecy may now have worked against him. Even if the SVR was aware that Hanssen had been betrayed, it had no fast, direct way to communicate with a mole whose identity it may not have known.

On November 7, 2000, around the time the file on the mole reached FBI headquarters, the voters of America had elected a president, although it was not at all clear that it was George W. Bush of Texas until December 12, when the United States Supreme Court intervened in the

---

*"Ann Manning" sold the house in September and vanished.

disputed Florida election results and by a vote of five to four blocked a recount, a decision that awarded the presidency to Bush.*

Now, in January, Bush was about to be inaugurated. For attorney general, he had chosen John Ashcroft, the conservative former Republican senator from Missouri, who had been defeated for reelection. Ashcroft's appointment to the cabinet was highly controversial, and was strongly opposed by a wide variety of liberal and minority groups because of his strong religious convictions, his opposition to abortion, and his views on race. Just before inauguration, Hanssen exchanged his last e-mails with his friend and former FBI colleague Jim Ohlson; the subject was John Ashcroft.

On January 18, Ohlson e-mailed Hanssen that the next day *The Wall Street Journal* would carry an op-ed piece by Jim Skillen, president of the Center for Public Justice, where Ohlson worked, that defended Ashcroft and began: "Do deeply held religious convictions pose a threat to government? May we trust a man like John Ashcroft, whose outlook appears to be saturated by faith, to serve as U.S. attorney general?"

In reply Hanssen messaged back: "Read Lord of the World, by Robert Hugh Benson. You are seeing the logical consequences of an idea as he predicted, an idea injected into a healthy society. The book is futuristic fiction from the past. In the end belief in God is the ultimate 'hate crime.' 'When the Lord comes will there be any faith left in the world.' "†

Later in January, when Hanssen had been in his new computer job less than two weeks, he began meeting with his friend Victor Sheymov, the KGB defector whom he had befriended in 1988—and betrayed by reporting about him to Moscow. Sheymov, a communications expert, had consulted with the NSA and then formed his own computer security company, Invicta, which claimed its new technology could protect computer networks from hackers.

Former CIA director James Woolsey was a prestigious board member of Invicta. Woolsey had represented Sheymov in a long-running bat-

---

*As it happened, December 12 was also the night that Hanssen drove three times by the Foxstone Park entrance and the FBI knew for certain for the first time that it had an active spy on its hands.
†After Hanssen was arrested, it was John Ashcroft who would decide whether to seek the death penalty. Ashcroft had been confirmed by the Senate on February 1 by a vote of fifty-eight to forty-two, after weeks of bitterly divisive debate.

tle with the CIA over money; Sheymov thought he had been promised a million dollars when he defected in 1980 with his wife and child. Woolsey won a settlement in 1994, but the terms were not revealed.

Hanssen led a team of FBI experts to inspect the technology, and he told Sheymov the bureau was interested in buying it, which would have been a big break for the new company. Experts who tested Invicta's system were impressed. According to one company official, the software embodied a new concept. "All virus protections build a firewall that lets some things through but not others. Clever hackers make bad stuff look like good stuff. Invicta's software moves the IP address of the computer, the Internet Protocol, and constantly changes it, so that a hacker can't find the computer. The system automatically tells who you are communicating with, the computer on the other end, when you change the IP address. The people who have tested this say, 'Huh, we can't find the computer.' "

On January 30, around the same time that Hanssen was dangling the prospect of a bureau contract to Sheymov, FBI agents secretly searched Hanssen's car, a Taurus. In the glove compartment they found a roll of white adhesive tape and a Crayola box with a dozen pieces of colored chalk. Both the tape and the chalk could be used for signaling. In the trunk, they found several dark-colored Hefty garbage bags of the sort that had arrived from Moscow with Hanssen's fingerprints. And in the trunk the agents also discovered a box containing seven classified documents that Hanssen had printed out from the FBI's Automated Case Support (ACS) system. Several related to then-current FBI counterintelligence investigations and were classified SECRET.

Six days later, on February 5, FBI agents searched Hanssen's office at headquarters and hit paydirt. They found several communications to and from the SVR, from 1999 on, still retrievable on a computer memory storage card in his office; these included the "Dear Friend: welcome!" letter from the Russians in October that marked the resumption of his spying after the eight-year interval.*

Hanssen, meanwhile, continued to be spooked. Whether or not he spotted any of the Gs, he seemed to know that for him, time was run-

---

*The last document in the KGB file brought out of Moscow is dated December 16, 1991. From 1999 on, all of Hanssen's instructions and his letters to and from the SVR were obtained by the FBI from the 8MB Versa memory card found in the search of his office. As Hanssen later told debriefers, he had retyped the letters from the SVR into his computer to preserve their instructions and requests.

ning out. On the same day that the FBI searched his office, Hanssen had lunch with Sheymov and another Invicta official. Sheymov thought they would be talking about the FBI's interest in the firm's technology. Instead, Hanssen astonished Sheymov by asking for a job. Sheymov, embarrassed, and not wanting to offend his friend or the FBI, stalled, asking what sort of timing Hanssen had in mind. "Right now," Hanssen replied.

Gently, Sheymov tried to explain that Invicta did not really have an opening for another executive. But Hanssen let it be known at headquarters that he was considering an offer from Invicta and would perhaps retire from the FBI.

Ominous signs may have lent fresh urgency to Hanssen's desire to bail out. Once, when he drove into the FBI garage, he thought he set off electronic alarms or buzzers in cars nearby. He also thought he detected radio signals, transmission bursts coming from his own vehicle, which would indicate that a tracking device had been planted in his car.*

And it had also begun to dawn on him by now that there was something fishy about his transfer to headquarters and sudden elevation to a higher status within the bureau. "He was very enthusiastic for the new assignment, at least at first," Gallagher recalled. "But he began to realize he didn't have a meaningful job. We didn't want him to have access to any classified or sensitive information. We gave him things to do, a lot of make-work."

On February 12, agents again searched Hanssen's Taurus. This time, they discovered a small plastic box in the glove compartment, and inside thumbtacks of various colors, including yellow and white, that the Russians had instructed him to use for signaling.

On the same day that the FBI found the thumbtacks, it also searched LEWIS, the new dead drop beneath the wooden stage of the amphitheater in the Long Branch Nature Center in Arlington, Virginia. They found a package inside two plastic garbage bags and took it to the FBI lab. When it was opened, they discovered it contained $50,000 in used hundred-dollar bills. The money was photographed and the package

---

*After Hanssen was arrested, he claimed he had heard radio transmissions from his car and had set off alarms in FBI cars. Ever the techie, Hanssen, within minutes of his arrest, warned the FBI agents who had him in custody that the bureau's tracking equipment was faulty. "We've had his car tested and were not able to reconstruct what he says occurred," Neil Gallagher said. "He was living on the edge and probably seeing surveillance that wasn't there and hearing things that did not actually happen."

rewrapped, taped, placed inside the two bags, and put back in the dead drop exactly as it had been found.

On Friday, February 16, Hanssen went to a meeting he had arranged at Invicta headquarters. To try to impress Sheymov, he stood up at a blackboard and described the new technology with extraordinary accuracy. "He did it as well as I could," Sheymov was quoted as saying.

On that same day, Hanssen dropped by the office of his old colleague Bill Houghton at headquarters. He seemed to want to chat. "We just talked for about an hour," Houghton said. "We talked about general stuff. He was going to retire later in the year and go to work for Victor Sheymov."

"I'm a section chief," Hanssen said.

"You bastard, you have a parking space now."

"Yeah, it's pretty great. I don't have a staff yet, but I'm going to be developing better systems for the bureau to keep our stuff secure."

By now, however, Hanssen was certain that his new job was a phony, and that his career as a Russian spy was rapidly coming to a close. He composed what was to be his last message to Moscow. It had the tone of a farewell letter—almost.

Dear Friends:

I thank you for your assistance these many years. It seems, however, that my greatest utility to you has come to an end, and it is time to seclude myself from active service.

Since communicating last, and one wonders if because of it, I have been promoted to a higher do-nothing Senior Executive job outside of regular access to information within the counterintelligence program. It is as if I am being isolate [*sic*]. Furthermore, I believe I have detected repeated bursting radio signal emanations from my vehicle. I have not found their source, but as you wisely do, I will leave this alone, for knowledge of their existence is sufficient. Amusing the games children play. In this, however, I strongly suspect you should have concerns for the integrity of your compartment concerning knowledge of my efforts on your behalf. Something has aroused the sleeping tiger. Perhaps you know better than I.

Life is full of its ups and downs.

My hope is that, if you respond to this constant-conditions-of-connection message, you will have provided some sufficient means of re-contact besides it. If not, I will be in contact next year, same time same place. Perhaps the correlation of forces and circumstances then will have improved.

> your friend,
> Ramon Garcia

Even with his warning that "Something has aroused the sleeping tiger," and that he was therefore in great danger, Hanssen could not quite bring himself to bid a final good-bye to his "friends." He needed them too much. So he promised to be back in touch, next year, same time.

In Moscow on February 17, Itar-Tass, the Russian news agency, carried a very brief news story reporting that Yevgeny Toropov had vanished from the Russian embassy in Canada in January and was believed to be in the United States. A Canadian foreign ministry official said Canadian authorities "have no information about the whereabouts of Toropov."*

Now, on Sunday, February 18, everything was in place for the final drama in the espionage career of Robert Hanssen. The FBI arrest team assembled, ready to move out. Hanssen, in turn, was preparing to keep his rendezvous at Foxstone Park.

Among the FBI officials waiting for this moment was Mike Waguespack. He could not help thinking back on his encounter with Hanssen at midnight mass on Christmas Eve. "I happened to see him as I walked out of St. Andrew's church in Clifton, Virginia," Waguespack recalled, "and we wished each other a merry Christmas. I thought to myself, *I hope you have a joyous Christmas, because this will probably be your last one.*"

---

*Once Toropov had helped the FBI to pinpoint the Russian source who provided the file from Moscow he vanished, presumably into the CIA's defector program.

27

The Arrest

Jack Hoschouer remembered it was a little after 4 P.M. on that Sunday, February 18, when Hanssen dropped him off at Dulles Airport to catch his flight to Phoenix.

The Special Surveillance Group, the Gs, had followed Hanssen to the airport. As he pulled out, heading east, they stayed on him. After days of preparation, everything was ready for the arrest, which officials at FBI headquarters and agents in the Washington field office expected to go down shortly after 8 P.M.

The bureau knew that Hanssen would appear at Foxstone Park that Sunday because it had found on his computer memory storage card the July 2000 letter from the SVR designating ELLIS as the dead drop to be used once a year on February 18.* And the FBI thought it knew exactly when he would show up at the park: when agents had searched Hanssen's Palm III computer, they found a reference to "ELLIS," February 18, and 8 P.M.

Neil Gallagher, the chief of the National Security Division, had arrived at FBI headquarters at 1 P.M. for a final briefing in the Strategic Information Operations Center (SIOC), the secure area on the fifth floor where officials monitor major operations. The floor of the SIOC is raised so that the space below it can be periodically swept for electronic bugs. The setting is what one might expect, with large television moni-

---

*In SVR parlance, this was a so-called iron site, a fixed location (i.e., one made of iron) to be used on a specified date every year. If all other means of communication should fail, the agent knows he can always make recontact at the iron site.

tors, computers, wall clocks set for time zones around the world, and sophisticated communications equipment. FBI director Louis Freeh planned to join Gallagher there that night to await word of the arrest.

In midafternoon, Gallagher returned to his office on the seventh floor at headquarters to grab a sandwich. Nothing was going to happen for a while.

The FBI, from the telephone taps on Hanssen's house, knew that his daughter, Jane, his son-in-law Richard Trimber, and their children were expected for Sunday dinner. Instead of heading back home from the airport to join them, however, Hanssen, in his silver Taurus, suddenly pulled into the Pike 7 Plaza shopping center in northern Virginia. As the Gs watched from a discreet distance, Hanssen opened his car trunk. He leaned into the trunk for a long time.

Tim Caruso and other FBI agents were sitting in the command van in a parking lot about a mile from the entrance to Foxstone Park. An agent in the van, relaying minute-by-minute reports from the watching Gs, exclaimed:

"He's got some documents and he's putting them in a plastic bag."

Caruso was as astonished as anyone, but he thought he knew what it meant. He looked around at the agents sitting in the van with him.

"He's going to do this right now," Caruso said. "In broad daylight."

Hanssen had previously prepared the package for the Russians, with four classified FBI documents and his "sleeping tiger" cover letter, but he had decided at the eleventh hour, racing back from Dulles, to add three more documents. He opened the package, put them in, and retaped the plastic bag.

All seven documents were classified SECRET. They dealt with current and proposed FBI counterintelligence operations against Russian agents in the United States.

At headquarters, Gallagher's phone rang. "I get a call around 4 P.M. saying that something unusual was occurring, you may want to get down to the SIOC right away. I get down there a minute or so later." Hanssen was at the shopping center, doing something in his trunk, he was told.

Gallagher began trying to reach Louis Freeh.

Hanssen slammed the car trunk shut, got back in the Taurus, and drove the short distance to Foxstone Park.

Debra Smith, the squad supervisor for the Hanssen case at the Washington field office, had been waiting for this moment. It was

Smith who was in charge of the investigation of GRAYDAY by WFO and the surveillance operations that had begun three months earlier. Smith was stationed in the command van with Caruso and Dan Cloyd, Caruso's deputy.

Now it was time. An FBI SWAT team was already in place, just out of sight of the entrance to Foxstone Park. They wore bulletproof vests, because no one knew whether Hanssen, who had boasted of his prowess with guns and owned an extensive personal armory, might start shooting when agents tried to arrest him.

Caruso was right; Hanssen was not waiting for dark. He pulled up across from the park entrance and got out of his car. He placed a piece of white tape vertically on the post of the park sign to indicate to the Russians that the drop would be ready to clear within minutes.

Washington field called the SIOC. He's at the park, WFO reported. "I'm still trying to find Louie Freeh," Gallagher recalled. "SIOC was paging him, we're beeping him, but we still haven't reached him. And in the next five minutes Hanssen's world would turn upside down."

Carrying the package, GRAYDAY disappeared into the woods. It was 4:34 P.M.

He walked deep into the narrow park, following the path that led to the weathered wooden footbridge that was dead drop ELLIS. It took him about four minutes. He looked around and, seeing no one, slipped the package under the bridge, out of sight. Then he walked back out of the park.

Despite Hanssen's increasingly jittery mood of late, it had, all in all, been a pleasant Sunday: church as usual, of course, playing Frisbee with the dog, seeing Jack again—good old Jack—then a visit to the dead drop so convenient to his house, leaving documents, for which the Russians had rewarded him so well. Now it was time to head home. Bonnie would have supper waiting. He crossed the road and was only a few feet from his car.

At that instant, two vans suddenly appeared from both directions, screeching to a halt, blocking Hanssen's Taurus. Four agents jumped out, some carrying huge MP-5 automatic weapons, and surrounded him. Four backup agents were ready to move in if needed.

It was the last second of freedom that Robert Hanssen would enjoy for the rest of his life.

"You're under arrest!" one of the FBI men said. "Put your hands in the air."

Hanssen did not comply immediately and the agent repeated the command.

"Do you have a weapon?" he was asked.

"No," Hanssen replied. The agents made sure.

Quickly, Hanssen was handcuffed with his arms behind his back and hustled into an SUV.

At almost the same moment, Gallagher finally reached Freeh, who started for headquarters.

Hanssen, meanwhile, was being driven to the FBI field office in Tysons Corner, not far from his home. Doug Gregory, the case agent for the GRAYDAY investigation, was in the car with the prisoner, along with another case agent, Stefan A. Pluta.

Hanssen was read his Miranda rights. In the car, the agents played for Hanssen the tape of his conversation of fourteen years earlier with KGB officer Aleksandr K. Fefelov. They showed him photographs of the drop sites he had used, and copies of his letters to the SVR that had been retrieved from his computer memory card. It was a kind of psychological warfare, designed to convince Hanssen that the evidence against him was irrefutable and overwhelming.

He was asked if he had ever spied for anyone other than the Russians. "No one but the Russians," he replied.

Then Hanssen claimed he had wanted to get caught.

For how long? he was asked.

"Since I started," he said.

He promised to tell everything now that it was over. He wanted to know how Bonnie would get the news.

Two agents were on the way to his house, he was told.

Hanssen's life is over, Doug Gregory was thinking. Despite everything, Hanssen had been a fellow FBI agent for twenty-five years.

"Bob, this is a sad day for all of us," Gregory said. "This is just terrible."

Expressionless, Hanssen replied: "Life has its ups and downs."

*   *   *

Bonnie was growing worried when Bob did not return home for dinner. It was getting past 6 o'clock. She waited a while, then served dinner to her daughter and son-in-law and their young children. Still no sign of Bob.

She tried his cell phone, but it wasn't turned on. Someone called the

FBI to see if they knew where Hanssen was. No, the word came back, they had no information. Then the Trimbers left.

Bonnie telephoned her mother in Chicago. Pray for Bob, she said, something odd is going on, he hasn't come home. Bonnie feared there might be a medical emergency; Bob had kidney problems, and his blood pressure had been way up lately. He might be lying in a hospital somewhere, unable to contact her.

Bonnie was becoming frantic. It was well after dark now, and Bob had still not returned from the airport. Nor had he called. What was keeping him?

Finally, she could stand it no longer. She got in her car with a friend and drove out to Dulles to look for him. She did not know what else to do.

The FBI followed her to the airport. In the parking lot, the Gs approached Bonnie and told her that her husband was unharmed and that an agent would be along in a minute or two to explain. The agents appeared and took Bonnie to a room inside the terminal. There she was told that her husband had been arrested for espionage.

"She was destroyed," one FBI man said. "She was in a very emotional state already, and more so afterward. She was devastated."

The agents drove Bonnie, weeping and overcome, from the airport back to her house. They stayed with her as she made a series of telephone calls to family members to tell them what had happened. She called her mother again and told her the dreadful news: Bob had been arrested. For espionage.

Jeanne Beglis, Bonnie's sister, and her husband, George, arrived from across the street to do what they could.

The FBI agents, although polite, weren't about to leave. The house was a crime scene and would have to be searched from top to bottom. The bureau had obtained search warrants two days earlier.

Bonnie was upstairs with a female agent, Peggy Casey Cash, throwing some clothes together. Upset as she was, Bonnie wanted to talk, and they did.

Downstairs, Special Agent Dave Lambert was already going through the house with Greg Hanssen, the couple's seventeen-year-old son. Lambert was asking about Bob Hanssen's guns: where were they? Greg knew exactly where they were, showing the FBI man the location of each firearm: in closets, under beds, seemingly all over the house.

Lisa, then fifteen, the only other Hanssen child still living at home, returned from a date with her boyfriend and stepped into the chaos.

When she heard that her father had been arrested as a spy, she broke down sobbing. Jeanne Beglis cradled Lisa in her arms.

The FBI agents pointed out to Bonnie that soon the house on Talisman Drive would become the center of a media frenzy, with yellow tape stretched across the lawn, television satellite trucks clogging the street, and reporters swarming the neighborhood. They offered to take her and the two children to a hotel to escape the mob scene. She accepted, and the agents escorted her and the children to the nearby Residence Inn at Tysons Corner.

As she left the house, Bonnie remarked: "He did it. He just did it."

While still at the house, and again in more detail at the hotel, Bonnie volunteered startling new information. Until then, the bureau's counterspies believed that Hanssen had begun spying in October 1985. That was the date on the first letter from Hanssen to the KGB in the file that the FBI, with help from the CIA, had purloined from Moscow.

Now, for the first time, the FBI learned from Bonnie that Hanssen had begun his espionage career in 1979 in New York. She revealed how she had come upon her husband in the basement of their home in Scarsdale writing a letter, which he had hastily tried to conceal. She told how he claimed he had been scamming the Soviets, providing worthless information—which, although she did not know it, was a lie. She had insisted he see Father Bucciarelli and said that Hanssen later contended he had given the money, $30,000, to Mother Teresa.

Not until months afterward, when Hanssen had pleaded guilty and was being debriefed, did the bureau learn from him that in 1979 he had betrayed to the GRU not worthless information but the identity of TOPHAT, General Dimitri Fedorovich Polyakov, one of the most important U.S. agents inside the Soviet military. TOPHAT was executed after he was also betrayed, in 1985, by the CIA's Aldrich Ames.

And it was only then, during the debriefing, that the FBI learned why the KGB's file on Hanssen contained no evidence of his earlier spying. The reason, Hanssen told the FBI, was that in 1979 he had volunteered his services to the rival GRU.

At the Residence Inn, Bonnie continued to talk and respond to questions almost until dawn. The agents seemed satisfied with her answers. The FBI appeared persuaded that she had really believed her husband's promises in 1980 that he would never spy again. She was clearly distraught and shocked by his arrest. It was 4 A.M. Monday before she fell, exhausted, into bed.

So far, the public knew nothing of the arrest of yet another world-class mole, this time not within the CIA, like Aldrich Ames, but inside the FBI itself. And to make matters worse, the spy was not only in the FBI, he was a counterintelligence agent in the National Security Division, the very part of the bureau responsible for catching spies. The FBI braced for the storm that was sure to come.

After the arrest, the FBI retrieved the package that Hanssen had left under the footbridge and substituted another, prepared in advance, containing only blank paper. It kept the drop site in Foxstone Park under surveillance, hoping to catch an SVR officer in the act of retrieving the package that Hanssen had left under the footbridge. Nabbing a Russian officer in the act would, at least a little, offset the bad news about Hanssen.

But no Russian showed up Sunday night, or the next day. On Monday night, the FBI continued to keep the drop site under surveillance. "We were hoping a Russian would come out," Gallagher said. "It didn't happen."

The FBI was not able to determine why. Perhaps, it was thought, the Russians were spooked. They might have had countersurveillance in the vicinity of the park and spotted the FBI cars in the area. That Sunday afternoon, the FBI knew, a number of Russians had left the embassy complex on Wisconsin Avenue. At 6 p.m., around the time that Bonnie and the Trimbers were having dinner, Gallagher said, "we still had some Russians unaccounted for."

For a week, agents had been lying in the woods in the cold and the rain at the Long Branch Nature Center, nine miles from Foxstone Park, watching the dead drop there, code-named LEWIS, where the SVR had left the $50,000 for Hanssen. About two hours after Hanssen's arrest agents also picked up the money at the Nature Center. Hanssen would not be needing it.*

Word of the arrest could not be held indefinitely, and on Tuesday, February 20, FBI director Louis Freeh scheduled an afternoon press

---

*The FBI concluded that the money had been left at the LEWIS drop site as a result of a breakdown in communication between the SVR and Hanssen. Normally, Hanssen and the Russians exchanged documents and money at the same drop site. Weather may have been partly to blame. "When the Russians placed the fifty thousand dollars at the amphitheater [at LEWIS], they put a piece of tape on a pole," Gallagher said. "It rained, the tape shriveled up and fell off the pole. We found it about two feet away."

conference. He was too late; at 7 A.M. NBC's *Today* show broke the story of Hanssen's arrest.

* * *

Aboard Air Force One on the way to St. Louis to speak to parents and teachers at an elementary school, President Bush issued a statement about the arrest a few minutes before Freeh faced the press. It was, he said, "deeply disturbing," but he had confidence in the FBI director and the men and women of the bureau. In language that foreshadowed the words he would use months later, after the September 11 terrorist attacks on the World Trade Center and the Pentagon, he added: "I thank the men and women who proudly serve our country. But to anyone who would betray its trust, I warn you—we'll find you and we'll bring you to justice."

* * *

Freeh looked grim as he faced a huge crowd of reporters and television lights in the FBI auditorium. The CIA director, George Tenet, sat on the stage, but said nothing and stole away early, before the news conference was over.

Attorney General John Ashcroft began with the obvious. "This is a difficult day for the FBI," he said.

Then Freeh took the microphone. Hanssen's arrest, he said, was the result of a mole hunt that followed the Aldrich Ames case. It had happened, he added, because of "a counterintelligence coup by the FBI," working with the CIA.

Freeh was attempting to put the best face on the capture of a penetration who had spied intermittently for almost twenty-two years. Yet his words were not an exaggeration. The arrest *was* the result of an extraordinary counterintelligence operation.

The FBI director did not spell out the details; he did not disclose the name of Mike Rochford, the secret meetings with the former KGB officer in the New York hotel room, the file the Russian had spirited out of SVR headquarters, or the $7 million paid to the ex-KGB man. He did let drop that the FBI had obtained "original Russian documentation" that had pointed to Hanssen. But that hint was as far as he went.

The damage Hanssen did, Freeh admitted, was "exceptionally grave." He added: "The criminal conduct alleged represents the most traitorous actions imaginable against a country governed by the rule of law. . . . I stand here today both saddened and outraged."

In Washington, when political figures find themselves in major hot water, they appoint a commission. Freeh announced that he had named William Webster, the respected former director of both the FBI and the CIA, to examine the bureau's internal security and procedures and recommend improvements. But Webster was investigating his own former agency; Ashcroft ordered the Justice Department's inspector general to launch a separate inquiry into what had gone wrong.

Soon afterward, although there was no public announcement, Paul Redmond, the former CIA counterintelligence expert, was named to run the intelligence community's detailed damage assessment of the Hanssen case. It was the task of Redmond's group, working in the shadows, to determine exactly which programs Hanssen had betrayed and destroyed, how costly were the compromises, and what changes U.S. intelligence agencies would have to make to repair the breach.

As FBI officials well understood, Congress and the public would focus on the fact that a mole had gone undetected among the counterspies for a very long time, not on the resourceful and imaginative way he was unmasked. For Freeh and the FBI, the public revelation that the bureau had harbored its very own Aldrich Ames in its ranks for more than two decades was only the latest in a seemingly endless series of disasters.

The string of debacles had begun at Ruby Ridge, Idaho, in 1992, when the wife of the white supremacist Randall Weaver was mistakenly shot and killed by an FBI sharpshooter. That was followed in 1993 by the FBI siege of the compound in Waco, Texas, that left seventy-five members of the Branch Davidian religious sect dead. Freeh did not become FBI director until later that year, but he was criticized for failing to crack down on subordinates in the cover-up that followed Ruby Ridge.

Then came the FBI's pursuit of Richard Jewell, initially a suspect but later cleared, in the bombing at the 1996 Summer Olympics in Atlanta; the disclosure of sloppy work in the bureau's crime lab, resulting in skewed testimony in court; and the mishandling of the case of Los Alamos scientist Wen Ho Lee.

During his eight-year tenure, Freeh had criticized President Clinton about the FBI files obtained by the White House, supposedly for political purposes, and he fought with Attorney General Janet Reno, who rejected his recommendation that she appoint an independent counsel to investigate fund-raising abuses in the 1996 Clinton-Gore presidential campaign. That won him strong Republican support on Capitol Hill, but at a price; it created the perception among the public that the FBI and its director had become embroiled in politics.

On May 1, 2001, Freeh announced he was leaving his post. He knew what was coming; nine days later, the Justice Department reported that the FBI had failed to provide what was eventually revealed to be a total of more than three thousand documents to defense lawyers for Timothy McVeigh. As a result, Attorney General Ashcroft was forced to postpone the scheduled execution of the Oklahoma City bomber for a month.*

By the time Freeh announced he was calling it quits, public confidence in the FBI had plummeted to 24 percent, according to a CBS News poll, down from 43 percent a year earlier.†

                    *   *   *

Jack Hoschouer had arrived in Arizona Sunday night to visit his elderly parents, who lived in Mesa during the winter months. On Tuesday morning, they were watching television when they heard the news.

"My mother said I turned white," he said. "At first I thought it had to be a mistake."

Hoschouer dialed his wife in Germany. "I told her to turn on CNN. My parents don't get CNN—they are in kind of a retirement community—so I went over to the clubhouse later and watched the press conference. I was devastated. I felt like Hiroshima the day after the bomb."

Jack Hoschouer knew the FBI would want to talk to him. He called the bureau's field office in Phoenix and arranged to fly back to Washington, where he was interviewed at length at the Washington field office.

In the course of the questioning, Hoschouer mentioned the Rolex that Hanssen had given to him in 1990. "They said, 'Give us the watch.'

---

*McVeigh, who built and set off the bomb that killed 168 people and destroyed the federal building in Oklahoma City in 1995, was executed by lethal injection on June 11, 2001, at the federal penitentiary in Terre Haute, Indiana.

†The telephone poll of 1,063 Americans found that only a quarter of respondents had a favorable view of the FBI. *The New York Times,* September 9, 2001, Section 4, p. 3.

I didn't have it right then. It was in repair." The Rolex was potential evidence, and Hoschouer understood why the government wanted it, "but I told them I want it back."

The Rolex was being repaired in Bonn. Hoschouer had to retrieve the timepiece from Germany to give it to the FBI. Later, he said, he tried to get the watch back and could not. Randy Bellows, the lead federal prosecutor in the Hanssen case, explained the reason. "Randy Bellows told me since it was a gift, and I didn't pay anything for it, they have a right to it. I paid $250 to get the watch fixed and had it for two days. If I'd known the government was going to take it, I wouldn't have had it fixed."

*   *   *

Bonnie Hanssen faced a bleak future, with no husband, six children, substantial debts, and Hanssen's FBI salary cut off. And there was always the possibility that the FBI would change its mind and come after her, even though they seemed to buy her story that she knew nothing about his espionage after 1980. There was also a chance that federal prosecutors would begin to place pressure on her, since she had known of Hanssen's earlier espionage, to try to get him to cooperate with the government and reveal the full extent of his treachery.

Under the circumstances, she decided she had better get herself a lawyer. She contacted Janine Brookner, a former CIA officer who had been awarded $400,000 by the intelligence agency for gender discrimination against her. The CIA had investigated Brookner and subjected her to various false accusations after she had disciplined several subordinates while she was station chief in Jamaica. Brookner, who went to law school after leaving the CIA, agreed to represent Bonnie Hanssen.

But who would defend her husband? When high-profile figures in Washington get into major trouble, there is one lawyer they often seek out. President Nixon's attorney general, John Mitchell; Aldrich Ames; and Monica Lewinsky had done so, among others. Bob would need a lawyer who could play in the big leagues. Espionage was punishable by death.

Bonnie Hanssen reached for the telephone and called Plato Cacheris.

28

Sex, Lies, and Videotape

It had begun in 1970, when Jack Hoschouer was serving in Vietnam as a U.S. Army adviser to a South Vietnamese battalion. The package from the States had arrived in a plain brown envelope.

Hoschouer remembered his amazed reaction when he opened it: holy Toledo! Out fell several photographs of Bonnie Hanssen, completely naked, some in provocative poses. Hoschouer wrote back to Bob Hanssen, asking, Did you make a mistake, sending these to me? But the next day a letter arrived from his friend. I hope you liked the little morale builder I sent you, Hanssen wrote.

More photos came while Hoschouer was in Vietnam. Along with them, in his letters Hanssen would ask, What kind of poses do you like? Hoschouer would tell him, and Hanssen would try to photograph Bonnie in the ways his friend would enjoy.

Bonnie Hanssen posed willingly for her husband of two years in the privacy of their bedroom. But she had no idea that he would ever share the photos with anyone.

At the time, Hanssen was studying accounting at Northwestern University. He looked up to Jack; there was his friend, risking his life for his country while he was safely in Chicago, getting his MBA, learning how to prepare a balance sheet and reconcile assets and liabilities. Over the years, Hanssen often told Jack he felt "rotten to the core," and that Jack was a better person. Men like Jack who fought in Vietnam were heroes, he would say.

Hoschouer did see combat in Vietnam; he was one of the first Americans into Cambodia when Richard Nixon ordered the incursion that led to the deadly clash between students and the National Guard on the campus of Kent State. He earned a bronze star when his unit came under heavy fire as helicopters lifted them out of Cambodia. Hoschouer decided to remain in the military and become a career Army officer. The following year, now a captain, he commanded an air infantry company in the 1st Air Cavalry Division in Vietnam; he received a purple heart after he was wounded in the left arm by shrapnel in an engagement with North Vietnamese forces.

So Hanssen may have rationalized that by secretly sending nude photos of Bonnie to his friend, he was doing his bit on the home front, running a bizarre one-woman U.S.O. show, starring his unwitting and unclad wife. But if that was his reason, it was soon forgotten; even after Hoschouer came home from the war, Hanssen continued to send him photos of his naked wife. It went on for years.

In Vietnam, Hoschouer had received negatives of some of the pictures so he could enlarge them, which he did. But, in time, he began to have qualms about what they were doing. He gave the negatives back to Hanssen. We've got to stop this, he told him.

That was in the 1980s, and Hanssen by now was a special agent of the FBI and had begun his second career as a Russian spy. For three or four years, he did stop sending the prurient photos to Jack. But then he started up again.

The photographs were only the beginning. In 1987, the Hanssens bought the house on Talisman Drive; Jack was a frequent visitor and would stay with them whenever he could get to Washington.

The Hanssens' house had three levels, with a living room, dining room, and kitchen on the ground floor. The Hanssens had added the spacious deck in the rear, just beyond the living room. Up five steps to the left of the front door were three bedrooms and two baths. The Hanssens' bedroom was one of these; all three boys in bunk beds shared another, and the couple's youngest daughter had her own small bedroom. Down five steps from the ground floor was another bedroom, where Jack would stay, with a den next to it and a powder room.

And it was in the house on Talisman Drive that Hanssen's fantasy to have other men, but Jack in particular, view his wife naked moved from photographs to reality. Again without Bonnie's knowledge, Bob proposed that Jack watch them having sex. Why he did so only he knows, but in an Internet posting about Bonnie in June 1998 on a pornographic website, he wrote: "Bob loved having men's tongues dangle out looking at his wife."

Whatever his motive, Hanssen was exposing secrets and at the same time exposing his wife. He betrayed his country and simultaneously betrayed his wife. And all the while he was confessing his sexual sins, and his espionage, to his priests, piously observing the rules and rites of Opus Dei, and urging his friends to get closer to God.

And so, at night, Hoschouer slipped out through the French doors onto the deck where, standing on a chair, he was able to look through the bedroom window and watch the Hanssens having sex. Because the deck backed onto the woods, there was little chance that anyone would see him standing there in the dark.

It was not enough for Hanssen to allow his close friend to watch the most intimate, private moments between a husband and wife; he also later felt compelled to write about it on the Internet. His language was raw and crude, and a few sentences are sufficient to capture the tone:

"He [Jack] could see her walking around the room naked and I'd position her in different ways on the bed while fucking her so he'd get a good look of my cock going in and out or of her tits bouncing. By pure chance, and his good fortune, she even bent over right in front of the window once when he was there, and he got a good view of her pussy from about a foot away. It was great. I was dying watching. . . . Anyway, Jack and I have our fun. Bonnie looks great. Jack and I love seeing her tits slapping together as she takes cock hard." And so on.

The live sex show had worked, and more than once, but Hanssen, ever the techie, decided there was a better way. Jack might get chilly standing in the night air, and there was always a chance, however remote, that one of the kids might spot him and wonder what Uncle Jack, as he liked to be called by the Hanssen children, was doing out there in the dark.

Starting sometime in the 1990s, Hanssen hid a small video camera in his bedroom and rigged it up so that Jack, sitting in the comfort of the downstairs den, could watch on television as Bob and Bonnie had sex in the upstairs bedroom.

Jack did, over a period of about three years. The den was cozy; there was a fireplace, a comfortable chair, and the television. Told by Hanssen on what nights to watch, Hoschouer would tune in to his own special, closed-circuit channel.*

---

*There were videotapes as well; at least one, of poor quality, was obtained by the FBI.

If Hoschouer was visiting for several days, Hanssen might ask his friend to watch the first night. Jack would agree. And the next day, Hanssen would ask, How was it? Hanssen would question his friend closely, to be sure Jack had tuned in. "I would tell him something specific I had seen," Jack said, "so he knew I had watched."

And the next night, Hanssen would say again, Do you want to watch? "I was uncomfortable, and a couple of times I told him the signal went away. I said this as an excuse when I did not want to watch."

By now Hoschouer had retired from the Army in Germany, where he worked for an arms dealer and lived in Trier, an ancient industrial city. Hanssen always looked forward to Jack's visits and their shared secret, of which Bonnie remained unaware.

According to Hoschouer, he never asked to view the sex show. "I never initiated it. I was always invited to watch. And sometimes I didn't want to. I didn't think it was right. But he wanted me to do it so bad." He paused, and added, "I've got no excuse."

Hoschouer could have said no, but he never did. He never told his friend to stop. And he could not deny that he was sometimes turned on by what he saw.

Once, but only once, he asked Hanssen:

"Why do you do this?"

"I'm a human and I'm weak," Hanssen replied.

When the bizarre story of the video camera in the bedroom and the televised sex show leaked to the media several months after Hanssen's arrest, Hoschouer struggled with the notoriety it brought.* The close bond formed between two teenagers had resulted, decades later, in an outcome that Hoschouer could hardly have foreseen; his friend in prison for life as a Russian spy, and his own participation as a voyeur exposed to the world.

In his late fifties, Hoschouer was a handsome man, still with a touch of military bearing, square-jawed but now gray haired, his face lined. He told the FBI and the Justice Department's internal inquiry how the sexual activity had begun with still photos and moved on to live watching, and then the closed-circuit television. He was also remarkably candid, if initially reticent, in a series of more than a dozen interviews by telephone from Germany and in person in Washington. He

---

*CBS's *60 Minutes* reported on the video sex show in the Hanssens' bedroom, and Hoschouer's role, on December 16, 2001.

appeared to be remorseful and vastly embarrassed by what he and Hanssen had done, but he did not attempt to deny any of it.

Their mutual preoccupation with sex and pornography had gone on for years, not only in the house on Talisman Drive but in their exchanges of transatlantic e-mails, their visits together to strip clubs in Washington, and once to a bordello in Germany, where Jack had watched as a prostitute performed oral sex on Bob.

Hanssen's obsession with the idea of other men seeing his wife naked was the consistent theme of his various Internet writings. In June 1998, he posted a story on an adult website, a fantasy about Bonnie, naked and fixing her hair in their apartment near the elevated railway in Chicago, when suddenly, at least in Hanssen's imagination, she spots a group of five men, track workers, staring at her through the window. At first, Bonnie tries to pull the shade, but it keeps rolling up, exposing her "cute little bush." Hanssen went on: "She felt aroused. 'If only Bob were here,' she thought, 'I'd show him even a better time.' " Then she performs a striptease for the track workers. "Bonnie was starting to enjoy this."

In another of Hanssen's Internet fantasies, at a party in their apartment Bonnie becomes groggy when she has a few drinks and puffs on a joint. She strips in the bedroom and he orders her to stay that way as two of the male guests wander in and see her. Then Hanssen enters the bedroom. "Bonnie was there lying completely nude on her bed, with her pussy held open, her legs splayed wide, just as I had told her. She was a good obedient wife." Was Hanssen, in his Internet fantasy, reenacting the punishment he had received when his father made him sit with his legs spread wide? The parallel was striking.

In the spring of 2001, some three months after Hanssen's arrest, Bonnie found out for the first time that Jack Hoschouer had been watching her make love to her husband for years, live, and on television.

Bonnie was told the horrendous truth, not directly by her jailed husband or by Jack Hoschouer, but by a psychiatrist hired—and soon thereafter fired—by Plato Cacheris. Dr. Alen J. Salerian was a fifty-four-year-old Armenian, born in Turkey, who received his medical education in Istanbul and in the United States, to which he emigrated in 1971. He had worked for the FBI and had previously consulted on cases for Cacheris. This time, however, their relationship went rapidly downhill.

The root cause was that Salerian, although warned not to do so by Cacheris, revealed to Bonnie that Jack had watched her for years having sex with her husband. Cacheris was also outraged that the psychiatrist planned to go on BBC television and talk about Hanssen, whom he had evaluated at the request of Cacheris.

Salerian had learned about the photographs, the video camera, and Jack's role when he met with Hanssen over a period of days in a small interview room at the Alexandria Detention Center.

"You're not a good Catholic and you cannot put this behind you until you confess to your wife," Salerian insisted. Salerian also told Hanssen that Jack had talked to the FBI. "We can assume everything Jack knows will surface," the psychiatrist said. "So it should also surface between you and Bonnie."

In mid-May, three months after Hanssen's arrest, Salerian went to Bonnie and told all. "I came to a conclusion in my work with Bob that Bonnie's knowledge was critical," he said. "There would be no relief for this man without her knowing. It was just a matter of time before Bonnie had this information. I thought his wife must be told. He totally agreed with me after many hours, tearful hours in prison. This happened in a crisis over the weekend. On Monday after, I talked with Bonnie. I told her everything. I spent four hours with her. Bonnie cried and hugged me. Bob said he was very happy about what I did."

Only afterward did Salerian tell Cacheris what he had done. The legendary defense attorney went ballistic when he heard the news. Cacheris was a gentleman of the old school. He felt Bonnie Hanssen had suffered enough when her husband was arrested as a Russian spy; her life had already been shattered; she did not need to know the rest. Moreover, at a meeting on May 14, Cacheris had explicitly warned Salerian not to reveal the sex show to Bonnie.

Cacheris called Salerian into his office. In a tense confrontation on the morning of May 17, Cacheris told the psychiatrist he had disclosed to Bonnie Hanssen, in Cacheris's words, "highly sensitive matters which we had specifically directed him not to disclose to her." According to Cacheris, Salerian replied, "It went over my head. I dropped the ball. I goofed."

Cacheris had also heard reports that Salerian was preparing to do an interview on BBC television to discuss the case.* It was true, and

---

*Salerian flew to London nine days later and taped an interview about Hanssen with Tom Mangold, the prominent British television journalist. The program, one in a series called *The Correspondent,* aired in England on June 17. Salerian liked to appear on television; his résumé devotes one whole page to "Media Experience."

Cacheris, declaring he no longer had confidence in the psychiatrist, handed him a letter dismissing him.

In defending his decision to inform Bonnie about what her husband had done, Salerian said, "In my mind I was part of the defense team, and I was working with them. I saw myself as a team member. I didn't think I was reporting to him [Cacheris]. I was joining the team as a forensic expert to offer my opinions and advice, but primarily to work with Bob and Bonnie Hanssen."

Cacheris disagreed, suggesting that Salerian had another agenda. "He [Salerian] got the idea there was a psychiatric defense, and I think he envisioned himself as the star witness in a highly public trial," Cacheris said.

Having fired Salerian, Cacheris still felt he needed a psychiatrist to evaluate his client. It was then that he turned to Dr. David Charney, an Alexandria, Virginia, psychiatrist who had made a specialty of studying the minds and motivations of spies.

The two psychiatrists who saw Hanssen disagreed sharply on whether his sexual obsessions were related in any way to his espionage. Salerian thought there was a link. "He felt extremely guilty about his psychological behavior," he said. "He wanted to get rid of and contain his sexual demons. He found some comfort in religion and in Opus Dei. Opus Dei told him to pray to heal the demons. He prayed and failed. He became increasingly despondent over his inability to help himself. He was a tormented soul as a result of his psychological wounds and sexual demons.

"The spying in some symbolic and psychological way was an attempt to keep his sexual demons at bay. The spying was a diversion, keeping his mind preoccupied. Spying was less of an evil than his own illness. It would keep him busy and away from his own demons."

Dr. Charney, on the other hand, saw little relationship between the kinky goings-on at Talisman Drive and Hanssen's spying for the KGB. "The sexual stuff has very little to do with the espionage," he said. "I'm not going to say zero, but I think it's very incidental to the true dynamics of his involvement with spying. He had a great hunger for not being lonely, and Jack was so valuable to him, he had to do with Jack what he thought it took to keep Jack's interest sustained. Jack had the same struggle within as Hanssen did, and one or the other would get very remorseful.

"Bob valued Jack's friendship a tremendous amount, and their relationship was sealed at the time they were eighteen years old. When you are eighteen, relationships are coarse, physical, athletic, towel-snapping in the locker room, bragging, sexual. I believe their relationship was arrested at that time psychologically. It [the live and video sex show] was a very middle-adolescent or late-adolescent thing."

Except for Jack, no one knew of Hanssen's infatuation with pornography. To his colleagues, he went out of his way to appear straitlaced and even prudish, as he did when he told Paul Moore that strip clubs were sinful.

"Bob never indicated any interest in sex," said Ron Mlotek, Hanssen's friend at the State Department. "He was to all intents and purposes almost asexual. In the cafeteria we'd see a short skirt go by. I'd say, 'Wow, look at that.' From Bob, no reaction, never."

There was one exception, however. When the FBI searched Hanssen's car, agents found two photographs of the sultry Welsh actress Catherine Zeta-Jones. "The only time I ever heard him talk about sex," Mlotek said, "was when he described the actress in the movie with Sean Connery about the bank heist. Catherine Zeta-Jones. He teams up with her because she is also a thief.* She was wearing tight-fitting bodysuits in the movie. He talked a lot about that. He said she looked really hot. He saw the movie five times. She did something for him."

But to Bonnie, Hanssen revealed nothing about his sexual escapades, the visits to strip clubs, his relationship with Priscilla Sue Galey, the trip to Hong Kong, the pornography on the Web, or, most of all, how he had turned their bedroom into an X-rated video for the amusement of his friend Jack.

One can only imagine Bonnie Hanssen's deep humiliation and anger, her utter devastation, when she learned the truth about what her husband had done to her. The intimacies they had shared in the privacy of their bedroom were not only seen by Jack but described by Hanssen and posted around the world on the Internet. Yet she continued to visit her husband in jail. She remained fully supportive of the man to whom she had been married for more than thirty-two years. Friends said she had forgiven him. "Her mission now is to save his soul," said one.

But there was an even more shocking sexual scheme hatched by Hanssen, worse, if that is possible, than allowing his friend Jack to watch him having sex with Bonnie.

---

*Entrapment, a 1999 caper film, starred Connery, Zeta-Jones, and Ving Rhames in a plot to steal $8 billion from a Malaysian bank.

Jack had no children, and over several years, Hanssen, the father of six, had often said how sad he was that the Hoschouers were childless. He suggested that if Bonnie and Jack could, one way or another, make love and have a baby boy—it was always a baby boy—they would be a three-person family. Hoschouer did not take these musings seriously; he knew there was no way that Bonnie would ever agree to it.

But in 1997 Hanssen sent the first of two e-mails on the subject to Jack in Germany. Suppose, Hanssen wrote, there were a relaxed, quiet evening, just the three of them. In the scenario Hanssen imagined, they would all be having drinks. The night would turn romantic, and lead to group sex. Bonnie would be impregnated with Jack's child.

The next e-mail took on a much more sinister cast. There was a drug, Hanssen wrote, called Rohypnol. The date-rape drug.* It was called that because teenagers and others have used it to sedate women and then have sex with them. Usually, the women who have been drugged cannot remember what happened. It might be the perfect solution to the problem. As Hanssen knew, Rohypnol is illegal in the United States, but the pills can be obtained by prescription in Europe. Could Jack get some?

Although the drug, if prescribed, is available in Germany, Jack had heard that it could be bought over the counter in the Netherlands. To his later regret, instead of saying no, Hoschouer sent an e-mail back to Hanssen saying he lived near Holland and would look for it.

As it happened, Hoschouer was teaching in Belgium that summer, on the Dutch border. He got on his bike and rode fifteen miles over the border to Eindhoven. "I had no intention of doing it, of buying the drug," he said. "I did not look for the drug. The only way would have been if someone jumped out of the bushes and gave it to me."

As for drugging and having sex with Bonnie, Hoschouer said, "There is no way I would do that. It would be rape." He also said he told Hanssen he could not participate in the scheme.

After Hanssen's arrest, Hoschouer did tell the FBI about watching the marital scenes in the Hanssens' bedroom over the years, both

---

*Rohypnol, the generic name for which is flunitrazepam, is similar to Valium but approximately ten times more potent. It is manufactured by Hoffmann-LaRoche and is prescribed widely in Europe and other countries as a sleeping pill and tranquilizer. Known as "roofies," the pills are often abused in combination with alcohol or other drugs. Rohypnol has no taste or odor and if slipped into a drink cannot be detected.

through the window and on TV, but he did not reveal the plan to drug Bonnie. At the request of the FBI, however, he turned over his computer hard drive to the bureau.

Jack usually deleted his e-mail exchanges with Hanssen about sex, and he thought he had done so with the two from 1997. But the bureau's computer technicians were able to retrieve them.

Much later, almost a year after Hanssen's arrest, Hoschouer thought he had figured out why his friend wanted him to father a child with Bonnie Hanssen. Maybe, he speculated, Hanssen reasoned that if Jack had the child he would be emotionally bound to the family, so that if Hanssen were caught and sent to prison, Jack would step in as a surrogate father and take care of his family. Their family.

It was a bizarre concept, but Hanssen's e-mail intrigue with Hoschouer to acquire Rohypnol and sedate Bonnie for sex with Jack was an almost natural progression from the still photos, the visual watching, and the video show. There was not much more Bob could do. He had already violated Bonnie in every other way.

Robert Hanssen, who took a stripper to Hong Kong, used his own wife as an unwitting porn star, and plotted to drug her for sex with his friend, had come a rather long way from the wide-eyed twenty-two-year-old who told Aya Hoschouer in the Playboy Club in Chicago that it was against the rules to touch the cottontails on the waitresses.

29

The Plea Bargain

Hanssen was denied bail—the federal judge said he posed "a severe risk of flight"—and he was locked up in the Alexandria Detention Center, the same redbrick jail where Aldrich Ames had been housed in the months after his arrest.

Plato Cacheris went to see Hanssen there after receiving the phone call from Bonnie Hanssen. "He asked me to be his lawyer," Cacheris said. "The government got a court order immediately freezing all his assets. So I am doing this pro bono." There was no way that Bonnie Hanssen could have afforded Cacheris's fees in any event; but few criminal defense lawyers would turn away from the public attention that inevitably accompanies a high-profile international spy case.

And Cacheris was no stranger to the bright lights and intense pressures of a major Washington legal drama. He thrived on the combat and controversy surrounding a big case. When he represented Monica Lewinsky during the scandal that led to the impeachment of President Clinton, there were television cameras staked out in front of his office building on Connecticut Avenue. He didn't seem to mind at all; he held sidewalk press conferences, as tourists and office workers gaped.

The son of a Greek immigrant who worked as a streetcar motorman in Chicago and a Greek mother who insisted he be named Plato, Cacheris had built a highly successful and lucrative law practice that allowed him to indulge his taste for expensive Savile Row suits, bright suspenders, and monogrammed shirts from Denman & Goddard of London. He grew up in the Maryland suburbs and in Washington, joined the Marines, graduated from Georgetown Law School, and married his longtime girlfriend, Ethel Dominick.

During the Watergate scandal, former Attorney General John Mitchell hired Cacheris and his partner to defend him against obstruction-of-justice charges. Cacheris got even more attention during the Iran-Contra scandal, when he represented Fawn Hall, Oliver North's statuesque secretary, who famously hid White House documents in her décolletage.

Despite his somewhat flamboyant public persona, Cacheris was a quiet professional who enjoyed a rock-solid reputation for integrity among his fellow lawyers. Although he might not admit it, he cared deeply about his clients, including those sentenced to prison, staying in touch with them and their families long after he would have any necessity to do so.

Since Cacheris had represented Aldrich Ames in the last big Washington spy case, he was a logical choice for Bonnie Hanssen to contact when she needed a lawyer for her husband.

In the tumult that followed the arrest, finding a lawyer was only one of a series of decisions that suddenly confronted her. To escape the turmoil, Bonnie moved in with her sister Peggy, who lived with her husband in Falls Church, Virginia. It was days before she was able to move back to Talisman Drive. The FBI was still there, searching every inch of the house. In any event, Bonnie did not want to reappear while the press was camped outside.

Hanssen's family was allowed to see him at the jail, and Bonnie was a frequent visitor. Separated by a thick glass barrier, they could talk there only by telephone. The children came to see him as well. In April, Vivian Hanssen flew up from Florida to visit her son.

"He's thinner but doing well," she said. "He's not depressed, thank God."

Behind the scenes, the maneuvering over Hanssen's fate began. Soon after Hanssen's arrest, Attorney General John Ashcroft told an interviewer: "I would not hesitate to include the death penalty among the options that are to be considered." In a news conference the same day, Ashcroft also said that in espionage cases the government might seek the death penalty to "send a signal," but might also explore the possibility of a "plea bargain."

Cacheris pounced. Federal prosecution guidelines, he pointed out to reporters, prohibit using the death penalty as a threat to gain advantage in a plea bargain. He lodged an official complaint in a letter to Ashcroft, charging that the attorney general's remarks were "not appropriate."*

Ashcroft's comment had come in answer to a question about whether the government would seek the death penalty for Robert Hanssen. Through a spokesperson, he claimed he was speaking only in general terms about the death penalty. True, Ashcroft had been careful to say he did not want to discuss "specific cases." But his blunder had given Cacheris an opening. If the government did in fact seek capital punishment, Cacheris said, "the attorney general has made himself our first witness in a motion to dismiss this case at an appropriate time."

A month after Hanssen's arrest, there were high-level repercussions. The Bush administration expelled fifty Russian diplomats in retaliation for his spying for Moscow. The State Department said that four of them were intelligence officers "implicated in the Hanssen investigation." They were declared persona non grata and told to leave immediately. The rest were given until July 1 to go. It was the largest number of Russians ordered out of the country since eighty Soviet diplomats were expelled by President Reagan in 1986. The next day, Moscow said it would expel an equal number of Americans, and it began by ordering four U.S. diplomats to leave.

Cacheris, meanwhile, had hammered out an agreement with the lead prosecutor, Randy I. Bellows, an assistant U.S. attorney in Alexandria, to postpone Hanssen's indictment for two months, a move that gave the defense early access to the government's voluminous evidence.

On April 18, Bellows and Cacheris met to discuss for the first time the possibility of a deal. The government wanted Hanssen to admit his spying in return for a sentence of life in prison. The prosecutor warned that the death penalty was still on the table. Cacheris listened, but made no commitment.

A month later, on May 14, they met again. The question of whether to seek the death penalty had still not been settled by the Justice Department, Bellows said. He asked for more time. Cacheris, playing hardball, refused and broke off the talks. The government then said it

---

*Cacheris's letter cited the *United States Attorney's Manual,* which is clear on the subject: "The death penalty may not be sought, and no attorney for the Government may threaten to seek it, solely for the purpose of obtaining a more desirable negotiating position." *USAM* 9–10.100.

would go ahead and issue a detailed indictment of Hanssen, which it did two days later.

Within the administration, officials were divided about whether to seek the death penalty for Hanssen. Ashcroft and Defense Secretary Donald Rumsfeld were reported to favor it; Freeh and CIA director George Tenet were opposed.

The debate was a classic argument about the merits of law enforcement versus intelligence. The CIA and the bureau were much more interested in getting Hanssen to cooperate as part of a plea bargain than in seeing him pay the ultimate penalty for his crimes. If Hanssen was executed, the intelligence agencies would never learn the full extent of what had been compromised.

That fact was Cacheris's strongest card, but he had others. The government's espionage case against Hanssen was powerful, because it had the incriminating file from Moscow. Moreover, the former KGB officer who provided the documents was portrayed as willing to testify at a trial if absolutely necessary. But the prosecutors, as Cacheris knew, were anxious to prevent that from happening; the FBI wanted to keep the source's identity secret if it could.

Beyond preserving the secrecy surrounding the operation to acquire the KGB file, the intelligence agencies were loath to have the secrets that Hanssen had betrayed broadcast to the world in a trial. The Classified Information Procedures Act of 1980 (CIPA) was passed to avoid "graymail" by defendants who might hope to avoid prosecution by threatening to reveal in court the very secrets they had betrayed to another country. But judges have the discretion to require that secrets be disclosed in a trial, so the law is not airtight.

Cacheris's partner, Preston Burton, a former assistant U.S. attorney, said that the government would have had difficulty prosecuting Hanssen without revealing the secrets he had passed. "Normally the government would seek to keep as many things as possible out of the trial under CIPA," Burton said, "but in a capital case the government would have had to produce much more evidence, including information about the source of the KGB/SVR file."

The government, in short, has a dual motive in often pressing for a plea bargain in spy cases. In addition to learning from the spy exactly what damage has been done, it hopes to avoid the exposure of the secrets that the spy had passed. There is an odd mind-set at work here. The secrets have long since been given to the country that paid for them, often, as in this case, the Soviet Union or Russia. Yet the American people are kept in the dark. The intelligence agencies are horrified at the thought of the public learning secrets that are already known to the adversaries from whom the secrets were primarily designed to be concealed. The counterargument by intelligence officials is that other countries might benefit from the disclosures of the stolen secrets.

If the evidence against Hanssen was compelling, the government's toying with the death penalty was on much shakier ground. In 1994, Congress restored the death penalty for espionage provided certain criteria were met. For example, the penalty might apply if a spy revealed to a foreign power information that resulted in the death of an intelligence agent, or data about a wide variety of other defense secrets.*

But Cacheris was prepared to argue that none of the secrets Hanssen passed after 1991 qualified for the death penalty. And the Constitution prohibits ex post facto laws that punish a person for acts that were not crimes at the time they were committed. Hanssen, in other words, could not be executed for secrets he revealed to the Russians prior to 1994.

"We had a strong ex post facto argument," Cacheris said. Even aside from that, in negotiations with the federal prosecutors Cacheris contended it was impossible to prove that his client was responsible for the deaths of the two KGB officers he betrayed. "We argued that you can't blame Hanssen for the deaths of Martynov and Motorin because Ames had already given them up months earlier.

"We also argued the government had a statute of limitations problem. Plus, there is a legal principle of duplicity—you cannot charge two crimes in a single count of an indictment. We argued that because of the long time span, and the fact that Hanssen had stopped spying at various intervals, the government could not charge that there was a single conspiracy, as they did. And somewhere in the middle of all this, the Soviet Union collapsed and now we are dealing with something called Russia."

On May 31, Hanssen pleaded not guilty in a two-minute appearance under heavy security at the federal courthouse in Alexandria. Judge Claude M. Hilton set a trial date for October 29.

---

*The list of secrets that, if passed to a foreign power, could bring the death penalty for espionage includes data about nuclear weapons, military spacecraft or satellites, early warning systems, war plans, codes or communications intelligence, major weapons systems, or any "major element of defense strategy."

But this was all part of the legal maneuvering being played out. Cacheris was not really willing to gamble on a trial. "You never know what a jury will do," he said. "And juries in Virginia can be particularly harsh. There are a lot of military people in northern Virginia. Virginia jurors are conservative, they are sophisticated, and they might find what he gave the Russians highly offensive."

Early in June, Cacheris telephoned Bellows and suggested they meet privately to see whether the talks about a plea bargain might be re-opened. By that time, Ashcroft was no longer trumpeting the death penalty, and Bellows had more room to negotiate. The deal was struck; Hanssen would plead guilty and promise to cooperate by revealing everything he had done.

Cacheris had saved Robert Hanssen from the death penalty. The compromise gave both sides what they wanted. But there was one cru-cial condition that would first have to be met. Before the plea bargain could be finalized, the government wanted to hear what Hanssen was prepared to reveal. The prosecutors would not sign the agreement un-less the former FBI man demonstrated that he was truly willing to co-operate.

The test, which is known as a "proffer," took place in a windowless room in the basement of the federal courthouse. There were two such meetings, and Hanssen was given a type of limited immunity from prosecution for what he revealed. In a proffer of this kind, with an im-munity agreement, the government cannot directly use against the de-fendant the information that is offered. But Preston Burton was worried about a double cross by the government.

"Our concern was, first, that the government could say he was not truthful, and then the deal could blow up and he would be back facing trial. In addition, we were well aware of reports of hostility by federal officials toward Hanssen and skepticism about his credibility. We were concerned that those people would sabotage the proffer by using it to obtain the full account of his activities and then falsely claiming he was being untruthful, thus depriving us of our main bargaining chip—the government's need to debrief Hanssen in detail to fully assess the dam-age he had caused."

On June 21, Cacheris and John C. Hundley, the firm's other partner, arrived for the meeting. As the lawyers for the government and for the defense chatted and milled about, federal marshals brought in Hanssen, wearing a green jumpsuit with the word "prisoner" on the back. They removed the manacles from his hands. The two sides took their places at a long, polished table in the underground room. Doug Gregory and the other FBI case agent, Stefan Pluta, sat across from Hanssen and the defense team. The Justice Department was represented by Randy Bellows and John Dion, the chief of the internal security section.

Doug Gregory did most of the questioning. Burton, delayed by a court appearance that morning, arrived late and immediately realized that Hanssen was not performing well. "I did not think he was being untruthful, but he seemed to hesitate and not be well focused on the events that the government was asking about."

Five hours later, the proffer session ended. Cacheris and his partners were dismayed; Hanssen might be blowing the deal. He would have one more chance to redeem himself, at another meeting set for a week later.

"I spent two days getting Bob ready for the next session," Burton recalled, "force-feeding him with every piece of paper we had, including the affidavit and the discovery materials we had received from the government. The second proffer session on June 28 went much better. In the first forty-five minutes, the clouds lifted. I could tell that the government side felt that he was now giving them the information they expected." After seven hours of questioning, it was clear that the deal would go through.

The court had agreed in advance that the plea bargain would be binding. Under federal rules, a judge does not have to accept a plea bargain worked out by the prosecution and the defense, but once the court accepts the arrangement, it becomes final.

In working out the details of the plea, the defense lawyers said that Hanssen was anxious to have access to a computer in prison. But the government, aware of Hanssen's technical skills, wanted to prohibit him from using a computer, even one with no modem that would allow him to dial out.

"Do you think this guy is the professor on *Gilligan's Island*?" Preston Burton asked. "Do you think he's going to make a radio out of a coconut?"

The defense lawyers eventually convinced the prosecutors to let the prison authorities decide how much computer access Hanssen could have. Hanssen was pleased; at least he might have a chance to get back to a keyboard, if not into cyberspace.

On July 6, Hanssen, looking gaunt in his green prison uniform, stood before Judge Hilton again and pleaded guilty to fifteen counts of espionage, attempted espionage, and conspiracy. Six counts were dropped by the government.

The deputy attorney general, Larry Thompson, told the court that "the interest of the United States would be best served" by allowing the government to assess the damage wrought by Hanssen, "an objective we could not achieve if we sought and obtained the death penalty against him."

During the debate over whether to seek capital punishment for Hanssen, CIA director George Tenet wrote to Ashcroft explaining how important it was to interrogate rather than execute the former FBI man. As Hanssen entered his guilty plea, Ashcroft, in a statement, said the decision to forgo the death penalty was based "on the strong recommendation of the intelligence community."

Under the agreement, Hanssen would be sentenced to life without the possibility of parole. He would forfeit the $1.4 million paid or set aside for him by the Russians, and he could not benefit from any book, film, or future publicity. And he was to be debriefed for six months about his spying. "We expect him to be candid with us and truthful with us and completely open about his espionage activities," said Ken Melson, the U.S. Attorney for the Eastern District of Virginia.

The formal sentencing of Hanssen was not to take place until after the debriefings were concluded and the prosecutors were satisfied. The government still held a club over his head. Should it decide Hanssen was not being frank, it could cancel the plea agreement, put him on trial, and seek the death penalty.

Under the bargain, and a 1996 law encouraging the families of spies to cooperate with the government, Bonnie Hanssen would receive a portion of her husband's pension, or about $40,000 a year, the same as a survivor benefit, assuming, Melson said, that she "continues to be fully cooperative." Bonnie was also allowed to keep the house and their three cars.

Soon after Hanssen's guilty plea, the twice-weekly debriefings began, in the same windowless room in the basement of the federal courthouse. Doug Gregory led the FBI team, and Paul Redmond, the former CIA counterintelligence specialist who led the damage assessment, was there along with other CIA officials.

But the September 11 attacks on America, combined with the deadly anthrax letters mailed to political and media figures, created new priorities for the FBI. The debriefings were interrupted for a time. In addition, various other government investigators wanted to talk to Hanssen. As a result, the debriefings, originally expected to be completed in January, stretched into the spring. A new sentencing date was set for May 10.

It was in the midst of the initial plea bargain talks, in mid-May 2001, that Bonnie Hanssen learned that her husband had allowed his best friend to watch them having sex, both live and later on closed-circuit television. She had reacted with shock and anger.

Her remark was buzzing around in the family, and for good reason. What Bonnie had told her sister Jeanne Beglis was brief and unforgettable:

"My husband is a traitor and a pervert."

30

The Mind of Robert Hanssen

Robert Philip Hanssen was a walking paradox—a zealous anti-Communist who spied for Moscow, a pious Catholic and ultrareligious member of Opus Dei who secretly televised his wife having sex and schemed to drug her so another man could father her child, a counter-spy who was himself a spy.

He led at least six lives: special agent of the FBI, devoted family man, Russian spy, devout Catholic, obsessed pornographer, and fantasy James Bond who took a stripper to Hong Kong and could, at least in his imagination, come up out of the Potomac shooting.

He fit into no known previous category of spies. He was not motivated entirely by money, and certainly not by ideology. James Woolsey, the former director of the CIA, conceded he was baffled by Hanssen.

"If you look at a hundred or so cases of Americans who spied for Russia, you don't have many ideological motives, as in the case of Philby or the Rosenbergs. You do have a few people who spy for ethnic or religious reasons—Larry Wu-Tai Chin, Pollard—but they are very small in number. Almost all are white guys. They break into two groups. Flaky young types, as in *The Falcon and the Snowman,* smoke a little grass, and hey, let's steal some secrets.* The other is the classic Aldrich Ames, the middle-aged guy in midlife crisis. Benedict Arnold was the same as Ames, both with new wives and a midlife crisis. This guy

---

*Woolsey was referring to the book by Robert Lindsey, and the 1985 movie based on it, about Christopher Boyce and Andrew Lee, two young affluent Californians who sold satellite secrets to the Soviets. Lee was sentenced to life, Boyce to forty years.

[Hanssen] is outside any of those patterns. He is not ethnic, not ideological, not a young guy who's flaky, and doesn't appear to be in a midlife crisis, despite the stripper. Everything is bottled up inside. It is truly odd."

Because Hanssen's character was so contradictory and complex, the extraordinary story of his more than two decades of espionage cannot be understood fully without exploring his motives and trying to fathom Hanssen himself. What drove him into such a dark place?

Dr. David L. Charney, the psychiatrist whom Plato Cacheris engaged to evaluate Hanssen, visited the spy in the Alexandria jail more than thirty times over many months. They met privately in a small, vaultlike room with white cinder-block walls and a camera, but no guards or other persons present.* Hanssen spoke freely to Dr. Charney about his childhood, his family, his FBI career, his spying, his religion, and his motives for betraying his country. As a result, Charney probably learned more about the experiences and influences that formed Hanssen, and his motives to spy, than anyone else in the world.

Normally, because of doctor-patient privilege, Charney could not discuss his conclusions or what Hanssen had confided to him. But Hanssen authorized Charney to speak to the author. He did so in a letter to his attorney, Plato Cacheris, with a copy to Charney, releasing the psychiatrist to discuss his findings.†

David Charney, who had previously spent time with Earl Pitts, the second convicted spy in the FBI's history, is a soft-spoken New Yorker whose psychiatric practice is based in Alexandria. He has in the past been a consultant to the CIA. At the time he evaluated Hanssen, he was also working on a paper on the psychology of spies that he hoped would help the government to better protect itself against them.

Charney identified several factors that led Hanssen to become a spy for Moscow. Many of these were raised by Hanssen himself in his often-weekly meetings with the psychiatrist.

---

*As Charney understood it, there was no microphone—no audio along with the camera—since the room was normally used for attorney-client meetings.

†Hanssen's extraordinary decision was based on his anger over statements to the news media by Dr. Alen Salerian, the first psychiatrist who saw him, that attributed his spying to an effort to alleviate his "sexual demons." With encouragement from Cacheris, he allowed Charney to talk exclusively to the author about their meetings. Cacheris said that in freeing Charney to be interviewed for this book, "Hanssen said, 'David Wise is the best espionage writer around.' "

But Charney had a word of caution. "People are complicated beings and motivations are multidetermined and evolve over time," he said. "Motives may get altered in memory, depending on rationalizations that people bring in explaining themselves to themselves."

Having said that, Charney affirmed that Hanssen himself pointed to "financial pressure" as one of the reasons he first crossed the line into espionage. To understand the motivation for espionage, Charney said, it is crucial to look at the six months leading up to when a spy first crosses that line. Nor can money be discounted as a continuing motive. For someone on the salary of a midlevel federal employee, the $600,000 that the Russians paid to Hanssen with the promise of another $800,000 is not inconsequential. Hanssen remodeled his house in Virginia at a cost of $70,000, sent six kids to private school, four to college, all of them to the orthodontist. He collected an armory of guns, all sorts of computers and related gadgetry, and spent some $80,000 on the stripper, including a sapphire-and-diamond necklace, the trip to Hong Kong, and a Mercedes, albeit used.

It would be simplistic, however, to say that Hanssen only spied for money. If it was only money, as Ed Curran and others have pointed out, Hanssen could have demanded millions for what he gave, because the secrets he passed to Moscow were not only of enormous value to the Russians but compromised U.S. intelligence-collection programs that cost hundreds of millions of dollars. Yet he never negotiated for more money, airily informing the KGB early on that he really had no need for more than $100,000.

Ironically, Hanssen's pension, had he not been arrested two months shy of his normal retirement date, could well have amounted to more than the total that the stingy KGB and SVR shelled out.* Hanssen was a budget spy, the actual cash and diamonds he received amounting to far less than the $2.7 million the Russians paid to Aldrich Ames.

---

*Until his bogus promotion just before he was arrested, Hanssen was earning about $115,000 a year. FBI agents can retire after twenty years at age fifty with a pension that is half of the average of their three highest years, a percentage that increases with up to seven additional years of service. Since Hanssen was planning to retire at the mandatory age of fifty-seven, assuming his salary base was about $111,000, his gross pension would have been $66,800 annually. If he lived for another ten years, he would have received $660,800 pretax, or more than he was paid by the KGB and the GRU combined. If he lived for twenty-one years, he would have received $1,402,800 pretax, or slightly more than he was paid or promised by the Russians, and with no jail time.

Where did the money go? Spread out over twenty-two years, the total Hanssen received was not a fortune. A senior FBI official said he believed most of it was "pissed away," into the gas tank and on other mundane, everyday household and living expenses. Some of it was parked in his two Swiss bank accounts, some in the box under his bed. The bureau had accountants trying to figure out exactly where the money went, but it was a daunting task.

According to Charney, Hanssen really wanted money for one reason: to assure his wife that he was not a failure. "Men are burdened by masculine pride. We put our public face into the world and want to be respected by our fellow men and by ourselves. The person we allow into our most intimate knowledge of our life is our wife. If our wife thinks we are an asshole, we have no protection. We have a chink in our armor; if our wife thinks we are a loser that is intolerable.

"Bonnie was the one person who brought light into his life. She was the last person he would want to think he was a failure. He reached to prove to her he was a good provider and a good husband. So that when she would express wishes for various things he would always buy them for her. He felt it was necessary to sustain his image in her eyes as successful. That put him into a financial corner, because he agreed to take on various financial burdens, like buying a house out of his reach financially, in Scarsdale.

"It's not that it's wrong to say that he did it for money; you have to go deeper and ask why he wanted the money. Why did Bob Hanssen get into a corner financially? Because he had to keep up his reputation with Bonnie. Because that was the one person in the world whose opinion mattered."

But Bonnie, Charney said, was not the sort to place burdensome financial demands on her husband. Hanssen did not blame her; he blamed himself. "She did not put pressure on him; it was his own inner drive to be the good provider and never disappoint her."

Aside from the money, many of Hanssen's colleagues in the FBI, including the friends he made there, strongly believed that Hanssen was motivated to spy because he was excluded from the inner club of counterintelligence agents and relegated to the back room.

"Bob was always seen as a computer guy, a weenie, a number cruncher," said David Major. "He was somebody you want on your team, to use. He was never going to lead the team. Don Stukey would be a quarterback, Bob's always on the sidelines; he would analyze the plays and know what they did right or wrong, but he would never get on the playing field."

Jim Ohlson reached much the same conclusion about his friend. "Although Hanssen was involved with and fascinated by CI and Soviet operations, he was never in the core group that actually conducted them. He may have felt excluded, his skills unappreciated. He had longed to be involved in spy work—so he turned to another government to do it.

"Hanssen had great respect for the KGB and its professionalism. He once said, 'They're the only target I want to work against. They're the only enemy worth fighting.' So he was drawn to the KGB."

Certainly, Hanssen may have felt passed over. He was never a field agent operating against the Soviets, except for a brief tour in New York, and even then he was in a back room in charge of POCKETWATCH, supervising agents with earphones who listened in on Amtorg and other Soviet commercial offices. POCKETWATCH was not the big leagues.

Joe Tierney, Hanssen's superior at headquarters in the early 1980s, tended to agree with this analysis. "He had never done anything operational himself," Tierney said. "He had not been involved in a recruitment or a successful espionage case. People tend to earn their bones in those cases, and then they're respected by their peers."

To Tierney, Hanssen's betrayal began as an intellectual exercise. "This is something he thought out in his head—this is how you could do it. He was flirting with it and it gets more and more concrete. Then he goes to New York and hits the New York real estate market and that pushes him over the edge."

A. Jackson Lowe, Hanssen's boss on his second New York tour, in the mid-1980s, also remembered him as an outsider. "He never got the respect he thought he deserved. There were always other agents out front getting the glory. Here was a guy who was very bright, he felt like he was not well accepted, an outcast. He did not fit in."

As a perennial outsider, Hanssen may have decided to create his own Soviet operation. The feeling of being excluded, combined with his self-image, at least partly justified, as a person of superior intellect and technical gifts, could have created bitterness, a desire to "show them." And underlying his decision to spy may have been a grandiose belief he could never be caught because he was too clever.

If Hanssen's resentment over being excluded led to his spying, however, he did not say that to Charney. He did tell the psychiatrist that "he came to think of himself as an outsider, a nerd." But Hanssen did not link that to his espionage.

Instead, Hanssen spent a good deal of time talking about his father. "In the very first meeting we had, that was the very first topic that he brought up," Charney recalled.

"You see this often in people. Troubled relationships with a father will affect their thinking for the rest of their life. Hanssen's father was a difficult father to grow up under, a strong personality. He was not a warm, mentoring person. Hanssen was an only child and his father did not hold him much in esteem. His father had very little time for him." Hanssen talked at length about the punishments and humiliations his father had imposed, such as wrapping him in the mattress so that his arms were pinned, or making him sit with his legs spread.

"Hanssen wished for his father to be a mentor and a coach and explain the world to him as a father should, welcoming him into manhood. Robert Hanssen didn't receive that and felt always out of step and lacking knowledge of how the world worked. His mother was a reasonably nurturing person but did not protect and defend him from his father. That is an abiding disappointment that he had.

"When a boy grows up without effective fathering, it leaves a tremendous empty place, a father hunger. Boys want to be welcomed into adult manhood by their fathers. If they don't get that, they are always feeling uneasy, not a true member of the club of men. That is one of the things that happened with Hanssen. He was belittled and made to feel inadequate. And yet he loved his father, he worshipped his father. That is not an unusual thing. The very person that abuses you is so powerful that one is in awe of that person."

At the same time, Charney said, Hanssen was "infuriated" with his father, his anger deep-seated and intense. Because he feared his father, however, "he had to bottle it up. He used the phrase 'bottled up' a lot. But now and then the cork would come out of the bottle. Not so much as a kid but as an adult. At a certain point he would blow like a volcano.

"Hanssen said when he spied that was the cork coming out of the bottle. He said that about the cork and used it many times." The way his father treated him, Hanssen said, was "unfair and unjust. That is a theme he brings up a lot.

"He has this strong sense of injustice. That attitude of being sensitized to unfairness you see throughout his life. He always wants to right things if he is able to do so. In the case of the stripper and others, he sees them as abused people, and if some way he can help them he wants to do that."*

Charney, based on his conversations with Hanssen, saw a direct link between Hanssen's fury at his father and his betrayal of the FBI. "Very often when a person joins an organization or a government agency, they are seeking an emotional resolution for unresolved questions. Any organization can be like a family. How that organization treats you is either going to replay those experiences or help you resolve them. But if you get disappointed a second time in your life, the thing you set up as your saving mechanism turns out to disappoint you again. That can bring about the fury and resentment that you were too overwhelmed to bring out when you were a little boy. And you may say, 'Now I'm going to get back.' He may have been replaying some things from his boyhood. But this time he had the capacity to get back."

Yet it would be a mistake, Charney said, to assume that Hanssen became a spy simply because his father treated him harshly. "Many people grow up emotionally damaged and nevertheless can overcome it and live normal adult lives. There are people who can rebound from any number of terrible circumstances of childhood. But even those who do can unexpectedly enter a period that puts them under tremendous strain and pressure that will reawaken problems of the past and push them into a psychological corner.

"Even people who are very well adjusted may be shoved into new territory that is quite unexpected and with which they can't really cope very well. It overwhelms them. Some people are so blighted by their early experiences they never seem to be able to overcome it. But thankfully most people do. A lot of people at the bureau have had rough childhoods. They don't become spies."

Hanssen told Charney his disappointment with the FBI was rooted, ironically, in his conviction that the bureau was focused too much on catching spies and was missing the real threat. "He felt that on a strate-

---

*Hanssen once urged Hoschouer to read Joseph Conrad's *Victory*. There are obvious parallels in the novel to parts of Hanssen's own life, including his escapade with Priscilla Sue Galey. The protagonist, Axel Heyst, has been emotionally damaged by his father and rescues a woman entertainer who is trapped in her job as a musician in an orchestra on an isle in the far Pacific. He eventually pays with his life for rescuing the damsel in distress.

gic level the FBI was failing to do what it needed to do to protect the country. That the main way the Soviets prosecuted their aims was through subversion of our institutions." By focusing on arresting people who stole documents, Hanssen told the psychiatrist, the bureau's resources were failing to come to grips with the enemy. He had made an effort to get the bureau to listen.

"He had tried, for example, to warn what the Japanese were doing to us economically, and he said the bureau was oblivious, the bureau did not have the depth to oppose those kinds of things. He attempted to say, 'Wake up,' and was regarded as an intellectual, not taken seriously; they didn't get it. He began to be disappointed and angry at the bureau for not paying attention. And that fired up some of his antipathy toward the bureau."

Hanssen, Charney said, considered himself a gadfly like John Boyd, a critic inside the Air Force, whom he saw "as a sort of role model." Hanssen invited Boyd to come to the FBI and give a talk, and he did, but the bureau had shown no interest in his ideas.

If Hanssen did regard the FBI as a father figure, and sought to vent his suppressed rage by striking back at it, his anger was certainly not the only factor that turned him into a spy. His fascination with James Bond, his desire for excitement, was surely an important element as well. He seemed to enjoy living on the edge. "He said he was bored before he started spying," Charney said. "The spying produced excitement and made him come alive. The excitement is from doing something different. The risk is part of the excitement."

Hanssen may have been seen as a computer nerd, a geek in the back room, but in his own mind he could at times apparently become 007 or something close to it. His attraction to Catherine Zeta-Jones, the Hong Kong interlude with Priscilla Sue Galey, the guns in his car trunk that led Ron Mlotek to call him "Machine Gun Bob"—these were all indicators of someone longing for the supposed glamour and thrills of a real-life spy.

Paul Moore, who knew Hanssen as well as anyone in the FBI did, once caught a glimpse of his friend's Bond-like romance with firearms. Hanssen had been down to the FBI's training academy in Quantico, Virginia, where agents practice shooting in a mock town known as Hogan's Alley. "He was talking about walking through a new, high-tech Hogan's Alley at Quantico using virtual reality. He said, 'I'm good with guns.'" Hanssen described how the computer simulation worked, like a video game. "He used a gun to chase the perp into an underground garage. You're taught how to fire to hit somebody hiding behind a pillar. You hit a cylindrical pillar just right and it spins the bullet around. He shot and got one of the people. He is still chasing the other guy. He shoots the guy on the ground again because he doesn't know if he's dead. 'Yeah,' he said, 'I put another one into him.' Bob used just those words, 'I put another one into him.' "

The tough-guy, Raymond Chandler dialogue and the fascination with guns fit with Hanssen's quest for something more exciting than the drudgery of the FBI's budget or analytical units.

"Bob was like the high wireman who wants to touch the wire," David Major said. "The fifty-thousand-volt wire that he knows will kill him, but he wants to see if he can touch it and get away with it." Ernie Rizzo, who had learned wiretap skills with Hanssen when they were both police officers in Chicago, compared espionage to skydiving: "Pretty soon you want to go further and further to see how high you can go."

Hanssen's curiosity may have also contributed to his journey into espionage, in Moore's view. "He was a special agent, he had the gun and the badge, but was never put into a situation where he'd use the gun and the badge. He was put in a position to talk to the analysts. His job is to ask, 'How are these people [the KGB] doing it to our country? What could we do to make the country safer?' Eventually you ask, 'How is it possible to attack the country?' That's going to land him into, 'How would one do it?' That's always going to be cooking on the stove.

"At some point he decides, 'It can be done and somebody like me can do it.' He knows all the cases, how people who spied against the U.S. were caught. And so he crosses the line. Once he got going he set out to be the best spy ever. He's trying to commit the perfect crime. He's really excessive in what he passes. In his day job he's being very helpful to the FBI.

"He's getting money he can't spend very well, and he's getting satisfaction he can't share with anyone. In the letters you see him forming a relationship with the Russians. The only people he can share his success with are the people on the other side."

David Charney, too, concluded that Hanssen spied, at least to an extent, because he wanted to peer inside the opposition. "The spying he did was partly out of curiosity: how did the KGB actually operate as opposed to how the FBI thought they operated? How would you ever know that if you did not get involved with them? He would give lectures, brilliant lectures, on how the KGB operated. Because he really knew. He knew better than anybody."

To many of his colleagues, Hanssen projected an irritating sense of superiority. That may have stemmed not only from his belief that he was smarter than others, but from his secret knowledge that he was a Russian spy, the spy who at one point directed the very study of moles in the FBI, so that he was looking for himself.

Hanssen exulted in his inside knowledge, Charney suggested. "He wound up in a position where he could regard himself as the puppet master, knowing more than anyone within the bureau or the KGB about the totality of what was happening."

David Major agreed. "Bob would get a sublime high by being the ultimate inside joke. Everybody is trying to uncover a spy and he's at the meeting where they are discussing it and he's the spy. Bob didn't have to tell that to anybody to get an inner joy out of it. I, Bob, have the greatest inside joke."

The flip side of his superior manner, however, was very different. According to Charney, one of the main threads in Hanssen's case "is a sense of failure. Spies may have an intolerable sense of personal failure as privately defined, a tremendous fear they will fail in a key experience in life and that will result in a shameful disclosure of their inadequacy. You might look at their career and say it is exemplary. But if a person does not meet his own standards and goals, then there is a sense of failure.

"Whatever motives a person has to spy, they are conflicted reasons. They are not just 'I want money, I hate the bureau.' At some deep level, the decision to spy in the first place represents a failure on the part of the person. They could not manage their lives, things were going wrong, they could not fix it, and they got thrown into a panic stage and the resolution in this cloud of panic was to do spying. They can clothe it in rationalizations but in truth it represents failure. Any time they can, they want to move back away from it and be their normal self."

Often, in his conversations with Charney, Hanssen compared himself to Dr. Jekyll and Mr. Hyde, the Robert Louis Stevenson character who could switch from good to evil and back.* "He has used the Dr. Jekyll and Mr. Hyde explanation several times. A constant struggle with the two sides of himself, the good and the bad. He's kind of proud and pleased he could quit for a time. He says, 'I was able to shut down the bad side of myself.' "

Sitting in his jail cell, Hanssen had plenty of time to think about his "bad side," including the video camera he hid in his bedroom for sev-

---

*In the novel *The Strange Case of Dr. Jekyll and Mr. Hyde,* published in 1886, Henry Jekyll, a physician, finds a drug that turns him into a monster, Mr. Hyde.

eral years so Jack Hoschouer could watch him having sex with Bonnie. He realized it was "sick and goofy," but he had gone to church and confessed it, and eventually stopped. He knew it was wrong, of course; in retrospect he saw it as some kind of attempt by him and Jack to hold on to their lost adolescence.

Hanssen talked a good deal with the psychiatrist about his fear of failure. "He, Bob, had many experiences that he considered failure. He was always afraid of flaming out in social situations where that would become apparent."

One night, at the Alexandria jail, "Hanssen explained that he actually had to deal with social situations by having preset stories and conversations. Like people who, as soon as you meet them, they start telling you jokes. He could be funny and charming in a sort of programmed way. But he could not be with someone for two hours in a row, because he would run out of stories."

Hanssen's sense of failure reached back to his early years. "Bob is a very bright man but did B work in college. He got into dental school, although his father wanted him to be a doctor. He was bored in dental school. When he thought of dropping out of dental school, he tried to switch over to medical school, but he could not because of his grades.

"Not having made it into med school was another confirmation he wasn't as good as he thought himself to be. He accepted his father's view of him. An abiding question for him is, 'Am I or am I not the thing I was led to believe I was?'

"People often have to prove something, but also they may have to prove what they are not. He may have said, 'I'm not the little schmuck my father said I was. I'll show him.' Then he doesn't get into med school and says to himself, 'Maybe my father was right.' We're talking about self-doubts."

Charney thought that Hanssen's religious beliefs were real, not a cover for espionage. "I believe it is sincere," Charney said. "He gave me extended lectures on Catholic theology." But Hanssen did not suggest that his religion, with its sacrament of confession, enabled him to spy. "He does not at all talk about how he can sin and get absolution. He doesn't suggest his religion gave him an easy pass. He believes his religion requires him to atone for what he has done and to suffer—he has used the term mortification—to come back to the proper relationship with God. His view is there is no easy pathway out of moral transgressions.

"Opus Dei believes everyone can become a saint. He believes even with everything he's done he still has to be working to become a saint."

Charney came to see Hanssen as an essentially lonely man. "The thing that was very painful throughout the first couple of decades of his life was loneliness. He was gawky and had thick bottle glasses for many years; at age fourteen he got contact lenses, he still wears them. What he yearned for were friends.

"But one of his friends when he was eleven or twelve was a little like him, an awkward but brainy kid. That kid had an aneurysm one day while they were playing together. Bob called the boy's mom, and she didn't respond right away. That kid was dead within a day. One of the few people he was able to get close to died on him. There were four people in his life he considered friends: one was someone in his FBI class, another died of leukemia, the fourth one, the only one that survived, was Jack. He was the only one that lived to tell the tale.

"I think a spy is the loneliest person in the world," Charney said. "The handlers of spies know this and know how to play them like a violin." That was certainly true of the KGB and the SVR, whose letters to Hanssen shamelessly played on his psychological need for their friendship and recognition. ("Your superb sense of humor and Your sharp-as-a-razor mind. We highly appreciate both." And so on.)

The mind of Robert Hanssen, which Charney explored with the author, was also a subject of great interest to American intelligence. By early 2002, the CIA was preparing a psychological profile of Hanssen as part of the damage assessment headed by former CIA counterintelligence expert Paul Redmond.

For the profile, the CIA asked Bonnie Hanssen to meet with an agency psychologist. It was a delicate request, but the CIA was anxious to question her, since she was obviously an important source of information about her husband. After consulting with her attorney, she agreed to the interview and met with the agency psychologist.

The purpose of the secret study was to try to identify those characteristics of Hanssen that might help intelligence agencies to spot potential traitors in the future. But Hanssen was so unusual a spy, his motives so mixed and complex, that one could only wish the CIA good luck in trying to draw universal conclusions from its study of the most damaging spy in the history of the FBI. The profilers attempting to understand the mind of Robert Hanssen were embarking on a voyage to the dark side of the moon.

31

"You Would Have to Be a Total Stupid Fucking Idiot to Spy for the KGB"

Could Robert Hanssen have been caught sooner?

There were certainly enough warning signs. Whatever else Mark Wauck said to his superior a decade before Hanssen was caught, there is no dispute that he mentioned his brother-in-law's unexplained cash. In 1991 Hanssen took a stripper to Hong Kong while on an official FBI inspection. Nobody noticed. Hanssen's attack on Kimberly Lichtenberg in 1993 should have triggered alarm bells that he was unstable, but did not. The bureau was content to administer a mild penalty.

That same year he broke into Ray Mislock's computer, but his colleagues accepted that transgression as an effort to point out the vulnerability of the bureau's system. A few years later, when informed he would have to take a lie detector test to join an interagency counterintelligence unit, he withdrew his name. In 1997, the FBI technicians discovered he had a password breaker on his hard drive, normally a sure sign of a hacker. He was told not to do it again. And in June of that year, Earl Pitts, when asked if he knew of any other moles in the bureau, said he did not, but added that he suspected Bob Hanssen. Nothing happened.

Other clues were missed as well. Hanssen told investigators for the Webster commission that no one ever questioned him when he made his own photocopies of documents, even though special agents of the FBI normally ask their assistants or secretaries to make copies. The FBI does periodic background checks of its employees; one reinvestigation of Hanssen noted he had money troubles, but "asserted that Hanssen's wife came from a wealthy family who assisted the Hanssens."*

---

*Webster commission, p. 60.

Perhaps none of these incidents and questions about Hanssen was enough, by itself, to lead the counterspies to suspect their own colleague, but taken together they should have triggered an investigation. The problem was that no one looked at the pattern, in part because of hubris, the ingrained belief in the bureau that, despite Miller and Pitts, the FBI did not harbor spies.

Ed Curran, the veteran counterspy, was blunt about it. "We should have got Hanssen a lot sooner than we did," he said. "There's absolutely no excuse for the FBI not, at some point, to have identified Bob Hanssen."

Other former and current bureau officials agreed, and recognized that, more broadly, the FBI's well-publicized errors over the past decade have cost it dearly. "I believe we should be criticized, and we will be a better organization for it," Tim Caruso said. "It will make us better and stronger."

To an extent, the bureau may have failed to detect Hanssen sooner because it was in love with its own image, carefully orchestrated over the years by J. Edgar Hoover—the cereal boxes with Junior G-Man badges, and the flood of movies, television dramas, news stories, and books glorifying the FBI. For decades, the vast majority of Americans admired the bureau and its agents, who were invariably portrayed as square-jawed and invincible. That image began to change only after Hoover's death, when congressional investigations revealed secret break-ins and various other abuses by the bureau, and again more recently with the disclosures of mismanagement and serious mistakes in the handling of several major cases.

It is a lot easier to catch a spy with the benefit of hindsight. Hanssen took care in his lifestyle not to draw attention to himself. He tooled around in an old Taurus, not a Jaguar, drank very little, and seemed outwardly a deeply religious, model family man, content to live a placid middle-class life in the Virginia suburbs.

Despite these precautions, Hanssen, contrary to popular belief, was far from the perfect spy. He was clever to try to conceal his identity from the Russians, but he made all sorts of mistakes, from repeated use of the same dead drops, whatever his rationale for doing so, to all the clues to his identity that he dropped like a trail of bread crumbs in his messages to Moscow. He even left incriminating letters to the Russians on his computer card in FBI headquarters.

As an experienced counterintelligence agent, Hanssen knew that his greatest risk was that he might, at any time, be turned in by an equivalent FBI or CIA mole inside the KGB. In the end, that was his undoing. The risk of such exposure is why both Hanssen and Ames betrayed Martynov and Motorin, the two FBI sources inside the KGB's Washington residency. The best way for a mole to protect himself is to betray and thereby kill the other side's mole.

Hanssen's friend Paul Moore summed up the stakes well. "The better you are, the more incentive for someone on to the other side to sell you out. The problem is that once you're in the game, you're in the game for life, and you're betting your life all the time.

"The only way you can get away with it is to die before U.S. counterintelligence finds you, because they will look for you and they will eventually get to you, because what you're doing is really dumb. The more successful you are, the more valuable it is to the U.S. to find you, and the more salable you are to somebody on the other side. Bob was playing smart moves at a very dumb game and he did not get away with it."

* * *

In the debris that follows a major spy case, usually the most difficult task is to assess the damage done to U.S. national security. What made the task somewhat easier in the Hanssen case is the file that was recovered from Moscow. The intelligence agencies were able to know much of what Hanssen had passed, and, because of the plea bargain worked out between Cacheris and the prosecutors, to question him directly and at length.

Ranking spies is probably not a very useful exercise. But if there is a pantheon of spies, certainly Hanssen would have to take his place in it, alongside such celebrated moles as Kim Philby and Aldrich Ames. That conclusion is almost inescapable, based on the materials that Hanssen is known to have given to the Russians and the extended length of his spying over twenty-two years.

For example, he disclosed U.S. analyses of Soviet nuclear missile strength, including the numbers and effectiveness of its ICBMs and warheads. He also passed to the KGB the CIA's estimate of what Moscow knew about U.S. early warning systems and about America's ability to retaliate against a massive nuclear attack.

In revealing the "continuity of government" plan, he enabled the Russians to discover exactly where top U.S. leaders, from the president on down, would be relocated in the event of a national emergency. That information took on even greater importance after the September 11 terrorist attacks on America.

Hanssen sold the Russians several documents describing highly sensitive satellite collection and other programs of the National Security Agency, the nation's supersecret code-making and global electronic eavesdropping arm. He revealed to the KGB that the NSA was exploiting a vulnerability in Soviet satellites that enabled the NSA to intercept their communications. He later disclosed a technical barrier that left the NSA unable to read certain Soviet communications. He betrayed the FBI/NSA tunnel under the Soviet embassy.

According to author James Bamford, an expert on the NSA, perhaps the most damage done by Hanssen was not to the FBI but to the NSA. Bamford expressed surprise at "the fact that he was able to get access to this information even though apparently he had no real need to know." He had damaged the NSA, Bamford believed, "probably worse than anybody since John Walker.

"By giving away to the Russians the details on which codes are being broken, which communication circuits are being listened to, Russia had two choices: they could either change the codes and cut off those circuits, which would have made NSA go deaf and basically put NSA out of business, or they could use the circuits to feed disinformation back to NSA. Either way it would have been one of the biggest blows to NSA since its founding."

But the major damage done by Hanssen did not end there. Among his worst actions was his betrayal of TOPHAT, one of the most valuable sources of U.S. intelligence inside the Soviet Union, who was later executed. The human costs were high; Hanssen also disclosed the names of the FBI's two KGB sources in Washington, who were also executed. All three had also been given up by Ames. Hanssen identified half a dozen other Soviet sources of the FBI. By tipping off the KGB to the FBI's investigation of Felix Bloch, he thwarted the espionage case the bureau was developing against the State Department official.

Cynics might ask, did it matter? After all, the Soviets lost the Cold War and the Communist system collapsed. But to argue that spying against the United States would only matter if America had lost the Cold War would be absurd. Hanssen's treachery endangered the security of the United States for more than two decades; along with Aldrich Ames, he betrayed three individuals who were executed, and he jeopardized the freedom of dozens of others.

Democracy rests on a compact between the governed, who give their consent, and their elected leaders; its citizens accept government and laws to protect them, preserve their liberties, and prevent chaos. Hanssen took the law into his own hands. That the Soviet Union failed to survive makes his acts no less reprehensible. Hanssen also spied for Russia, which did not collapse. No one would seriously contend that a distinction should be made between spying for the two countries, Russia and the Soviet Union, because one survived and the other did not.

Robert Hanssen's actions did not demonstrably alter the course of history. But the Communist system was built on quicksand and sank largely under the weight of its own inefficiency and corruption. It was doomed long before Hanssen sold American secrets to the Soviets.

Whenever a major spy case comes along, as they have in recent years with alarming frequency, there are headlines, investigations, a secret damage assessment, and calls in Congress and elsewhere for new procedures and safeguards. Hanssen might have been detected earlier, some suggested, if he had been given a lie detector test. He was never subject to a polygraph examination in his entire FBI career. In the wake of the outcry over his arrest, the bureau somewhat expanded its use of lie detectors.

The fallibility of polygraphs is well known, however, and the FBI has never been as enchanted with them as the CIA has.* Aldrich Ames, the worst mole in the history of the CIA, passed his polygraph tests. Lie detectors can notoriously result in false positives that may damage the lives of loyal employees. In the fallout from the Ames disaster, it will be recalled, some three hundred CIA employees were placed on the "A-to-Z list" because they had shown "SPRs," significant physiological responses, on their lie detector tests. Some careers were affected as a result, but no spies were caught.

Psychological testing, at least for agents in the FBI's counterintelligence division, has also been proposed as a tool to detect potential or actual spies. Former FBI counterintelligence chief John Lewis, who has

---

*Greater use of polygraphs had been debated for years within the FBI. But the bureau was split over the issue along functional lines. Some counterintelligence officials, because of the sensitive nature of their work, pressed for more lie detector tests; the criminal division was opposed, arguing that it was unnecessary and would injure morale and tarnish the careers of innocent agents.

thought a good deal about the problem, did not object to such screening before employment but was dubious that psychological testing "could reveal that an individual has committed a crime or was about to." Lewis favored better periodic background checks, greater awareness by coworkers, and broader use of polygraphs.

There are limits to what defensive measures can achieve, however. All the major powers spy on each other. The SVR is willing to pay large amounts of money to its best sources, and its principal target remains the United States. Washington, in turn, spends some $35 billion a year trying to steal and collect secrets from Russia and other nations, as well as to gather intelligence on terrorists.

In the end, spying will continue as long as there are secrets and a market for them. Espionage has been called the second oldest profession, and with good reason. It is no more likely to disappear than the first.

*   *   *

In July 2001, Jack Hoschouer wrote a letter to Bonnie Hanssen. "I said, 'I've sinned against you, please forgive me. I beg your forgiveness.' " About six weeks later, in mid-August, after fortifying himself with several drinks, "I called her from London and asked her to forgive me. I said, 'I understand if you don't want to see me.' She said, 'I forgive you.' " But Uncle Jack was no longer a welcome guest in the house on Talisman Drive.

Vivian Hanssen gave up her home in Venice, Florida, after twenty-seven years, and moved in with Bonnie to be closer to her son. It was difficult at age eighty-nine to pack up, let go of many of her possessions, and say good-bye to friends and neighbors. It was even more difficult, family members said, for her to see her son caged and behind glass, but it was better than not seeing him at all. He was still her son, and she loved him.

A year after her husband's arrest, Bonnie Hanssen was thinking about an annulment. In the eyes of the church, an annulment means that a marriage never existed. They are rarely granted, and only for grave cause.

The Hanssen children made it clear to their mother they would not be opposed to an annulment. Her mother and other family members had indeed urged it. Bonnie was only fifty-five. With an annulment and a civil divorce, she could remarry and change her name. But Bonnie, despite all she had been through, might never be able to bring herself to break her marriage vows to Bob, the father of her children. In the meantime, she was back teaching full-time at Oakcrest.

In her visits to the Alexandria jail, Bonnie asked her husband why he had spied, and why he had allowed Jack to watch them in their marital bed. He had very little to say about either subject, Bonnie told family members.

When the story surfaced about his relationship with Priscilla Sue Galey, Bonnie asked him point-blank whether he had had sex with the stripper. At first she thought he admitted he had, in Hong Kong, but when she asked about it on a subsequent visit to the jail, he said no, she had misunderstood. It was noisy in the background when we spoke before, he said; nothing had happened with the stripper.

In March, Bonnie went to the Justice Department to answer questions by the lawyers conducting the internal inquiry of the case. They took her into the bubble, a soundproof, secure room, for the all-day session. They still harbored suspicions that she knew of her husband's continued spying after he said he had stopped.

Two months later, just before her husband was sentenced, she was read her Miranda rights by the department lawyers and given a polygraph. Her lawyer, Janine Brookner, who watched through a one-way mirror, said she had passed it. During the polygraph examination, Bonnie denied she had any knowledge of Hanssen's later spying career, which began in 1985. She also denied finding any large amount of cash on her dresser.*

Bonnie Hanssen also insisted to *The New York Times* that after her husband said he had stopped spying, in 1980, she repeatedly questioned him to make sure he was, over time, paying the $30,000 he had received from the Russians to the Mother Teresa charity. He said he was. Ac-

---

*The prosecutors and the FBI found Bonnie Hanssen to have been "fully cooperative" with the government, as did the damage assessment group, which noted she had "met with our psychological evaluation team . . . to discuss various aspects of her husband's psychological makeup and disposition." The Justice Department's inspector general said, more cautiously, "based on the evidence available to us now, we cannot state that she has been untruthful in answering . . . questions." As a result of her cooperation, the prosecutors informed the court she was entitled to her husband's survivor's benefit.

cording to Brookner, Bonnie Hanssen also said during the lie detector test that over the next few years she asked her husband whether he was again working for the Russians, and he always denied it, acting as though he was hurt that she did not trust him.*

Bonnie also heard from Opus Dei, which was not at all happy to be linked to Robert Hanssen, whose arrest led to a flurry of news reports about the controversial organization. Early in 2002, the prelature of Opus Dei in Rome wrote to Bonnie, urging her to make no statements about her husband. Opus Dei may have been particularly anxious to avoid more adverse publicity in the months before October of that year, when the organization's founder, Josemaria Escriva de Balaguer, was to be elevated to sainthood by the Vatican.

*   *   *

A few weeks after Hanssen's arrest, Tom Burns received the red, white, and blue diplomatic license plate with the name BOB in big black letters, the present that had been made up for Hanssen's going-away party when he left the State Department. Wherever Hanssen was sent by the Federal Bureau of Prisons, he would not be needing it, Burns decided. "I think I will keep it as a memento," he said.

A year later, the lives of the actors in the Hanssen drama had changed.

Neil Gallagher had retired from the FBI to an executive position in the private sector.

Tim Caruso was the bureau's number two official in charge of counterterrorism; he had been named to that post only two months before the September 11 attacks. He retired in the summer of 2002.

Mike Rochford was the unit chief for Russian espionage at FBI headquarters.

The now-wealthy former KGB and SVR officer who produced the file that led to Hanssen's arrest was living comfortably somewhere in the United States under a new identity. With his $7 million.

Viktor Cherkashin, who had retired from the KGB a decade earlier, was living in Moscow, enjoying his three grandchildren and, he said, "in private security business now." Asked whether in all the years that

---

*James Risen, "Spy's Wife Speaks, after Taking a Lie Test," *The New York Times,* May 16, 2002, p. A16.

Hanssen had spied for the KGB and the SVR they ever learned who he was, he replied: "I never heard any name, of Hanssen or any other. I don't think anyone knew his identity."

Brian Kelley, cleared at last, was back at work at the CIA, but in a different job. He and his lawyer had not ruled out a possible legal claim against the government to compensate him for the three lost years when he was secretly and wrongly suspected as the mole.

John Lewis had retired from the FBI. He wondered sometimes, in the middle of the night, whether Moscow was playing mind games with American intelligence. "Pelton and Howard were handed to us. Their usefulness was at an end, as was true for Ames and Hanssen. Could it be that every so often they throw one our way? And look what it does to the community; we're disrupted. There's a part of you that has to ask, could a small group orchestrate these things on a periodic basis when someone has exhausted his usefulness?" Lewis didn't pretend to know the answer, just the question.

When Cherkashin was asked whether Hanssen could have been given up deliberately to protect another mole, he replied: "No, no, no, I have heard these theories before. It is out of the question, in general. That is not the way the intelligence community operates, in general, either Russian or American. If you start giving up sources deliberately, sooner or later that will become the practice, and no one will believe you. Even if a source is not important at all. With an important source, it is more ridiculous. The most important thing is to protect him in any way possible. It's out of the question."

Boris Yuzhin, who survived although betrayed by both Ames and Hanssen, was living quietly in northern California with his wife, Nadya, and daughter, Olga. Gray-haired at sixty, he was trying to forget his years in the harsh Soviet prison camps and build a new life in America.

Milt Bearden, the former head of the CIA's Soviet division, had been Aldrich Ames's boss for a time. He did not claim to understand Robert Hanssen. "There is an old Russian proverb," he said. " 'Another man's soul is darkness.' Does anybody ever really know anybody else?"

David Major headed the CI Centre, a private institution, and Paul Moore taught courses there. "I know what I see when I look at Bob Hanssen," Moore said. "But what does Bob Hanssen see when he looks in the mirror?"

Ron Mlotek was still at the State Department. Hanssen's arrest had been a terrible shock to him for months; the two had been so close. Something Hanssen once told him was particularly hard for him to forget.

"Bob said, 'A person would have to be a total stupid fucking idiot to spy for the KGB because you would be caught. Because we're [the FBI] going to get you.'"

*   *   *

In the Alexandria jail, Hanssen was housed in a separate wing reserved for federal prisoners. Because he did not want to mingle with the other inmates, guards awoke him at midnight to shower alone.

From the jail, Hanssen wrote long letters to his family. At first they were moralizing in tone: always live in the present, he advised his children, never in fantasy. He offered advice to his son-in-law on how to be a good husband and father. After a time, the letters were more practical; he counseled Bonnie on how to take care of the house, when to check the gutters. He wrote lengthy, technical letters to the children about computers.

In December 2001, Zacarias Moussaoui, a French citizen of Moroccan descent, was brought to the Alexandria facility to await trial in federal court on charges of conspiring in the September 11 terrorist attacks. Moussaoui, who authorities said was meant to be the twentieth hijacker, was arrested a month before the attacks after he aroused suspicion at a flight school in Minnesota, where he wanted to train to fly jumbo jets. When Moussaoui arrived, Hanssen was moved from his cell to another floor to make room for the new prisoner, and his privileges were curtailed; for a time, at least, he had no access to books or TV.

"I'm being treated like a common criminal," he complained to Bonnie.

Most of the debriefings had gone without incident, until he was given a polygraph test that same month. Afterward, the FBI polygraph operator sat down with Hanssen and said there were problems with the results. There was a conflict between his account and that of Priscilla Sue Galey.

The trouble started when the first question the polygrapher asked was whether Hanssen had a sexual relationship with the stripper. Hanssen angrily denied it, and his anger apparently affected his responses to other questions as well. Later, Hanssen explained to the

Webster commission that he felt a one-time event in Hong Kong was not a sexual relationship, a rationale that echoed President Clinton's famous finger-wagging denial of sex with Monica Lewinsky.

Priscilla Sue Galey had also told the FBI that at one point Hanssen said he wanted to buy a house for her. In retrospect, she believed that was part of a plan he had to use her somehow in his spying. Hanssen, when polygraphed, denied he offered to buy her a house or intended to enlist her as a spy.

There was another problem, the polygraph operator told Hanssen, aside from the conflicts between his account and Galey's. The peaks and valleys on the readout from the machine suggested that he had not fully disclosed what happened to all the cash he had received from the Russians. Hanssen insisted he had accounted for all of the money. But the polygraph operator was not satisfied. He told Hanssen he had failed his test, and that as a result Bonnie's pension might be taken away.

Hanssen lost it. He lunged for the man, who jerked backward out of the way. Hanssen landed no blows and the fracas was quickly over. Afterward, Cacheris went to see Randy Bellows, the federal prosecutor, to assure him that Hanssen was cooperating fully. "There were a few glitches on the polygraph," Cacheris said, "but there always are."

The episode was smoothed over, and Hanssen for the most part satisfied his FBI interrogators and the Webster commission. But the Justice Department's inspector general and Paul Redmond's damage assessment team at the CIA suspected Hanssen had not revealed all that he knew.

The split created a dilemma for the prosecutors. The plea bargain hinged on Hanssen's full cooperation in the debriefings. The prosecutors told the court that the government, despite the reservations of two of the four investigating groups, could not prove that Hanssen had broken the agreement. They asked that the sentencing proceed as scheduled.

On May 10, Hanssen, gaunt in his green prison uniform—he had lost seventy pounds in jail—appeared before Judge Claude Hilton in the Alexandria federal courthouse. The courtroom was packed with grim-faced FBI agents, most of whom had worked with Hanssen in counterintelligence.

Before the sentencing, Hanssen arose and read a statement. "I apologize for my behavior," he said. "I am shamed by it. I have opened the door for calumny against my totally innocent wife and children. I have hurt so many deeply."

Moments later, Judge Hilton sentenced Hanssen to life in prison with no possibility of parole.

Bonnie Hanssen and the children were not in the courtroom.

Afterward, Van Harp, the special agent in charge of the bureau's Washington field office, said the sentence had brought an end to "the darkest chapter in the history of the FBI."

Two months later, Hanssen was transferred from Alexandria to the maximum security federal prison in Florence, Colorado, a high-tech facility opened in 1994 and mainly reserved for violent and dangerous felons. In the prison, nicknamed Super Max, inmates are isolated and confined to their concrete cells twenty-three hours a day for at least two years, and, because of the prison's design, they cannot make eye contact with other inmates. The move was a disappointment to Hanssen's family, which hoped he would be sent to Allenwood, the federal prison in Pennsylvania, only a few hours' drive from Washington.

More than a year earlier, in the hours before he was arrested, Hanssen had given the copy of *The Man Who Was Thursday,* G. K. Chesterton's allegory, to Jack Hoschouer and urged him to read it. The elusive, supernatural figure of Sunday worked for Scotland Yard, but simultaneously seemed to be England's leading anarchist. There is a sentence near the end of the book that might serve as an epitaph to the strange career of Robert Hanssen. Inspector Ratcliffe says to Sunday:

"It seems so *silly* that you should have been on both sides and fought yourself."

The epitaph might have been written much earlier. All his life, Robert Hanssen had fought with himself. As a chemistry major at Knox, he had easy access to chemicals in the lab. For the last two years of college, he kept a vial on his dresser. He later said he never felt impelled to use it, never came close. But it was nevertheless reassuring to have it there, a silent witness to his despair and self-doubts. It was there if life became too much.

The vial contained potassium cyanide.

Author's Note

I began work on this book when an intelligence source alerted me to the arrest of Robert Philip Hanssen the day before it was announced publicly.

The FBI counterintelligence agent had spied for the Russians intermittently for almost twenty-two years. There were many questions to be answered, but it seemed to me that the most difficult and challenging were two: what was Robert Hanssen's motive in betraying his country—and how was he finally caught?

To resolve the first question meant trying to understand who Robert Hanssen really was, what forces had shaped him and ultimately led him to cross a line from which there was no turning back. To pursue the second question, the real story of how he was unmasked, the trail led me deep inside the FBI's secretive counterintelligence arm, where I discovered the extraordinary answer.

Under the terms of Hanssen's plea bargain with the government, he could not be interviewed during the time that I researched and wrote this book. He was barred from talking to any writer or to the news media until the FBI and other federal authorities were through questioning him. However, I had the good fortune to gain access to the mind of Robert Hanssen through an unusual means. With the assent of his defense attorney, Plato Cacheris, Hanssen authorized Dr. David L. Charney, the psychiatrist who spent many hours and days with him in the months after his arrest, to speak with me at length.

Hanssen apparently held little, if anything, back in his conversations with Charney. His secret life as a spy finally revealed, he unburdened himself freely in these sessions. My access to the psychiatrist, whose views struck me as particularly incisive, provided me with exclusive insights into Hanssen's state of mind, his personal and family background, and his complicated, interlocking web of motivations.

In researching the dramatic story of how Hanssen was finally caught, I was able to speak with a number of counterintelligence agents and officials, many of whom had directly participated in the FBI investigation that led to his arrest. My thanks go to all of them. Although the counterspies were circumspect, even silent, on some aspects of how the FBI, with help from the CIA, managed to extract from Moscow the actual secret KGB file that enabled the bureau to identify Hanssen, I was able in a series of interviews to piece together the essentials of the story—and of the investigation that ended when Hanssen emerged from a dead drop in a park in northern Virginia on a peaceful Sunday afternoon and was captured.

Although it might be assumed that the FBI was eager to cooperate in this exercise, the truth was rather the opposite. Hanssen had gone undetected for more than two decades, and the case was seen as another in a series of disasters that had battered the bureau and its public image. It took more than six months of constant badgering, importunings, e-mails, faxes, letters, and telephone calls before I was able to sit down with the first FBI counterintelligence official to discuss the Hanssen case and the innovative operation that led to his arrest. And although I was gratified that the bureau had, in effect, expressed confidence in my objectivity, at one point the interviews temporarily and mysteriously stopped. The counterspies, I was told, were alarmed that I had found out too much!

To research this book, I conducted more than 350 interviews with approximately 150 persons. Wherever possible, they are identified by name. I drew as well on a number of court documents, including the detailed FBI affidavit in the case and the government's indictment.

Although Hanssen was prohibited from speaking publicly while he was being debriefed, and his wife, Bonnie, declined to be interviewed, I was able to talk with several of her siblings, including her sister Jeanne Beglis, as well as with her parents, Dr. Leroy Wauck and Frances Wauck. I also spoke with Hanssen's mother, Vivian, several times over many months. I greatly appreciate the willingness of family members to talk to me about what has surely been a painful and terribly difficult experience for all of them.

I am grateful as well to Jack Hoschouer, who described himself aptly as closer than a brother to Robert Hanssen, and who figures at many points in the story. Although mortified by the highly public exposure of his participation in Hanssen's bizarre sexual activities, Hoschouer agreed to speak to me at length in a series of interviews by telephone to Germany and in person in Washington. I felt he showed considerable courage in doing so; another man might have retreated behind a wall of silence. I thank him for his openness, his patience, and his help. His wife, Aya, also was kind enough to share with me her recollections of Robert Hanssen. His mother, Jeanette Hoschouer, told me of her encounters with Howard Hanssen.

I am particularly indebted to Plato Cacheris, the defense attorney who saved Hanssen from a possible death penalty, and to Dr. David L. Charney, whose insights into Hanssen's psyche were invaluable. My thanks as well go to Preston Burton, Plato Cacheris's law partner.

Among the FBI counterintelligence officials interviewed, I am especially grateful to Neil J. Gallagher, then the assistant director in charge of the National Security Division, as well as to James T. Caruso, Michael J. Waguespack, Leslie G. Wiser, Jr., and James D. Lyle. Still other FBI counterintelligence specialists were helpful but preferred not to be named; I am no less grateful for their assistance.

I also greatly appreciate the help of John E. Collingwood, the FBI assistant director in charge of the Office of Public and Congressional Affairs; Michael P. Kortan, chief of the public affairs section of that office; Bill Carter, the acting unit chief of the FBI national press office; and Supervisory Special Agent Steven W. Berry of the national press office, whose assistance was unstinting and invaluable. Others in the FBI helped as well, including Bill Houghton, Kimberly Lichtenberg, Candy Curtis, Kevin Wilkinson, and James H. Davis.

More than thirty former FBI agents and officials were also interviewed, and I thank them all for their assistance. I must begin with William H. Webster, former director of the FBI and the CIA, who headed the special commission that reviewed FBI security programs for the Department of Justice. John F. Lewis, Jr., the former assistant director in charge of the FBI's National Security Division, provided many valuable insights, and his patience with my endless questions never flagged. I am grateful as well to James D. Ohlson, Edward J. Curran, and Thomas E. Burns, Jr.; to David G. Major and Paul Moore of the Centre for Counterintelligence and Security Studies; to Raymond A.

Mislock, Jr., Joseph Tierney, Donald E. Stukey, James E. Nolan, Jr., Phillip A. Parker, Thomas J. Pickard, Robert M. Bryant, A. Jackson Lowe, John F. Mabey, Harry B. "Skip" Brandon, R. Patrick Watson, Dick Alu, Robert B. Wade, Thomas K. Kimmel, Jr., Pete O'Donnell, Dale H. Pugh, James A. Werth, Theodore M. Gardner, and Bill Westberg.

I also appreciate the generous help I received from Charles C. Stuart, the prizewinning producer and president of Stuart Television Productions, and Chris Szechenyi, his talented and tireless field producer, who together created the documentary on the Hanssen case for the A&E cable network, on which I served as a consultant. Emily Ratliff, their production assistant, was always marvelously helpful.

I am obliged as well to Professor Chester Gillis of Georgetown University; Brian Finnerty, the U.S. spokesman for Opus Dei; Father C. John McCloskey III, director of the Catholic Information Center in Washington, D.C.; Father Franklyn M. McAfee of St. Catherine of Siena Catholic church; and Father Robert P. Bucciarelli. To understand the legal aspects of the Roman Catholic sacrament of confession, I relied principally on Michael J. Mazza's "Should Clergy Hold the Priest-Penitent Privilege?" in the *Marquette Law Review* 82, no. 1 (fall 1998), pp. 171–204.

Several former CIA officials were interviewed, including former CIA director James Woolsey, Milton A. Bearden, Paul J. Redmond, Jr., John C. Platt, Gordon C. Oehler, Colin R. Thompson, and Suzanne Spaulding. My thanks as well go to Mark Mansfield, the CIA deputy director for public affairs. Other current and former CIA officials preferred to speak only on background. To tell the story of GRAY DECEIVER, the CIA official who was erroneously thought to be the mole, I interviewed his attorney, John Moustakas, and drew as well upon several intelligence sources and on published accounts by James Risen and David Johnston of *The New York Times* and Dan Eggen, Brooke A. Masters, and Vernon Loeb of *The Washington Post.*

Viktor Cherkashin, the former KGB counterintelligence officer who ran the Hanssen case in Washington, was reached at his home in Moscow and interviewed at length. His comments provided an intriguing perspective from the Russian side of the drama.

Many other individuals helped me to tell the story of Robert Hanssen. The list is too long to include everyone, and a few preferred to remain anonymous. But I thank Thomas B. Ross, coauthor with me of three books; James Bamford, Priscilla Sue Galey, Dr. Alen J. Salerian, Herb Romerstein, William Schulz, Edward S. McFadden, Momcilo Rosic, Mike and Judi Shotwell, John C. Sylvester, H. Keith Melton, Ed Pound of *USA Today,* John Carl Warnecke, Benny Pasquariello, Ronald Sol Mlotek, and Boris Yuzhin.

Sarah J. Albertini provided vital computer advice and research assistance along the way. Ida Sawyer made sure my newspaper files were up to date.

I am especially grateful to Robert D. Loomis, my editor at Random House on this and eight previous books, whose editorial skills and dedication are unsurpassed and reflected throughout these pages.

Finally, and as always, I am indebted beyond measure to my wife, Joan, who, without complaint, heard more about Robert Hanssen and the murky world of spies he inhabited than she probably wanted to know.

—David Wise
Washington, D.C.
July 30, 2002

Afterword

In the Supermax federal prison in Florence, Colorado, Robert Hanssen's world had shrunk to a seven-and-a-half-by-fifteen-foot cell in the high security wing. There he lived in solitary confinement, taken out by guards only for an hour and a half on weekdays to exercise in a wire cage. To and from the cage, he was in shackles. The former FBI agent was now a number, 48551-083.

It was the toughest prison in the federal system, a warehouse for the nation's worst, most violent, and dangerous criminals—serial killers, terrorists, Mafia hit men. One third have committed murder in prison.

Like all inmates at the Supermax, Hanssen was isolated, alone in his cell behind bars and a steel door. But unlike the others, by order of the attorney general of the United States, John Ashcroft, Hanssen was placed under even harsher restrictions. These "special administrative measures," or SAMs, were designed, in theory, to prevent Hanssen from disclosing classified information. Ashcroft's order meant that Hanssen could not have contact with anyone other than his wife, members of his immediate family, his priest, and his attorney.*

---

*I discovered this when I attempted to send a letter to Hanssen in July 2002, seeking an interview. In return, I received a stern letter from Warden Robert A. Hood informing me that "at the direction of the attorney general" the special restrictions on Hanssen prohibited him from contact with the news media because there was "a substantial risk of disclosure" of secrets that "would pose a threat to the national security of the United States." Hanssen was also prohibited from receiving mail or writing to anyone except his family and his lawyer. Under federal regulations, the restrictions can be imposed for one year, but may be extended indefinitely by the attorney general. In March 2003, Ashcroft extended the restrictions for another year.

No convicts in the Supermax have cellmates, and the prison is designed with staggered cells so that the inmates do not have eye contact with each other. Even so, Hanssen caught a glimpse of another resident of the high security wing and recognized him: Theodore Kaczynski, the Unabomber.

The prison, advertised as "escape-proof," is one hundred ten miles due south of Denver in the barren foothills of the Rockies. It was opened in 1994 to house up to 490 inmates. Fourteen hundred electronically controlled gates clang shut to seal off the units. The facility is ringed by watchtowers and there are laser beams and sensors to detect any movement in the area between the prison walls and the perimeter razor wire. To date, no one has escaped from the Supermax.

In late October 2002, Bonnie Hanssen, accompanied by her second daughter, Susan, and Hanssen's ailing ninety-year-old mother, Vivian, visited him at the Supermax. No physical contact with Hanssen was permitted; they spoke to him through thick glass. The family had hoped Hanssen would be sent to Allenwood, the federal prison in central Pennsylvania, where he could be visited more often, but the Bureau of Prisons, a division of the Justice Department, decided otherwise.

To Bonnie, Hanssen seemed enormously sad. He appeared to have difficulty articulating words, perhaps, his family thought, from his months in solitary confinement.

He described the harsh conditions in the Supermax, how the only time he could leave his cell was when he was taken out in restraints to an exercise cage, some days outdoors, other days indoors. His bed was a concrete slab with only a thin mattress and he complained he was developing hip trouble because of it. This is really hard time, Hanssen told his family.

He was receiving visits from a Greek Orthodox priest who provided him with some books by C. S. Lewis. Later, at Bonnie's request, a young Catholic priest was allowed to see Hanssen. Like all inmates at the Supermax, Hanssen had a small television in his cell, the channels controlled by the prison guards. He was curious enough to turn on the CBS two-part miniseries about his espionage, but he was so disgusted with the portrayal of him, he thought it so bad, that he had turned it off.

To Bonnie, at least, Hanssen seemed repentant. Yet, according to one source close to the family, Hanssen tried to persuade her that what he did was somehow good for the country, because it alerted the FBI to the flaws in its security.

In his last conversations with Dr. Charney before he was transferred from the Alexandria, Virginia, jail to Colorado, Hanssen had unburdened himself further about his spying. He told the psychiatrist that as a Russian mole within the FBI he had enjoyed a sense of power, he was pulling all the strings.

"He wound up in a position where he could regard himself as the puppetmaster," Charney said, "knowing more than anyone within the bureau or the KGB about the totality of what was happening."

And to the psychiatrist Hanssen had elaborated further on excitement as a motive for his spying. "It was not mere excitement," Charney said. As Hanssen had explained his actions, "It was more a matter of stretching oneself, employing the fullest range of one's powers. He did this by spying."

Hanssen also told Charney that part of the excitement he derived from spying was that he was able "to let his mind run like a racehorse. His father was into racehorses, and that is why he used that metaphor."

In the Supermax, Hanssen was no longer the puppetmaster. He had become the puppet. He had no control over his life. Confined to his cell almost twenty-three hours a day, his meals were brought to him by a guard and shoved through a food slot. And as long as he was housed in the Supermax, he had little hope of any change.

Most convicts are sent to the Colorado prison for at least three years. In the second year, some are rewarded for good behavior by having a few restrictions removed. They may be allowed out of their cells, for example, for group meetings. In the third year, according to the prison's supervising attorney, Christopher B. Synsvoll, "they can walk with escort to the commissary, the prison store, and can go to the main line, to group meals." But none of that would be possible for Hanssen as long as the attorney general's restrictions remain in effect.

Even if those restrictions are lifted, the most Hanssen would have to look forward to in the Supermax would be a prison job: "mopping up, cleaning, or in the federal prison industries, which are the more desirable jobs," Synsvoll said. "He would be making orange jumpsuits for the inmates. Or stamping envelopes with the prison's return address."

Hanssen, the quintessential computer nerd, would never have access to a computer in the Supermax; no inmate does. If he were ever transferred to a less harsh prison, computer access would be up to the warden. In no event would he be allowed online; the FBI, obviously, does not want Robert Hanssen ever again to be able to communicate with Moscow.

Bonnie, whose religion remained central to her life, confided to a friend that Hanssen, in prison for the rest of his years, was now truly doing penance for his acts. She lamented that she would have to continue to see him behind glass on her visits; it was unfair to any human being unless there was a physical danger.

It all remains a deep mystery, Bonnie added, how such a loving husband and father could have done all this and seem so totally sad and repentant now; there was something so utterly odd and tragic about the whole thing. It was beyond her understanding.

If Hanssen's espionage continued to baffle his wife, one complaint he voiced to his family was an indicator of how, even now, he had failed to grasp fully the enormity of what he had done and the reality of where he was. Hanssen said he thought he might be treated better in prison because of his long years of government service.

Apparently Robert Hanssen chose to overlook the fact that for almost twenty-two of his twenty-five years in the FBI, he had, intermittently, betrayed the country he had sworn to protect.

One may also wonder whether Hanssen, when he was an FBI counterintelligence agent, viewed a brief video of the arrest of Dimitri Fedorovich Polyakov (TOPHAT), the first agent he betrayed to the Russians. The footage made its way to the West a few years ago and was even aired on CNN.

It showed General Polyakov, his arms handcuffed behind his back, as KGB goons rip off his shirt. Fingers appear from behind on each side of his face, forcing him to look at the camera. Dignified, despite all of this, TOPHAT stares straight ahead, knowing full well that when the long months of interrogation are over, he will be executed.

He never knew the name of his betrayer.

Index

ACS (Automated Case Support System, FBI), 189–90, 236
Albertini, Sarah J., 299
Albright, Madeleine, 194
Alu, Dick, 30–32, 76, 101, 134, 298
Ames, Aldrich H.
  arrest of, 24, 79n, 168, 170, 171, 199, 211, 220, 261, 290
  at CIA, 83n, 168, 246, 290
  debriefing, 175
  defense lawyer, 10, 250, 262
  and espionage penalties, 124n
  and FBI-CIA mole hunts, 168–71, 176, 180, 200, 205–7, 217, 220, 229, 247, 286
  motives for spying, 270
  and polygraph tests, 34, 286
  spy career of, 23, 24, 48n, 50, 51–52, 56, 74, 79, 139, 168–70, 187, 200, 245, 248, 265, 272, 284, 285
  unawareness of Bloch case, 170
Amtorg (Soviet commercial trading agency), 20, 21, 58–60, 62, 274
Angleton, James J., 71, 208
ANLACE, 169, 173
Arnold, Benedict, 270
Ashcroft, John, 125, 235, 247, 248, 262–64, 266, 268, 301, 301n, 303

Bakatin, Vadim V., 109
Bamford, James, 87, 116, 165–67, 285, 299
Bannerman, Laine, 173
Barnett, David H., 47–48
"Bart, Pierre." See Gikman, Reino
Bates, John D., 156
Bearden, Milton A., 141, 290, 298

Beglis, George, 121–23, 130, 244
Beglis, Jeanne Wauck, 120–23, 125, 130, 244, 245, 269, 296
Bellows, Randy I., 250, 263, 266, 267, 292
Bereznay, Timothy, 219, 226
Berlin, spy tunnel in, 108
Berry, Steven W., 297
Blake, George, 108
BLINDSWITCH, 174–75
Bloch, Felix, 99, 111–19, 128, 166, 170, 199, 203, 205–7, 210, 285
Bloch, Lucille Stephenson, 112, 119
Boeckenhaupt, Herbert W., 22n
Bogart, Humphrey, 149
Bond, James, 146, 149, 189, 270, 277
Borovikov, Vacheslav Z., 107
Borrasca, Adelia, 166
Borrasca, Barton A., 162–67
BOURBON. See Polyakov, Dimitri Fedorovich
Boyce, Christopher, 270n
Boyd, John, 277
Brandon, Harry B. ("Skip"), 161
Brookner, Janine, 250, 288–89
Brown, Ron, 165
Bryant, Robert M. ("Bear"), 170, 181, 298
Bucciarelli, Robert P., 25–27, 120, 141, 245, 298
BUCKLURE, 199–201, 219, 223
Burke, Edmund, 186n
Burns, Thomas E., Jr., 37–39, 42, 87, 93, 184, 231–32, 289, 297
Burton, Preston, 264, 266–67, 297
Bush, George H. W., 113, 200
Bush, George W., 215, 234–35, 247, 263
Byrne, Frank, 44

C-5 (Chicago Police Department intelligence unit), 17
Cacheris, Ethel Dominick, 262
Cacheris, Plato, 10, 26, 250, 255–57, 261–67, 271, 284, 292, 295, 297
Camden, Pat, 17
Carlson, Rodney W., 39
CART (Computer Analysis Response Team), 188
Carter, Bill, 297
Caruso, James T. ("Tim"), 169, 174, 219, 241–42, 283, 289, 297
Casablanca (film), 149, 150–51
Casey, Robert P., 13
Cash, Peggy Casey, 244
Charney, David L., 10, 257–58, 271–73, 278–81, 295–97, 303
Cherkashin, Viktor I., 23, 30, 54, 57, 61–62, 75, 166–67, 200–1, 207, 289–90, 298
Chin, Larry Wu-Tai, 46, 270
Chuvakhin, Sergei D., 52, 169
CI-3 (FBI counterintelligence section), 4, 29, 32, 37
CI-4 (FBI KGB squad), 221
CIA (Central Intelligence Agency)
    and agent betrayals, 21, 67, 168–69
    and Berlin spy tunnel, 108
    and Bloch case, 112–14
    Brookner suit against, 250
    Counterespionage Group, 128, 171, 172, 176, 217
    data collection devices, 95, 102n
    directorates, 164
    and fall of Soviet Union, 141
    Hanssen case damage assessment, 281, 292
    and Hanssen sentencing, 264
    "illegals" specialists at, 206, 207, 214
    Kelley suspension by, 212–14, 218
    killings outside headquarters of, 186
    mission of, 172
    and mole hunts, 3, 71, 128, 168–73, 175–76, 179, 199–200, 208, 221, 229, 245, 286, 290
    in Moscow, 220, 229, 245
    and Nixon administration, 183
    Nonproliferation Center, 162, 164
    and polygraphs, 33, 34, 176–77, 286
    relations with FBI, 24, 39, 45, 47–48, 68, 70, 169, 171–73, 175–77, 181, 199, 209–10, 221, 224, 229, 245
    and Russian defectors, 45, 57, 61, 71, 80, 132, 141, 208, 222, 229, 239
    secrets passed to KGB, 47–48, 51–52, 82–83, 95, 140, 225, 284
    and Soviet agent recruitment, 39, 78–79, 169, 199–201
    and Soviet embassy tunnel, 109
    Special Investigations Unit, 171–73, 175, 176, 179, 199, 217
    spy camera, 47, 49
    surveillance techniques, 208
    and TOPHAT, 22–24
    training base, 59, 175
    See also Ames, Aldrich H.; Chin, Larry Wu-Tai; Nicholson, Harold James
CIC (CIA Counterintelligence Center), 211
CIPA (Classified Information Procedures Act of 1980), 264
CKTWINE. *See* Yuzhin, Boris
Classification levels, of documents, 20n
Clinton, Hillary Rodham, 14, 165
Clinton, William J.
    and counterintelligence reorganization, 171, 172, 176
    Freeh criticism of, 248–49
    and gays in armed services, 122
    Hanssen distaste for, 165, 186
    and Lewinsky affair, 261, 292
    rumored FBI surveillance of, 164–65
Cloyd, Dan, 242
COINS-II (Community On-Line Intelligence System), 79
Colby, William E., 71
Collingwood, John E., 297
Community Nonproliferation Committee (CNPC), 162–63
Confession, as Catholic sacrament, 85–86, 298
Confidentiality, legal rulings on, 26n
Connery, Sean, 258
"Continuity of government" plan, U.S., 248–49
Counterintelligence Group (interagency task force), 83, 184
COURTSHIP (FBI-CIA unit), 39
Curran, Edward J., 31, 59, 76, 171–73, 175, 179, 217, 272, 283, 297
Curtis, Candy, 154, 155, 156, 297

Daley, Richard J., 137, 140, 186, 227
Davis, James H., 297
DeConcini, Dennis, 170
Defector, meanings of term, 132n
Degtyar, Viktor M., 50, 52–54, 61, 64, 65, 81
Dion, John, 267
Documents, classification levels of, 20n
Double agents (DAs), 38
Drummond, Nelson C. ("Bulldog"), 22n
DST (Direction de la Surveillance du Territoire), 114–15, 118
DTP (Dedicated Technical Program), 29–30, 98
Duffy, Barbara, 158

Duggan, Jack, 164
Dulles, Allen W., 108
Dunlap, Jack E., 22n
Dzheikiya, Rollan G., 174–75

EASY CHAIR, 102
Eddleman, Joseph K., Jr., 40
Eggen, Dan, 298
Embassies. *See* Soviet embassy (D.C.);
	United States embassy (Moscow)
Entrapment (film), 258
Escriva de Balaguer, Josemaria, 90–91, 289
Espionage
	difficulty of proving, 210
	early detection of, 286–87
	inevitability of, 287
	penalties for, 8, 124, 202, 211, 235n, 250,
		262–65
	prosecution of, 264–65
	risks of, 284
	usual motives for, 270–71, 279, 281

Falcon and the Snowman, The (Lindsey), 270
Fasano, Jerome, 87
FBI (Federal Bureau of Investigation)
	and Ames arrest, 168, 220
	analysis techniques, 66–68
	"Black Vault," 173
	and Bloch case, 111–19, 128, 285
	and CNPC, 162–63
	and computer security, 161, 187–89,
		235–36
	counterintelligence arm, 4, 59, 122, 123,
		126, 128, 137, 169, 183, 193, 219–21,
		241, 246, 286, 291, 295–97
	crises of public confidence in, 181,
		248–49, 283, 296
	and double agents, 38, 80–81, 159–60
	foreign offices of, 148, 220, 282
	and GRAYDAY-Hanssen investigation, 20,
		159, 219–39, 241–42, 243, 296
	and Hanssen arrest, 239–50
	Hanssen career with, 18–21, 28–39, 42,
		44–46, 50, 58–60, 62, 66–68, 100, 134,
		137, 139, 140, 148, 153–58, 160–66,
		227, 246, 248, 273–74, 276–79, 282–83
	and Hanssen post-arrest investigation,
		130–31, 145, 159, 262, 292, 295
	Hanssen warning signs overlooked by,
		158, 282–83
	inspection division, 134, 179
	intelligence division, 3–4, 37–39, 44,
		66–67, 122, 179, 181
	and Kelley investigation, 205–19, 226
	mission of, 172
	and mole hunts, 3–4, 25n, 38–39, 67–73,
		82–83, 123–27, 160, 166, 168–76,
		179–81, 199–202, 205, 209–10,
		219–29, 283
	National Security Division, 179, 181, 187,
		215, 230, 240, 246, 297
	in New York City, 19–20, 42, 45, 50,
		58–60, 74, 83, 122, 126, 172
	and NSA, 165
	and Pitts case damage assessment, 178–82
	and polygraphs, 33–35, 177, 205, 214,
		282, 286
	promotions system, 134
	Quantico training academy, 149, 277–78
	recruitment of KGB agents, 38–39,
		196–201
	relations with CIA, 24, 39, 45, 47–48, 78,
		169, 171–73, 175–77, 181, 199, 216
	retirement parties, 145–46
	and Russian informants, 3, 38–42, 47–49,
		61–62, 70–71, 83, 96, 99, 132, 136,
		168–69, 174, 211–18, 220–30, 264
	SIOC, 240–41
	and Soviet embassy tunnel, 98–99, 100–1,
		103, 104–11, 285
	spy arrests by, 44–46, 175, 178
	surveillance techniques, 29–30, 59, 60,
		78, 83, 146n, 170–71, 208–9, 213,
		233–34, 236
	and White House surveillance, 164–65
FBInet, 187–89
FEDORA, 69–71
Fefelov, Aleksandr K., 62–64, 65n, 225, 243
Finnerty, Brian, 91, 298
Florence, Colorado, Supermax federal
	prison in, 301, 301n, 302–4
Forden, David, 61
Foreign Intelligence Surveillance Court,
	208, 233
Fox, Charlie, 144
Freeh, John, 91n
Freeh, Louis, 91, 173–74, 180–81, 214, 215,
	217n, 229, 241–43, 246–49, 264
Fuller, Gwen, 221

Galey, Priscilla Sue, 143–52, 227, 258, 260,
	276, 277, 288, 291–92, 299
Gallagher, Neil J., 180, 182, 215–16, 219,
	226, 228–29, 231, 233, 237, 240–43,
	246, 289, 297
"Garcia, Ramon" (Hanssen alias), 7, 62, 65,
	75–77, 82, 141, 160, 189, 192, 223,
	225, 239
Gardner, Theodore M., 198, 298
Gessford, Ben, 221
Gibson, Grover, 197
Gikman, Reino, 113–18, 206
Gillis, Chester, 85–86, 298
Golitsin, Anatoly M., 71

Good Guys (strip club), 145–46
Gorbachev, Mikhail S., 109, 135, 138
GRAY DECEIVER (Brian Kelley), 206, 216, 218, 225–27, 298
GRAYDAY (Robert Hanssen), 227, 228, 231, 233, 242, 243
GRAYSUIT, 206, 218, 219, 222
Gregory, Doug, 211, 212, 243, 267, 268
Grimes, Sandy, 169
GRU (Glavnoye Razvedyvatelnoye Upravlenie)
 CIA spies in, 39
 and FBI operations, 37, 38, 126, 159–60
 Hanssen espionage for, 20–22, 42, 245, 272n
 and Hanssen revolunteer attempt, 159–60
 rivalry with KGB, 24, 160
 U.S. activities of, 20, 37, 59
 See also Polyakov, Dimitri Fedorovich
"Gs, the" (Special Surveillance Group, FBI), 208–9, 230, 236, 240, 241, 244
GTBEEP. See Polyakov, Dimitri Fedorovich
GTGAUZE. See Motorin, Sergei
GTGENTILE. See Martynov, Valery
GTGLAZING, 78
GTJOGGER, 47, 48n
Guerin, Rudy, 211, 212
Gundarev, Victor, 61–62, 167
Gusev, Stanislav, 193–94

Hagarty, Robert, 13, 86
Hall, Fawn, 262
Hanna, H. Russell, Jr., 105–6
Hanssen, Bernadette Wauck ("Bonnie")
 background, 13–15
 and Catholicism, 6, 13, 86, 88, 124
 disillusionment with husband, 269, 287–88, 293
 and Hanssen arrest, 25n, 243–46, 250, 258, 261, 262
 and Hanssen cash displays, 120, 123, 125–28, 130, 134, 288
 and Hanssen espionage, 24–27, 53, 120, 127, 130, 141, 245, 269, 273, 281, 288–89
 and Hanssen FBI career, 19, 273
 Hanssen letters to, 291
 and Hanssen pension, 268, 292
 and Hanssen in Supermax, 302, 304
 and Hanssen voyeurism, 252–60, 269, 270, 280, 287, 288
 and husband's liaisons, 15, 25, 145, 288
 and in-laws, 19, 43
 nude photos of, 251, 252
 and Opus Dei, 13, 15, 25–26, 86, 88, 124, 289

personality, 121, 131, 273
 teaching career, 43, 234, 288
Hanssen, Greg, 244
Hanssen, Howard
 background, 9
 death, 160
 move to Florida, 43
 police career, 9, 10, 15–17, 135, 186
 relationship with son, 10–11, 19, 126, 255, 275, 276
 and son's career choices, 12, 16–17
Hanssen, Jack, 88, 166
Hanssen, Lisa, 244–45
Hanssen, Robert Philip
 arrest of, 8, 10, 25n, 130, 158, 167, 181, 189, 213–14, 218, 229, 239, 261–63, 290, 295
 background, 4–6, 9–18, 207, 216, 293
 and Catholicism, 6, 15, 25–26, 43–44, 85–93, 120, 150, 167, 184, 187, 253, 257, 270, 280–81
 and Clinton surveillance rumor, 164–65
 conservative views, 32, 121–22, 154, 167, 186, 258, 270
 counterintelligence training, 17–18, 187, 278
 evidence against, 181, 221–30, 233, 234, 236–38, 243, 264, 282–84, 289
 extramarital relationships, 15, 143–52, 227, 258, 260, 270–72, 276, 282, 288, 291–92
 family suspicions about, 25, 120–31, 282
 FBI career, 18–21, 28–39, 42, 44–46, 50, 58–60, 62, 66–68, 100, 134, 137, 140, 148, 153–58, 160–66, 173, 184, 187, 230–31, 233, 236–38, 252, 272n, 273–74, 276–79
 FBI database searches by, 160, 188–89, 191, 192, 233
 FBI GRAYDAY surveillance of, 230–31, 233–34, 236–42
 as FBI mole study director, 3–4, 67–69, 73–74, 82–83, 119, 173, 181
 FBI-CIA damage assessment on, 248, 266–69, 284–86
 and harassment of co-worker, 153–58, 160
 health problems, 244
 as mole hunt target, 160, 181, 191, 202, 216–18, 223, 225–28
 motives for spying, 21, 53–54, 189, 191–92, 257, 270–81
 and NACIC, 176–77
 nicknames, 31, 153, 185, 277
 at Office of Foreign Missions, 184, 187, 189
 and Opus Dei, 6, 15, 25–26, 43, 86–92, 120, 124, 147, 153, 167, 184, 253, 257, 270, 280, 281, 289

Pitts suspicions about, 181
and plan to drug wife, 259–60, 270
and plea bargain, 262–69, 284, 292, 295
and polygraphs, 34–35, 176–77, 282, 286, 291–92
and pornography, 5, 252–53, 255, 258, 260, 270
in prison, 261–62, 267, 287–88, 291–93, 301–4
prosecution of, 215
psychological profile of, 10–11, 17, 30–32, 83, 89, 93, 94, 121, 187, 257–58, 270–81, 290, 293, 297
sentencing of, 268, 269, 292–93
sources betrayed by, 132, 159–60, 168–69, 235, 245, 248, 265, 284, 285
spending habits, 43, 122, 128–29, 134–35, 146, 149–50, 184, 272
spy career, 4, 7–8, 15, 20–24, 42, 46, 49, 50–58, 60–65, 74–84, 94–99, 103, 107, 108, 114n, 115, 117–20, 123, 132–42, 159–60, 166–67, 169, 170n, 189–95, 200, 202–3, 231, 234, 236, 238–39, 243, 245, 247–48, 265, 272, 274, 282–86, 290
and strip clubs, 145–46, 255, 258
tape recording of, 225–26
technical expertise, 4, 29–30, 32–35, 55, 60, 97, 121, 160–62, 181, 185, 192–93, 230–31, 237n, 238, 253, 267
and voyeurism, 251–60, 279–80
and weapons, 147, 149, 166, 185–86, 242, 244, 270, 272, 277–78
Hanssen, Susan, 302
Hanssen, Vivian Baer, 9–10, 15, 16n, 43, 262, 275, 287, 296, 302
Harp, Van, 293
Harriman, Averell, 101
Harris, Linda, 151
Hathaway, Gardner R. ("Gus"), 168, 206–7
Hengemuhle, Joseph F., 42
Hilton, Claude M., 265, 268, 292, 293
Höbart, Helga, 113, 115
Holt, Jim, 39, 169
Honorary Consul, The (Greene), 197–98
Hood, Laura, 234
Hood, Perry, 234
Hood, Robert A., 301n
Hoover, J. Edgar, 30, 70, 283
Horan, Sheila, 219
Hoschouer, Ayako Matsuda ("Aya"), 6, 13, 19, 249, 260, 297
Hoschouer, Jack Delroy
    background, 5–6, 11–13, 138, 251–52
    and Clinton surveillance rumor, 164
    and Hanssen arrest, 240, 242, 249
    on Hanssen's father, 10, 17
    on Hanssen's religiosity, 92
    and KGB, 138–39
    and pornography, 5, 255, 260
    and Rolex watch, 134–35, 249–50
    and strip clubs, 145, 255
    ties to Hanssen family, 5–7, 11, 12, 97, 254, 257–60, 276n, 287, 297
    and voyeurism, 252–60, 269, 270, 280, 297
Hoschouer, Jeanette, 11, 249, 297
Houghton, Bill, 16, 97, 135, 297
Howard, Edward Lee, 45, 46, 51n, 172, 290
Huffines, Steve, 157
Hundley, John C., 266

"Illegals," definition of, 206
Invicta (computer security company), 235–38
Iran-Contra scandal, 262
Itar-Tass news agency, 239
    See also Tass
Ivanov, Boris, 70

Jackson, Donald, 18
Jackson, Thomas Penfield, 157
Jewell, Richard, 248
Jirousek, Tina, 111–12
Joanna's 1819 Club, 143, 144–45, 147
John Paul II (pope), 90–91
Johnston, David, 298
Justice, U. S. Department of, 125, 130, 131, 156, 233, 248, 249, 288, 292, 297

Kaczynski, Theodore, 302
Kansi, Mir Aimal, 186
KARAT, 217–18
Karlow, Peter, 102, 208
Kelley, Brian, 205–19, 226, 227, 290, 298
KGB (Komitet Gosudarstvennoi Bezopasnosti)
    and Aldrich Ames, 23, 24, 34, 50, 51–52, 139, 168–69
    and Bloch case, 113–19, 166, 170, 285
    CIA efforts to recruit officer of, 78–79
    and CIA secrets, 47–48, 82–83
    compartmentalization from GRU, 24, 42, 160
    defectors to CIA, 45, 141, 198, 235–36
    double agents, 38, 80, 132
    FBI analyses of, 37, 42, 67, 68
    and FBI informants, 45, 46, 71–73, 99, 174–75, 179, 180, 217–30, 264, 284, 285, 289
    and FBI mole hunts, 38–39, 67–73, 119, 170–71, 174, 219–230
    FBI-CIA pitches to, 196–201, 247
    file on Hanssen, 221–30, 233, 234, 236n, 247, 264, 289

KGB (Komitet Gosudarstvennoi
    Bezopasnosti) *(cont'd)*
  fraternization with U.S. agents, 200
  Hanssen dealings with, 46, 50–58, 61–65,
    74–84, 94–99, 103, 107, 108, 114n,
    115, 117–20, 123, 132–39, 159,
    166–67, 226–28, 245, 272, 274,
    278–79, 281, 284–85, 290, 298
  "illegals" in, 59, 113–18, 206
  Norwegian spy for, 49
  promotions within, 48, 198
  recruitment efforts against CIA, 78–79, 82
    in Singapore, 113
  surveillance techniques, 49, 75–76,
    101–3, 109, 183n
  U.S. operations of, 20, 30, 37, 39, 42,
    47–48, 59, 74, 105, 137, 187, 207, 290
  See also SVR
Kimmel, Husband E., 178
Kimmel, Thomas K., Jr., 178–82, 298
King, Bob, 4, 67, 68, 83, 226
Kirdyanov, Vladimir A., 190n
Knox, Ronald, 44
Kortan, Michael P., 297
Kryuchkov, Vladimir A., 79, 80, 83, 94, 99,
    138, 139
Kulak, Alekei Isidorovich (FEDORA), 69, 71

Lamb, Robert E., 116
Lambert, Dave, 244
Lee, Andrew, 270n
Lee, Wen Ho, 248
Lewinsky, Monica, 10, 250, 261, 292
Lewis, John F., Jr., 31, 96, 107–8, 110, 170,
    179–80, 218, 286–87, 290, 297
Lichtenberg, Kimberly Schaefer, 153–58,
    160, 282, 297
Lichtenberg, Michael, 153, 155–56, 158
Lie detectors. *See* Polygraphs
Lieberman, Joseph I., 185
Listening devices, in U.S. Moscow embassy,
    101–3
Lodge, Henry Cabot, 102n
Loeb, Vernon, 298
Loomis, Robert D., 299
Lord of the World (Benson), 235
Lowe, A. Jackson, 174, 274, 298
Lyle, James D., 125–29, 131, 297
Lysov, Valentin, 69–70

Mabey, John F., 22, 298
Major, David, 35–36, 68, 69n, 75, 89, 134,
    173n, 273, 278, 279, 290, 297
Malakhov, Boris M., 64, 74, 76, 77
Man Who Was Thursday, The (Chesterton),
    6–7, 293
Mangold, Tom, 256n

Mansfield, Mark, 298
Martynov, Natalya, 57
Martynov, Valery
  betrayal of, 4, 23, 49, 51, 55–56, 65, 99,
    265, 284
  execution of, 3, 57, 168–69, 265
  FBI-CIA recruitment of, 39–42, 51
Mary Dominga, 27
MASINT (measurement and signature
    intelligence) program, 95, 96
Masters, Brooke A., 298
McAfee, Franklyn M., 87–88, 298
McCloskey, C. John, III, 43, 88–89, 92–93,
    298
McFadden, Edward S., 299
McMahon, Joe, 157, 158
McVeigh, Timothy, 249
McWethy, John F., 116
MEGAHUT, 59
MEGAS. *See* Motorin, Sergei
Melson, Ken, 268
Melton, H. Keith, 299
MI5 (British internal security service), 102n,
    109
MI6 (British secret intelligence service),
    108, 109, 222
Milburn, James P., 4, 67, 68, 83, 169, 173,
    221
Miller, Richard, 45, 46, 72, 283
Mislock, Raymond A., Jr., 128, 160–62, 181,
    188, 200–1, 282, 297–98
Missionaries of Charity, 26–27, 245, 288
Mitchell, John, 250, 262
Mitrokhin, Vasili, 222
Mlotek, Noah, 185
Mlotek, Ronald Sol, 92, 93, 184–87, 258,
    277, 291, 299
Mole hunts
  CIA, 3, 71, 128, 168–72
  FBI, 3–4, 38, 67–73, 82–83, 123–27, 160,
    166, 168–76, 179–81, 219–30
  by joint task force, 168–69, 179, 202,
    205–19, 229, 245, 247
  techniques of, 174, 216, 220
Molehunt (Wise), 208n
MONOLITE, 78
MONOPOLY (FBI tunnel project), 98–99,
    100–1, 103, 104–11, 170n, 285
Moore, Paul D., 32–34, 43, 44, 66–68, 73,
    89, 146, 216, 258, 277, 284, 290, 297
Morton, Mike, 41
Mother Teresa, 26–27, 245, 288
Motorin, Sergei
  betrayal of, 4, 23, 49, 51, 55–56, 65, 99,
    265, 284
  execution of, 3, 57, 168–69, 265
  FBI recruitment of, 40–42, 51

Moussaoui, Zacarias, 291
Moustakas, John, 210–17, 298
Mueller, Robert S., III, 129, 215
Mullins, Dep, 145
My Fair Lady (musical), 151

NACIC (National Counterintelligence
    Center), 176–77
National HUMINT Collection Plan (NHCP),
    84
National Security Threat List (NSTL), 140,
    153
New York City
    FBI operations in, 19–20, 42, 45, 50,
        58–60, 74, 83, 122, 126, 172, 173–75,
        178, 207, 219, 221, 274
    Hanssen in, 245, 273, 274
    mole hunts in, 173–75
    Soviet activity in, 20, 58–60
NFIP (National Foreign Intelligence
    Program), 35
Nicholson, Harold James ("Jim"), 175–76,
    199
NIGHTMOVER, 170, 173
Nixon administration
    and Cambodia, 251–52
    and CIA, 183
Nolan, James E., Jr., 183, 298
Nosenko, Yuri I., 71
NROC (National Resettlement Operations
    Center), 229, 239n, 289
NSA (National Security Agency)
    Bamford books on, 165, 167
    defector employed by, 235
    and electronic intercepts, 165
    and FBI, 165, 172
    Hanssen damage to, 225, 285
    Hanssen job application to, 15, 18
    intelligence collection, 55, 59, 61, 65,
        80
    and polygraphs, 33, 172
    and Soviet embassy surveillance, 98,
        104–5, 108n
NSC (National Security Council), 76

O'Donnell, Pete, 178, 179, 298
Oehler, Gordon C., 162–63, 298
Office of Foreign Missions (OFM), 183–84,
    187, 189
Ogorodnikov, Svetlana, 45
Ohlson, James D., 9, 28–29, 42, 43, 60, 66,
    187–88, 235, 274, 297
OPERATION GOLD, 108
Opus Dei
    Hanssens' participation in, 6, 15, 25–26,
        43–44, 86–92, 120, 124, 126, 147, 153,
        167, 184, 257, 270, 280, 281, 289

history of, 90–91
    membership of, 90, 91, 164
    purpose of, 25, 44, 89, 90, 281
    schools, 43, 44, 66, 91
    study centers, 25, 43–44, 87, 90, 91
    warning to Bonnie Hanssen, 289
    and Wauck family, 13, 15, 25–26, 86, 88,
        124

Parker, Phillip A., 31, 198, 298
Pasquariello, Benny, 104, 106, 299
Patton, George S., Jr., 140, 141, 194, 226
Pelton, Ronald W., 46, 74, 172, 290
Penkovsky, Oleg, 39
Philby, Harold A. R. ("Kim"), 117, 192, 203,
    270
Pickard, Thomas J., 174, 214–15, 298
Piguzov, Vladimir M., 48n
PIMENTA. *See* Martynov, Valery
Pitts, Earl Edwin, 72n, 174–75, 178–81,
    199, 271, 282, 283
Platt, John C., 78–79, 298
PLAYACTOR/SKYLIGHT, 169, 173
Playboy Club, 13, 260
Pluta, Stefan A., 243, 267
POCKETWATCH, 58, 59, 274
Podlesny, John A., 34
Pollard, Jonathan Jay, 45–46, 270
Polyakov, Dimitri Fedorovich (TOPHAT),
    21–24, 42, 65, 103, 245, 285, 304
    derivation of code name, 22n
Polygraphs, 33–35, 176–77, 282, 286–88
Pound, Ed, 299
Pugh, Dale H., 40, 196–97, 298
Putin, Vladimir, 202

RACKETEER, 199–201
"Ramon" (Hanssen alias), 7, 62, 65, 75–77,
    82, 141, 160, 189, 192, 223, 225, 239
RAMPAIGE. *See* Yuzhin, Boris
Ratliff, Emily, 298
Reagan, Ronald
    expulsion of Soviet diplomats by, 263
    Hanssen admiration for, 186
    staff members in Opus Dei, 90
    and U.S. Moscow embassy, 103
Redmond, Paul J., Jr., 171, 172, 175, 248,
    268, 281, 292, 298
Reno, Janet, 249
Risen, James, 298
Rizzo, Ernie, 18, 278
Roberts, Jerry, 144
Rochford, Mike, 201, 207, 209, 216, 217,
    219, 220–24, 226, 247, 289
Romerstein, Herb, 299
Rosic, Momcilo, 12, 299
Ross, Thomas B., 298

Ruby Ridge (Idaho), 248
Rumsfeld, Donald, 264
Russia, post-Soviet
  and Hanssen 1993 approach to GRU,
    160
  political prisoner release in, 56
  and spy operations, 187, 202, 265, 286,
    287
  See also GRU; KGB; Soviet Union; SVR
Russian embassy (D.C.)
  as diplomatic cover for spies, 193–94,
    201, 263
  and Hanssen arrest, 246
  See also Soviet embassy (D.C.)

Safehouse (cabin cruiser), 166
Safeway supermarket, as FBI "pitch" site,
    196–97
Salerian, Alen J., 255–57, 271n, 299
Samson, David T., 113
Samsonov, Igor S., 49
SATYR, 102n
Sawyer, Ida, 299
Schulz, William, 299
SCIF (Sensitive Compartmented
    Information Facility), 157
SCOTCH, 69
Scowcroft, Brent, 200
SDI (Strategic Defense Initiative), 81
Sheymov, Victor, 80, 81, 235–38
Shotwell, Judi, 299
Shotwell, Mike, 299
SIOC (Strategic Information Operations
    Center, FBI), 240–42
SIU (Special Investigations Unit, CIA),
    171–73, 175, 176, 179, 199, 217
Skillen, Jim, 235
Skotzko, Waldimir ("Scotty"), 22
Smith, Debra, 221, 241–42
Smits, Bill, 48, 49
Sommer, Mary, 173
Soviet embassy (D.C.)
  communications interception by, 101, 105
  construction project, 98, 100–1, 103–4
  FBI informants in, 3, 23, 39–42, 67, 284
  FBI surveillance of, 52, 98, 100–1, 104,
    170–71, 183–84
  FBI tunnel under, 98–99, 100–1, 103,
    104–11, 170, 285
  GRU agents in, 160
  KGB agents in, 62–65, 169, 196–98,
    200–1, 263, 284
  location of, 101, 183, 196
  See also Russian embassy (D.C.)
Soviet Union
  CIA operations within, 67, 83
  fall of, 99, 109, 137, 138, 139, 141, 142,
    162, 175, 187, 190, 200, 265, 285–86

Hanssen views on, 89, 92, 147, 187, 277
intelligence operations in U.S., 20, 24, 37,
    59, 60, 69, 70, 78, 82
missile technology assessments, 84, 132,
    284
U.S. embassy bugs in, 102–3
U.S. intelligence sources from, 3–4, 51,
    80, 285
U.S. spies for, 45–46, 270
U.S. surveillance of, 102n, 103, 140, 285
  See also GRU; KGB; Russia, post-Soviet;
    SVR
Spaulding, Suzanne, 164, 298
SPIDERWEB, 170–71
Spycraft, 54–55, 76–77, 201, 208
SSG (Special Surveillance Group, FBI),
    208–9, 230, 236, 240, 241, 244
"Star Wars" (Strategic Defense Initiative),
    81
Stassinos, James O., 197
State Department, U.S.
  and Hanssen license plate, 232, 289
  Office of Foreign Missions, 183–84, 187,
    189
  SVR bug inside, 193–94
*Strange Case of Dr. Jekyll and Mr. Hyde,
    The* (Stevenson), 279
Strauss, Robert S., 109
Stuart, Charles C., 298
Stukey, Donald E., 31, 117, 118, 128, 273,
    298
Sullivan, William C., 72
Supermax federal prison, 301–4
SVR (Sluzhba Vneshnei Razvedki)
  and CIA source, 175–76
  and CIA-FBI mole hunts, 202, 219, 220
  file on Hanssen, 221–30, 233, 234, 247,
    264, 289
  Hanssen contacts with, 7–8, 139–42,
    190–95, 202–4, 234, 236, 240, 243,
    246n, 272, 281, 290
  and "iron sites," 240n
  retaliation for defection, 224
  U.S. operations of, 30, 193–94, 287, 290
  See also KGB
Sword and the Shield, The
    (Andrew/Mitrokhin), 222n
Sylvester, John C., 299
Synsvoll, Christopher B., 303
Szechenyi, Chris, 298

Tass (Soviet wire service), 20, 47, 48
  See also Itar-Tass news agency
Tenet, George, 210, 211–12, 247, 264, 268
Terrorism
  9/11/2001 attacks, 247, 268–69, 285, 289,
    291
  U.S. efforts against, 287

Third Man, The (film), 111
Thompson, Colin R., 298
Thompson, Larry, 268
Thorne, Juan Luis Cipriani, 91
Tierney, Joseph L., 29–31, 33n, 34–35, 274, 298
TOPHAT. *See* Polyakov, Dimitri Fedorovich
Toropov, Yevgeny, 220, 239
TRAPDOOR, 168, 173
Treholt, Arne, 49
Trimber, Jane Hanssen, 7, 241, 243, 246
Trimber, Richard, 7, 241, 243, 246, 291
Tropel (spy camera), 47, 49

U-2 spy plane, 102n
United Nations, Soviet mission to (SMUN), 20, 59, 60, 69, 70, 78, 136, 174, 175, 196
United States embassy (Moscow), 101–3, 106, 107, 109, 183, 263
United States v. *Nixon,* 26n
UNSUB DICK, 68–71
Ushakov, Yuri V., 110

VALBEL, 70
Vasilenko, Gennady, 78–79, 80
Vertefeuille, Jeanne R., 168, 169, 171, 172
Victory (Conrad), 276n

Waco (Texas), 248
Wade, Robert B., 128, 174, 199, 222, 298
Waguespack, Michael J. ("Wags"), 129, 176–77, 225–26, 230–31, 239, 297
Walker, Arthur, 45n, 46
Walker, John A., Jr., 45, 46, 285
Walker, Michael, 45n, 46
Walpole, Bob, 163
Walsh, Nick, 155
Ware, Mitchell, 17
Warnecke, John Carl, Sr., 105, 299
Watson, R. Patrick ("Pat"), 161, 169, 298
Wauck, Frances Hagarty, 14, 43, 86, 244, 296

Wauck, Greg, 124, 125, 130
Wauck, John Paul, 13, 86
Wauck, Leroy A., 14, 32, 43, 86, 87, 296
Wauck, Mark A., 86–87, 122–31, 282
Wauck, Mary Ellen, 123, 125, 130
Way, The (Escriva de Balaguer), 90
Weaver, Randall, 248
Webster, William H., 21, 248, 297
Webster commission, 21, 248, 282, 292, 297
Werth, James A., 298
Westberg, Bill, 298
WFO (Washington Field Office, FBI), 211, 217, 219–20, 241–42, 293
See also FBI
Whalen, William H., 22n
Whitworth, Jerry A., 45n
Wilkinson, Kevin, 297
Willis, Homer, 106
Wise, David
access to Hanssen's psychiatrist, 271, 295–96
and Felix Bloch, 114n, 115
and Victor Gundarev, 61n
Wise, Joan, 299
Wiser, Leslie G., Jr., 170, 220, 221, 297
Wojtyla, Karol (Pope John Paul II), 90–91
Woolsey, James, 214, 235–36, 270, 298
Worthen, Diana, 172–73

Yakushkin, Dimitri I., 196–98
Yakushkin, Irina, 196–97
Yeltsin, Boris, 56, 138
Yurchenko, Vitaly, 45, 46, 57, 61n, 79, 172, 198, 201
Yuzhin, Boris, 47–49, 51, 55–56, 65, 99, 290, 299
Yuzhin, Nadya, 290
Yuzhin, Olga, 290

Zeta-Jones, Catherine, 258, 277